You may be reading the wrong way!

This book reads right to left to maintain the original presentation and art of the Japanese edition, so action, sound effects and word balloons are reversed. This diagram shows how to follow the panels. Turn to the other side of the book to begin.

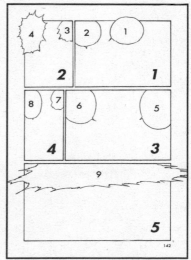

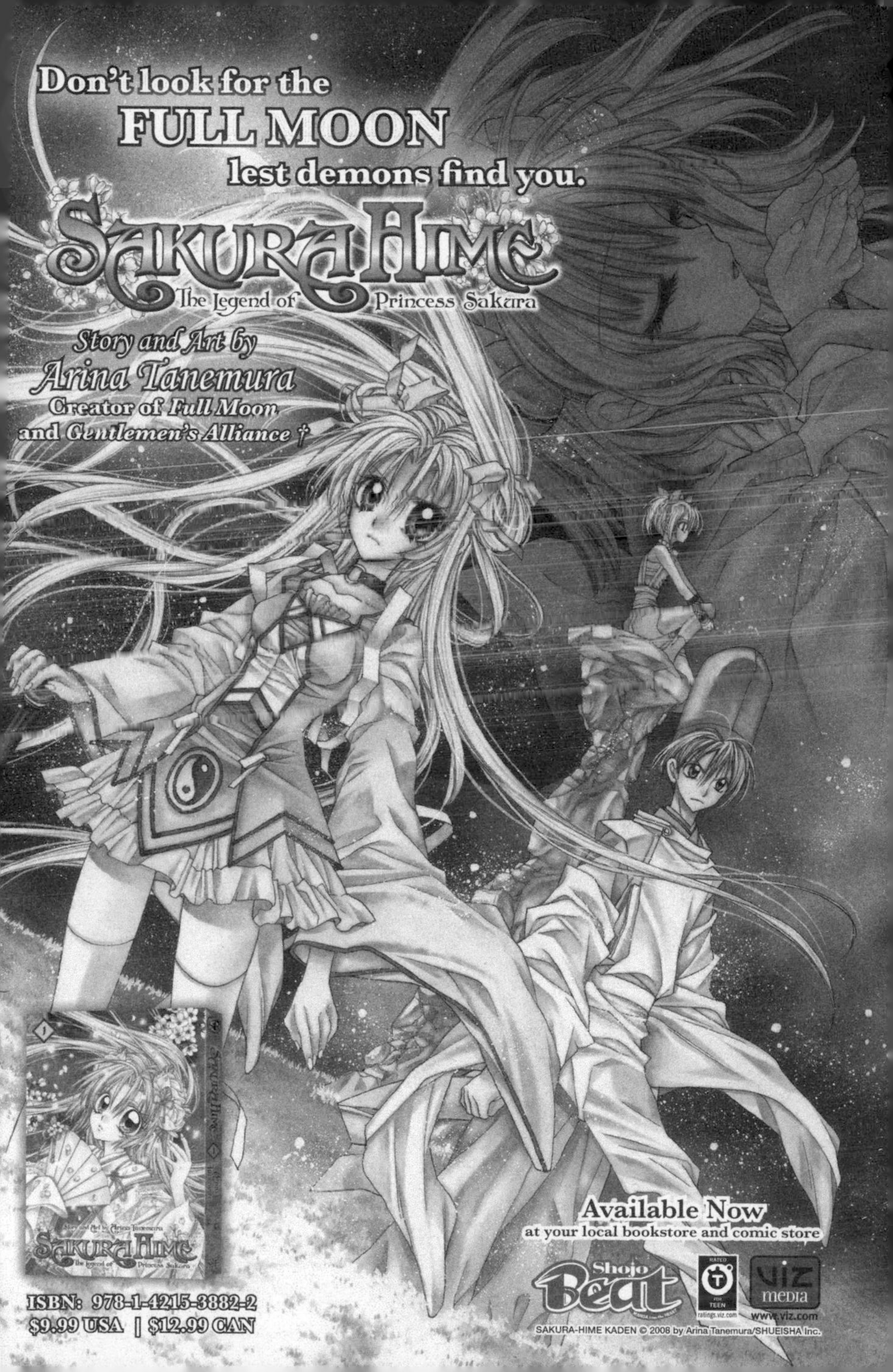

Don't look for the
FULL MOON
lest demons find you.
SAKURA HIME
The Legend of Princess Sakura
Story and Art by
Arina Tanemura
Creator of Full Moon
and Gentlemen's Alliance †
ISBN: 978-1-4215-3882-2
$9.99 USA | $12.99 CAN
Available Now
at your local bookstore and comic store
Shojo Beat
RATED T TEEN
ratings.viz.com
VIZ media
www.viz.com
SAKURA-HIME KADEN © 2008 by Arina Tanemura/SHUEISHA Inc.

Honey
So Sweet

Story and Art by
Amu Meguro

Contents

#06 Suddenly 3

#07 Just the Two of Us 43

#08 I Need to Tell You Something 81

#09 The Path to Happiness 117

#10 Can We Be Friends? 153

Story Thus Far

One day during junior high, the nervous and cowardly Nao comes across a beat-up delinquent in the middle of a downpour. She leaves him her umbrella and a box of bandages before running away. Now in high school, she runs into the very same delinquent, and he unabashedly asks her to date him with marriage in mind.

At first Nao is afraid of Onise, but she soon discovers he's a gentle soul, and the two become friends. Before long, Yashiro, the "cool beauty" of the school, and foul-mouthed pretty boy Misaki join their circle.

Onise asks Nao who she likes, and she says she has a crush on her uncle Sou. When Sou injures his wrist, Onise steps in to help at the café. The first meeting between Onise and Sou is awkward, but Nao sees the good job that Onise does, and a mysterious sensation begins to grow in her heart...

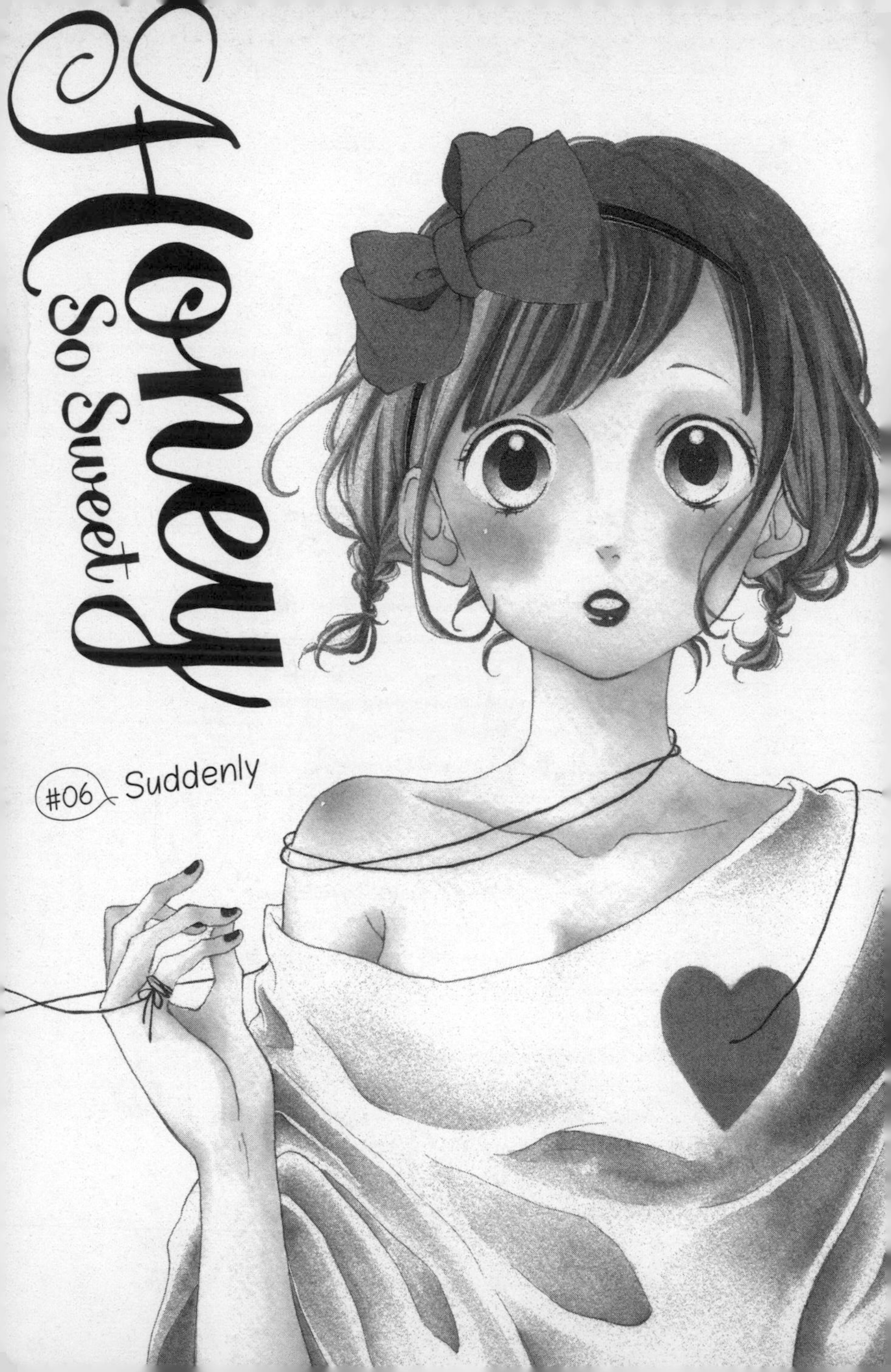
Honey
So Sweet
#06 Suddenly

This is volume 2!
In the midst of working on this volume I came down with the stomach flu, and I ruined some pages by spilling ink all over them. What a mess! I'm just glad I was able to finally finish. (laugh) I hope you enjoy volume 2!

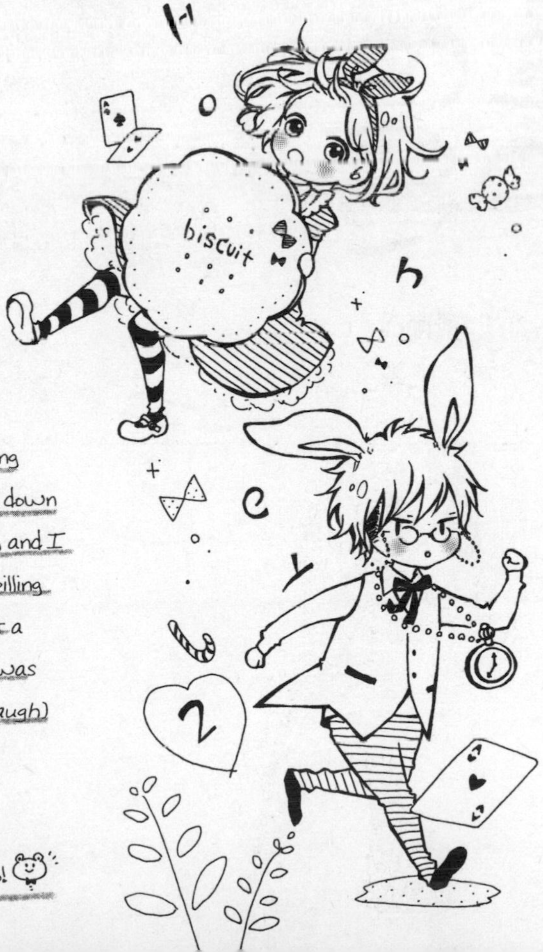
biscuit
2

That was my hello!

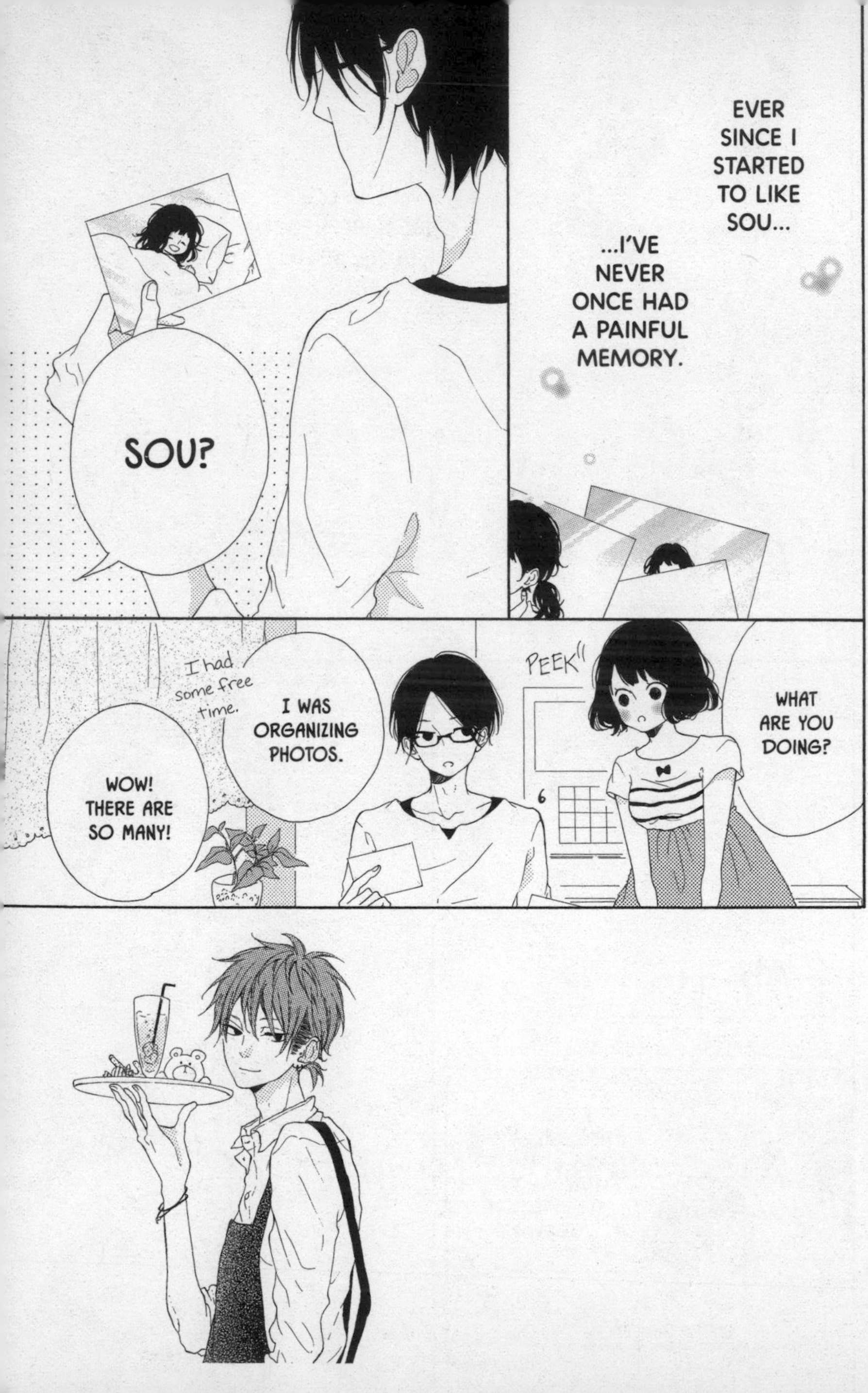
EVER SINCE I STARTED TO LIKE SOU...
...I'VE NEVER ONCE HAD A PAINFUL MEMORY.
SOU?
WHAT ARE YOU DOING?
PEEK
I WAS ORGANIZING PHOTOS.
I had some free time.
WOW! THERE ARE SO MANY!

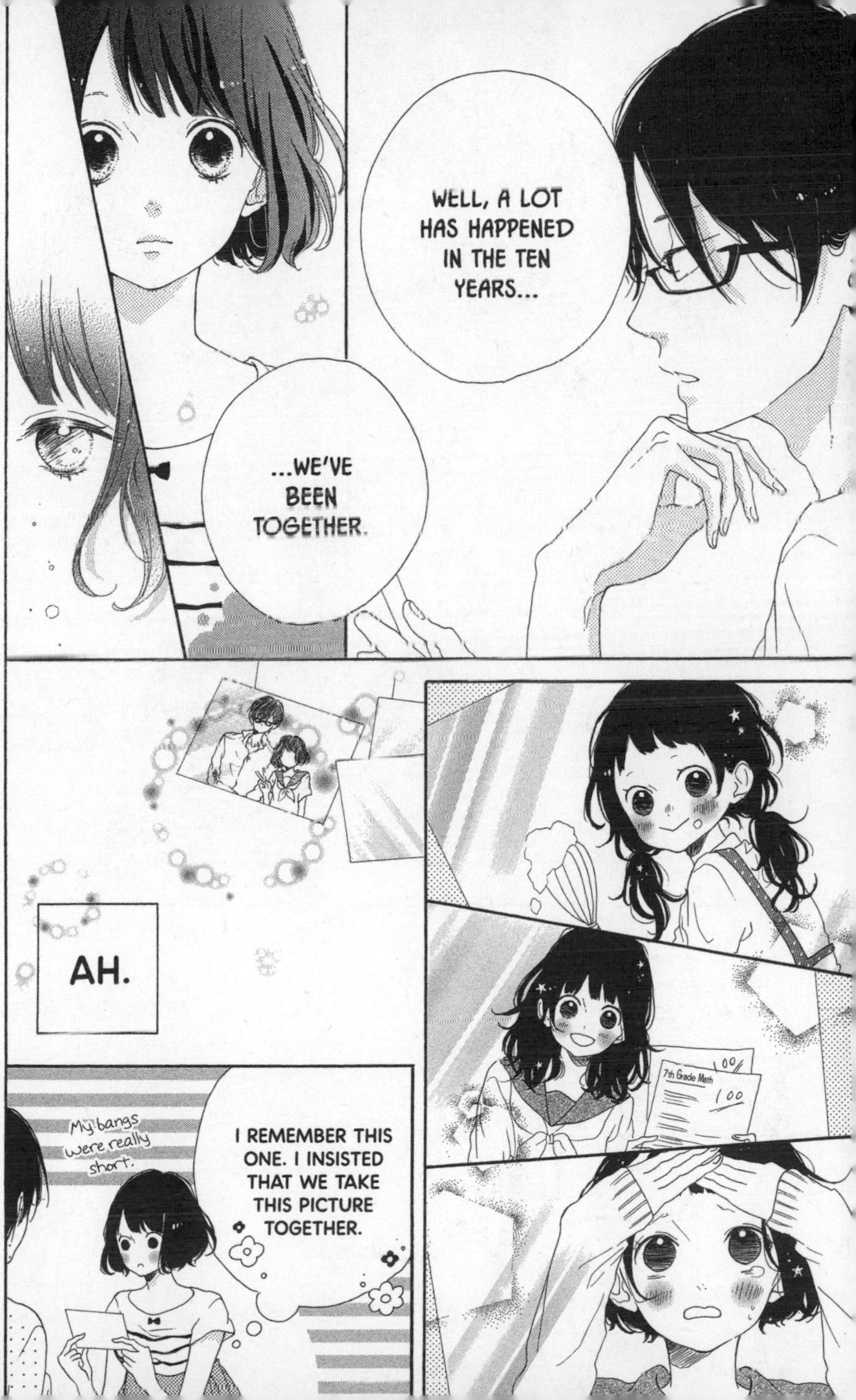
WELL, A LOT HAS HAPPENED IN THE TEN YEARS...
...WE'VE BEEN TOGETHER.
7th Grade Math
100
100
AH.
I REMEMBER THIS ONE. I INSISTED THAT WE TAKE THIS PICTURE TOGETHER.
My bangs were really short.

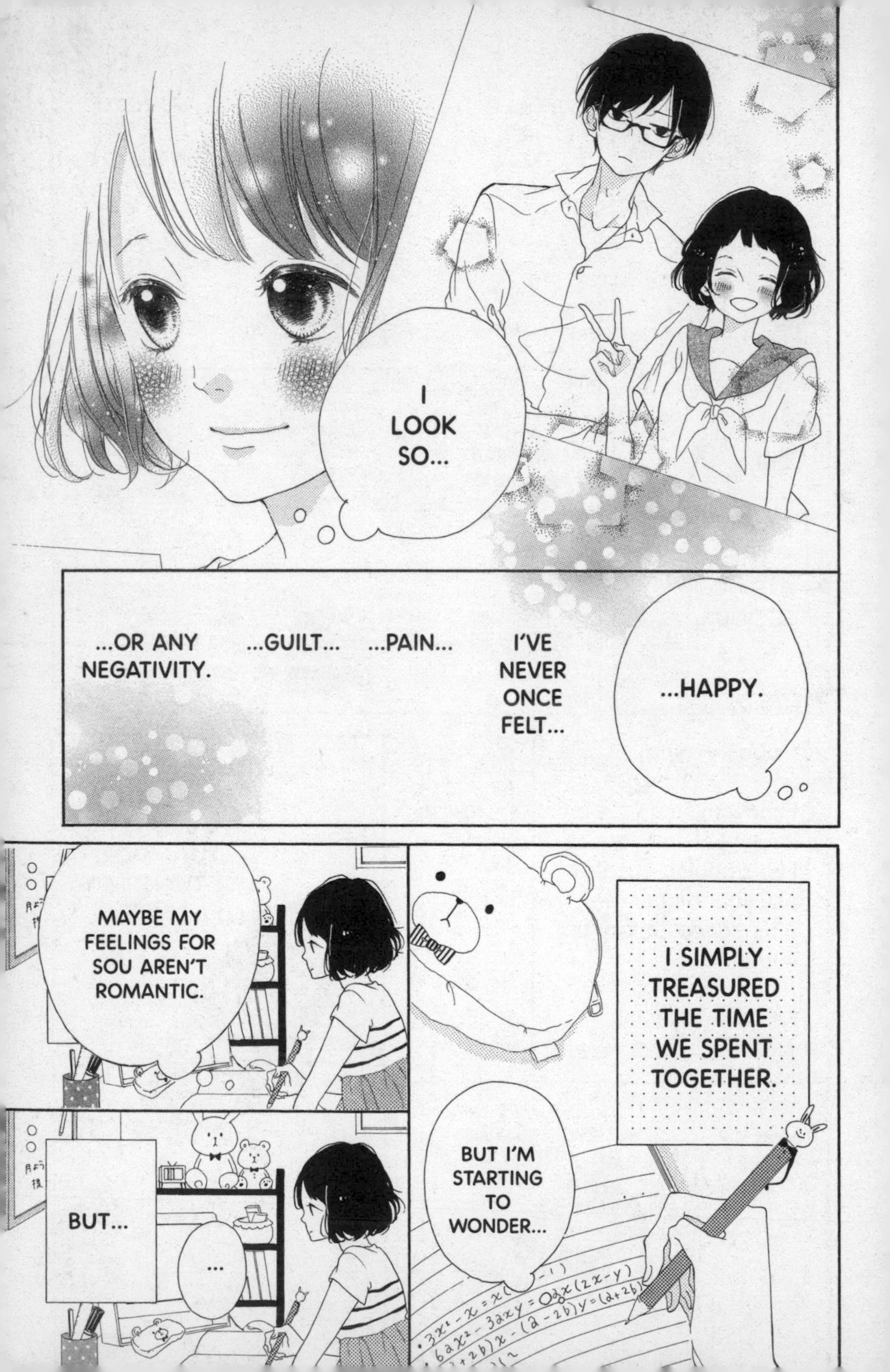
I LOOK SO...
...HAPPY.
I'VE NEVER ONCE FELT...
...PAIN...
...GUILT...
...OR ANY NEGATIVITY.
I SIMPLY TREASURED THE TIME WE SPENT TOGETHER.
BUT I'M STARTING TO WONDER...
MAYBE MY FEELINGS FOR SOU AREN'T ROMANTIC.
BUT...
...

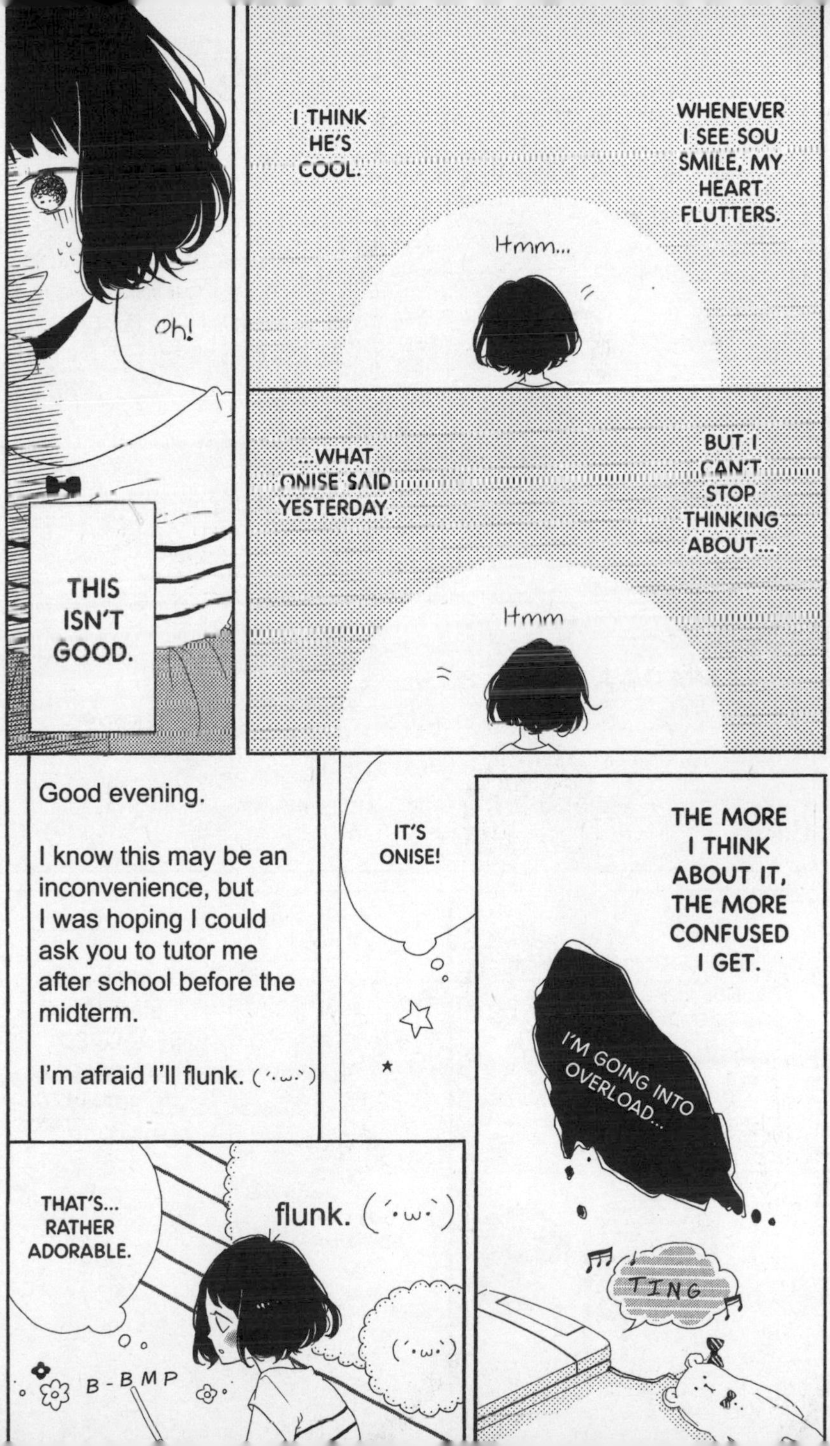
WHENEVER I SEE SOU SMILE, MY HEART FLUTTERS.
I THINK HE'S COOL.
Hmm...
BUT I CAN'T STOP THINKING ABOUT...
...WHAT ONISE SAID YESTERDAY.
Hmm
Oh!
THIS ISN'T GOOD.
THE MORE I THINK ABOUT IT, THE MORE CONFUSED I GET.
I'M GOING INTO OVERLOAD...
TING
IT'S ONISE!
Good evening.
I know this may be an inconvenience, but I was hoping I could ask you to tutor me after school before the midterm.
I'm afraid I'll flunk. (´・ω・`)
flunk. (´・ω・`)
THAT'S... RATHER ADORABLE.
(´・ω・`)
B-BMP

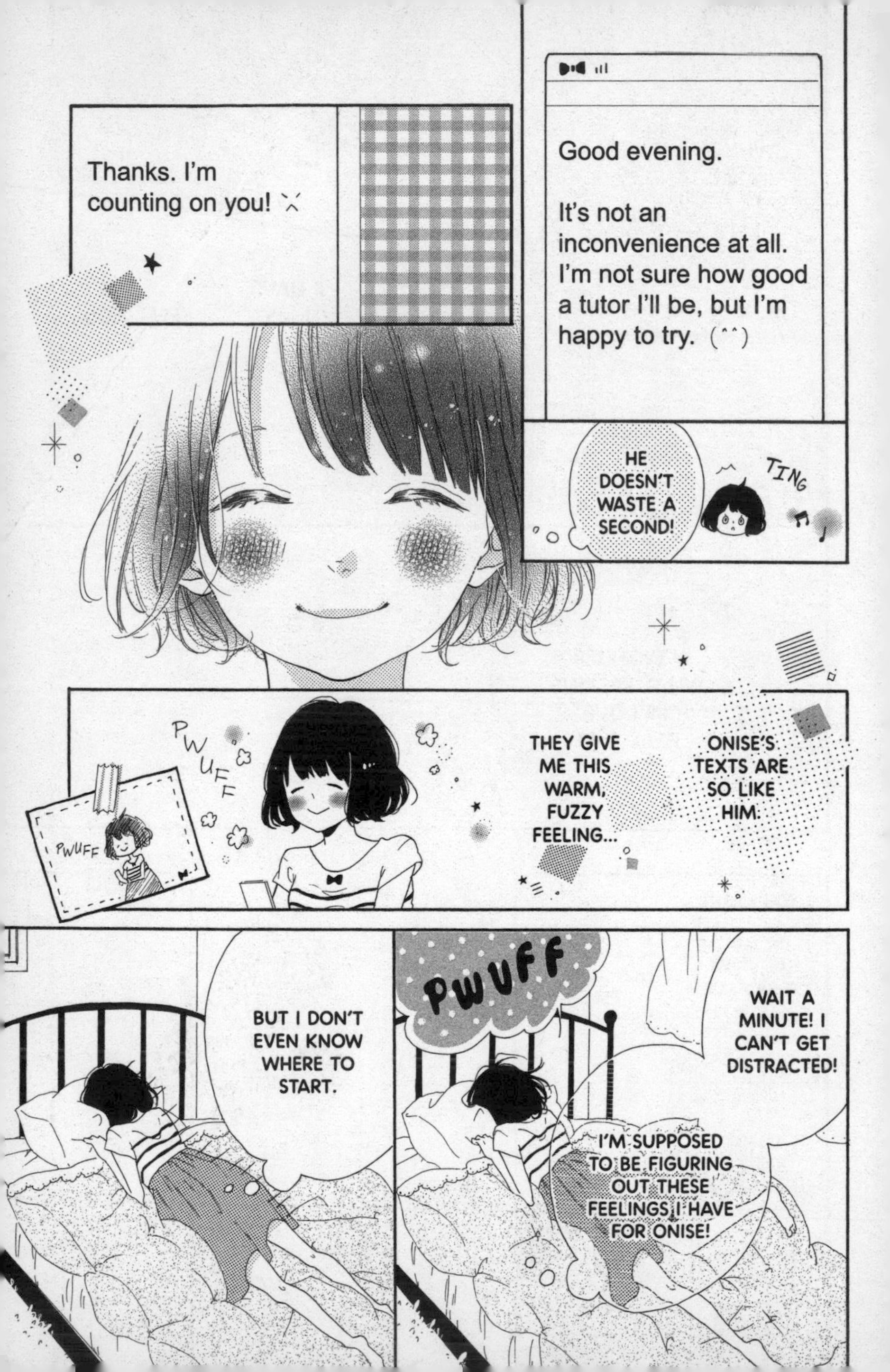
Good evening.
It's not an inconvenience at all. I'm not sure how good a tutor I'll be, but I'm happy to try. (^^)
HE DOESN'T WASTE A SECOND!
TING
Thanks. I'm counting on you!
ONISE'S TEXTS ARE SO LIKE HIM.
THEY GIVE ME THIS WARM, FUZZY FEELING...
PWUFF
PWUFF
WAIT A MINUTE! I CAN'T GET DISTRACTED!
I'M SUPPOSED TO BE FIGURING OUT THESE FEELINGS I HAVE FOR ONISE!
PWUFF
BUT I DON'T EVEN KNOW WHERE TO START.

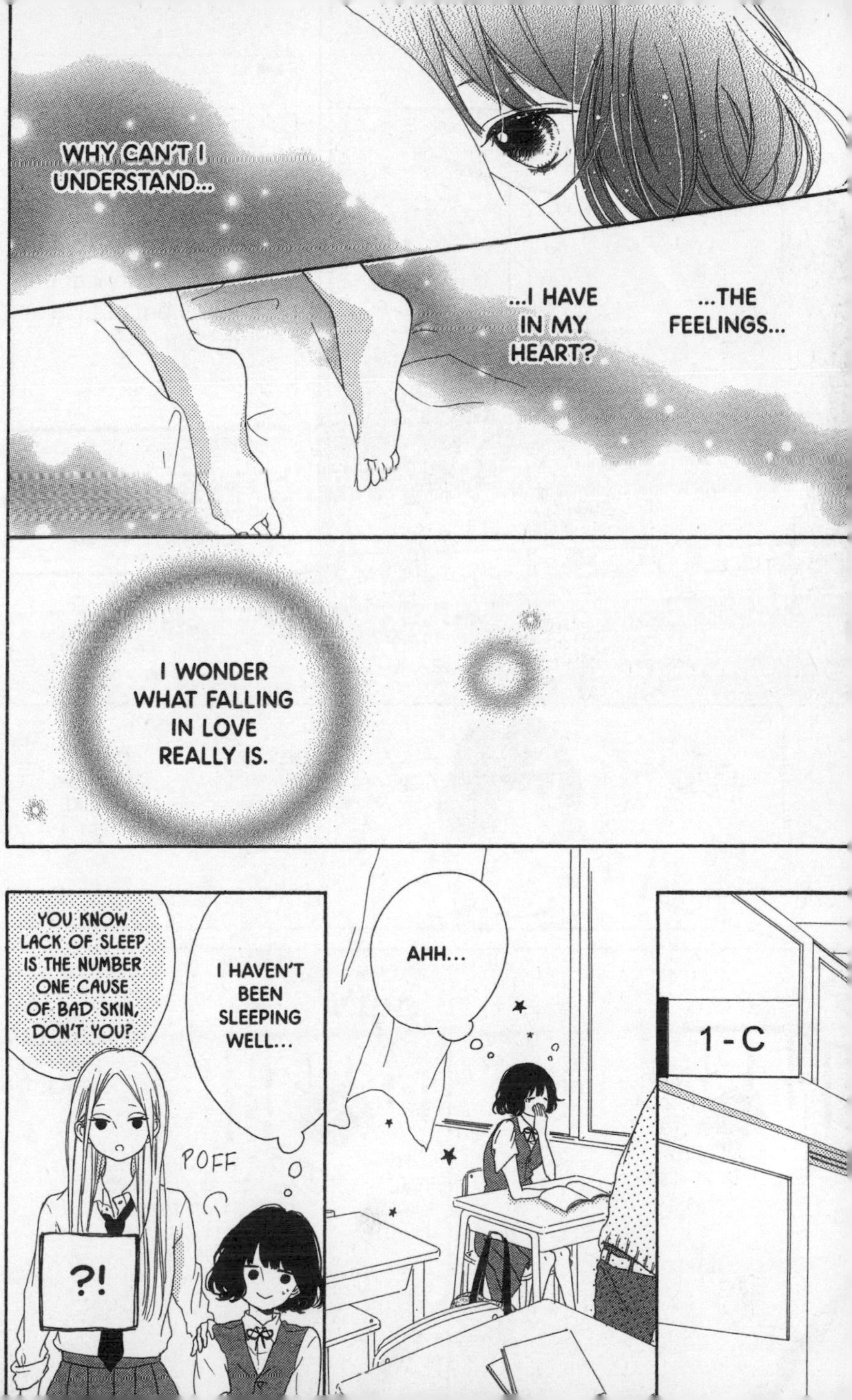
WHY CAN'T I UNDERSTAND...
...THE FEELINGS...
...I HAVE IN MY HEART?
I WONDER WHAT FALLING IN LOVE REALLY IS.
1 - C
AHH...
I HAVEN'T BEEN SLEEPING WELL...
YOU KNOW LACK OF SLEEP IS THE NUMBER ONE CAUSE OF BAD SKIN, DON'T YOU?
POFF
?!

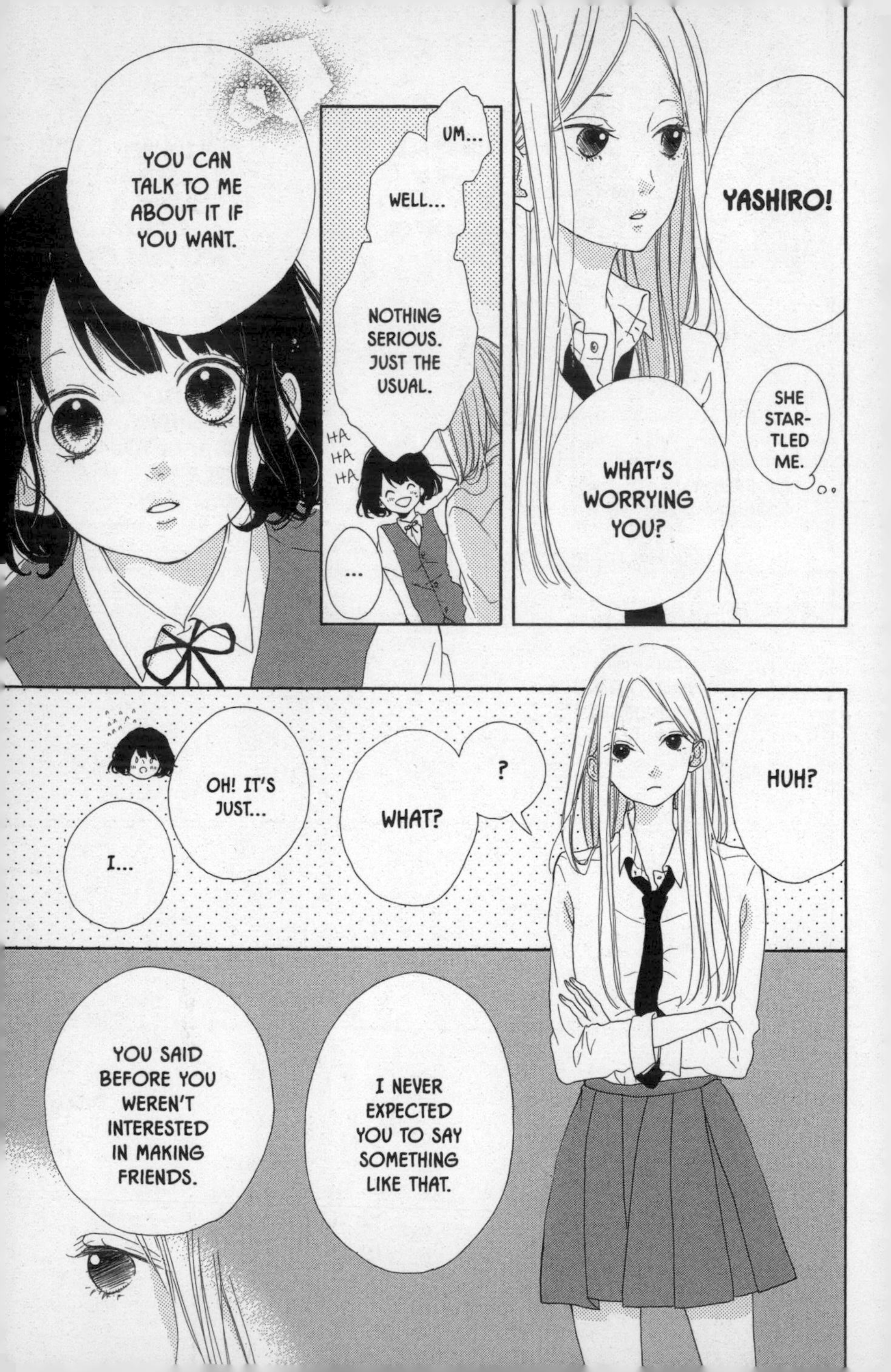
YASHIRO!
SHE STARTLED ME.
WHAT'S WORRYING YOU?
UM...
WELL...
NOTHING SERIOUS. JUST THE USUAL.
HA HA HA
...
YOU CAN TALK TO ME ABOUT IT IF YOU WANT.
HUH?
?
WHAT?
OH! IT'S JUST...
I...
I NEVER EXPECTED YOU TO SAY SOMETHING LIKE THAT.
YOU SAID BEFORE YOU WEREN'T INTERESTED IN MAKING FRIENDS.

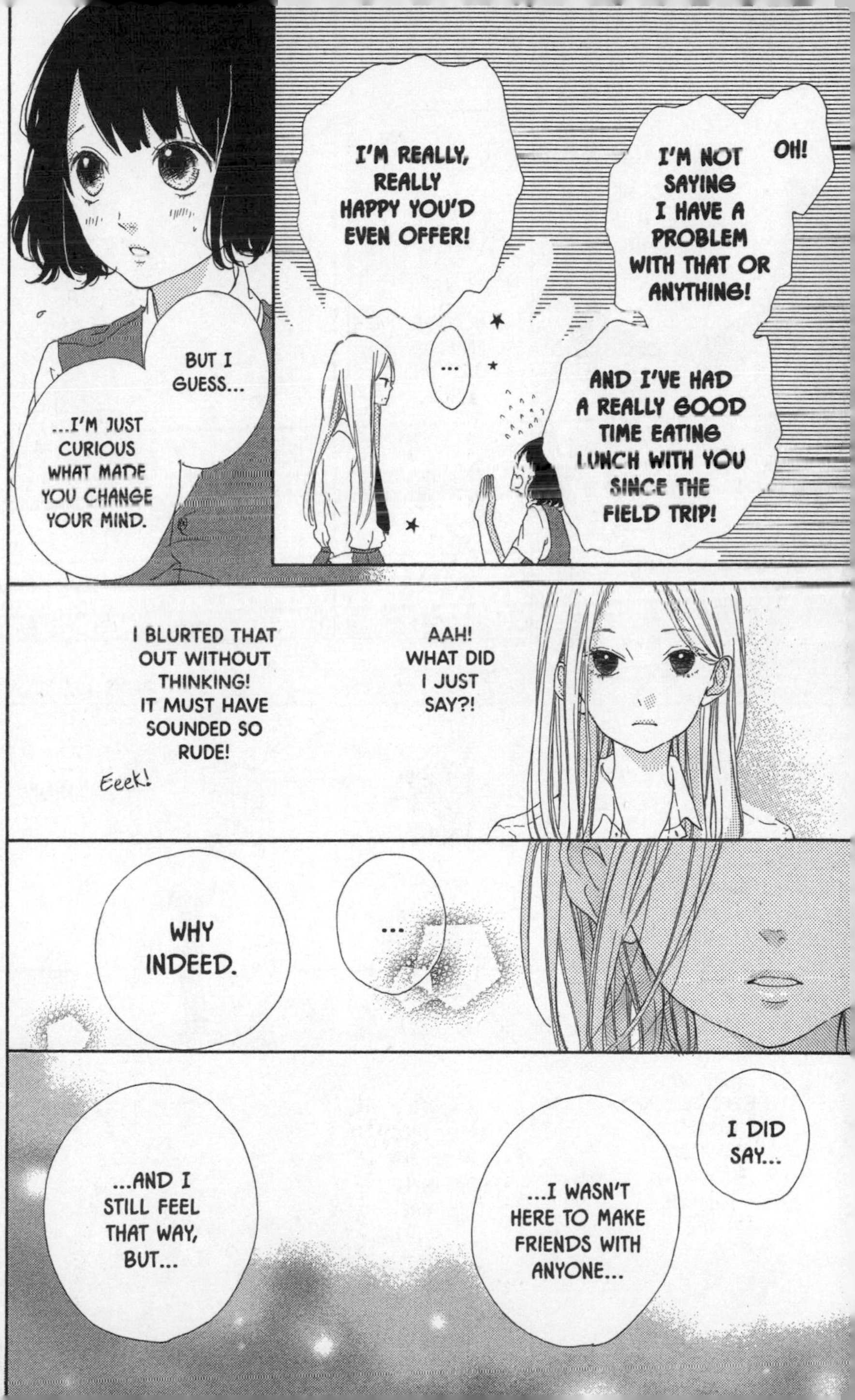
OH!
I'M NOT SAYING I HAVE A PROBLEM WITH THAT OR ANYTHING!
I'M REALLY, REALLY HAPPY YOU'D EVEN OFFER!
AND I'VE HAD A REALLY GOOD TIME EATING LUNCH WITH YOU SINCE THE FIELD TRIP!
...
BUT I GUESS...
...I'M JUST CURIOUS WHAT MADE YOU CHANGE YOUR MIND.
AAH! WHAT DID I JUST SAY?!
I BLURTED THAT OUT WITHOUT THINKING! IT MUST HAVE SOUNDED SO RUDE!
Eeek!
...
WHY INDEED.
I DID SAY...
...I WASN'T HERE TO MAKE FRIENDS WITH ANYONE...
...AND I STILL FEEL THAT WAY, BUT...

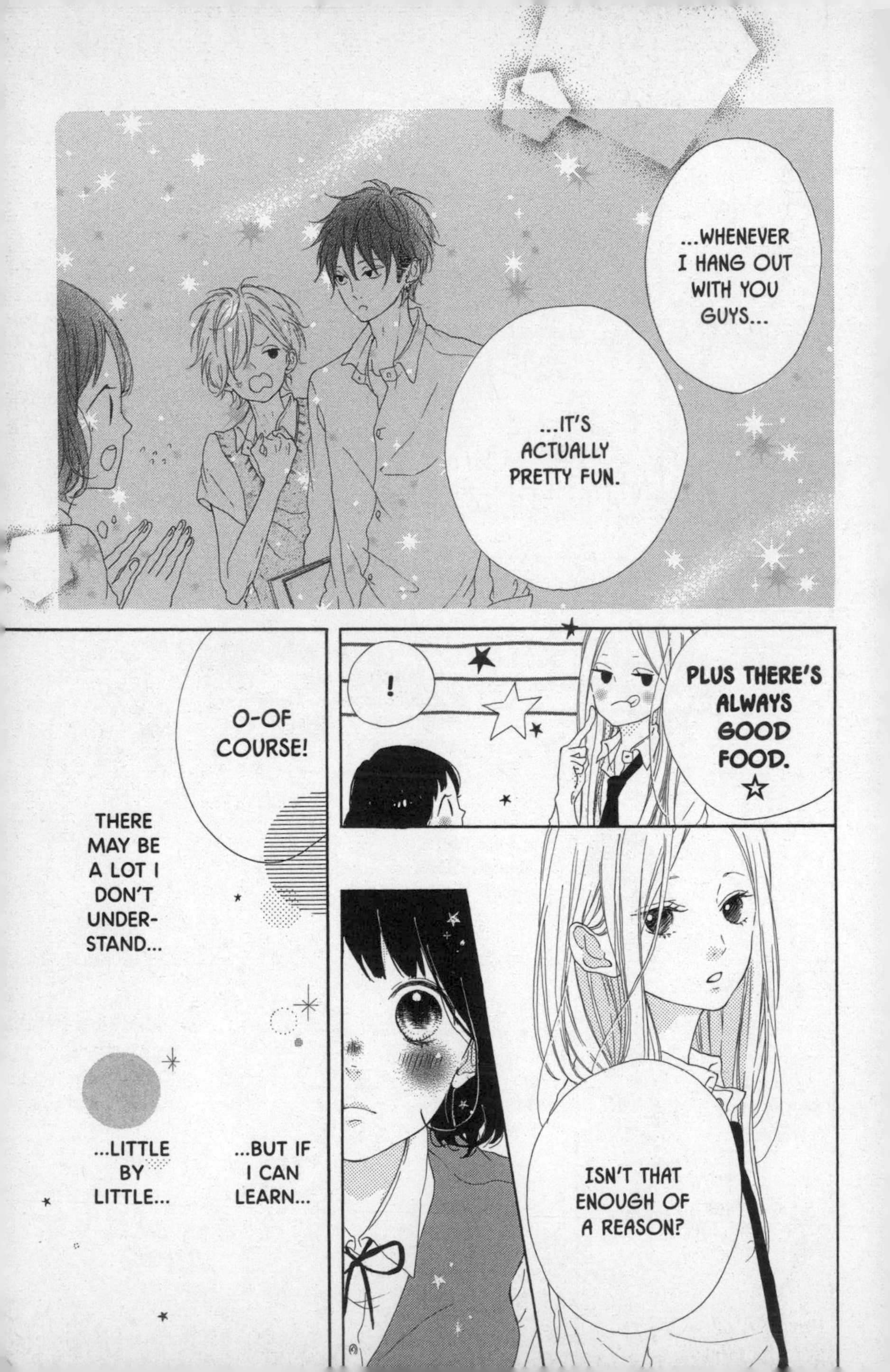
...WHENEVER I HANG OUT WITH YOU GUYS...
...IT'S ACTUALLY PRETTY FUN.
PLUS THERE'S ALWAYS GOOD FOOD. ☆
!
ISN'T THAT ENOUGH OF A REASON?
O-OF COURSE!
THERE MAY BE A LOT I DON'T UNDER-STAND...
...BUT IF I CAN LEARN...
...LITTLE BY LITTLE...

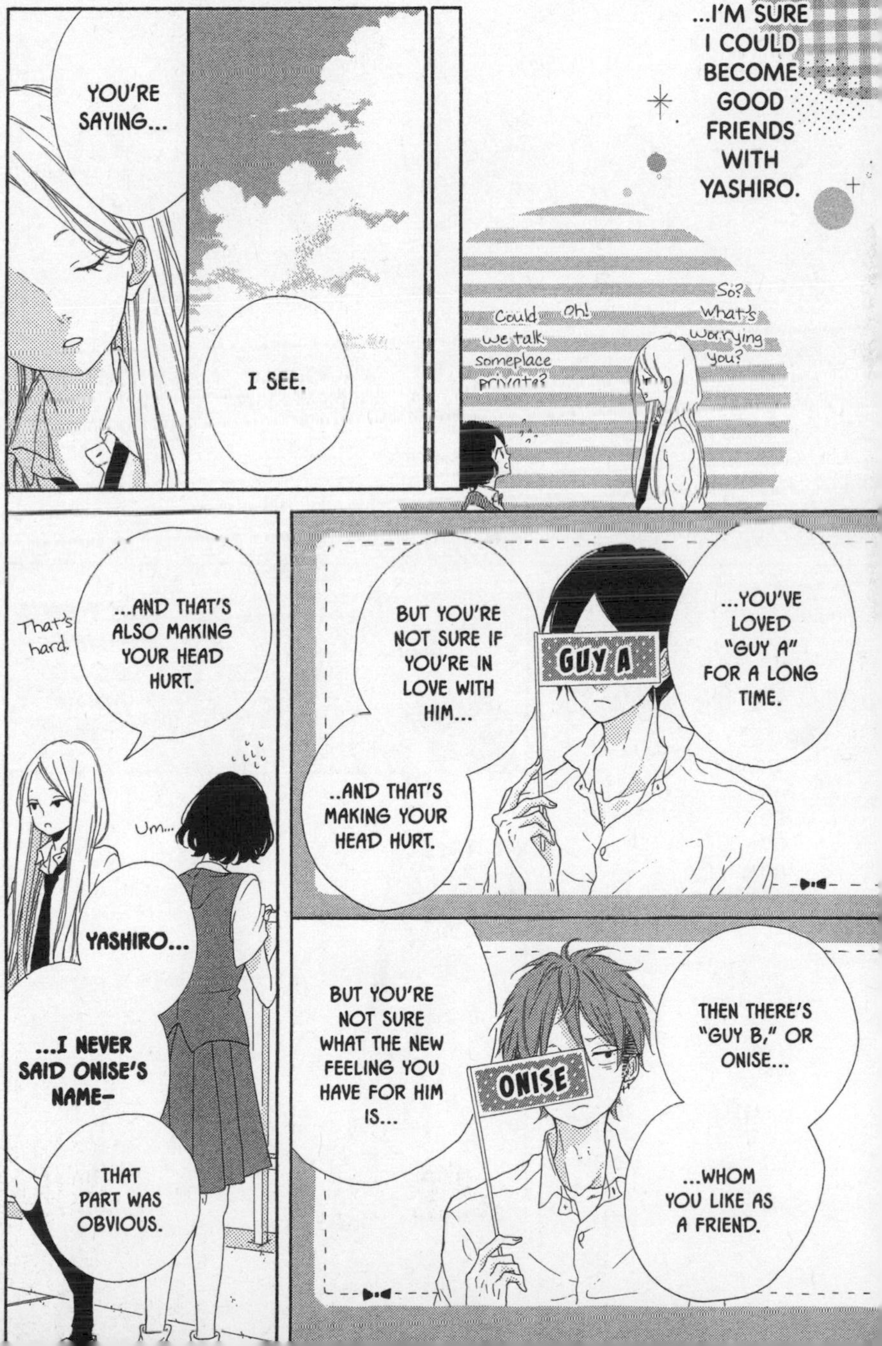
...I'M SURE I COULD BECOME GOOD FRIENDS WITH YASHIRO.
So? What's worrying you?
Oh!
Could we talk someplace private?
I SEE.
YOU'RE SAYING...
...YOU'VE LOVED "GUY A" FOR A LONG TIME.
GUY A
BUT YOU'RE NOT SURE IF YOU'RE IN LOVE WITH HIM...
..AND THAT'S MAKING YOUR HEAD HURT.
THEN THERE'S "GUY B," OR ONISE...
...WHOM YOU LIKE AS A FRIEND.
ONISE
BUT YOU'RE NOT SURE WHAT THE NEW FEELING YOU HAVE FOR HIM IS...
...AND THAT'S ALSO MAKING YOUR HEAD HURT.
That's hard.
Um...
YASHIRO...
...I NEVER SAID ONISE'S NAME—
THAT PART WAS OBVIOUS.

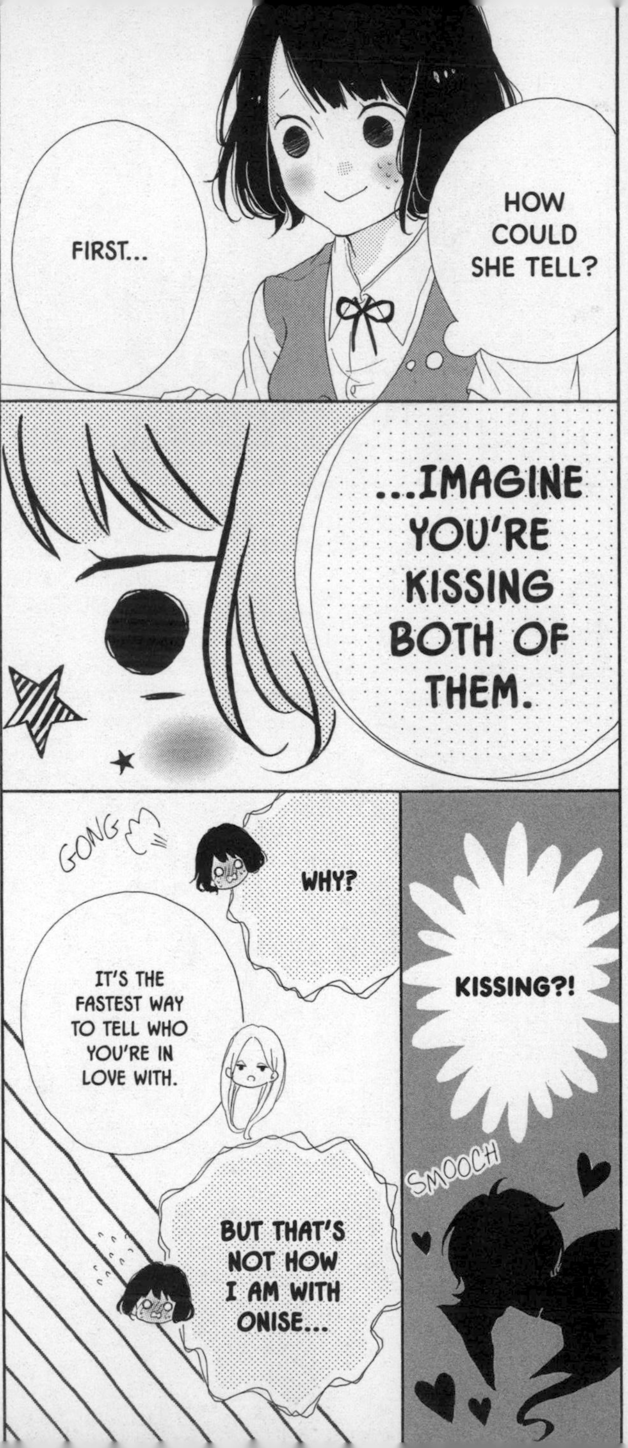
HOW COULD SHE TELL?
FIRST...
...IMAGINE YOU'RE KISSING BOTH OF THEM.
KISSING?!
SMOOCH
GONG
WHY?
IT'S THE FASTEST WAY TO TELL WHO YOU'RE IN LOVE WITH.
BUT THAT'S NOT HOW I AM WITH ONISE...

Pencil Sketch Corner 1

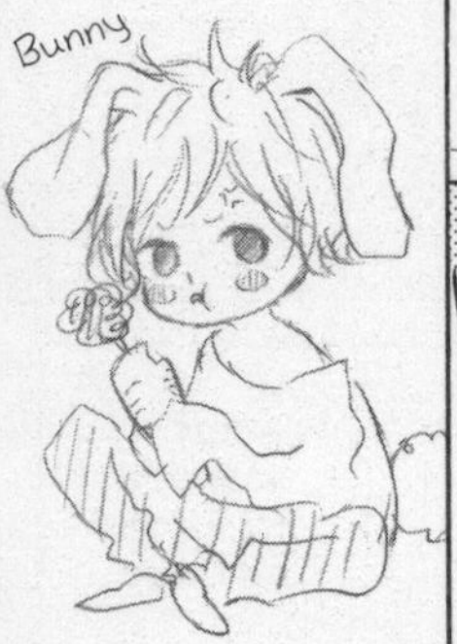
Bunny

Once when I went to Tokyo with Aoka Tsuchii, we visited a bunny café! It was heavenly! They were adorable! I highly recommend going!

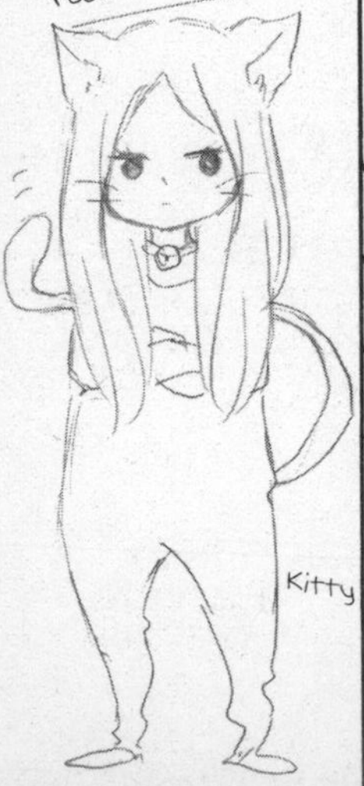
Kitty

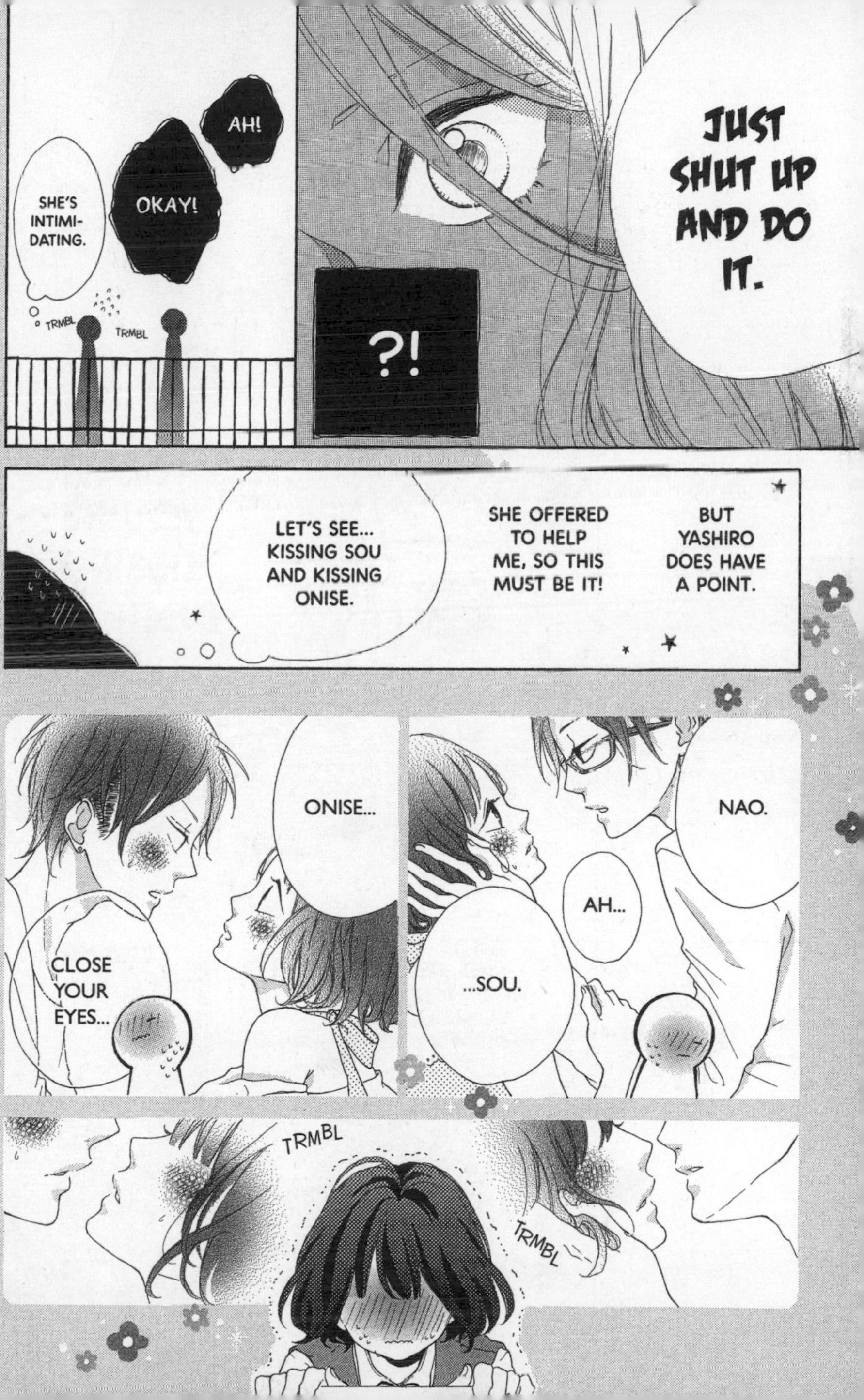
JUST SHUT UP AND DO IT.
?!
AH!
OKAY!
SHE'S INTIMI-DATING.
TRMBL
TRMBL
BUT YASHIRO DOES HAVE A POINT.
SHE OFFERED TO HELP ME, SO THIS MUST BE IT!
LET'S SEE... KISSING SOU AND KISSING ONISE.
NAO.
AH...
...SOU.
ONISE...
CLOSE YOUR EYES...
TRMBL
TRMBL

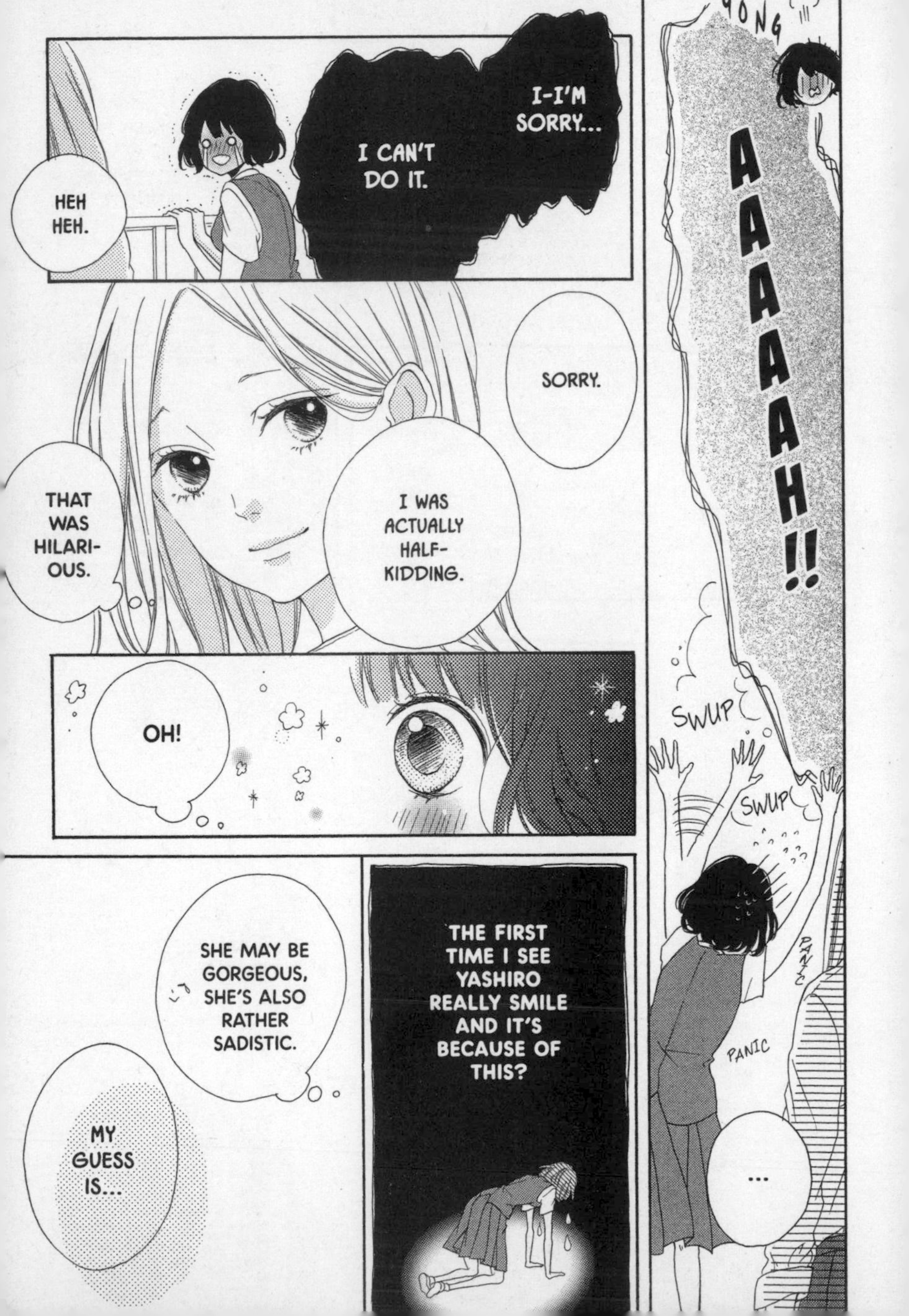
GONG
AAAAAH!!
SWUP
SWUP
PANIC
PANIC
...
I-I'M SORRY...
I CAN'T DO IT.
HEH HEH.
SORRY.
I WAS ACTUALLY HALF-KIDDING.
THAT WAS HILARI-OUS.
OH!
THE FIRST TIME I SEE YASHIRO REALLY SMILE AND IT'S BECAUSE OF THIS?
SHE MAY BE GORGEOUS, SHE'S ALSO RATHER SADISTIC.
MY GUESS IS...

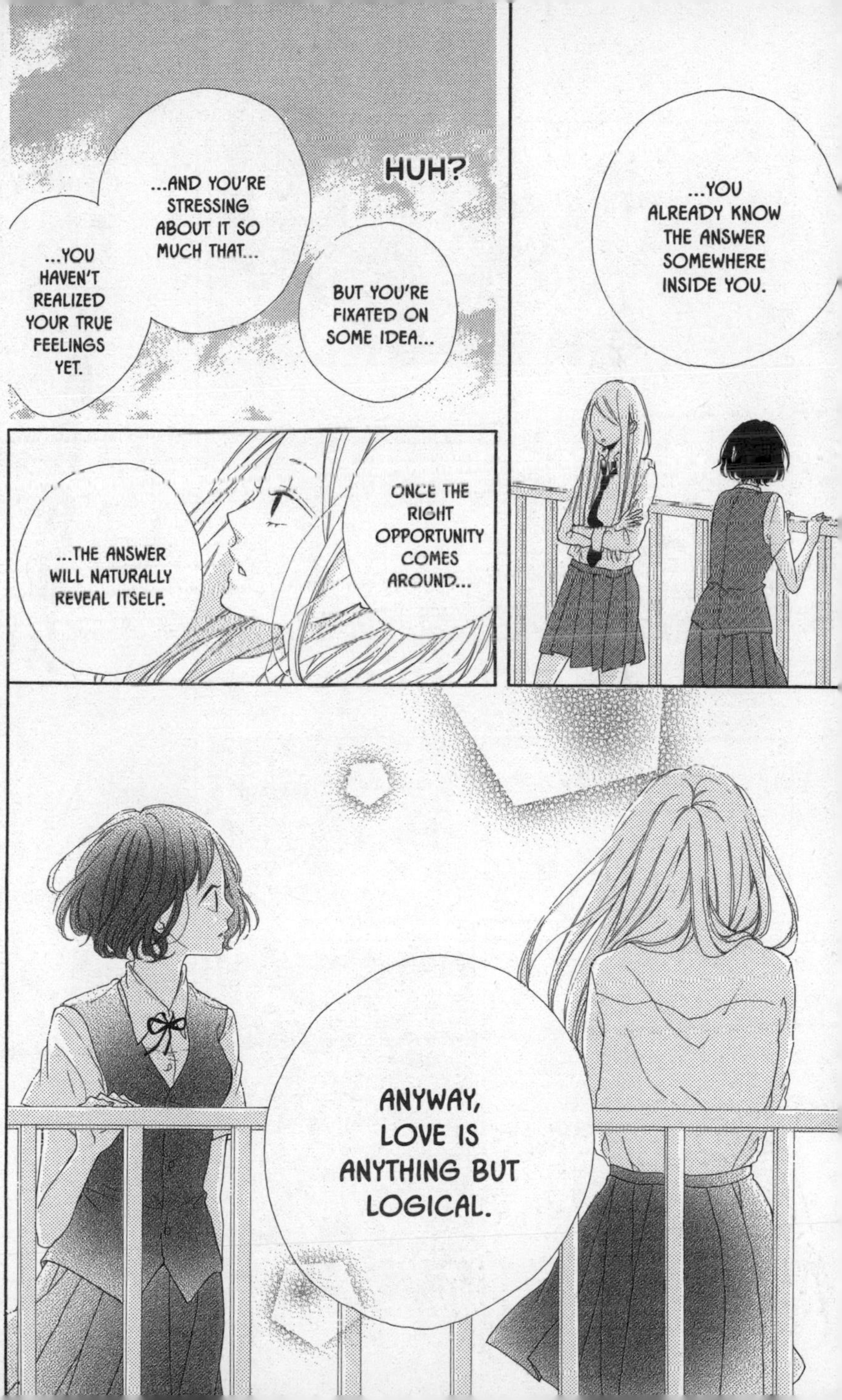
...YOU ALREADY KNOW THE ANSWER SOMEWHERE INSIDE YOU.
HUH?
BUT YOU'RE FIXATED ON SOME IDEA...
...AND YOU'RE STRESSING ABOUT IT SO MUCH THAT...
...YOU HAVEN'T REALIZED YOUR TRUE FEELINGS YET.
ONCE THE RIGHT OPPORTUNITY COMES AROUND...
...THE ANSWER WILL NATURALLY REVEAL ITSELF.
ANYWAY, LOVE IS ANYTHING BUT LOGICAL.

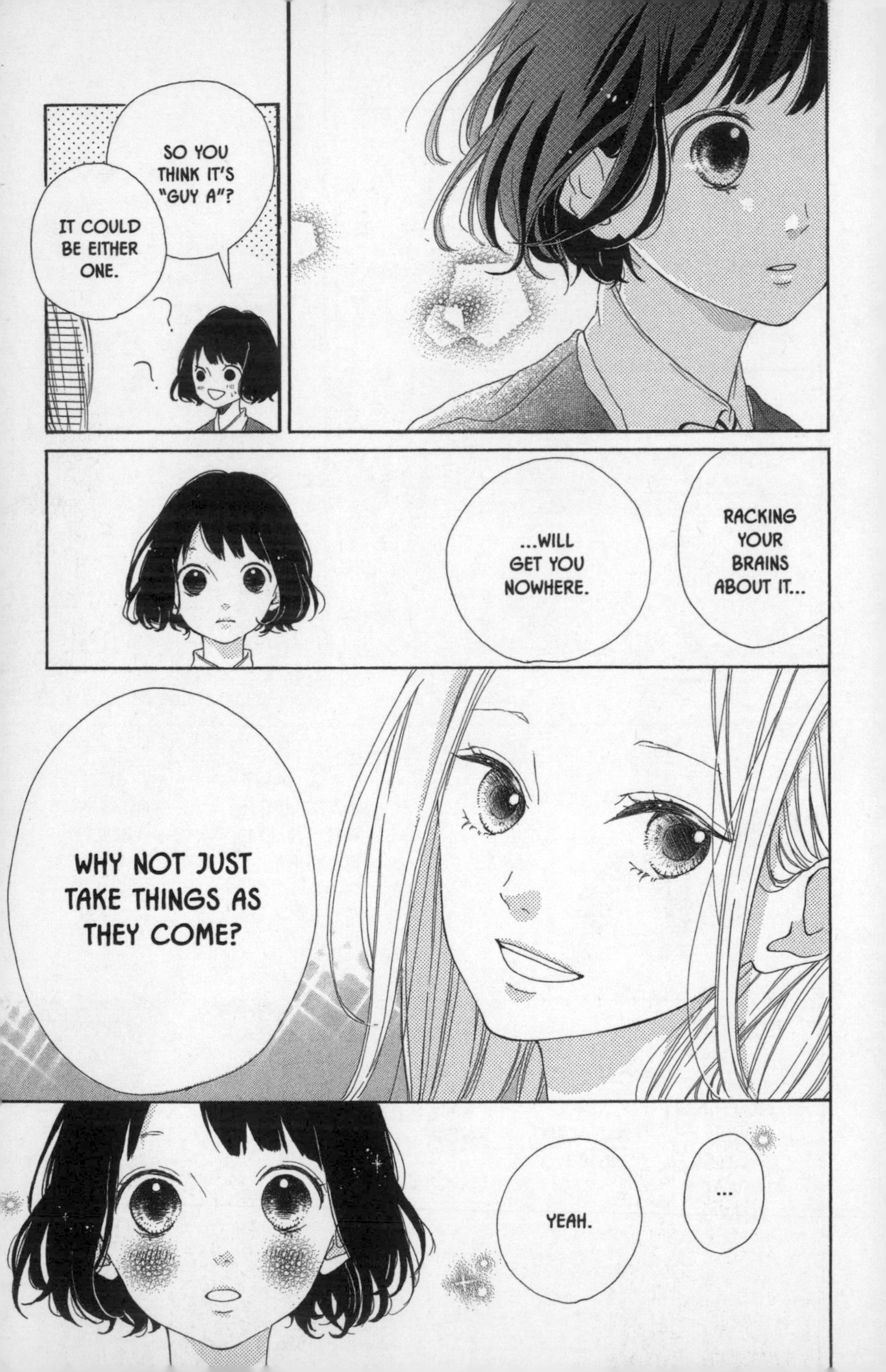
SO YOU THINK IT'S "GUY A"?
IT COULD BE EITHER ONE.
RACKING YOUR BRAINS ABOUT IT...
...WILL GET YOU NOWHERE.
WHY NOT JUST TAKE THINGS AS THEY COME?
...
YEAH.

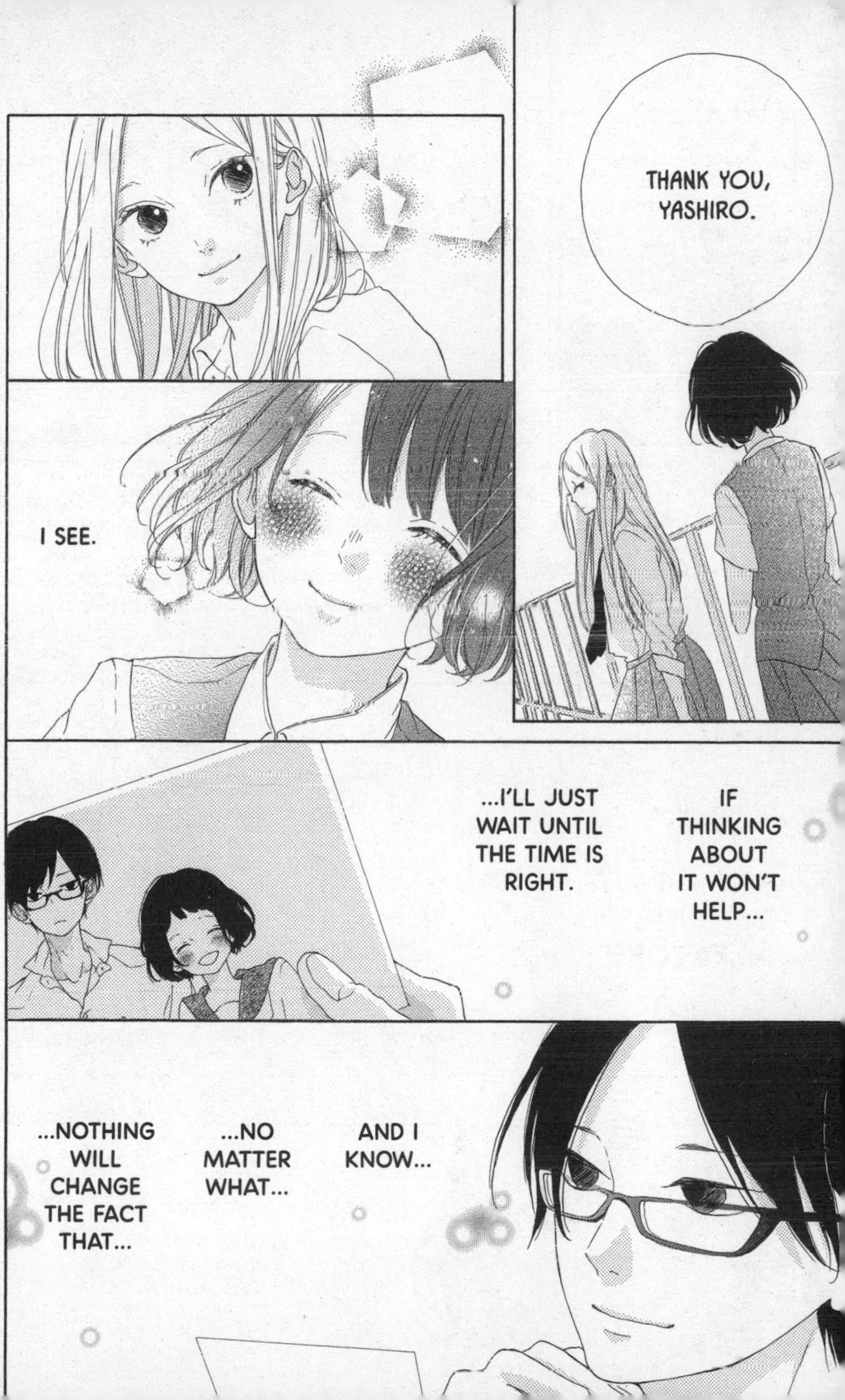
THANK YOU, YASHIRO.
I SEE.
IF THINKING ABOUT IT WON'T HELP...
...I'LL JUST WAIT UNTIL THE TIME IS RIGHT.
AND I KNOW...
...NO MATTER WHAT...
...NOTHING WILL CHANGE THE FACT THAT...

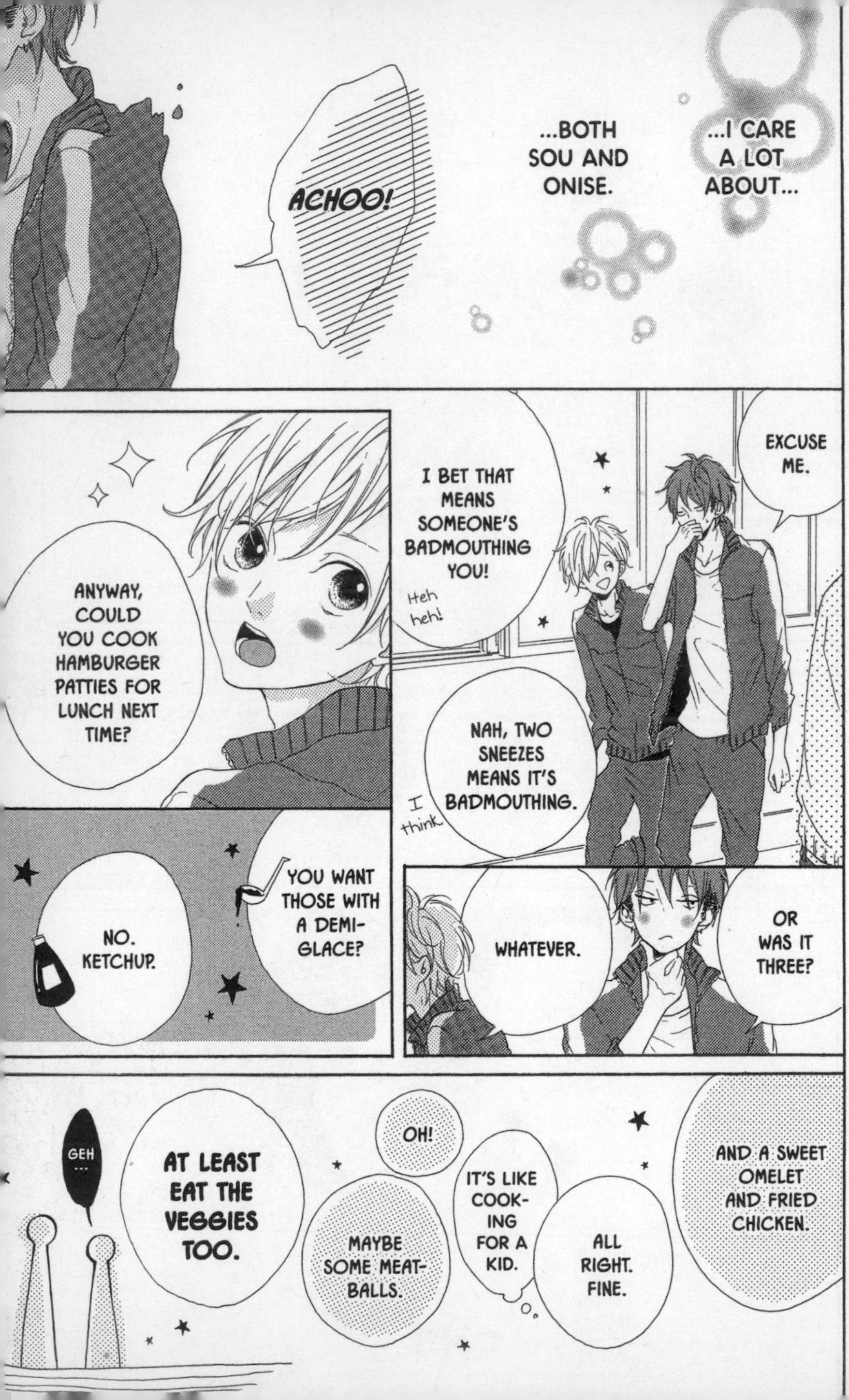
...I CARE A LOT ABOUT...
...BOTH SOU AND ONISE.
ACHOO!
EXCUSE ME.
I BET THAT MEANS SOMEONE'S BADMOUTHING YOU!
Heh heh!
NAH, TWO SNEEZES MEANS IT'S BADMOUTHING.
I think.
OR WAS IT THREE?
WHATEVER.
ANYWAY, COULD YOU COOK HAMBURGER PATTIES FOR LUNCH NEXT TIME?
YOU WANT THOSE WITH A DEMI-GLACE?
NO. KETCHUP.
AND A SWEET OMELET AND FRIED CHICKEN.
OH!
IT'S LIKE COOKING FOR A KID.
ALL RIGHT. FINE.
MAYBE SOME MEATBALLS.
AT LEAST EAT THE VEGGIES TOO.
GEH...

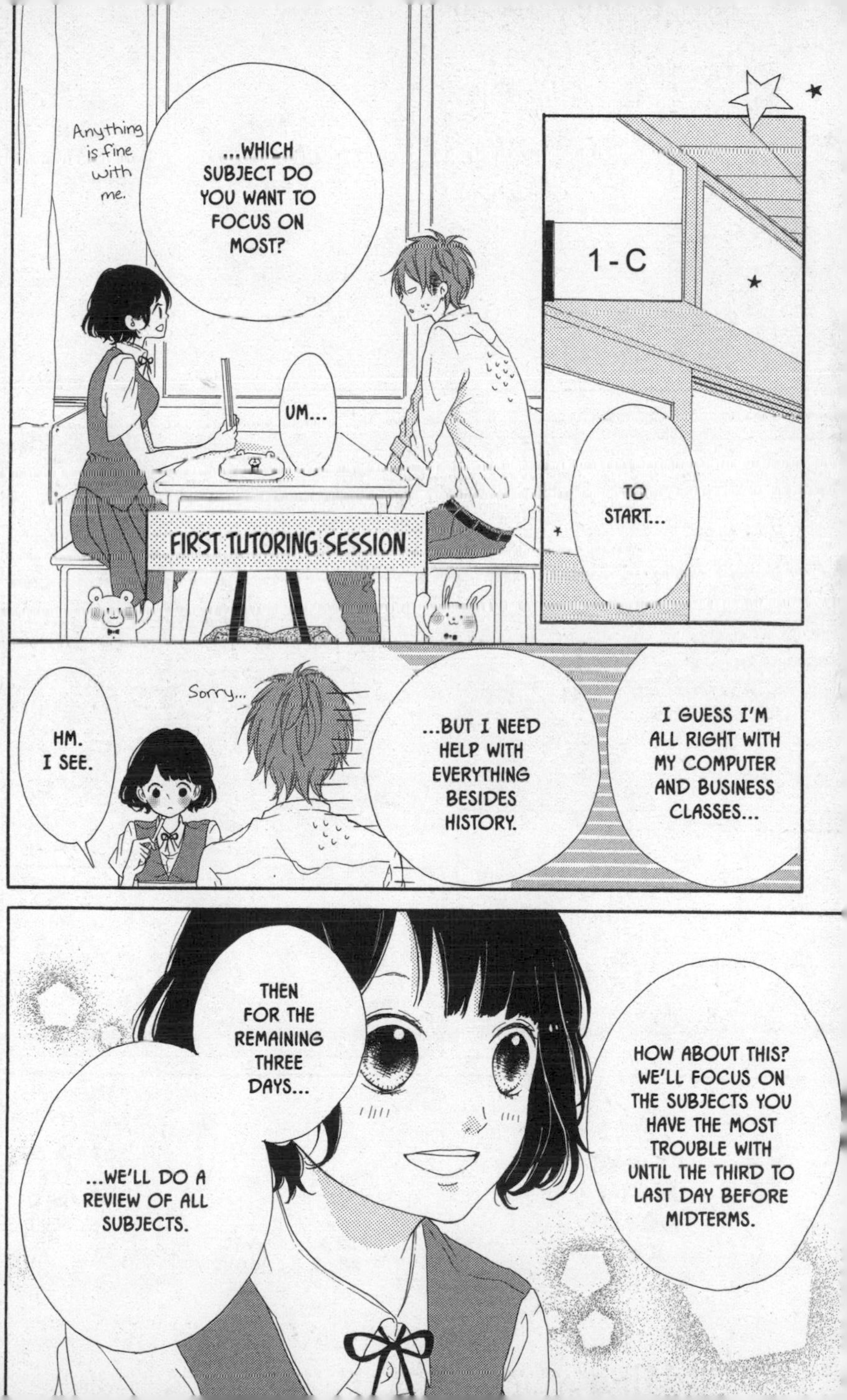
1 - C
TO START...
...WHICH SUBJECT DO YOU WANT TO FOCUS ON MOST?
Anything is fine with me.
UM...
FIRST TUTORING SESSION
I GUESS I'M ALL RIGHT WITH MY COMPUTER AND BUSINESS CLASSES...
...BUT I NEED HELP WITH EVERYTHING BESIDES HISTORY.
Sorry...
HM. I SEE.
HOW ABOUT THIS? WE'LL FOCUS ON THE SUBJECTS YOU HAVE THE MOST TROUBLE WITH UNTIL THE THIRD TO LAST DAY BEFORE MIDTERMS.
THEN FOR THE REMAINING THREE DAYS...
...WE'LL DO A REVIEW OF ALL SUBJECTS.

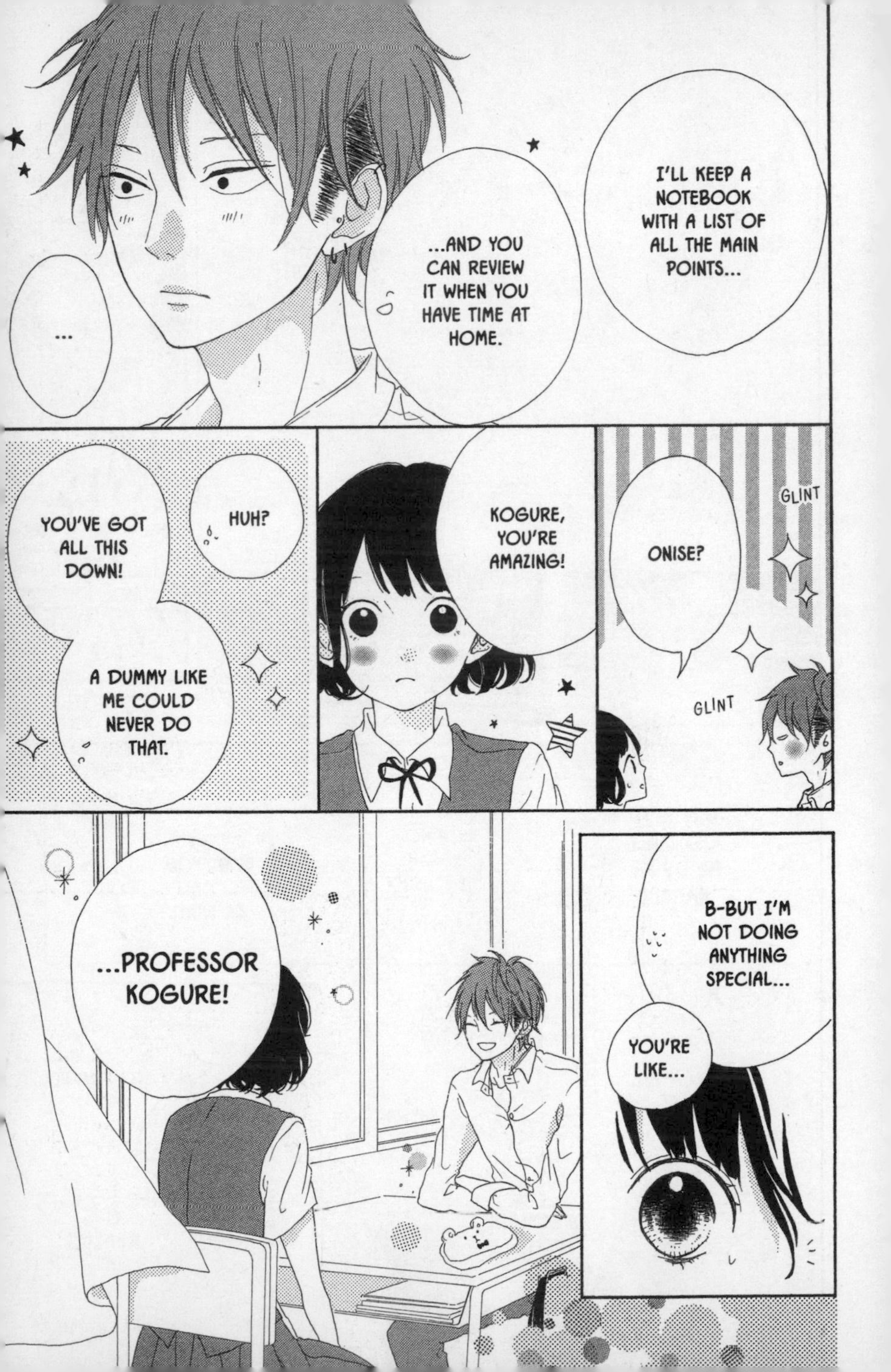
I'LL KEEP A NOTEBOOK WITH A LIST OF ALL THE MAIN POINTS...
...AND YOU CAN REVIEW IT WHEN YOU HAVE TIME AT HOME.
...
ONISE?
GLINT
GLINT
KOGURE, YOU'RE AMAZING!
HUH?
YOU'VE GOT ALL THIS DOWN!
A DUMMY LIKE ME COULD NEVER DO THAT.
B-BUT I'M NOT DOING ANYTHING SPECIAL...
YOU'RE LIKE...
...PROFESSOR KOGURE!

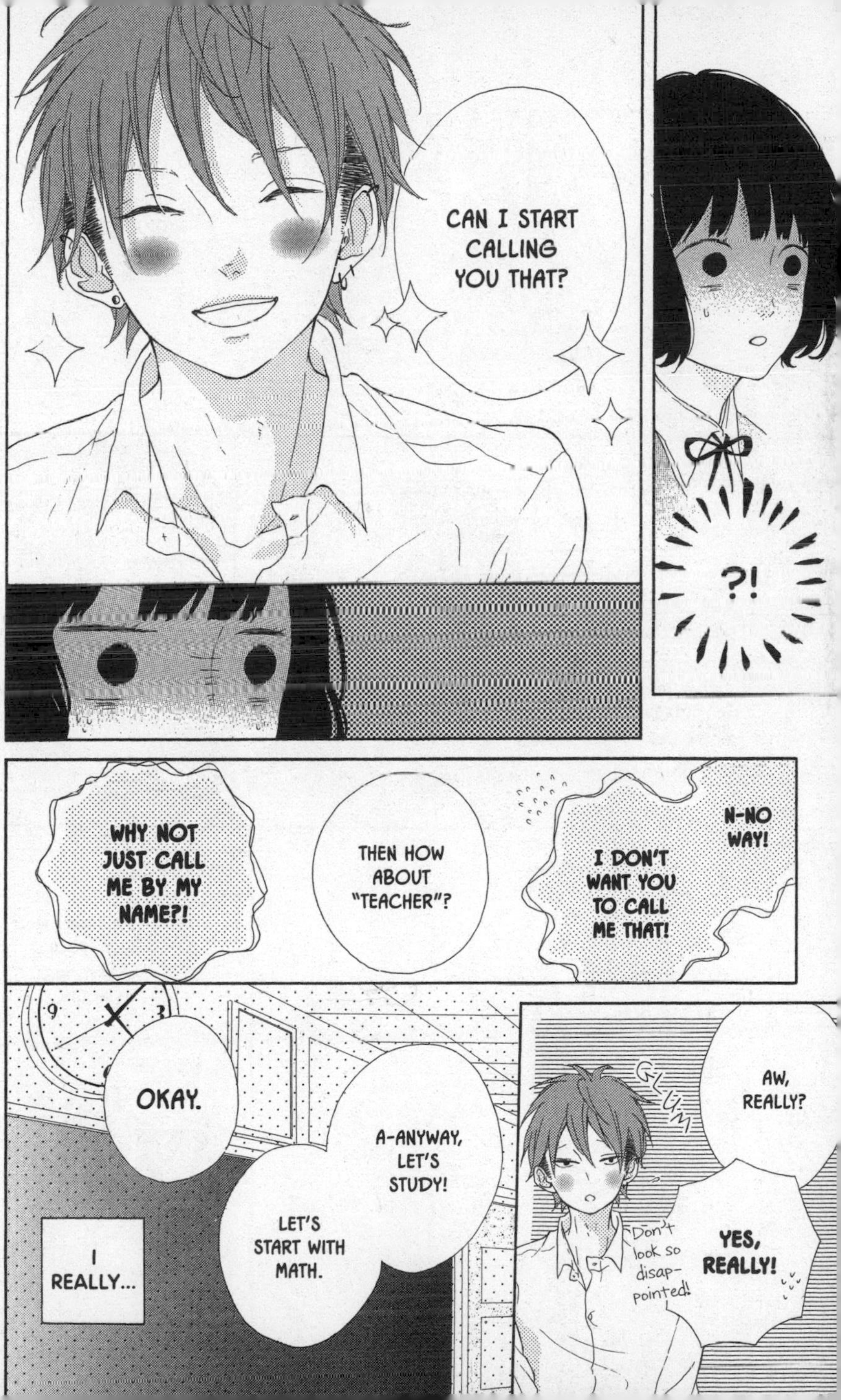
?!
CAN I START CALLING YOU THAT?
N-NO WAY!
I DON'T WANT YOU TO CALL ME THAT!
THEN HOW ABOUT "TEACHER"?
WHY NOT JUST CALL ME BY MY NAME?!
AW, REALLY?
GLUM
YES, REALLY!
Don't look so disap-pointed!
A-ANYWAY, LET'S STUDY!
LET'S START WITH MATH.
OKAY.
I REALLY...

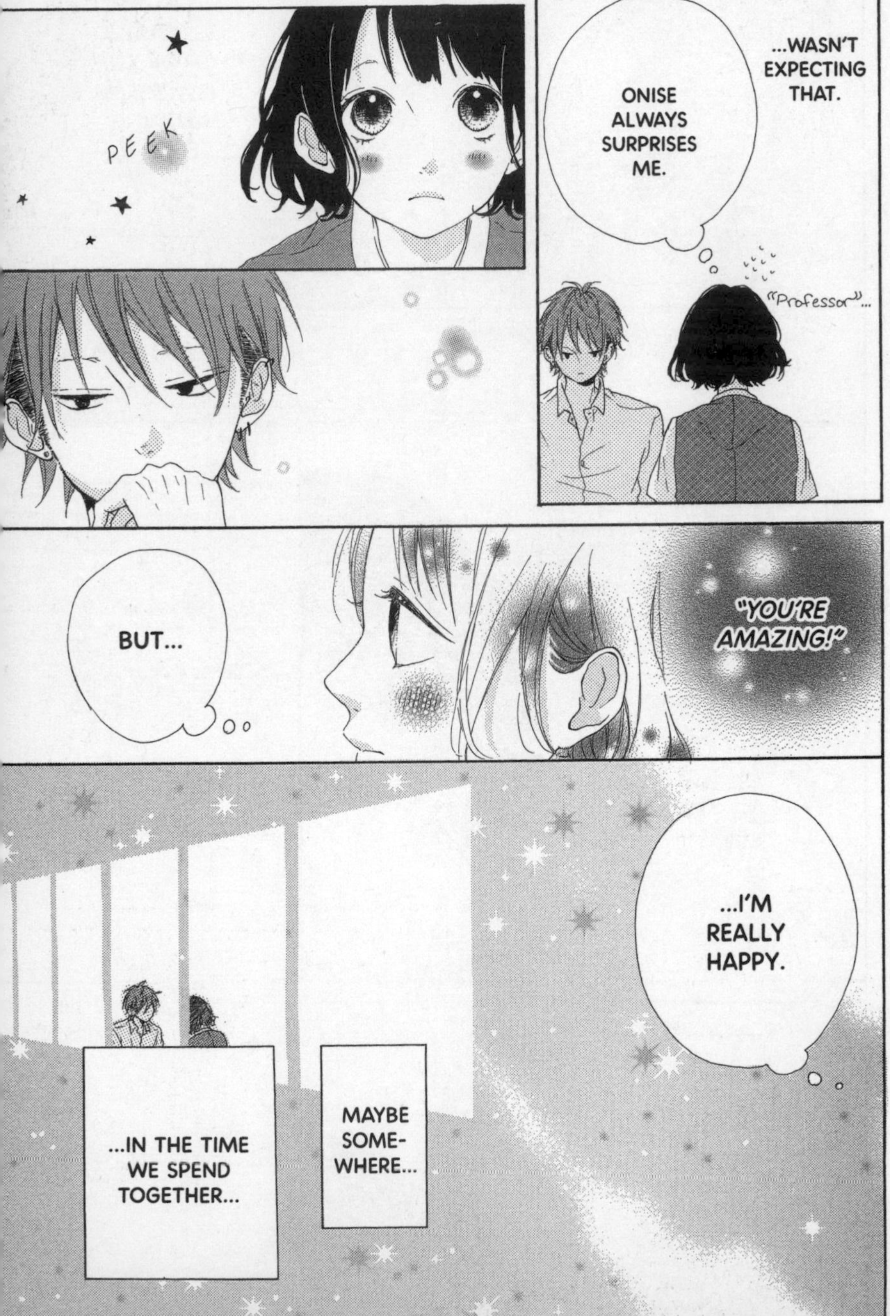
...WASN'T EXPECTING THAT.
ONISE ALWAYS SURPRISES ME.
“Professor”...
PEEK
"YOU'RE AMAZING!"
BUT...
...I'M REALLY HAPPY.
MAYBE SOME-WHERE...
...IN THE TIME WE SPEND TOGETHER...

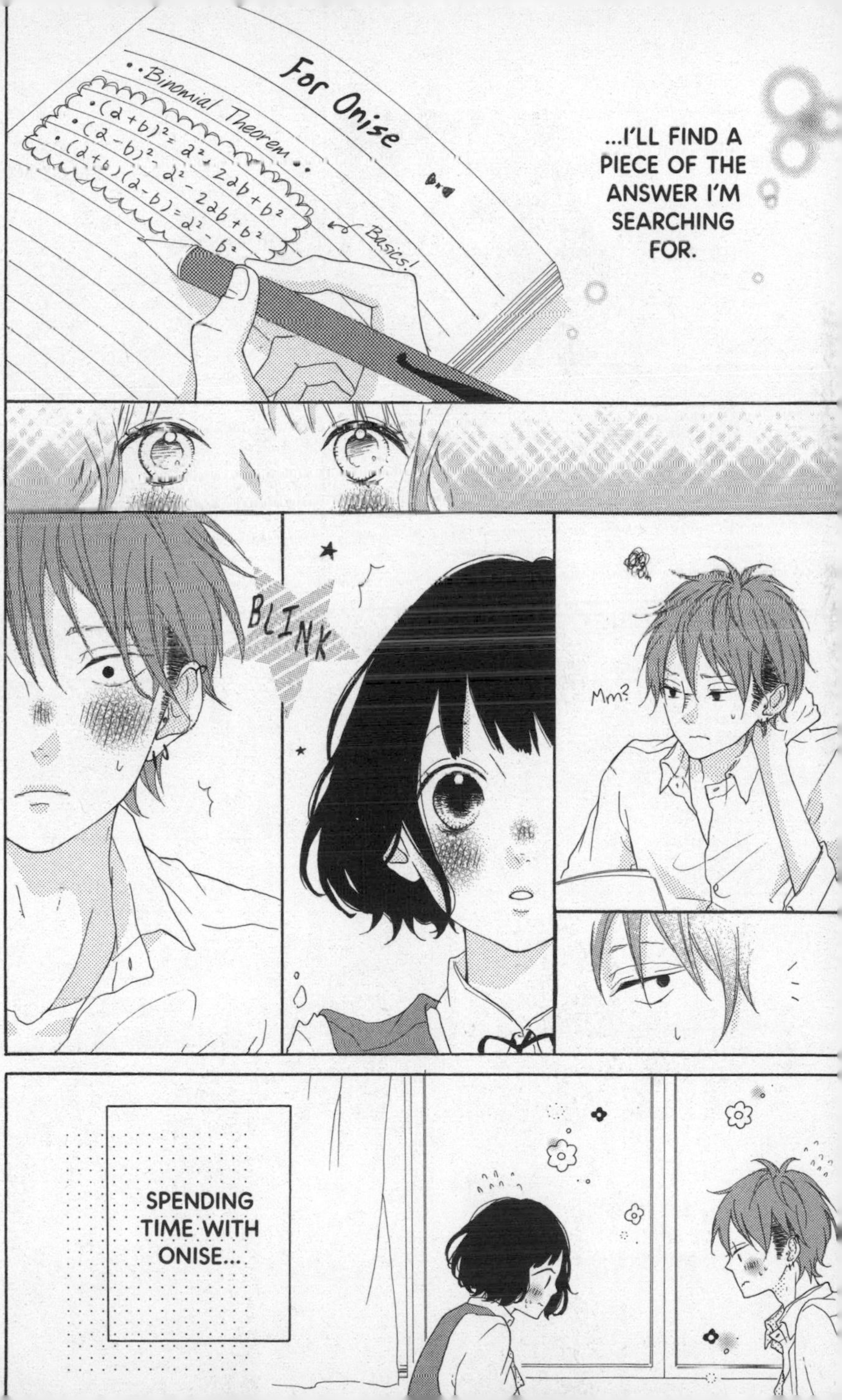
...I'LL FIND A PIECE OF THE ANSWER I'M SEARCHING FOR.
For Onise
••Binomial Theorem••
•$(a+b)^2 = a^2 + 2ab + b^2$
•$(a-b)^2 = a^2 - 2ab + b^2$
•$(a+b)(a-b) = a^2 - b^2$
Basics!
Mm?
BLINK
SPENDING TIME WITH ONISE...

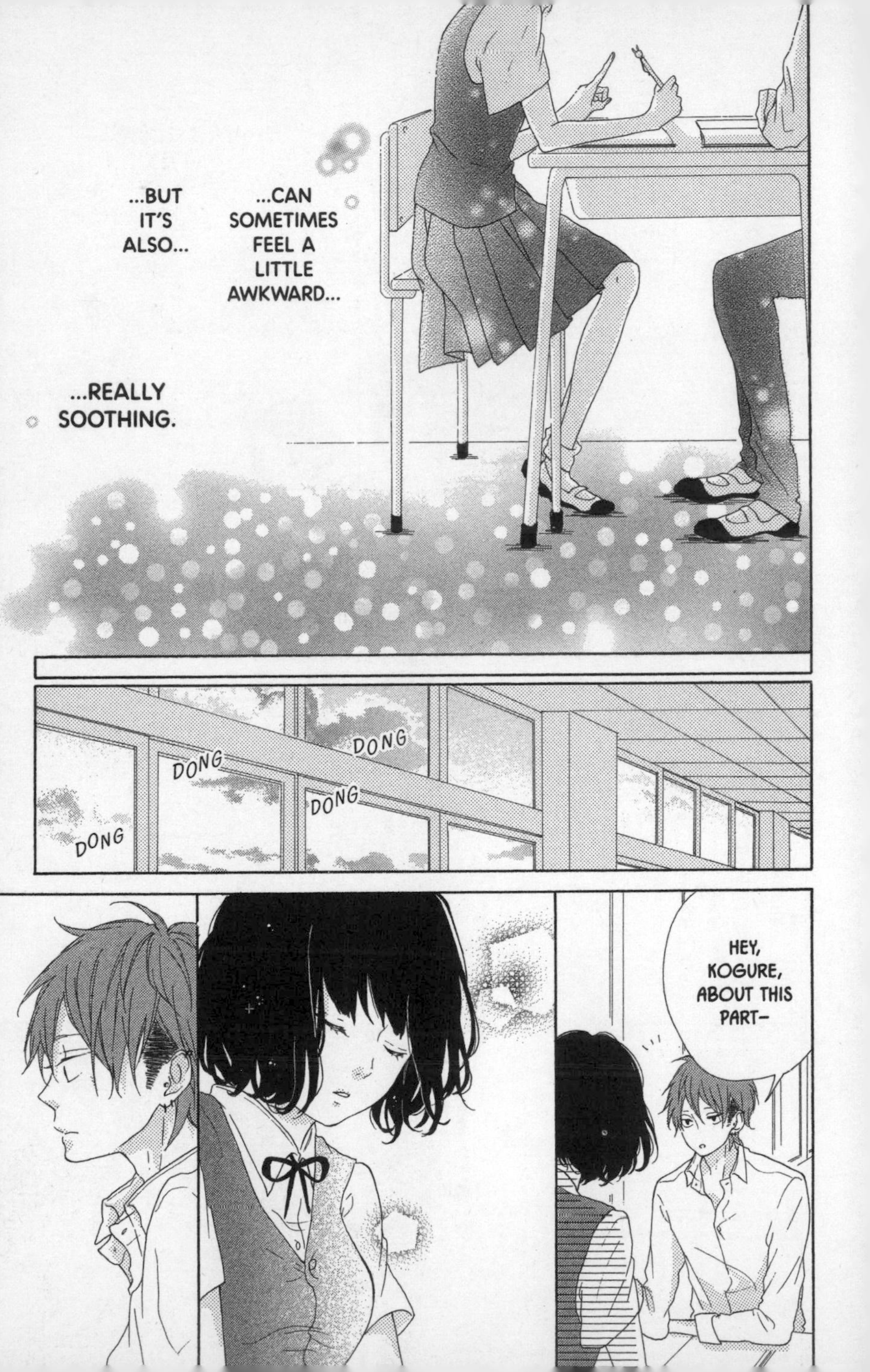
...CAN SOMETIMES FEEL A LITTLE AWKWARD...
...BUT IT'S ALSO...
...REALLY SOOTHING.
DONG
DONG
DONG
DONG
HEY, KOGURE, ABOUT THIS PART–

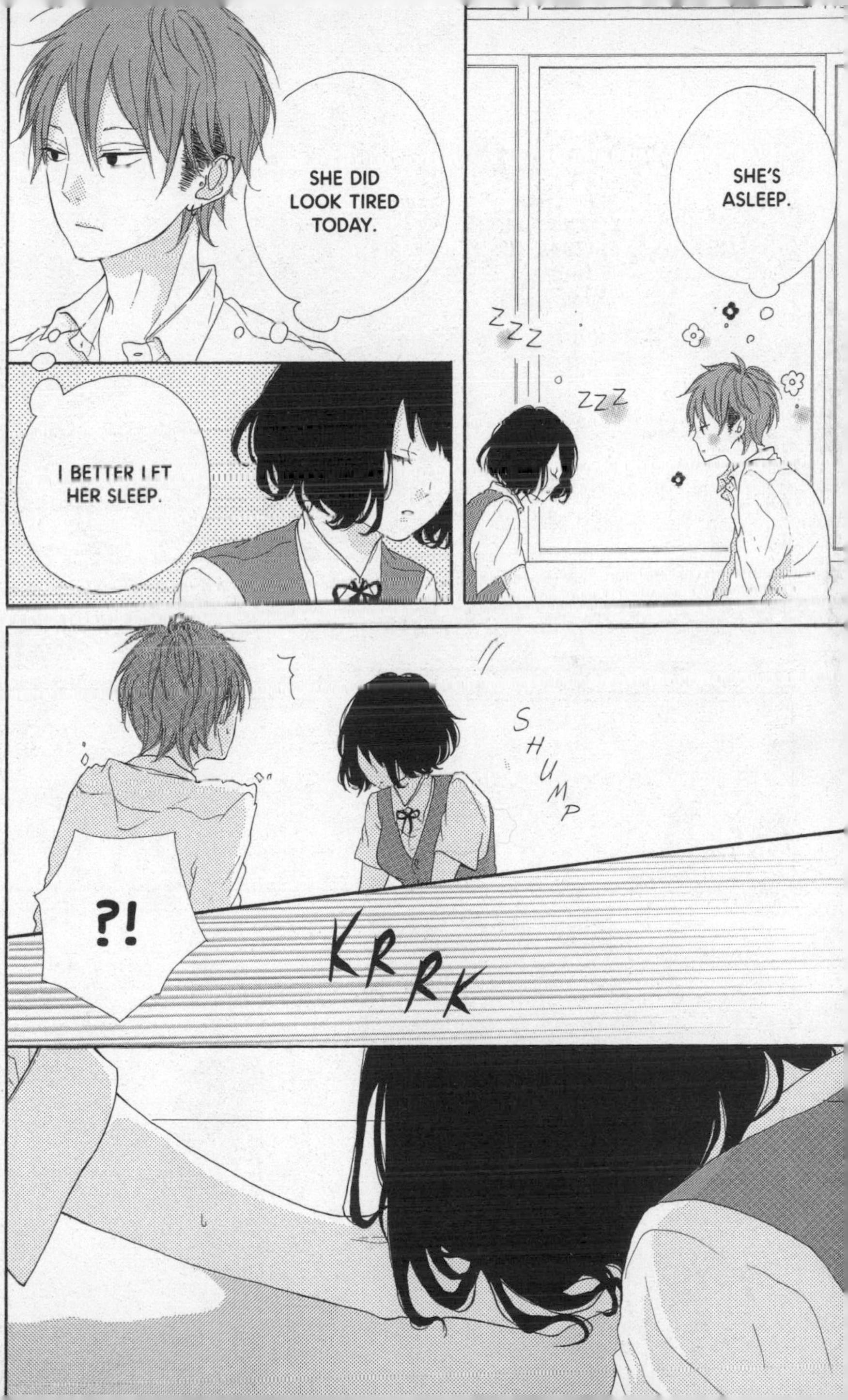
SHE'S ASLEEP.
ZZZ
ZZZ
SHE DID LOOK TIRED TODAY.
I BETTER LET HER SLEEP.
SHUMP
?!
KRRK

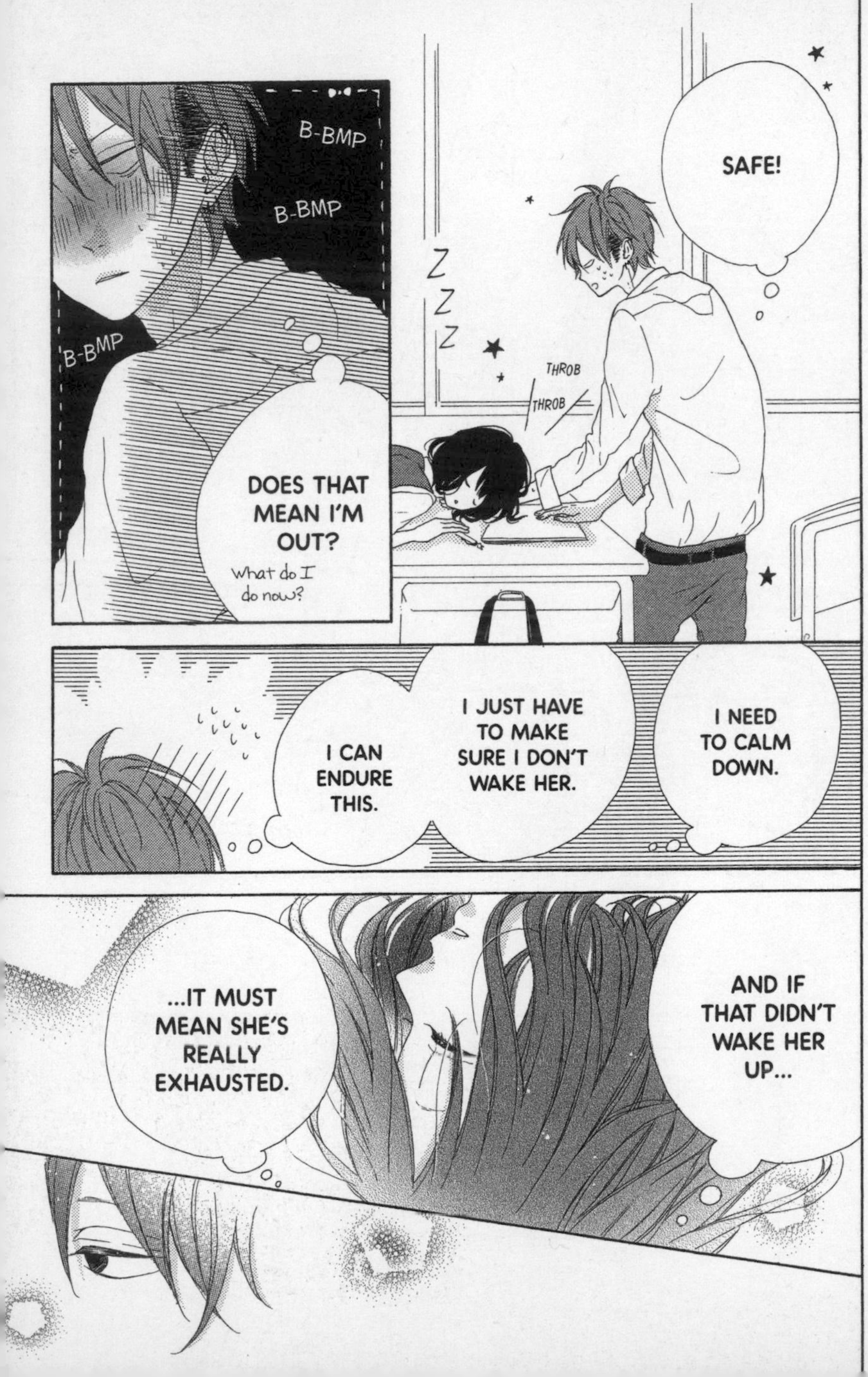
SAFE!
Z Z Z
THROB THROB
B-BMP B-BMP B-BMP
DOES THAT MEAN I'M OUT?
what do I do now?
I NEED TO CALM DOWN.
I JUST HAVE TO MAKE SURE I DON'T WAKE HER.
I CAN ENDURE THIS.
AND IF THAT DIDN'T WAKE HER UP...
...IT MUST MEAN SHE'S REALLY EXHAUSTED.

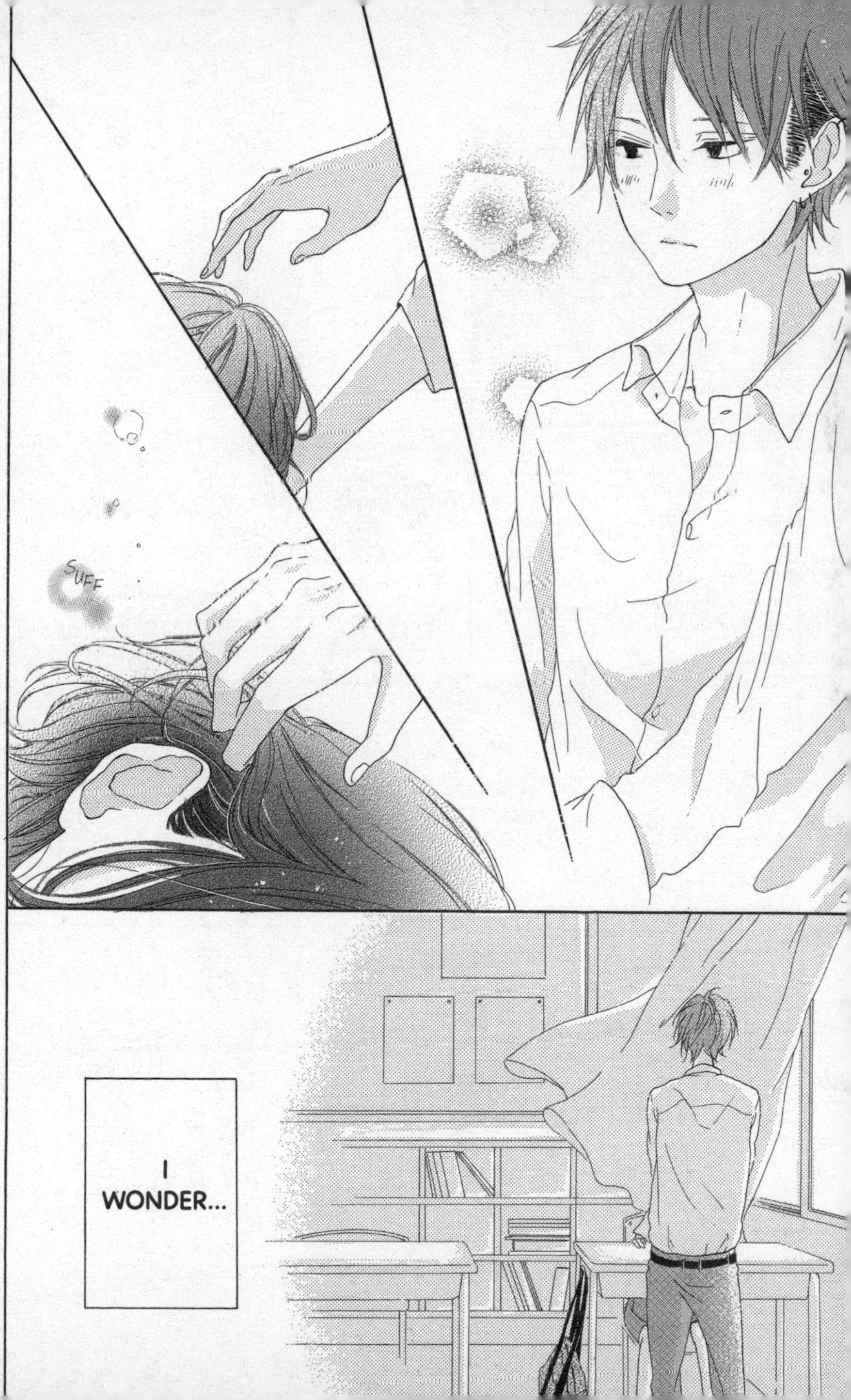
SUFF
I WONDER...

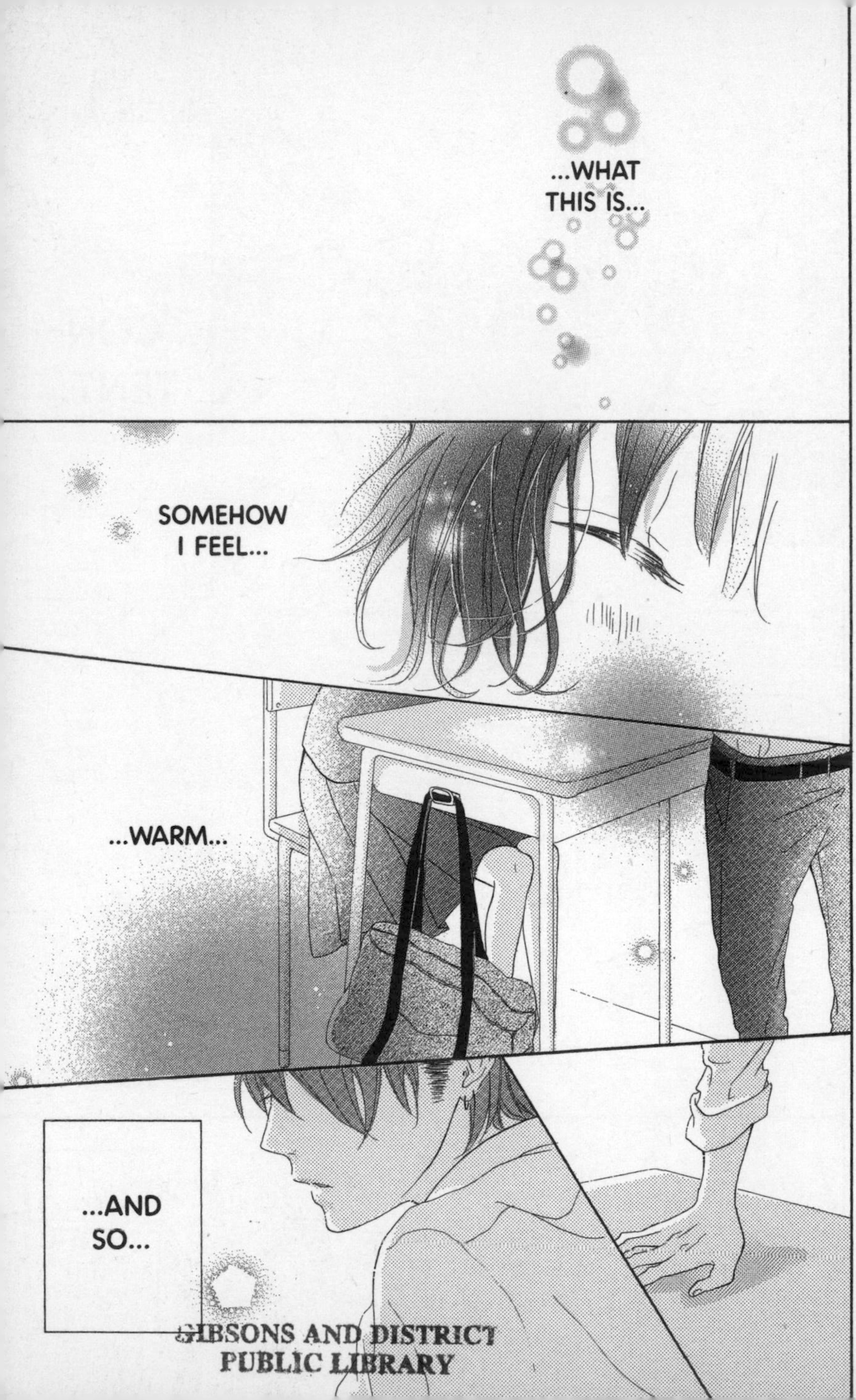
...WHAT
THIS IS...
SOMEHOW
I FEEL...
...WARM...
...AND
SO...

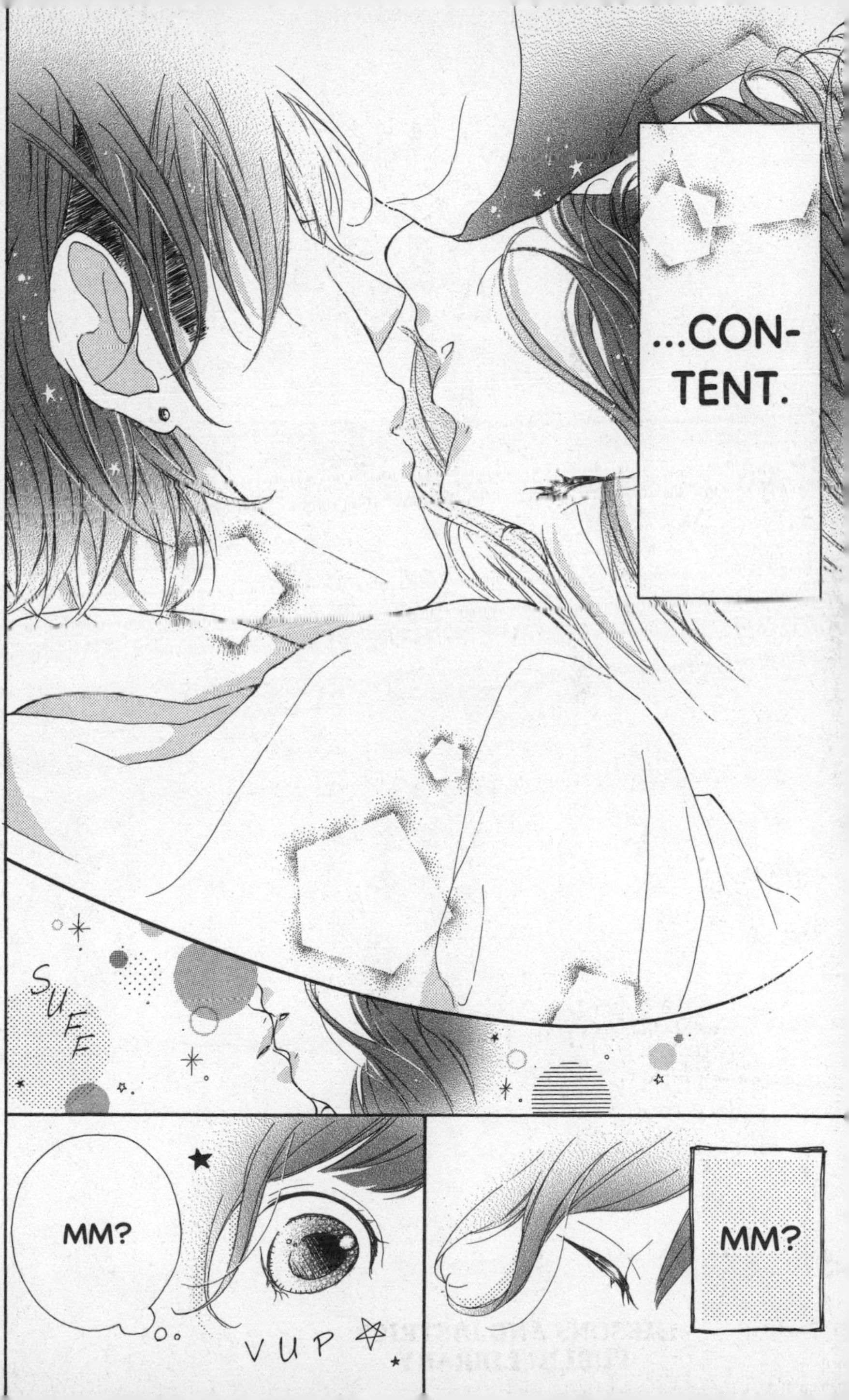
...CON-
TENT.
SUFF
MM?
MM?
VUP

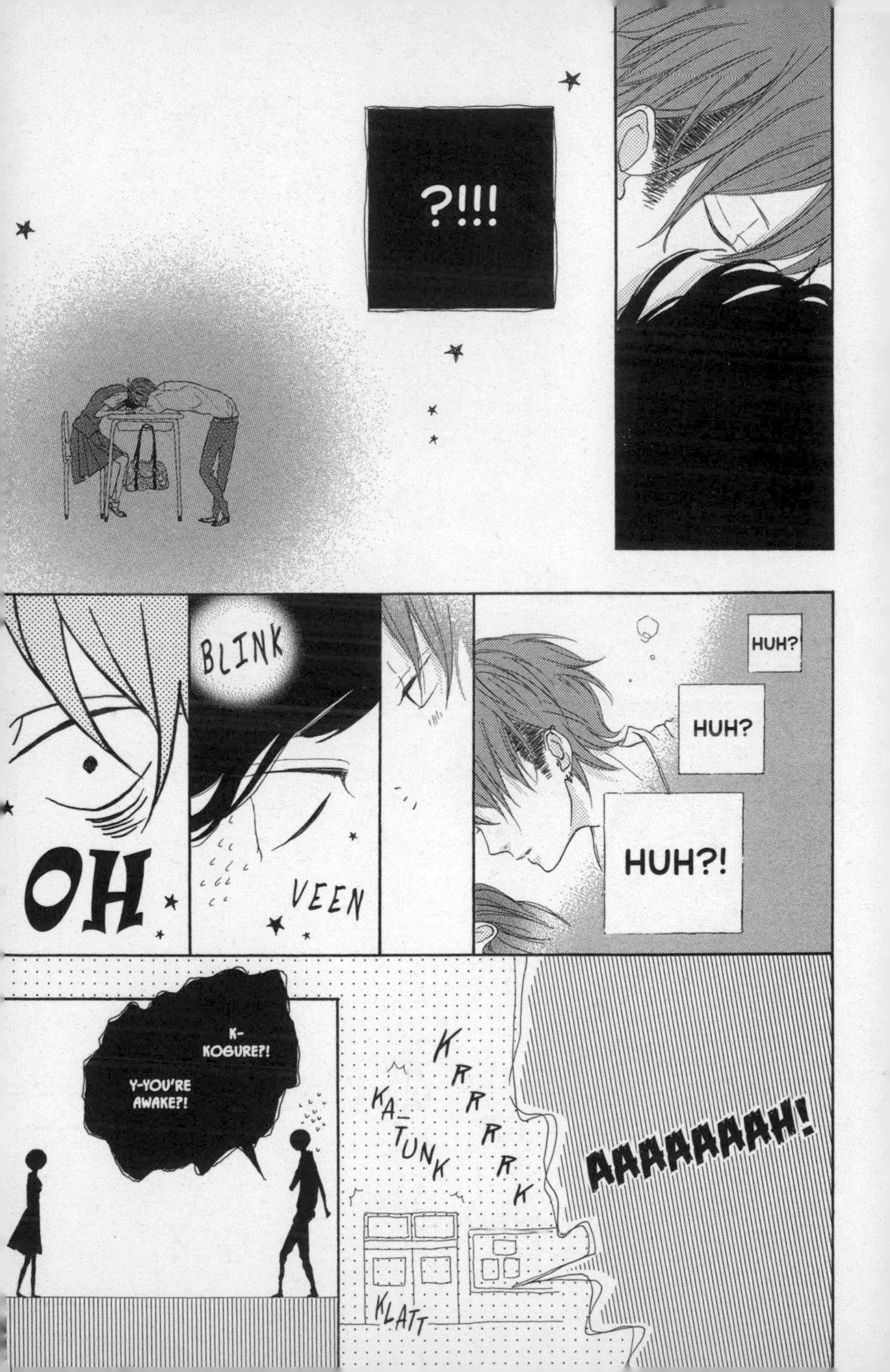
?!!!
HUH?
HUH?
HUH?!
BLINK
VEEN
OH
AAAAAAAH!
KRRRRRK
KA-TUNK
KLATT
K-KOBURE?!
Y-YOU'RE AWAKE?!

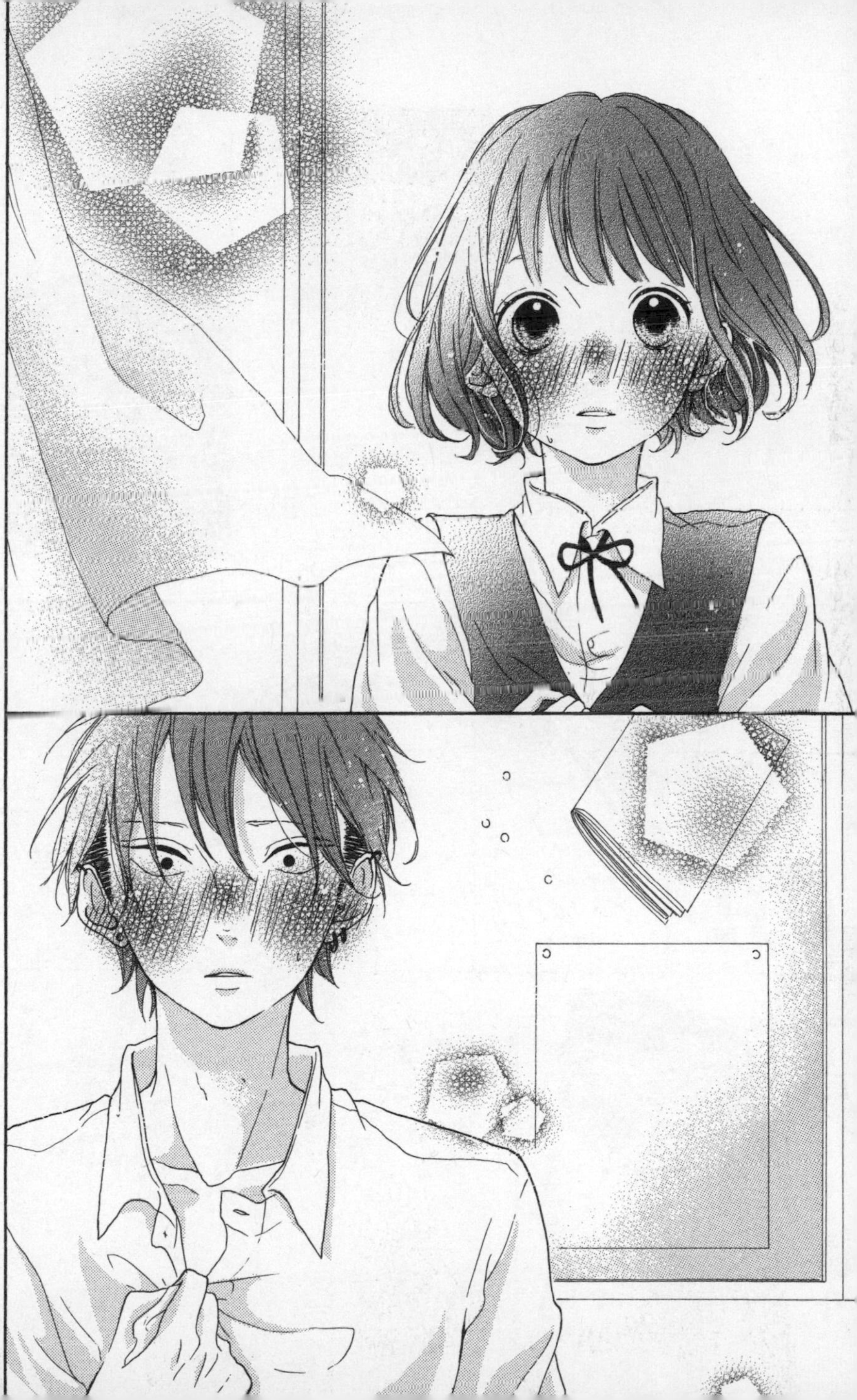

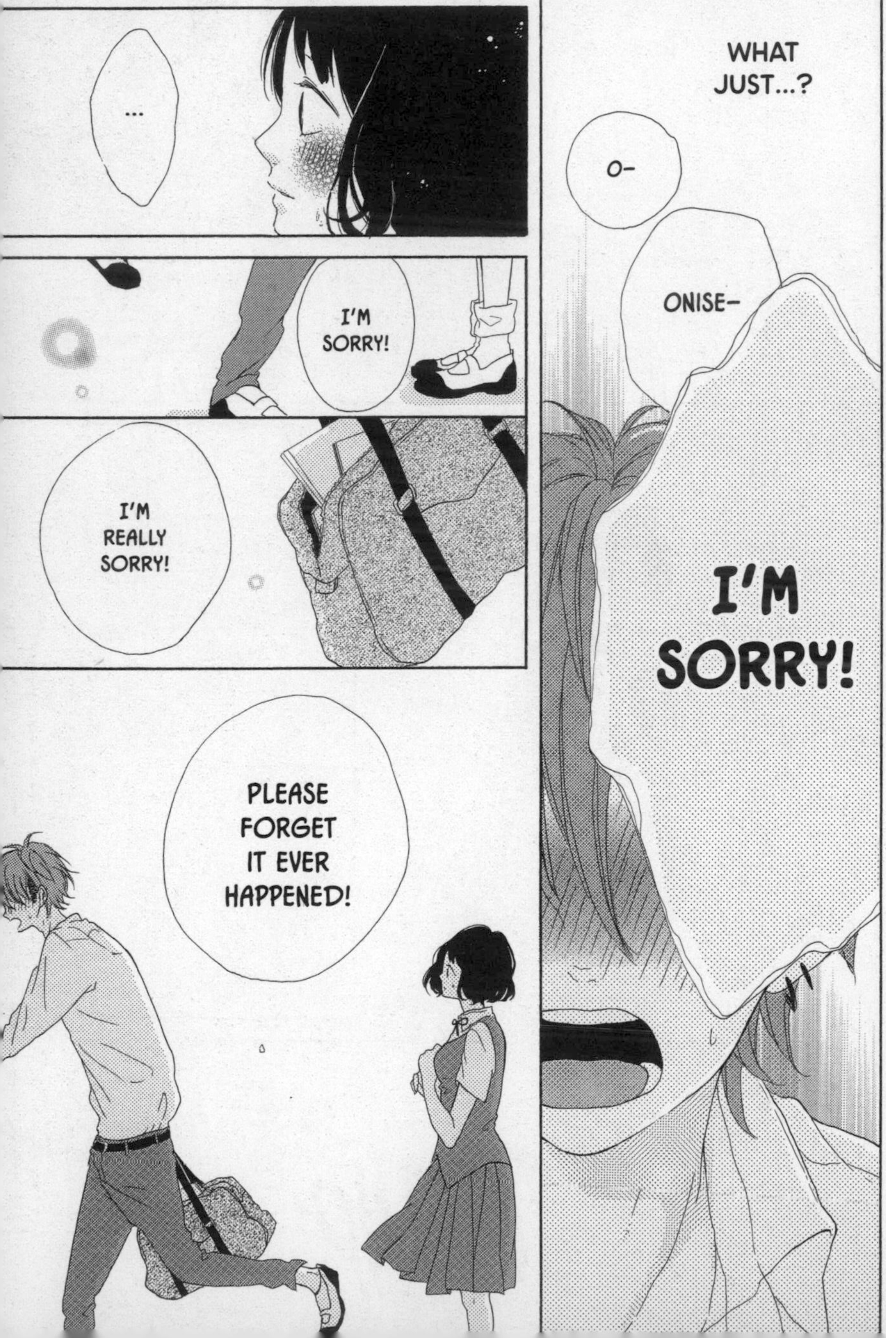
WHAT JUST...?
O-
ONISE-
I'M SORRY!
...
I'M SORRY!
I'M REALLY SORRY!
PLEASE FORGET IT EVER HAPPENED!

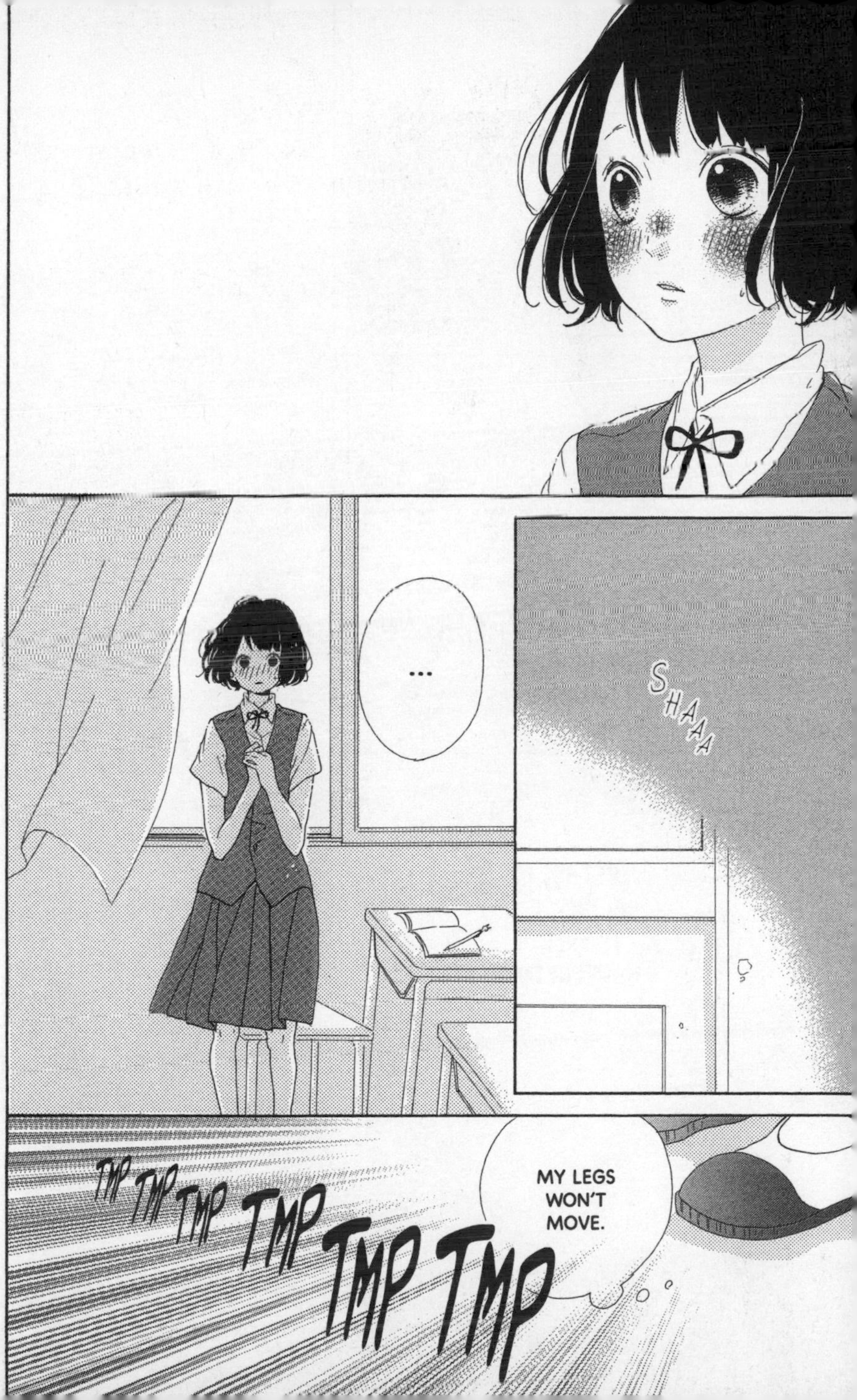
SHAAA
...
MY LEGS WON'T MOVE.
TMP TMP TMP TMP TMP TMP TMP

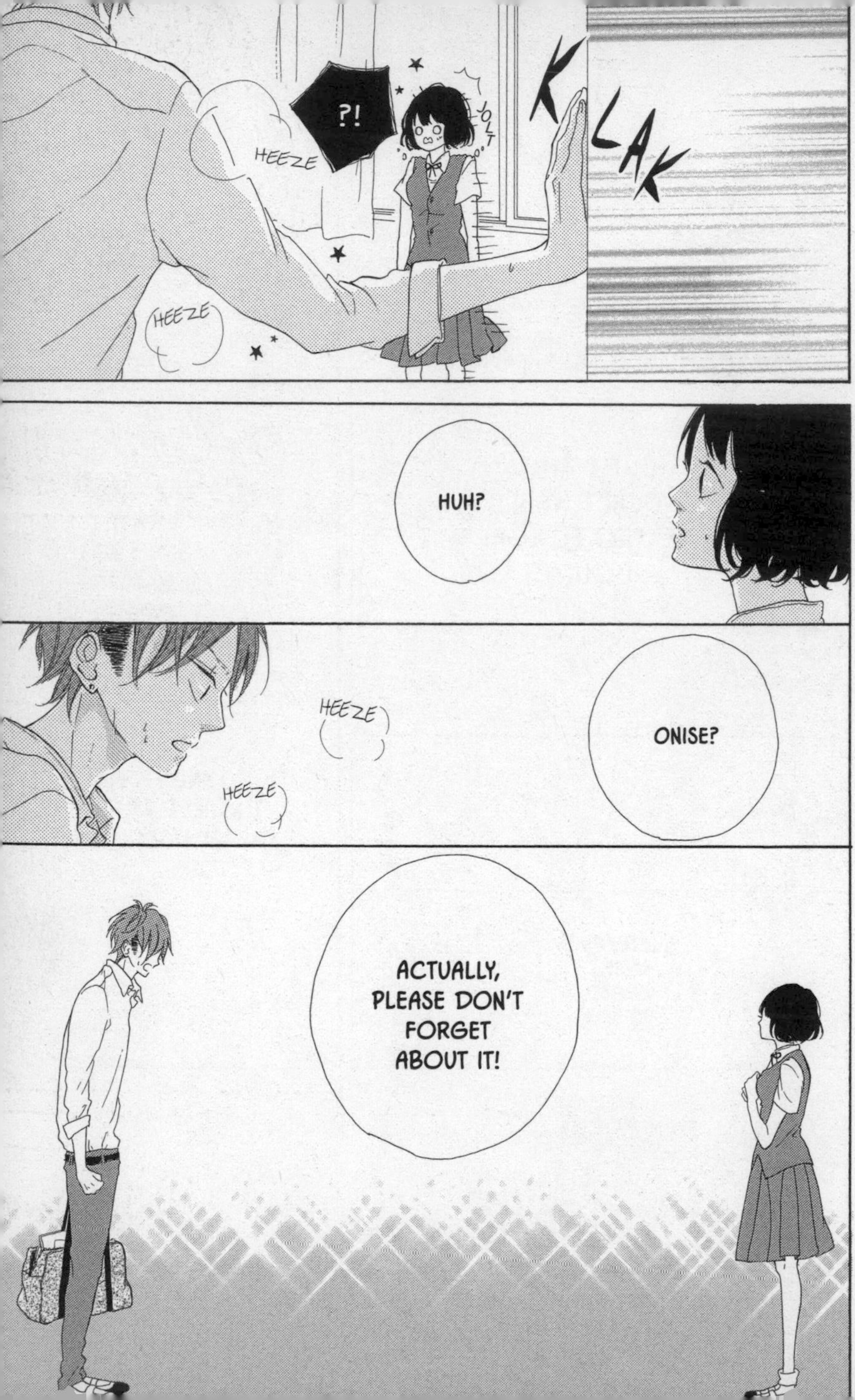
KLAK
JOLT
?!
HEEZE
HEEZE
HUH?
ONISE?
HEEZE
HEEZE
ACTUALLY, PLEASE DON'T FORGET ABOUT IT!

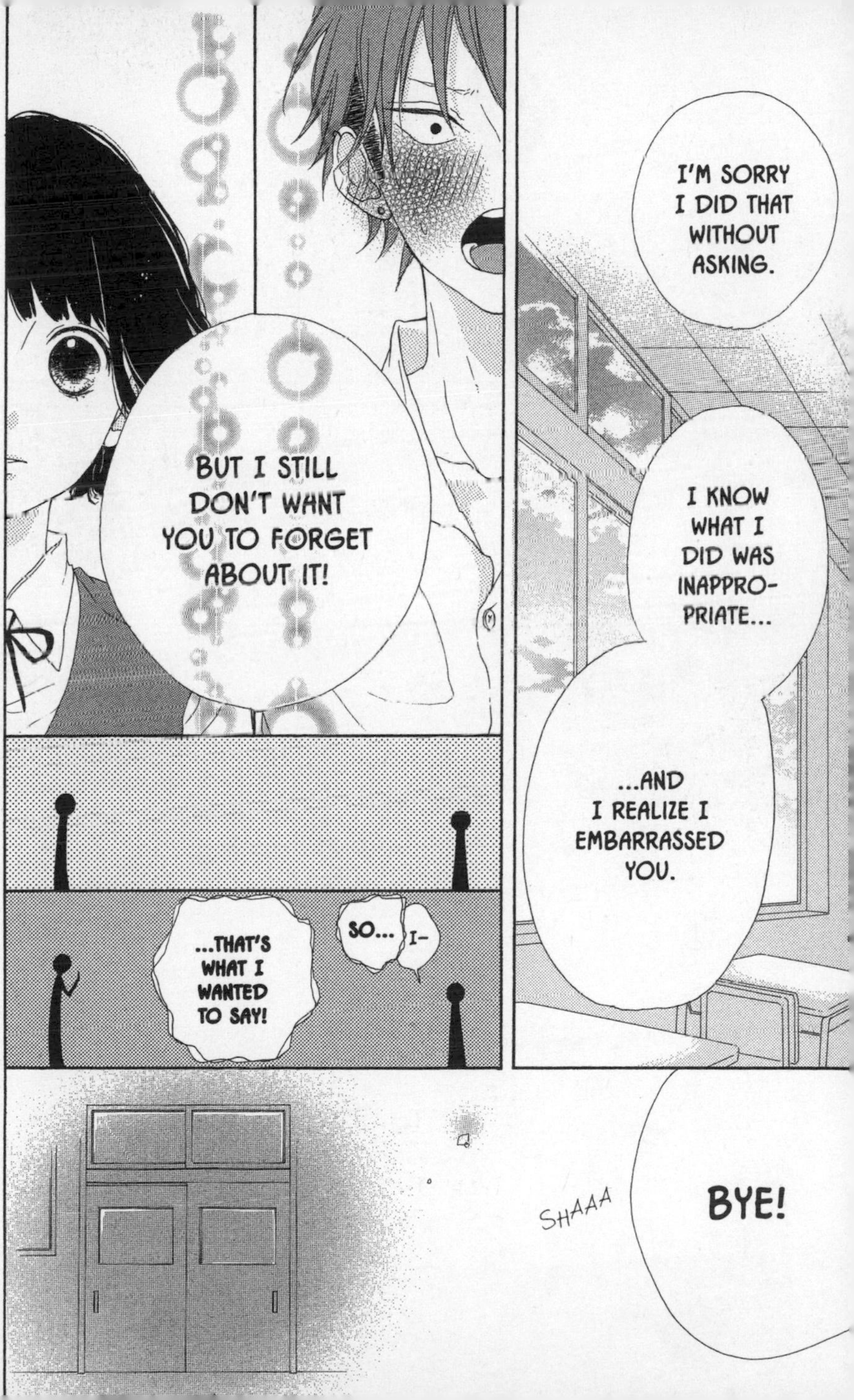
I'M SORRY I DID THAT WITHOUT ASKING.
I KNOW WHAT I DID WAS INAPPROPRIATE...
...AND I REALIZE I EMBARRASSED YOU.
BUT I STILL DON'T WANT YOU TO FORGET ABOUT IT!
SO...
I-
...THAT'S WHAT I WANTED TO SAY!
BYE!
SHAAA

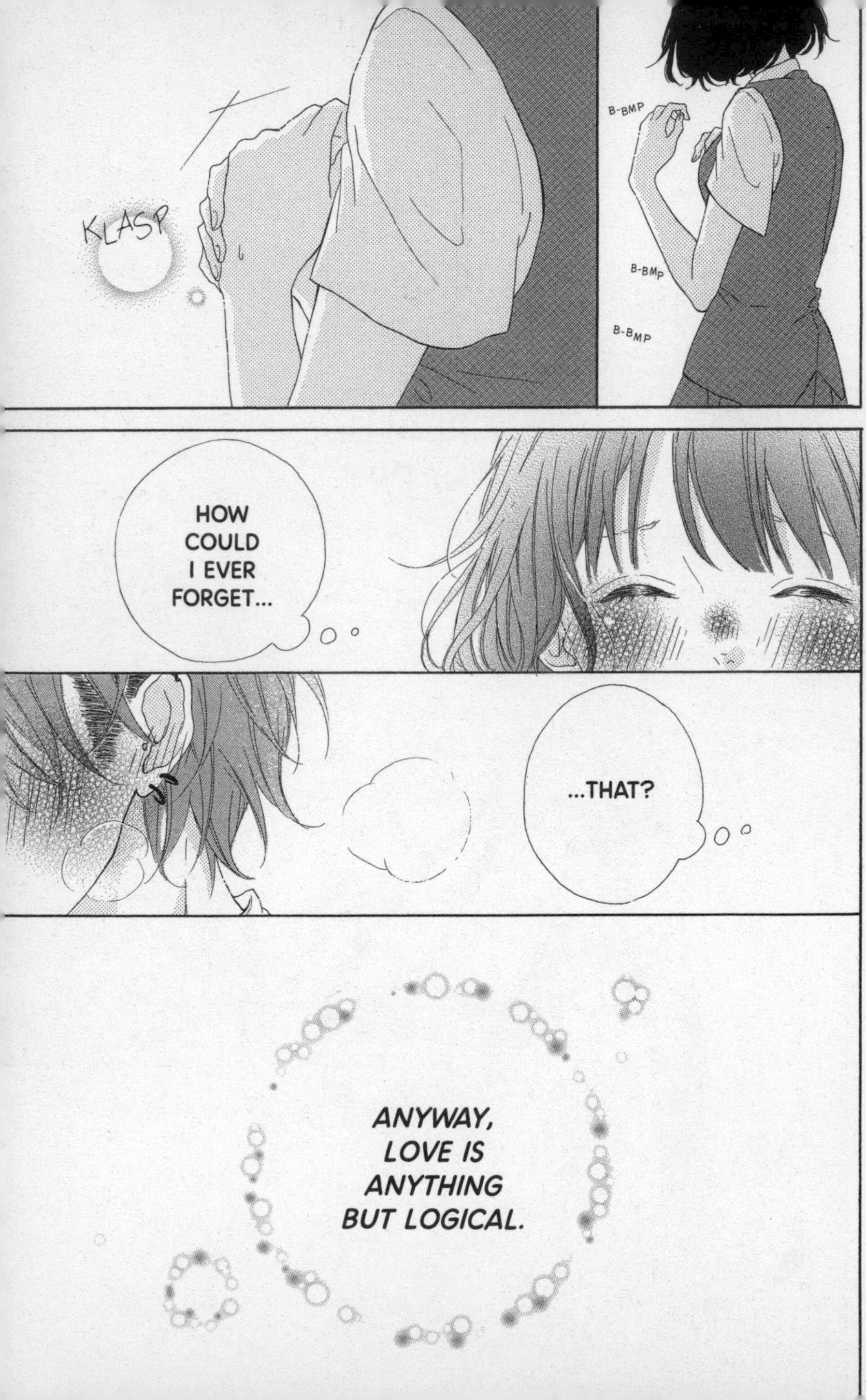
B-BMP
B-BMP
B-BMP
KLASP
HOW COULD I EVER FORGET...
...THAT?
ANYWAY, LOVE IS ANYTHING BUT LOGICAL.

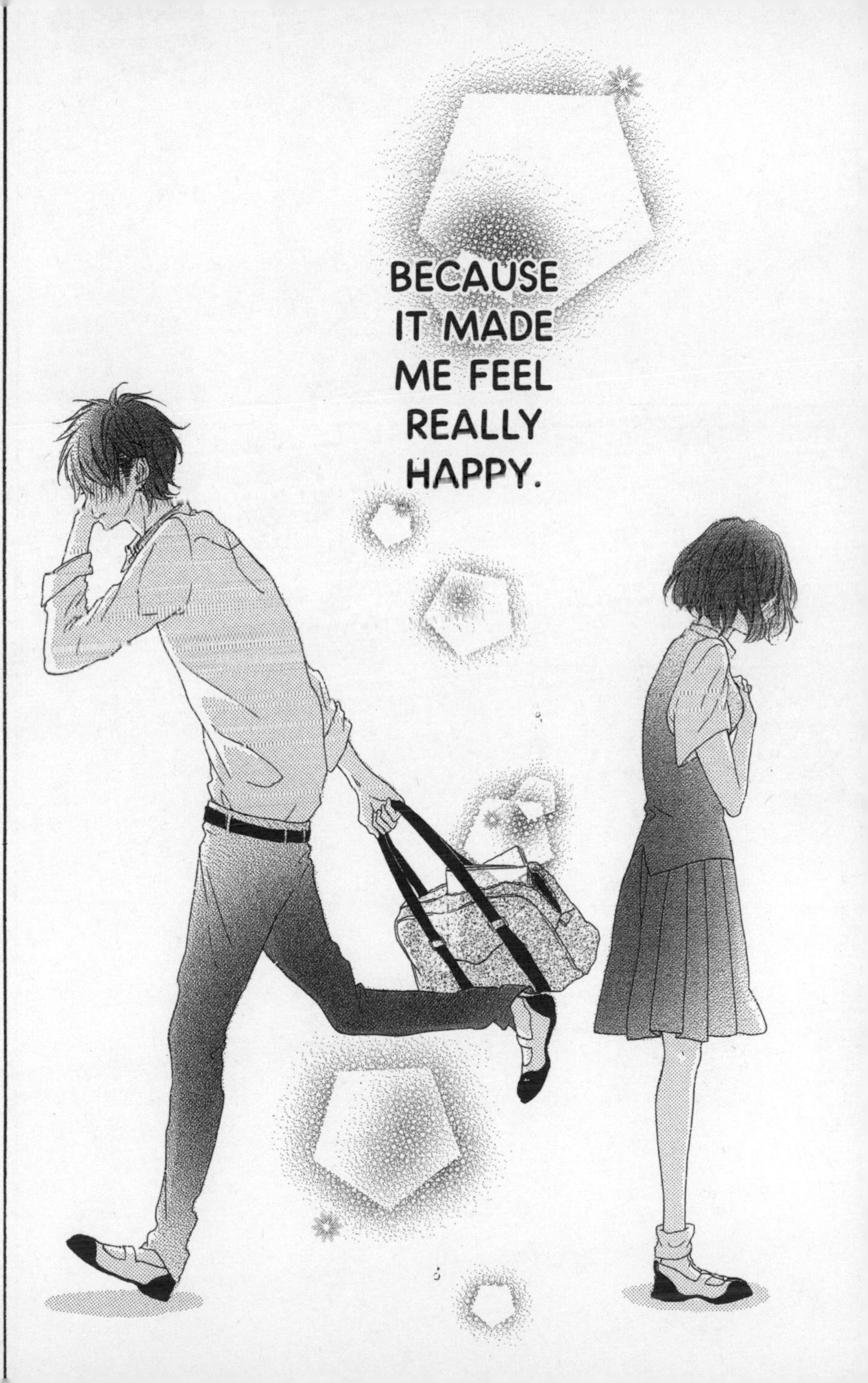
BECAUSE IT MADE ME FEEL REALLY HAPPY.

I love kids so much that

I love to draw them too!

That's how I came up with this.

Honey Kindergarten: Nectar Class!

(This has nothing to do with the actual story.)

Cast of Characters

A quasi-manga starts on the next page!

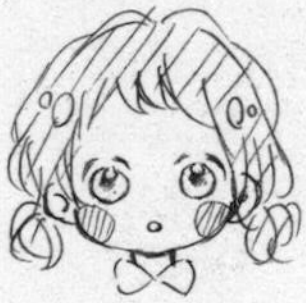

★ Nao ★

A nervous scaredy-cat.

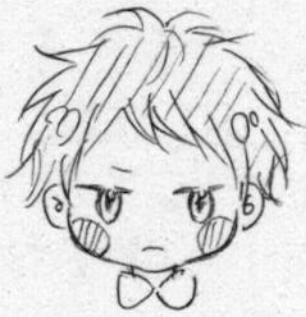

★ Taiga ★

Looks just like the baddies in action shows.

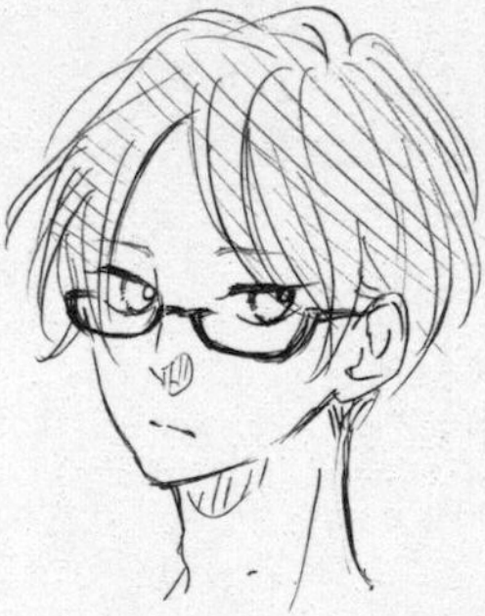

★ Teacher Sou ★

Nectar Class's teacher. Age unknown.

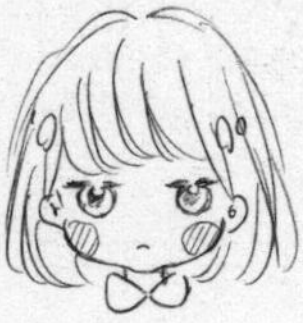

★ Kayo ★

Mature for her age.

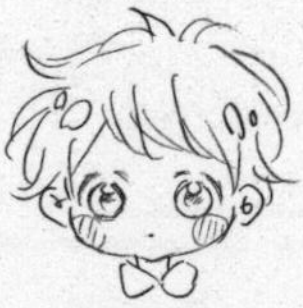

★ Ayumu ★

An angel when he's quiet.

Misunderstanding

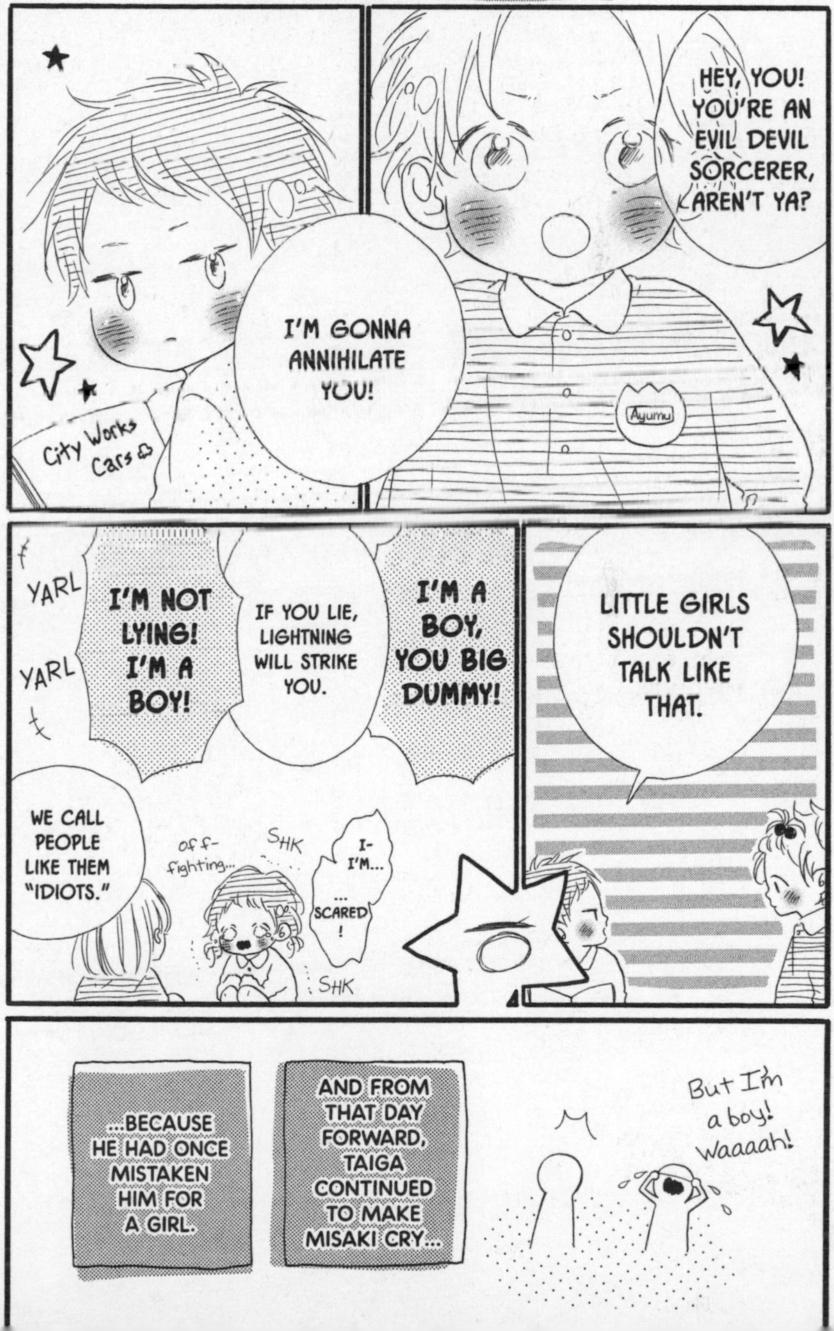
HEY, YOU! YOU'RE AN EVIL DEVIL SORCERER, AREN'T YA?
I'M GONNA ANNIHILATE YOU!
City Works Cars
Ayumu
LITTLE GIRLS SHOULDN'T TALK LIKE THAT.
I'M A BOY, YOU BIG DUMMY!
IF YOU LIE, LIGHTNING WILL STRIKE YOU.
I'M NOT LYING! I'M A BOY!
YARL
YARL
I- I'M... ...SCARED!
SHK
SHK
off f-fighting...
WE CALL PEOPLE LIKE THEM "IDIOTS."
But I'm a boy! Waaaah!
AND FROM THAT DAY FORWARD, TAIGA CONTINUED TO MAKE MISAKI CRY...
...BECAUSE HE HAD ONCE MISTAKEN HIM FOR A GIRL.

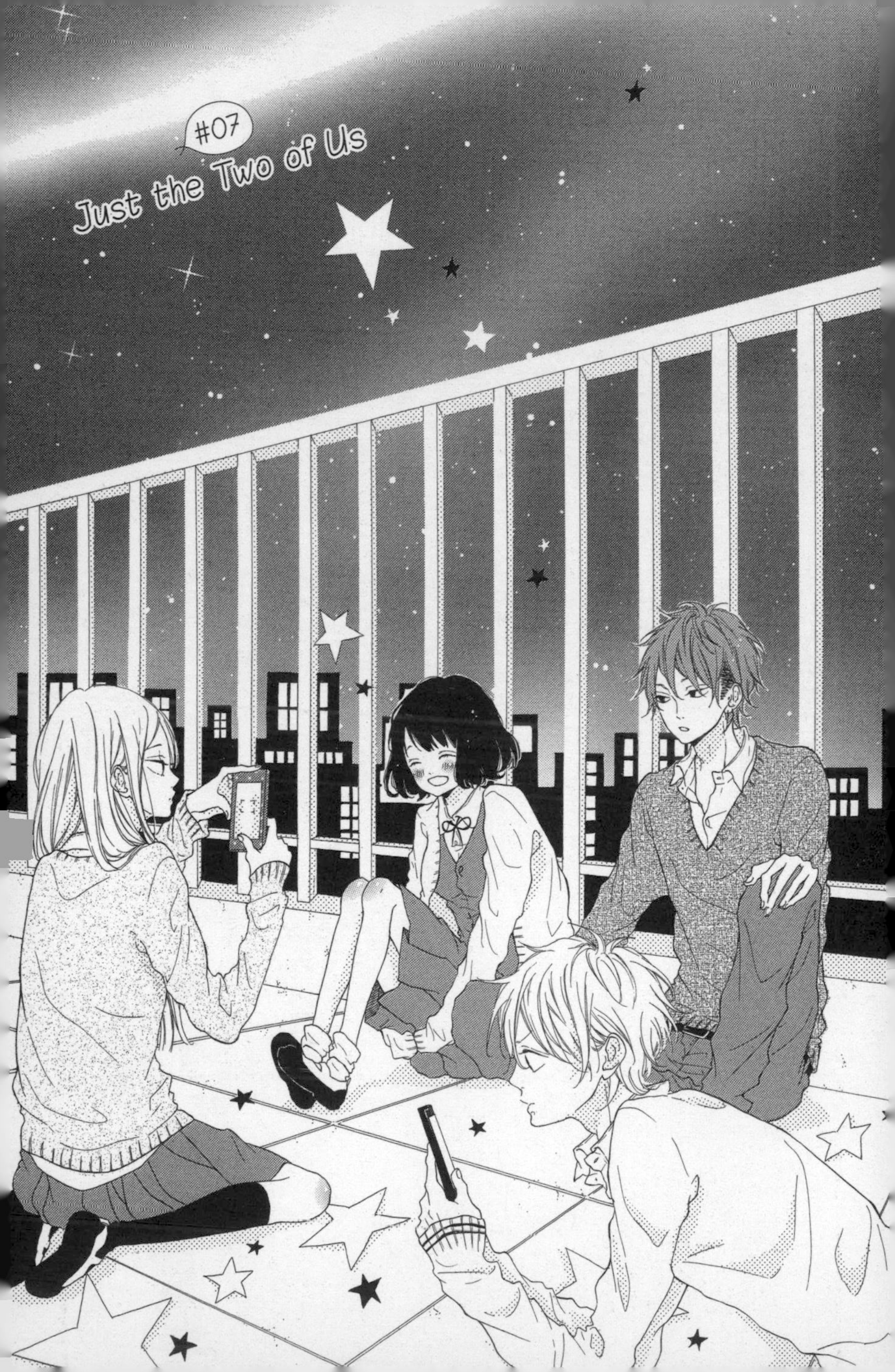

#07
Just the Two of Us

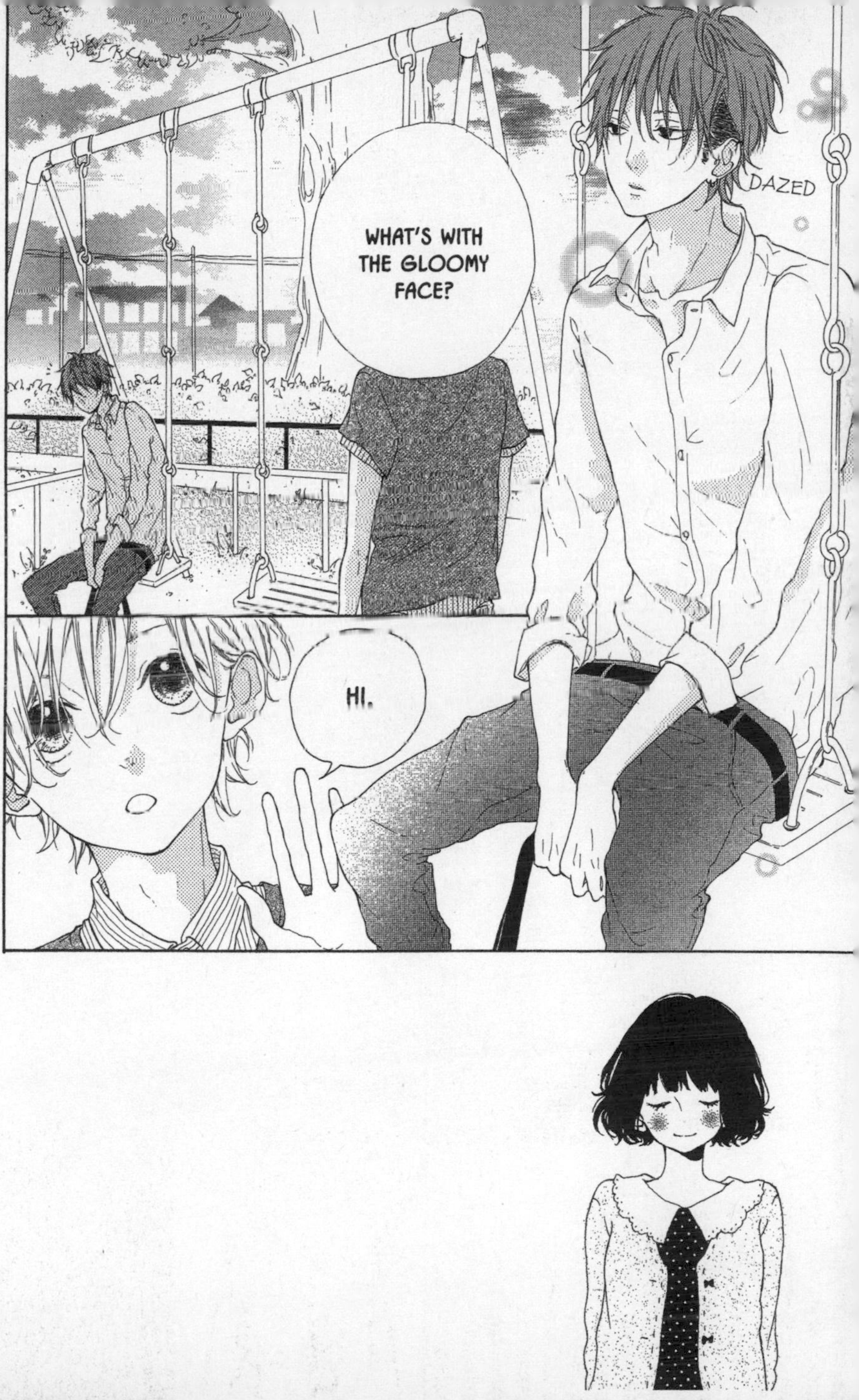
DAZED
WHAT'S WITH THE GLOOMY FACE?
HI.

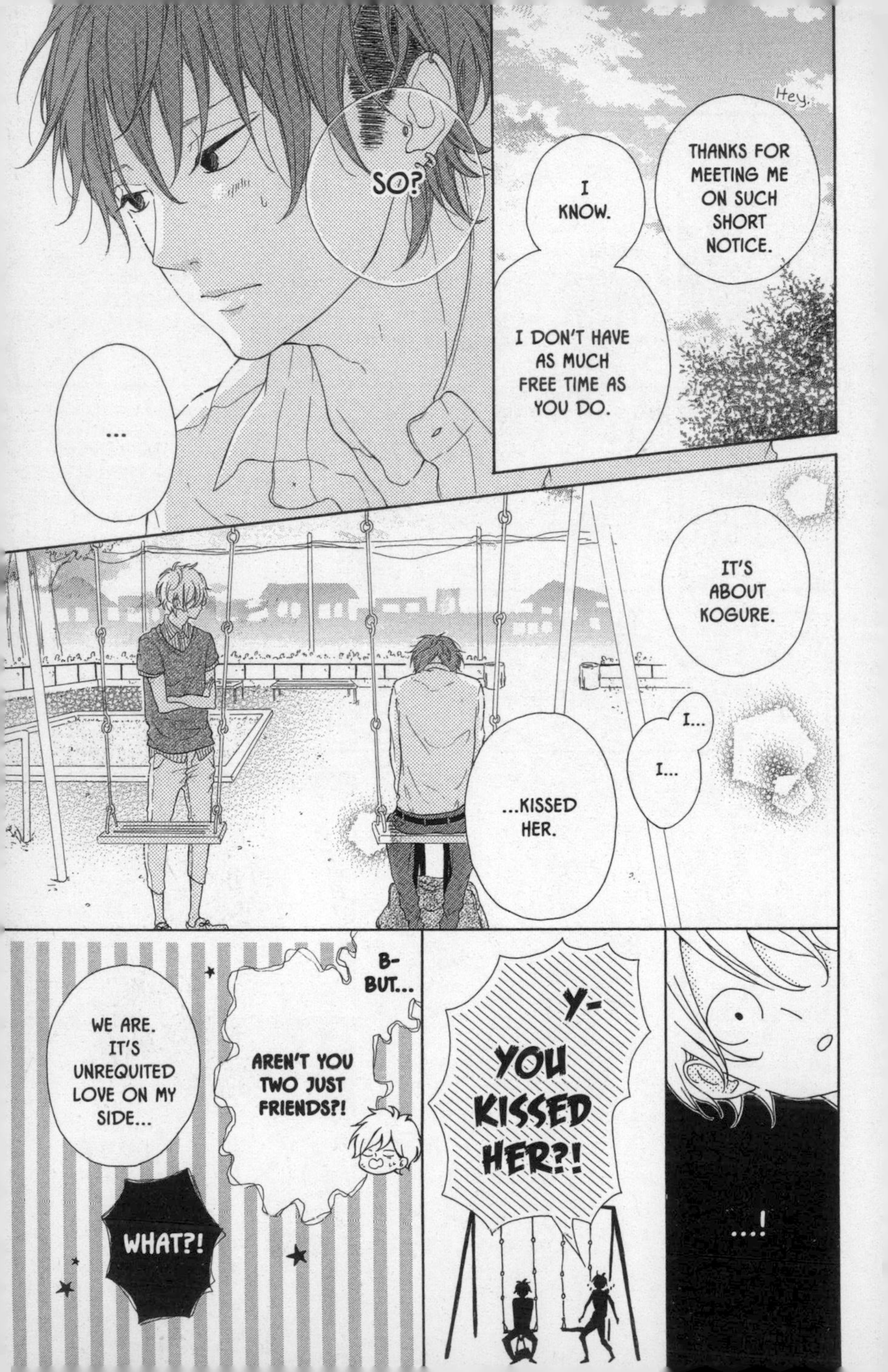
Hey.
THANKS FOR MEETING ME ON SUCH SHORT NOTICE.
I KNOW.
I DON'T HAVE AS MUCH FREE TIME AS YOU DO.
SO?
...
IT'S ABOUT KOGURE.
I...
I...
...KISSED HER.
...!
Y- YOU KISSED HER?!
B- BUT...
AREN'T YOU TWO JUST FRIENDS?!
WE ARE. IT'S UNREQUITED LOVE ON MY SIDE...
WHAT?!

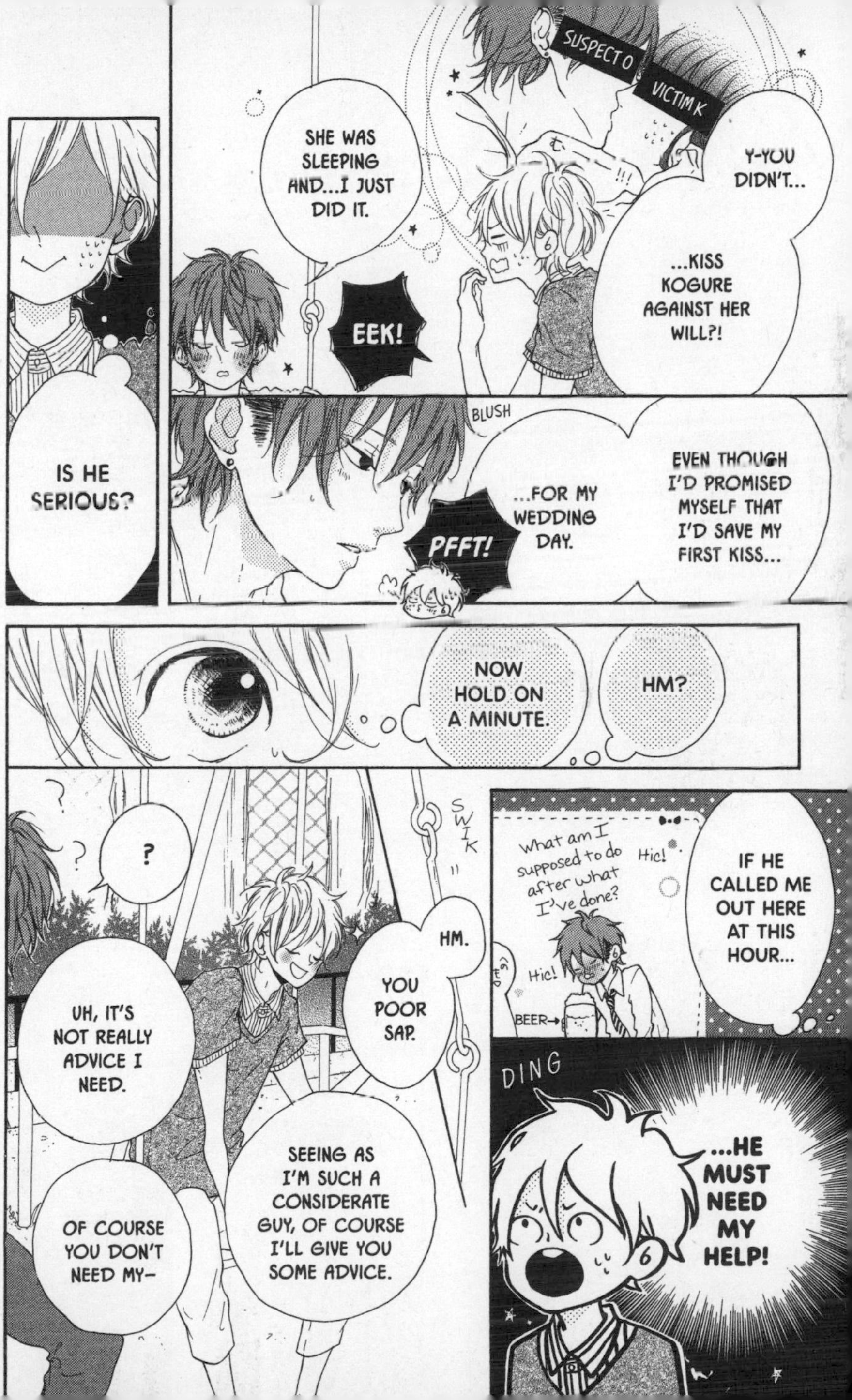
SUSPECT O
VICTIM K
Y-YOU DIDN'T...
...KISS KOGURE AGAINST HER WILL?!
SHE WAS SLEEPING AND...I JUST DID IT.
EEK!
BLUSH
EVEN THOUGH I'D PROMISED MYSELF THAT I'D SAVE MY FIRST KISS...
...FOR MY WEDDING DAY.
PFFT!
IS HE SERIOUS?
HM?
NOW HOLD ON A MINUTE.
IF HE CALLED ME OUT HERE AT THIS HOUR...
What am I supposed to do after what I've done?
Hic!
Hic!
BEER→
DING
...HE MUST NEED MY HELP!
SWIK
HM.
YOU POOR SAP.
?
SEEING AS I'M SUCH A CONSIDERATE GUY, OF COURSE I'LL GIVE YOU SOME ADVICE.
UH, IT'S NOT REALLY ADVICE I NEED.
OF COURSE YOU DON'T NEED MY–

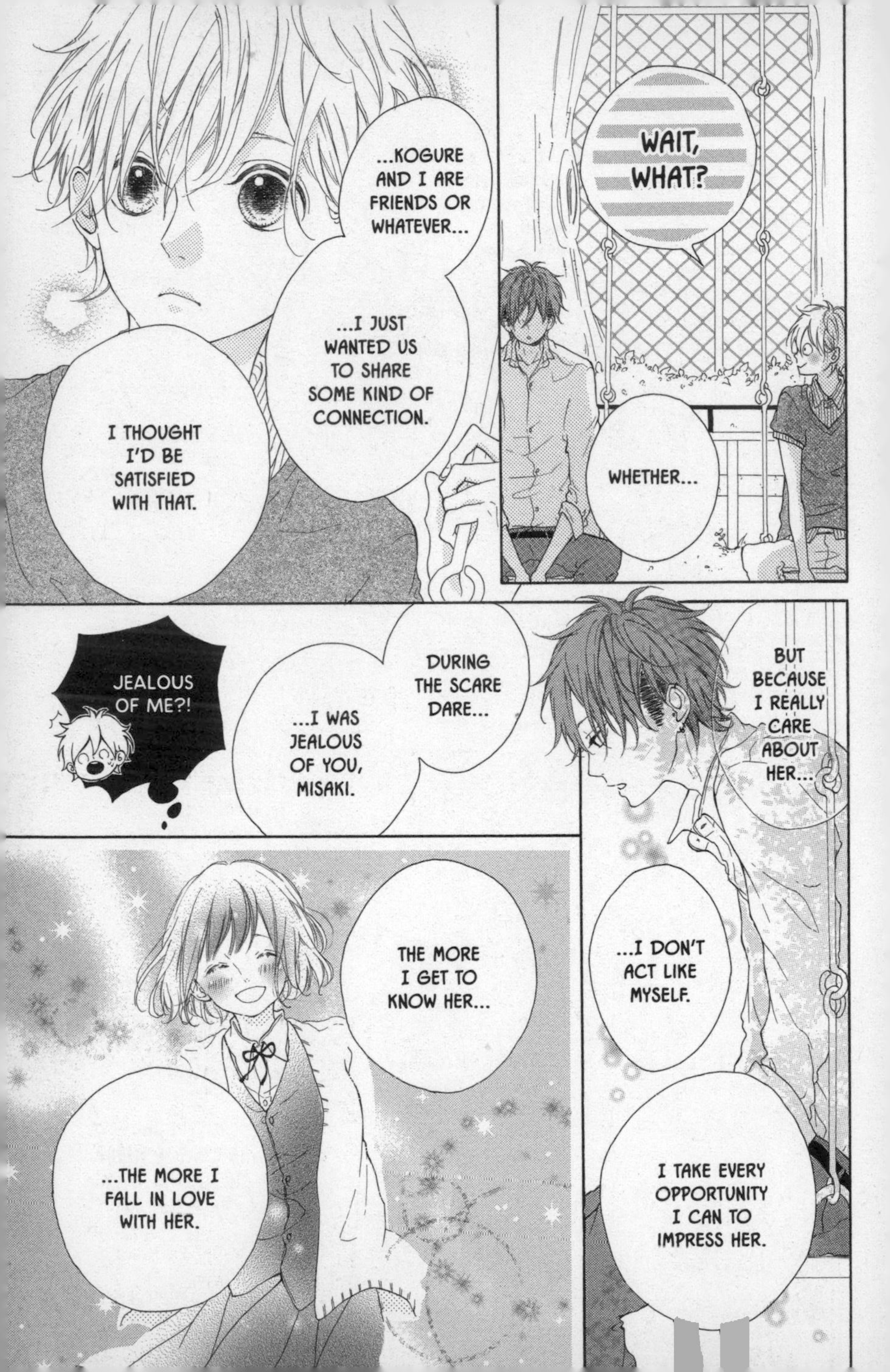
WAIT, WHAT?
WHETHER...
...KOGURE AND I ARE FRIENDS OR WHATEVER...
...I JUST WANTED US TO SHARE SOME KIND OF CONNECTION.
I THOUGHT I'D BE SATISFIED WITH THAT.
BUT BECAUSE I REALLY CARE ABOUT HER...
...I DON'T ACT LIKE MYSELF.
I TAKE EVERY OPPORTUNITY I CAN TO IMPRESS HER.
DURING THE SCARE DARE...
...I WAS JEALOUS OF YOU, MISAKI.
JEALOUS OF ME?!
THE MORE I GET TO KNOW HER...
...THE MORE I FALL IN LOVE WITH HER.

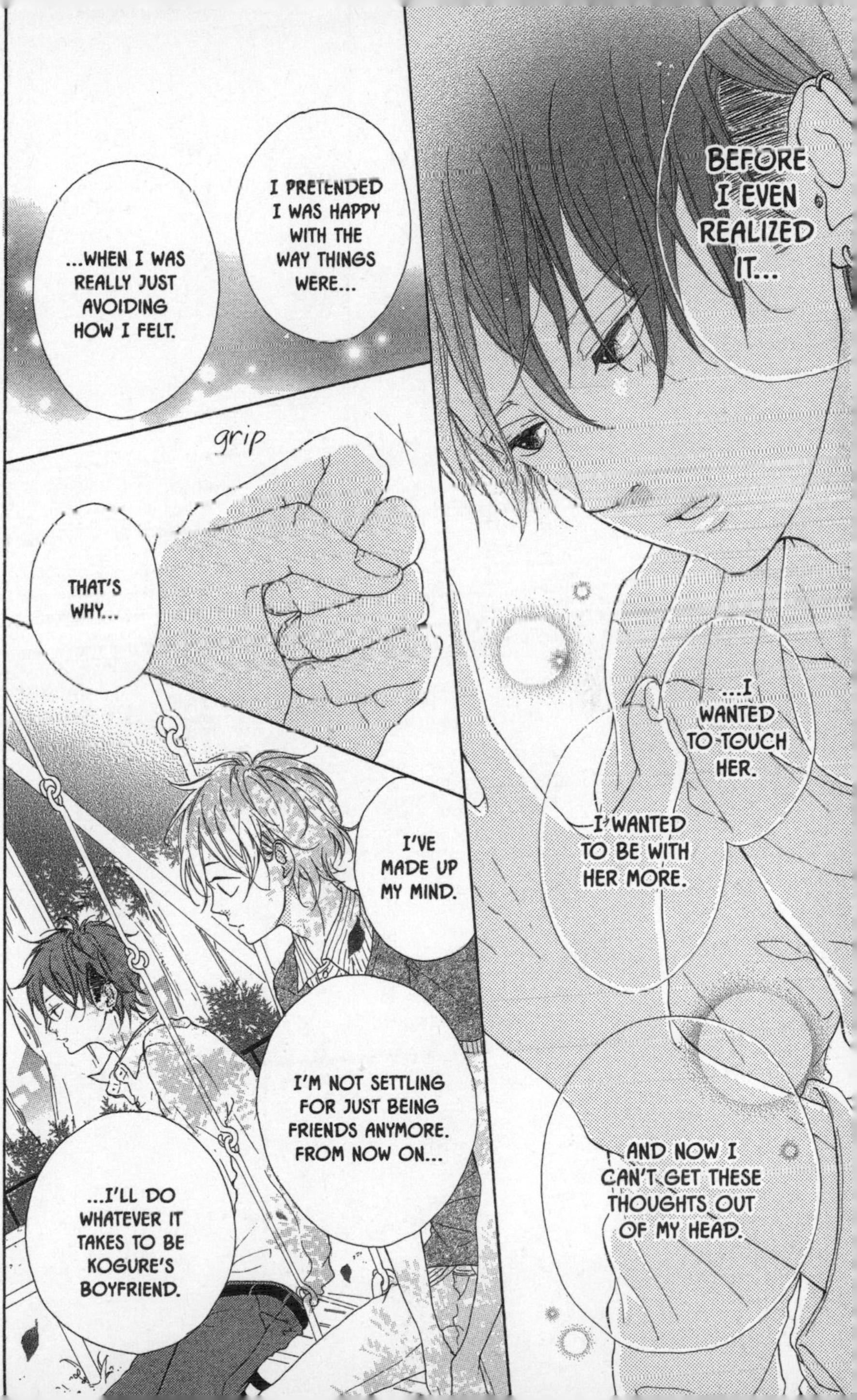
BEFORE I EVEN REALIZED IT...
...I WANTED TO TOUCH HER.
I WANTED TO BE WITH HER MORE.
AND NOW I CAN'T GET THESE THOUGHTS OUT OF MY HEAD.
I PRETENDED I WAS HAPPY WITH THE WAY THINGS WERE...
...WHEN I WAS REALLY JUST AVOIDING HOW I FELT.
grip
THAT'S WHY...
I'VE MADE UP MY MIND.
I'M NOT SETTLING FOR JUST BEING FRIENDS ANYMORE. FROM NOW ON...
...I'LL DO WHATEVER IT TAKES TO BE KOGURE'S BOYFRIEND.

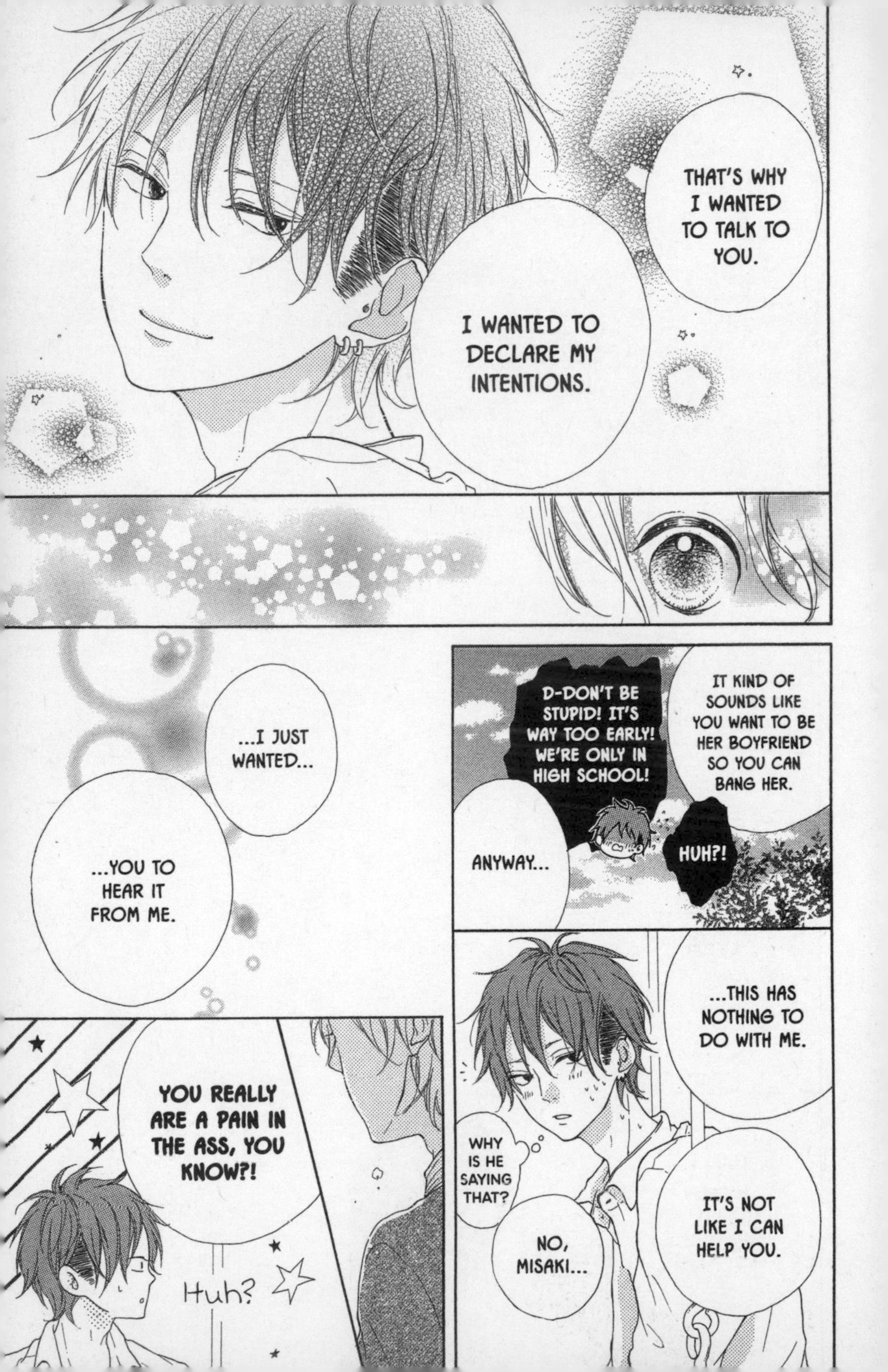
THAT'S WHY I WANTED TO TALK TO YOU.
I WANTED TO DECLARE MY INTENTIONS.
IT KIND OF SOUNDS LIKE YOU WANT TO BE HER BOYFRIEND SO YOU CAN BANG HER.
HUH?!
D-DON'T BE STUPID! IT'S WAY TOO EARLY! WE'RE ONLY IN HIGH SCHOOL!
ANYWAY...
...THIS HAS NOTHING TO DO WITH ME.
IT'S NOT LIKE I CAN HELP YOU.
WHY IS HE SAYING THAT?
NO, MISAKI...
...I JUST WANTED...
...YOU TO HEAR IT FROM ME.
YOU REALLY ARE A PAIN IN THE ASS, YOU KNOW?!
Huh?

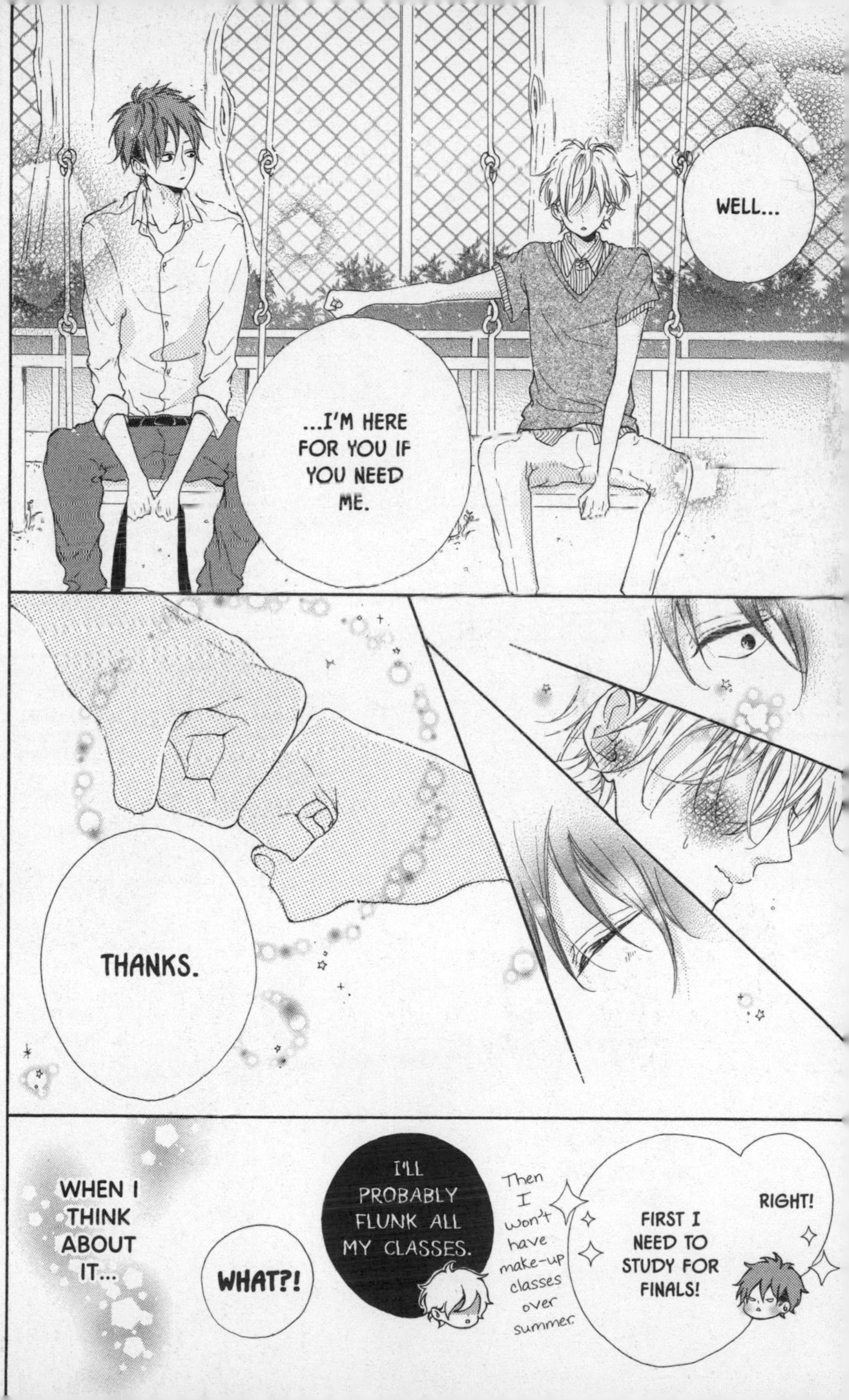

WELL...
...I'M HERE FOR YOU IF YOU NEED ME.
THANKS.
RIGHT!
FIRST I NEED TO STUDY FOR FINALS!
Then I won't have make-up classes over summer.
I'LL PROBABLY FLUNK ALL MY CLASSES.
WHAT?!
WHEN I THINK ABOUT IT...

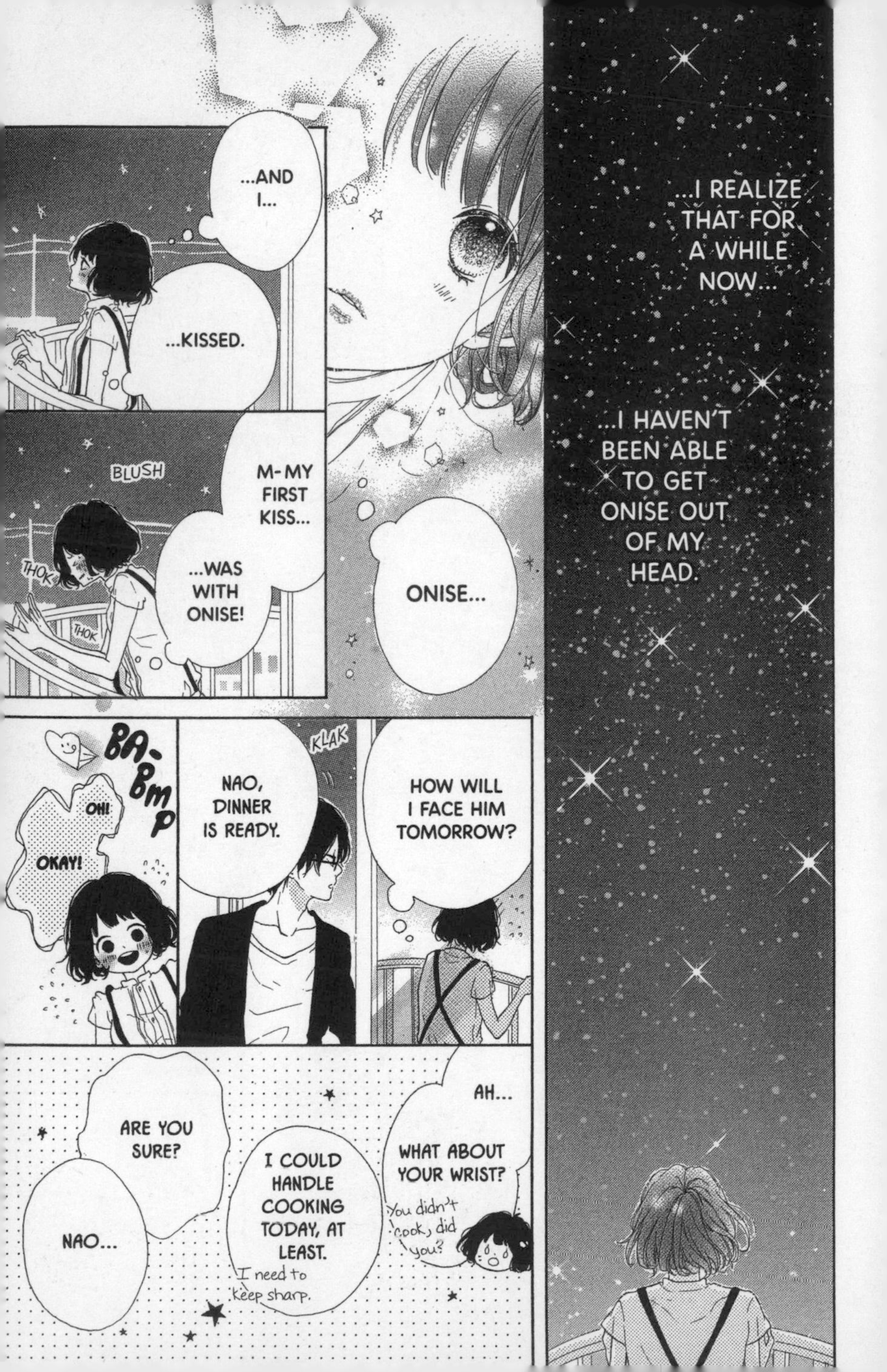
...I REALIZE THAT FOR A WHILE NOW...
...I HAVEN'T BEEN ABLE TO GET ONISE OUT OF MY HEAD.
...AND I...
...KISSED.
BLUSH
M-MY FIRST KISS...
...WAS WITH ONISE!
THOK
THOK
ONISE...
HOW WILL I FACE HIM TOMORROW?
KLAK
NAO, DINNER IS READY.
BA-BMP
OH!
OKAY!
AH...
WHAT ABOUT YOUR WRIST?
You didn't cook, did you?
I COULD HANDLE COOKING TODAY, AT LEAST.
I need to keep sharp.
ARE YOU SURE?
NAO...

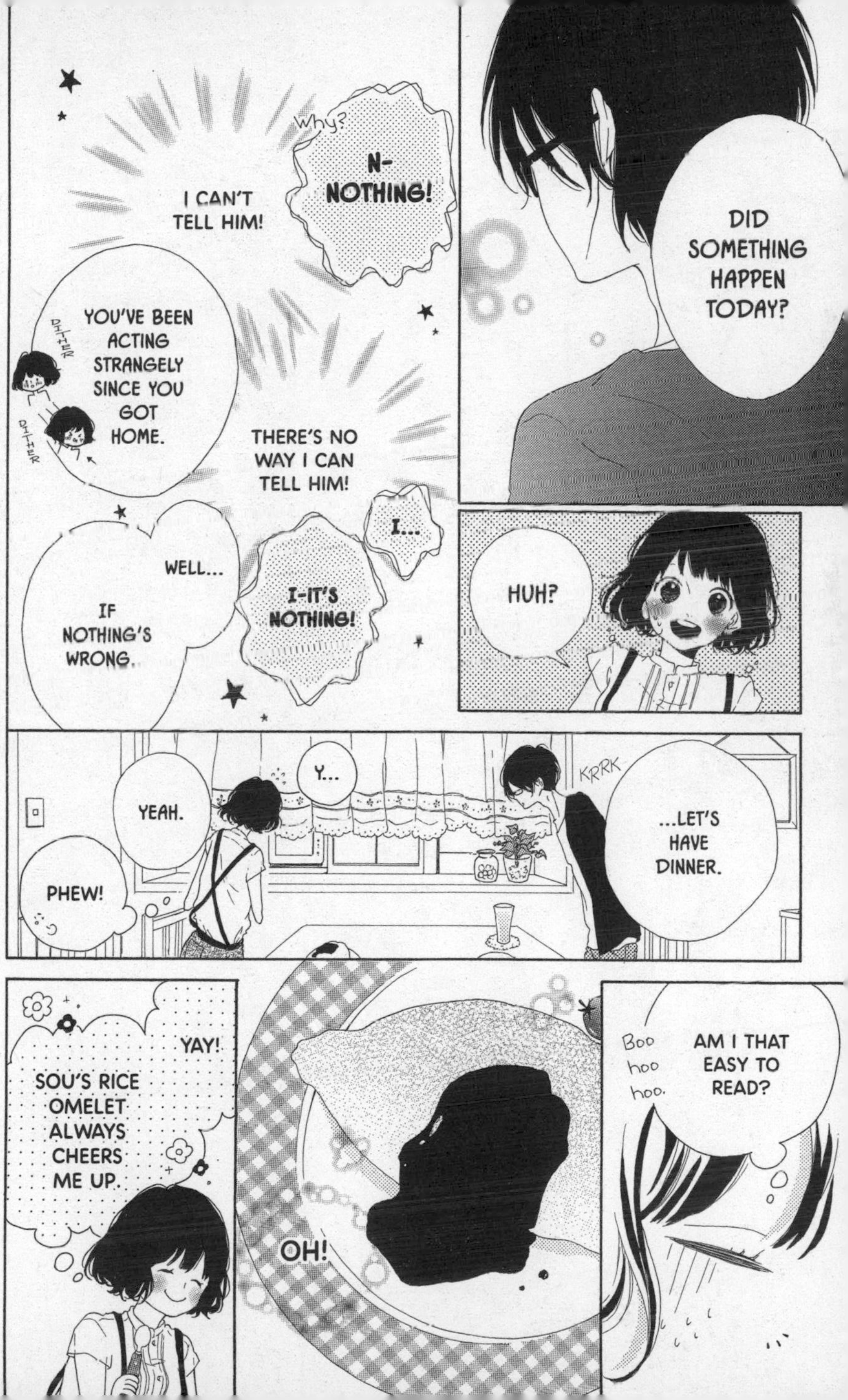
DID SOMETHING HAPPEN TODAY?
HUH?
Why?
N- NOTHING!
I CAN'T TELL HIM!
YOU'VE BEEN ACTING STRANGELY SINCE YOU GOT HOME.
DITHER
DITHER
THERE'S NO WAY I CAN TELL HIM!
I...
I-IT'S NOTHING!
WELL...
IF NOTHING'S WRONG...
KRRK
...LET'S HAVE DINNER.
Y...
YEAH.
PHEW!
AM I THAT EASY TO READ?
Boo hoo hoo.
OH!
YAY!
SOU'S RICE OMELET ALWAYS CHEERS ME UP.

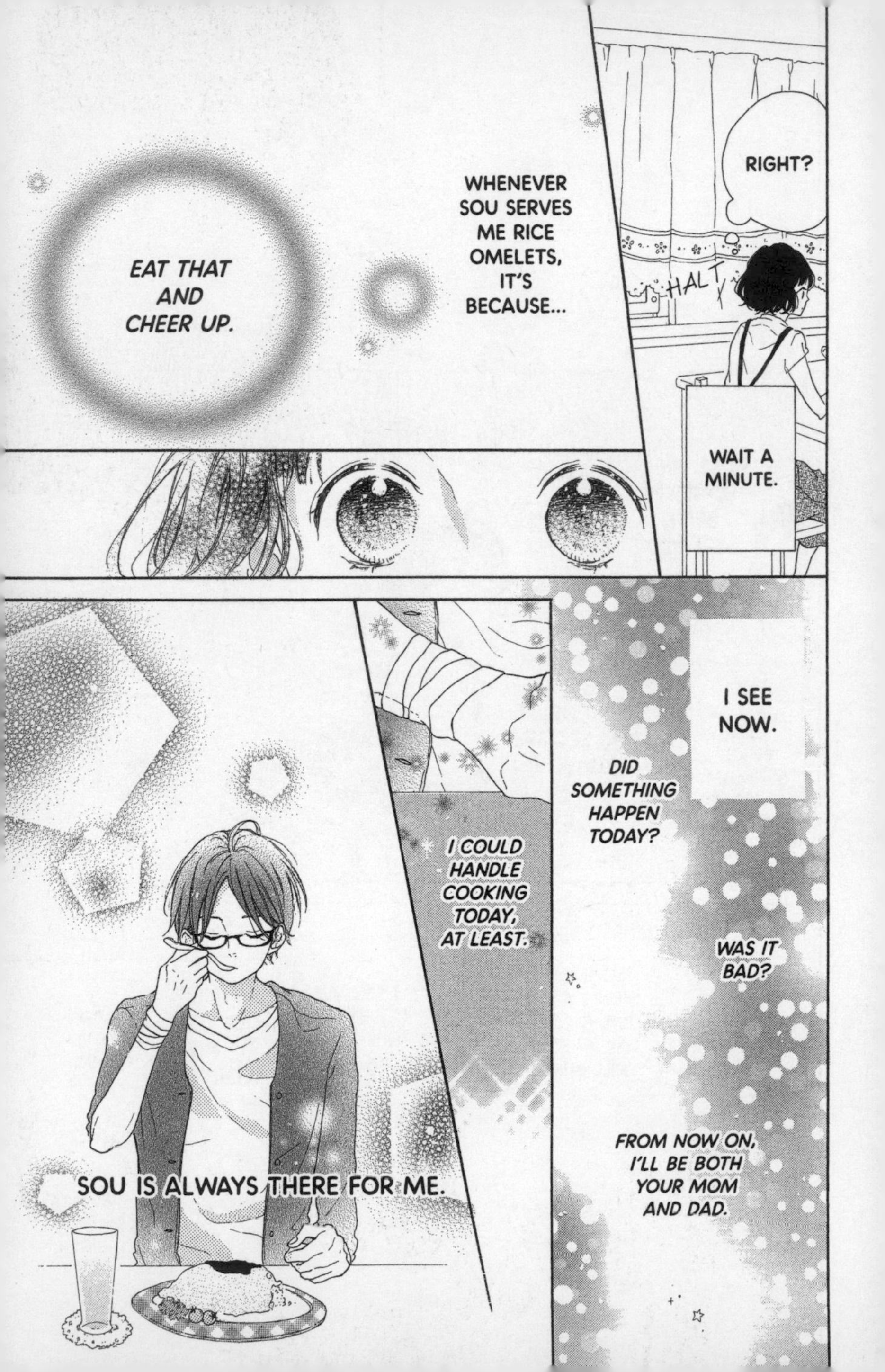
RIGHT?
HALT
WAIT A MINUTE.
WHENEVER SOU SERVES ME RICE OMELETS, IT'S BECAUSE...
EAT THAT AND CHEER UP.
I SEE NOW.
DID SOMETHING HAPPEN TODAY?
WAS IT BAD?
FROM NOW ON, I'LL BE BOTH YOUR MOM AND DAD.
I COULD HANDLE COOKING TODAY, AT LEAST.
SOU IS ALWAYS THERE FOR ME.

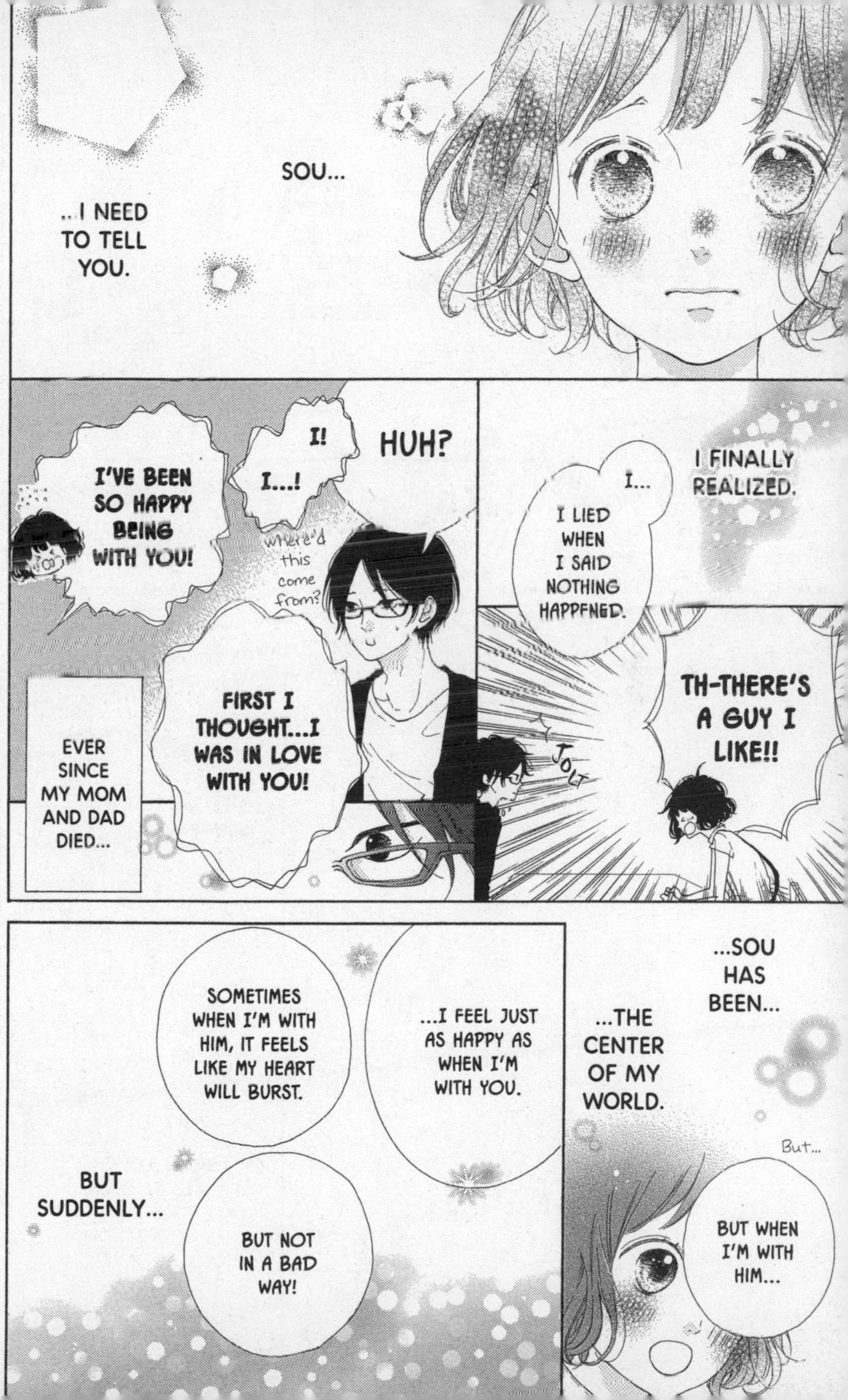
SOU...
...I NEED TO TELL YOU.
I FINALLY REALIZED.
I...
I LIED WHEN I SAID NOTHING HAPPENED.
TH-THERE'S A GUY I LIKE!!
JOLT
HUH?
I!
I...!
where'd this come from?
I'VE BEEN SO HAPPY BEING WITH YOU!
EVER SINCE MY MOM AND DAD DIED...
FIRST I THOUGHT...I WAS IN LOVE WITH YOU!
...SOU HAS BEEN...
...THE CENTER OF MY WORLD.
But...
BUT WHEN I'M WITH HIM...
...I FEEL JUST AS HAPPY AS WHEN I'M WITH YOU.
BUT SUDDENLY...
SOMETIMES WHEN I'M WITH HIM, IT FEELS LIKE MY HEART WILL BURST.
BUT NOT IN A BAD WAY!

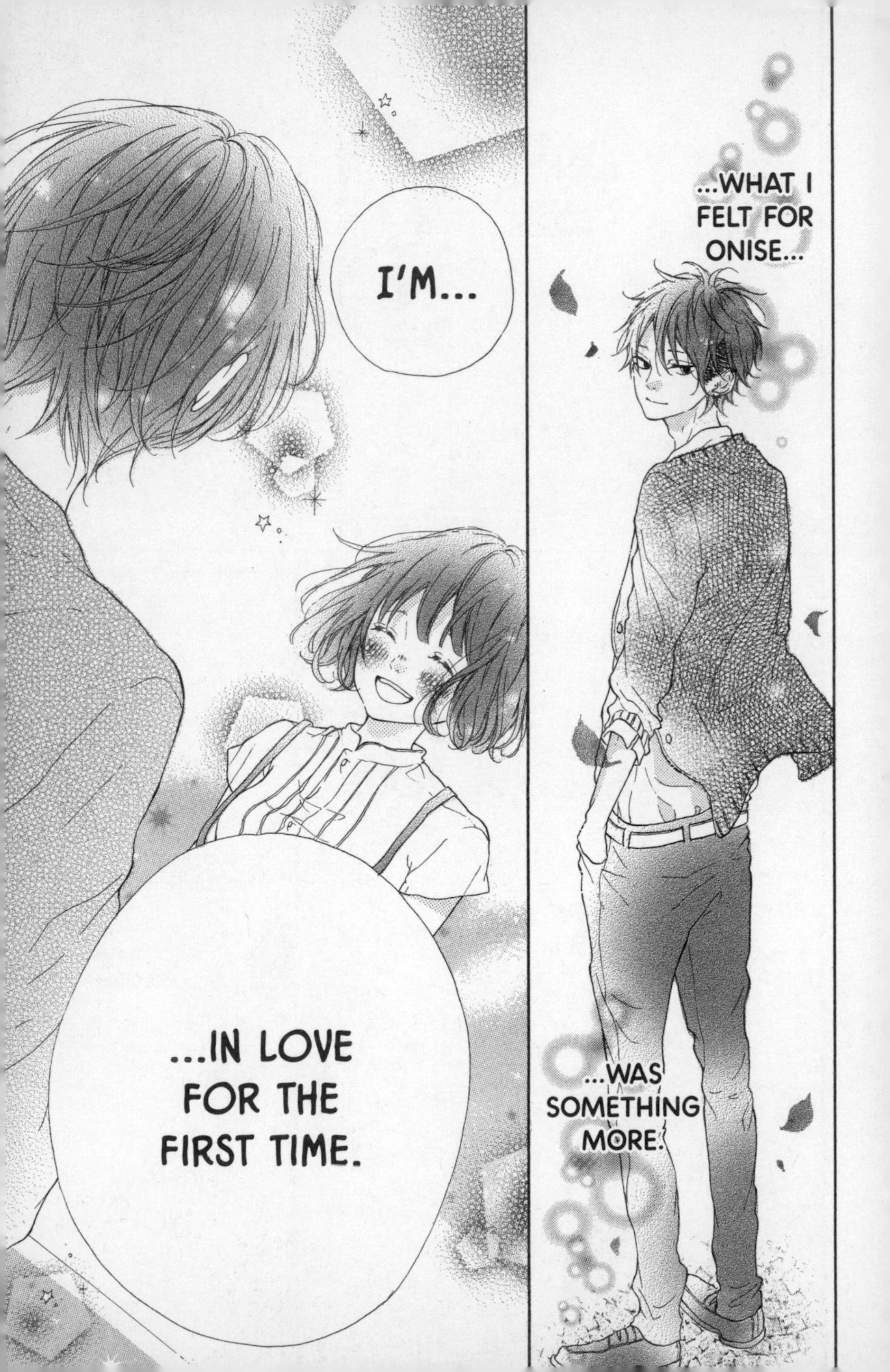
...WHAT I FELT FOR ONISE...
...WAS SOMETHING MORE.
I'M...
...IN LOVE FOR THE FIRST TIME.

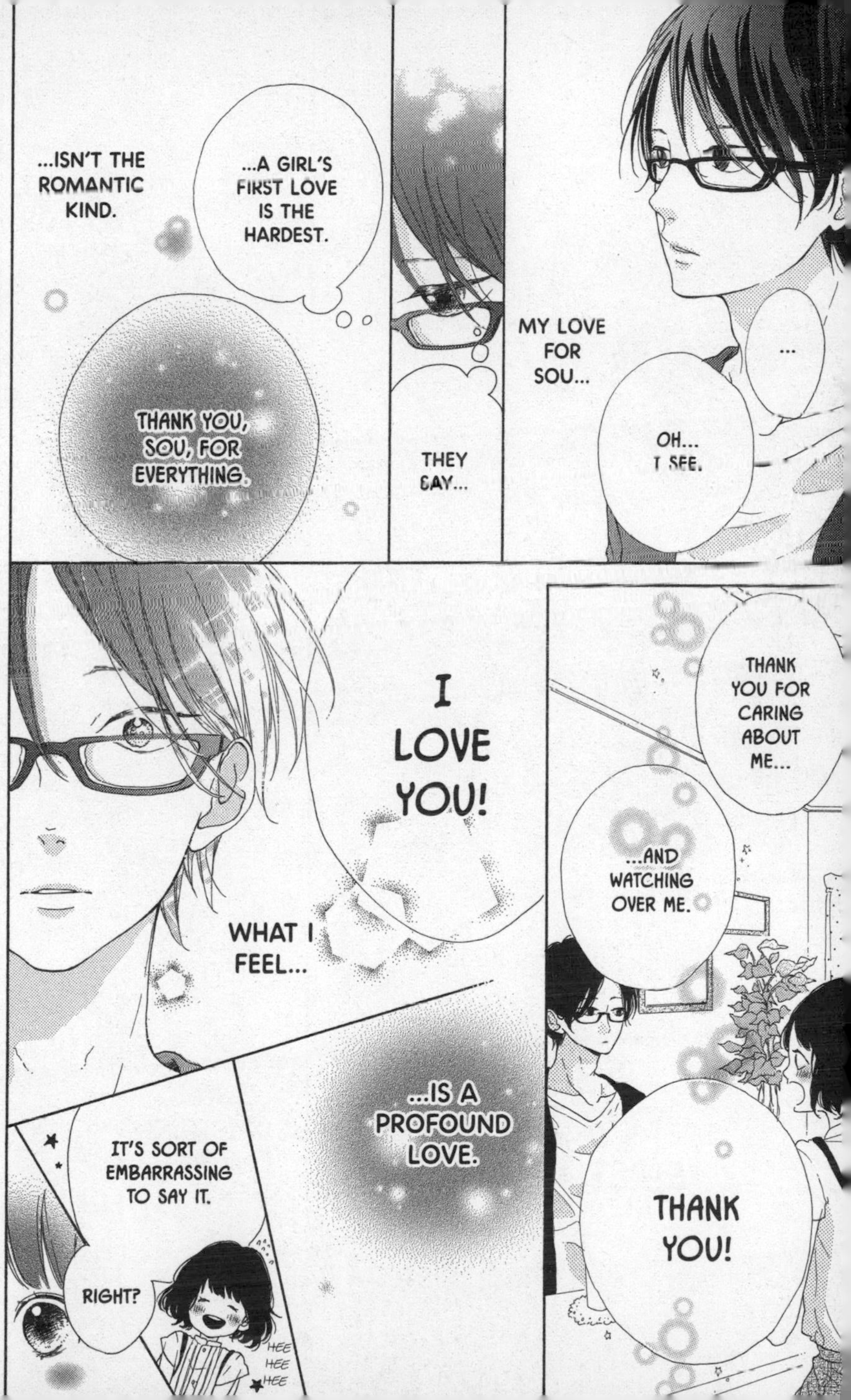
...
OH... I SEE.
MY LOVE FOR SOU...
THEY SAY...
...A GIRL'S FIRST LOVE IS THE HARDEST.
...ISN'T THE ROMANTIC KIND.
THANK YOU, SOU, FOR EVERYTHING.
THANK YOU FOR CARING ABOUT ME...
...AND WATCHING OVER ME.
THANK YOU!
I LOVE YOU!
WHAT I FEEL...
...IS A PROFOUND LOVE.
IT'S SORT OF EMBARRASSING TO SAY IT.
RIGHT?
HEE HEE HEE

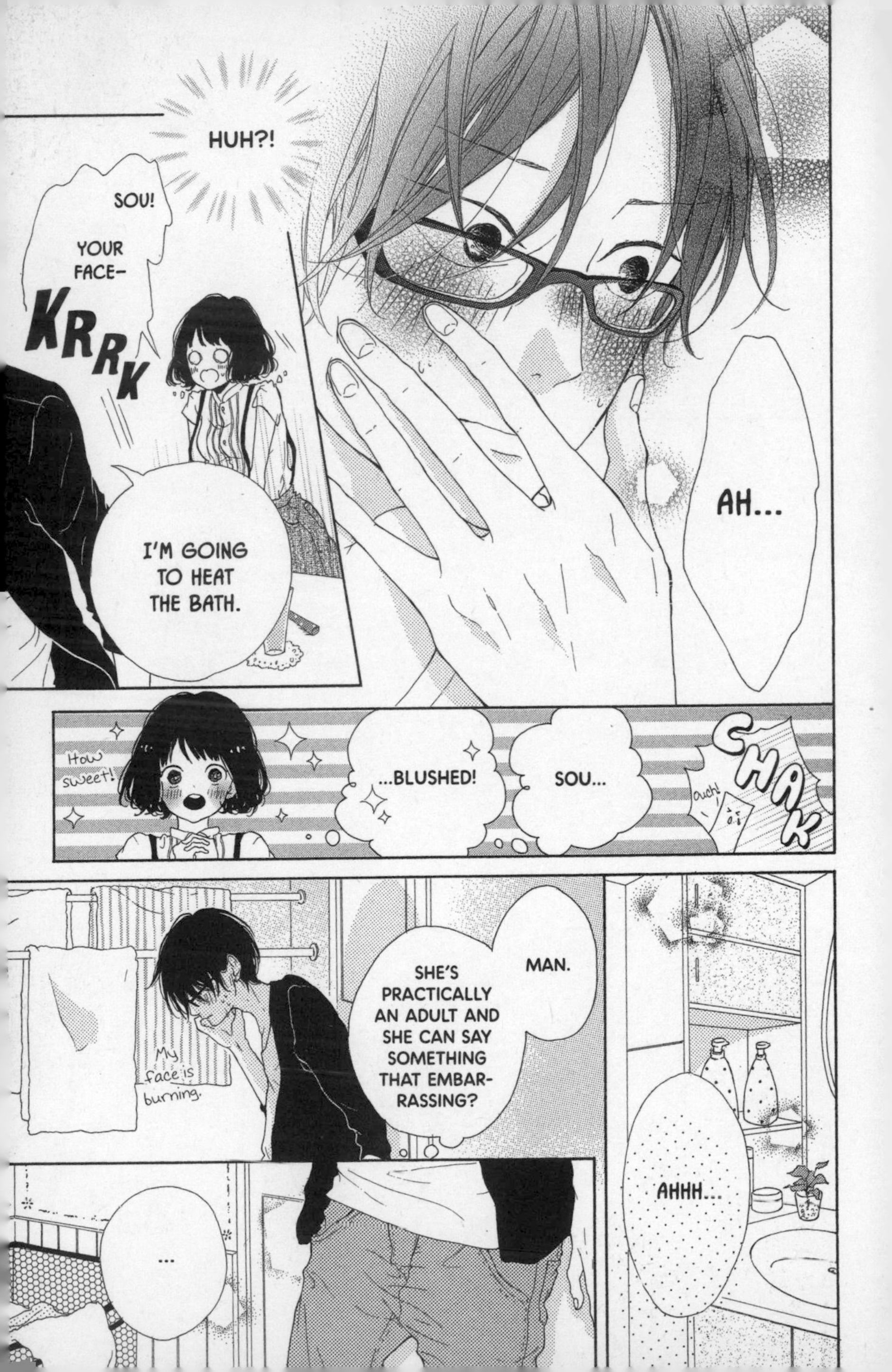
AH...
HUH?!
SOU!
YOUR FACE—
KRRK
I'M GOING TO HEAT THE BATH.
CHAK
ouch!
SOU...
...BLUSHED!
How sweet!
AHHH...
MAN.
SHE'S PRACTICALLY AN ADULT AND SHE CAN SAY SOMETHING THAT EMBARRASSING?
My face is burning.
...

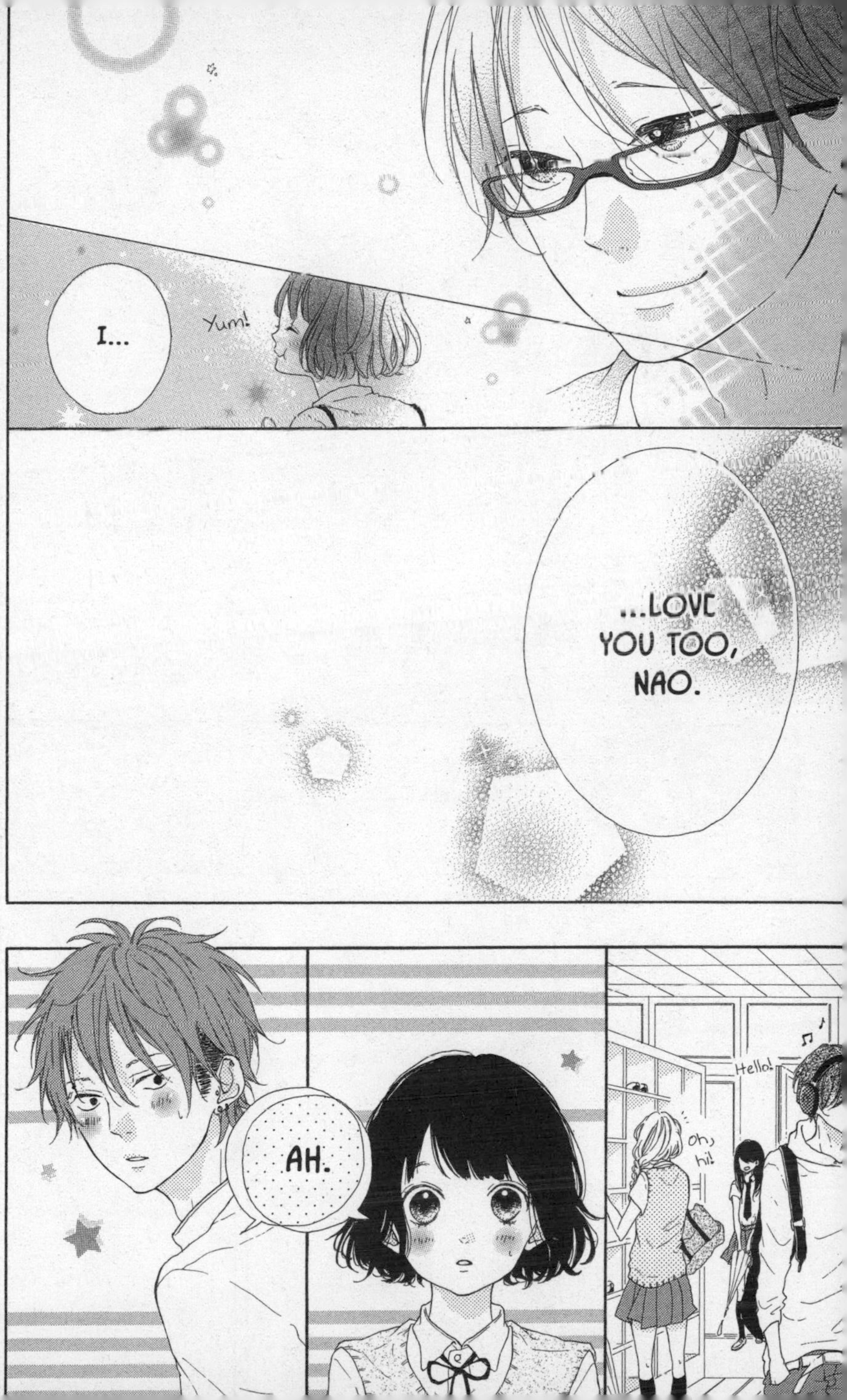
I...
Yum!
...LOVE YOU TOO, NAO.
Hello!
Oh, hi!
AH.

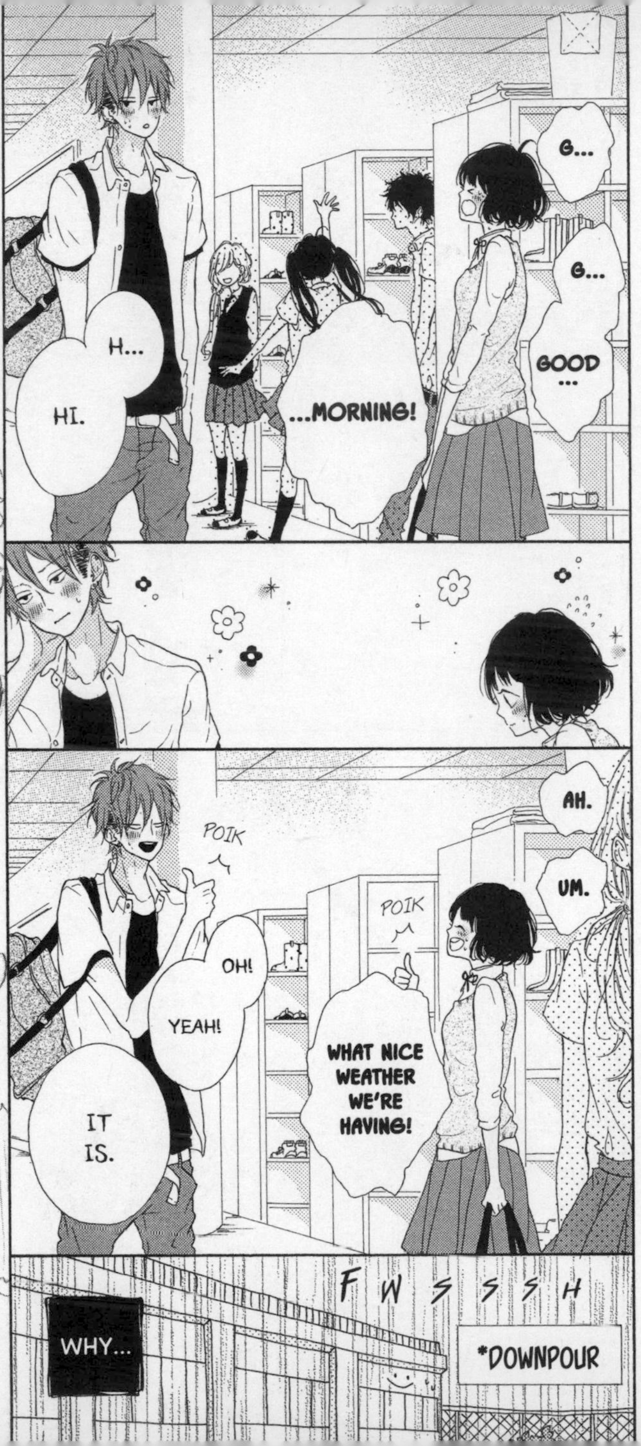
G...
G...
GOOD...
...MORNING!
H...
HI.
AH.
UM.
WHAT NICE WEATHER WE'RE HAVING!
POIK
OH!
YEAH!
POIK
IT IS.
*DOWNPOUR
FWSSSH
WHY...

Pencil Sketch Corner 2

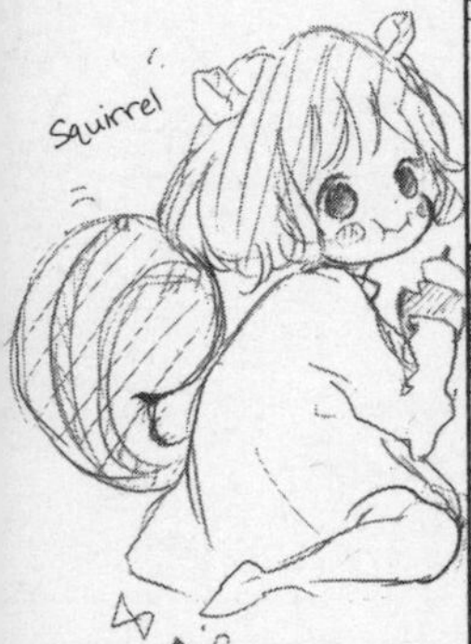
Squirrel

I love animal ears and tails. And butts. I'd like to meet an alpaca someday.

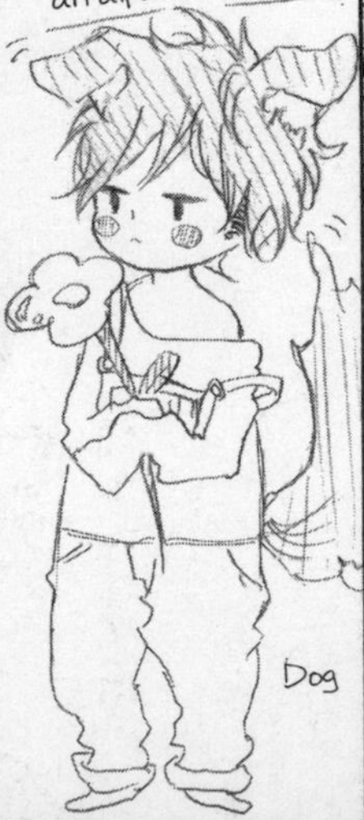
Dog

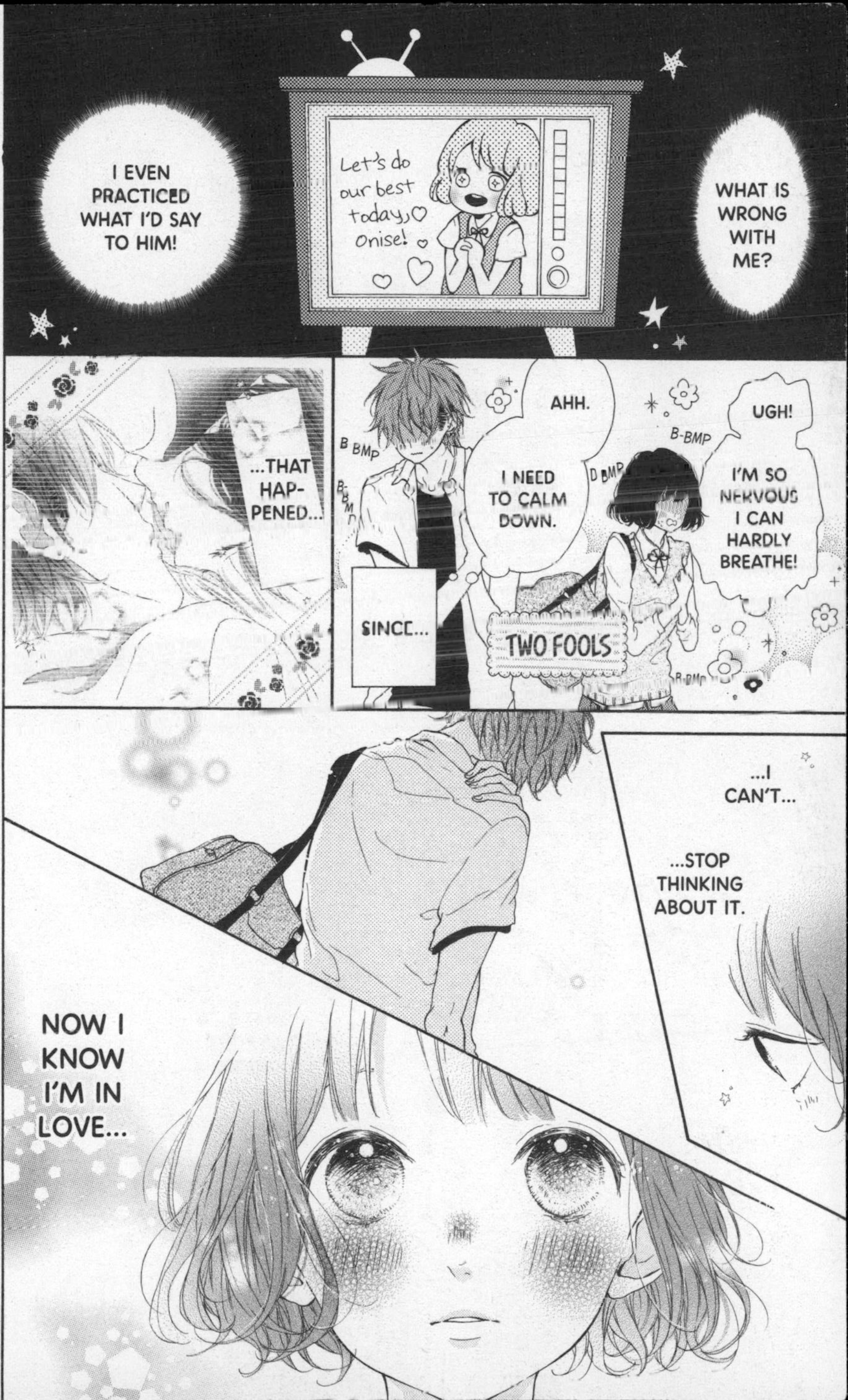
WHAT IS WRONG WITH ME?
Let's do our best today, Onise!
I EVEN PRACTICED WHAT I'D SAY TO HIM!
UGH!
B-BMP
I'M SO NERVOUS I CAN HARDLY BREATHE!
D BMP
B-BMP
AHH.
I NEED TO CALM DOWN.
B BMP
B-BMP
TWO FOOLS
SINCE...
...THAT HAPPENED...
...I CAN'T...
...STOP THINKING ABOUT IT.
NOW I KNOW I'M IN LOVE...

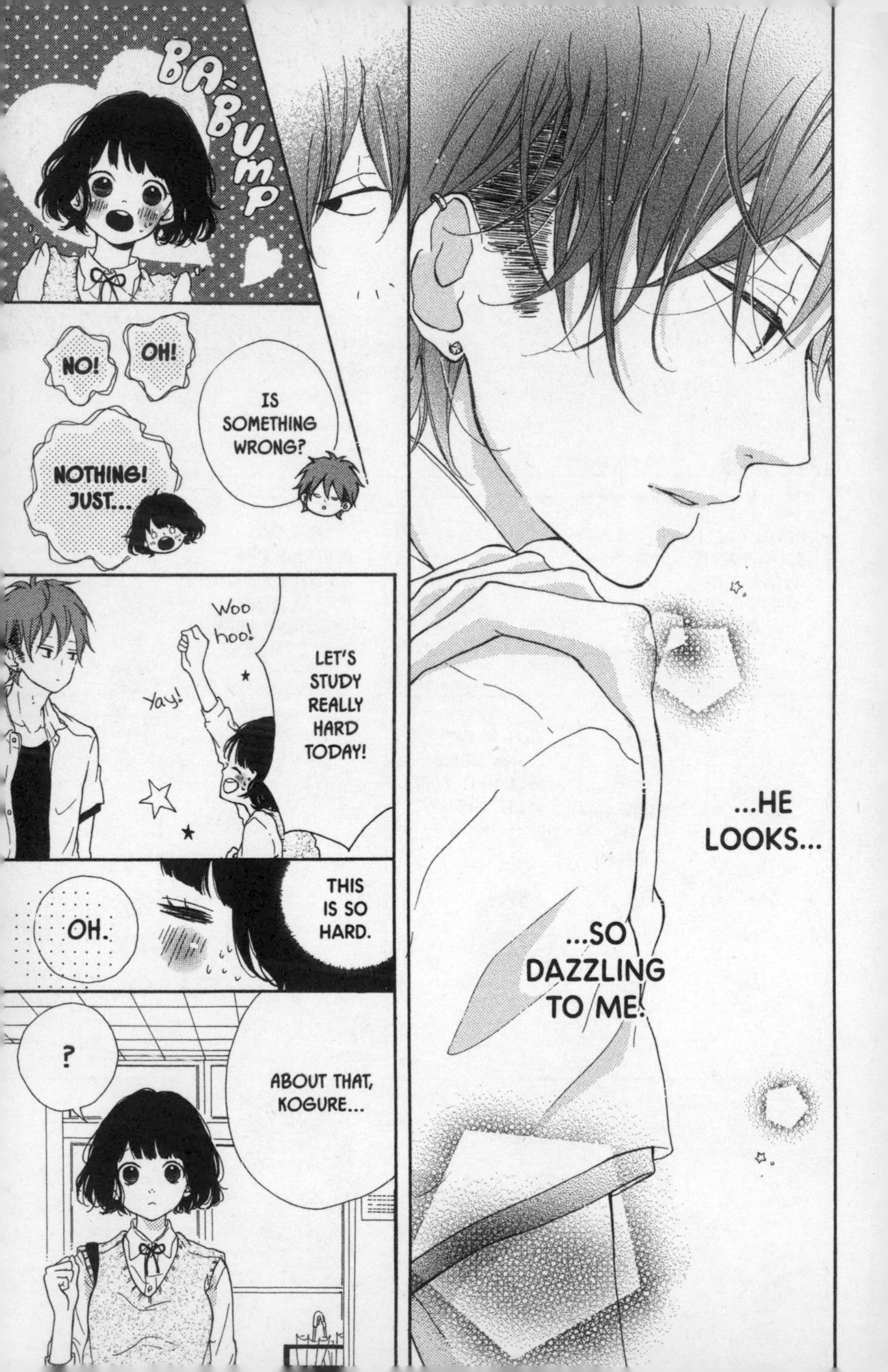
...HE LOOKS...
...SO DAZZLING TO ME.
BA-BUMP
IS SOMETHING WRONG?
OH!
NO!
NOTHING! JUST...
LET'S STUDY REALLY HARD TODAY!
Woo hoo!
Yay!
THIS IS SO HARD.
OH.
ABOUT THAT, KOGURE...
?

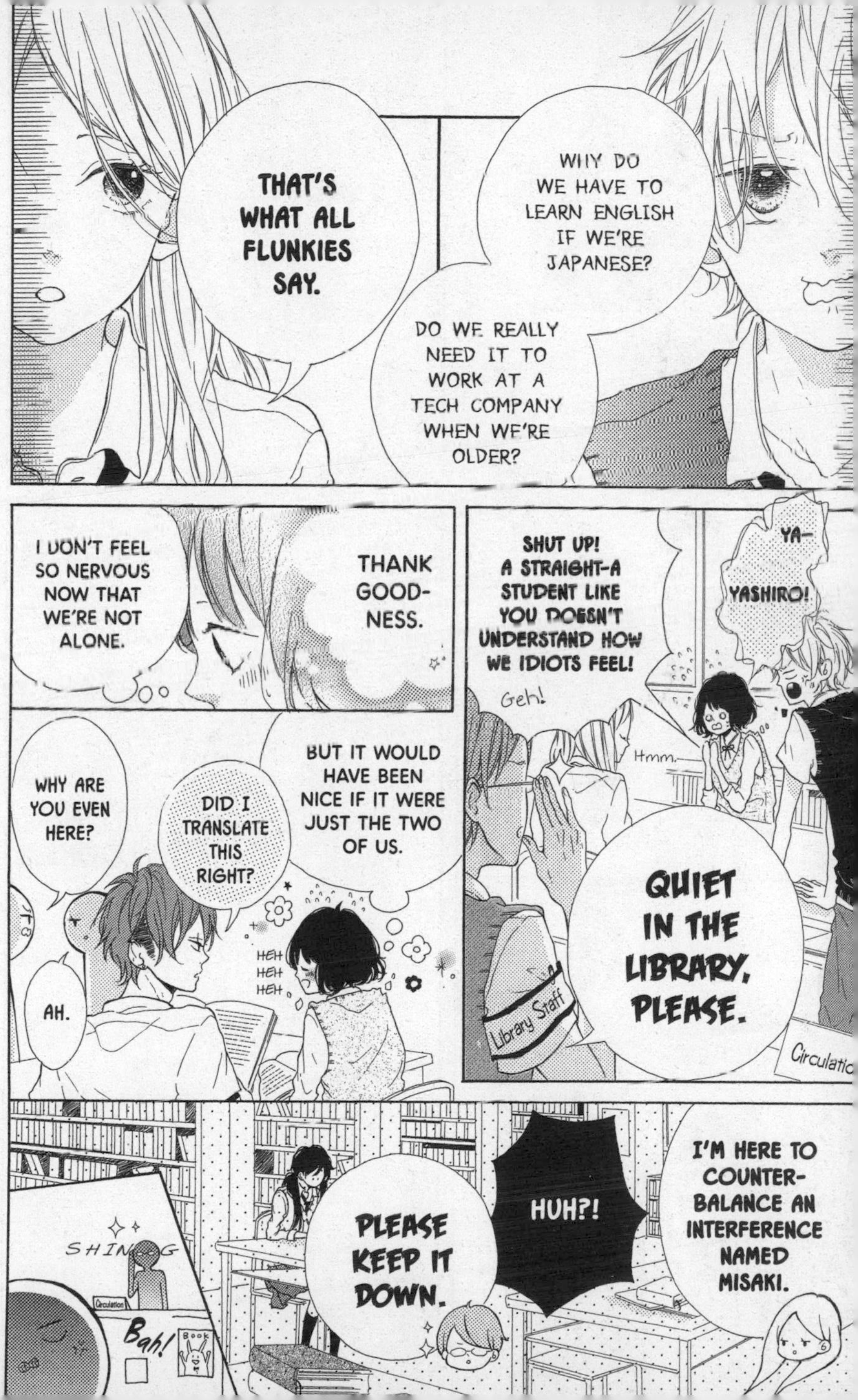

WHY DO WE HAVE TO LEARN ENGLISH IF WE'RE JAPANESE?
DO WE REALLY NEED IT TO WORK AT A TECH COMPANY WHEN WE'RE OLDER?
THAT'S WHAT ALL FLUNKIES SAY.
YA- YASHIRO!
SHUT UP! A STRAIGHT-A STUDENT LIKE YOU DOESN'T UNDERSTAND HOW WE IDIOTS FEEL!
Geh!
Hmm.
QUIET IN THE LIBRARY, PLEASE.
Library Staff
Circulatio
THANK GOODNESS.
I DON'T FEEL SO NERVOUS NOW THAT WE'RE NOT ALONE.
BUT IT WOULD HAVE BEEN NICE IF IT WERE JUST THE TWO OF US.
DID I TRANSLATE THIS RIGHT?
WHY ARE YOU EVEN HERE?
HEH HEH HEH
AH.
I'M HERE TO COUNTER-BALANCE AN INTERFERENCE NAMED MISAKI.
HUH?!
PLEASE KEEP IT DOWN.
SHINING
Circulation
Bah!
Book

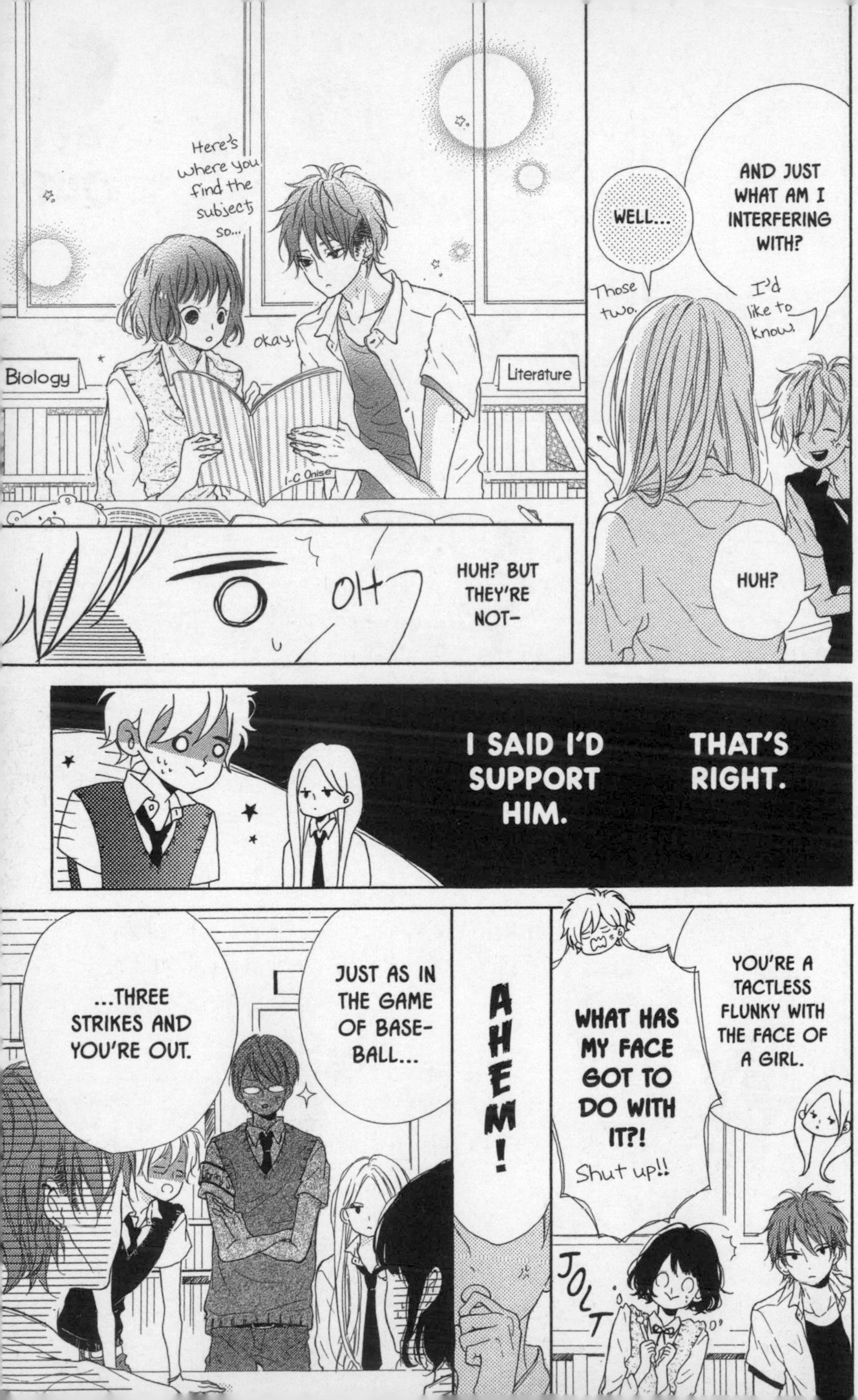
AND JUST WHAT AM I INTERFERING WITH?
I'd like to know.
WELL...
Those two.
HUH?
Here's where you find the subject, so...
okay.
Biology
Literature
1-C Onise
OH
HUH? BUT THEY'RE NOT-
THAT'S RIGHT.
I SAID I'D SUPPORT HIM.
YOU'RE A TACTLESS FLUNKY WITH THE FACE OF A GIRL.
WHAT HAS MY FACE GOT TO DO WITH IT?!
Shut up!!
JOLT
AHEM!
JUST AS IN THE GAME OF BASE-BALL...
...THREE STRIKES AND YOU'RE OUT.

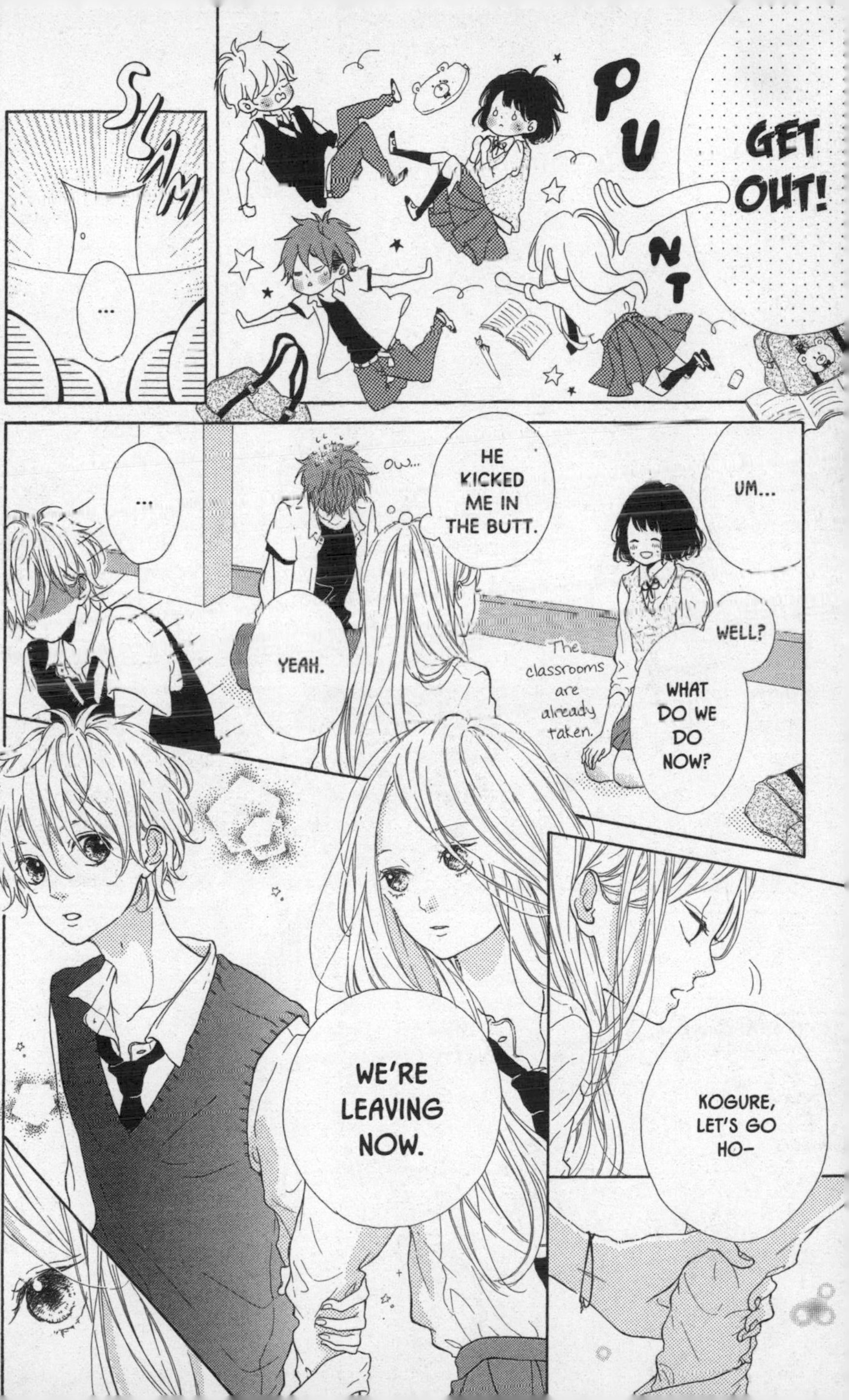
GET OUT!
PUNT
SLAM
...
UM...
HE KICKED ME IN THE BUTT.
OW...
...
WELL?
WHAT DO WE DO NOW?
The classrooms are already taken.
YEAH.
KOGURE, LET'S GO HO-
WE'RE LEAVING NOW.

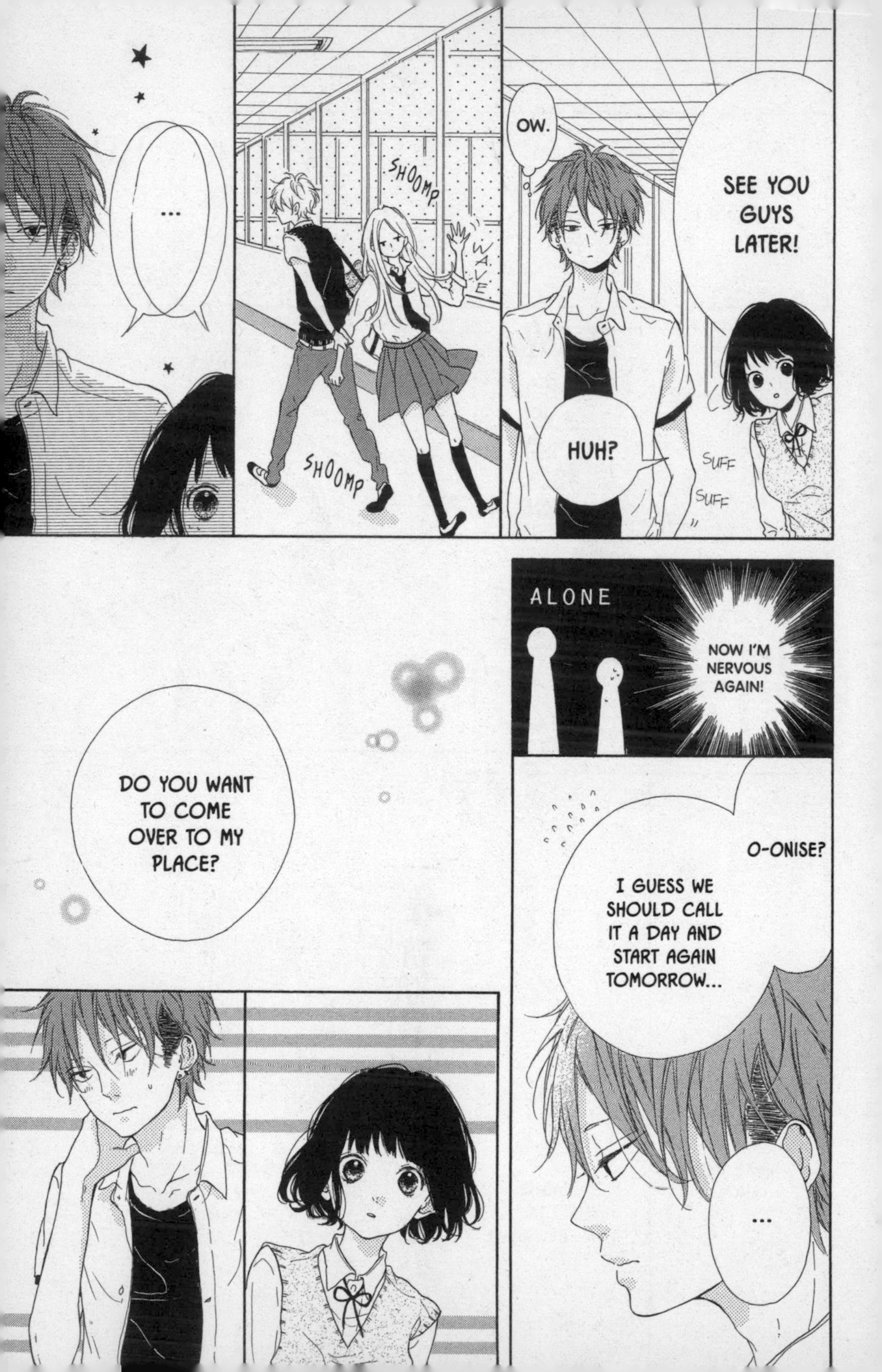
SEE YOU GUYS LATER!
OW.
HUH?
SUFF
SUFF
SHOOMP
WAVE
SHOOMP
...
ALONE
NOW I'M NERVOUS AGAIN!
O-ONISE?
I GUESS WE SHOULD CALL IT A DAY AND START AGAIN TOMORROW...
...
DO YOU WANT TO COME OVER TO MY PLACE?

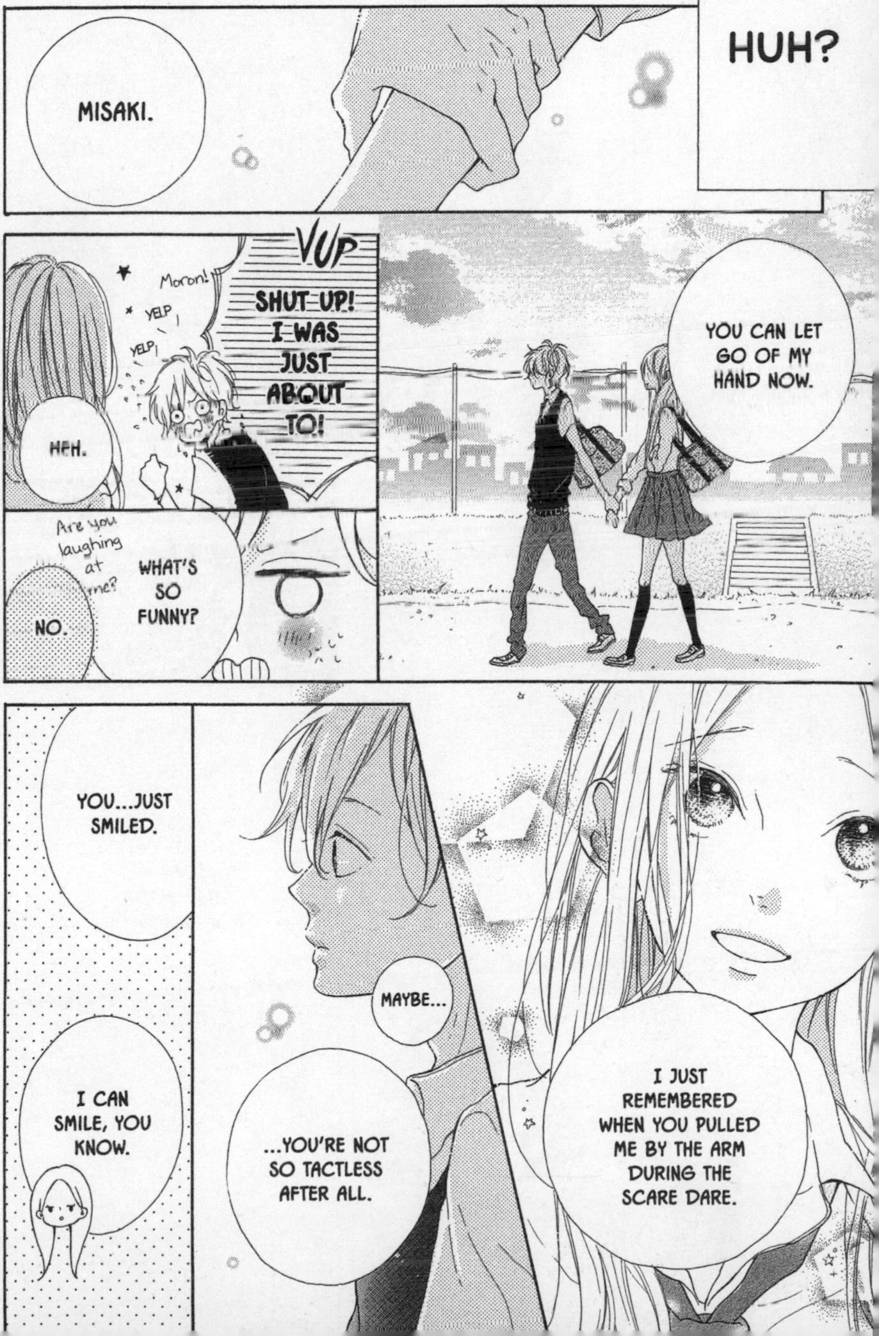
HUH?
MISAKI.
YOU CAN LET GO OF MY HAND NOW.
VUP
SHUT UP! I WAS JUST ABOUT TO!
Moron!
YELP
YELP
HEH.
Are you laughing at me?
WHAT'S SO FUNNY?
NO.
MAYBE...
I JUST REMEMBERED WHEN YOU PULLED ME BY THE ARM DURING THE SCARE DARE.
...YOU'RE NOT SO TACTLESS AFTER ALL.
YOU...JUST SMILED.
I CAN SMILE, YOU KNOW.

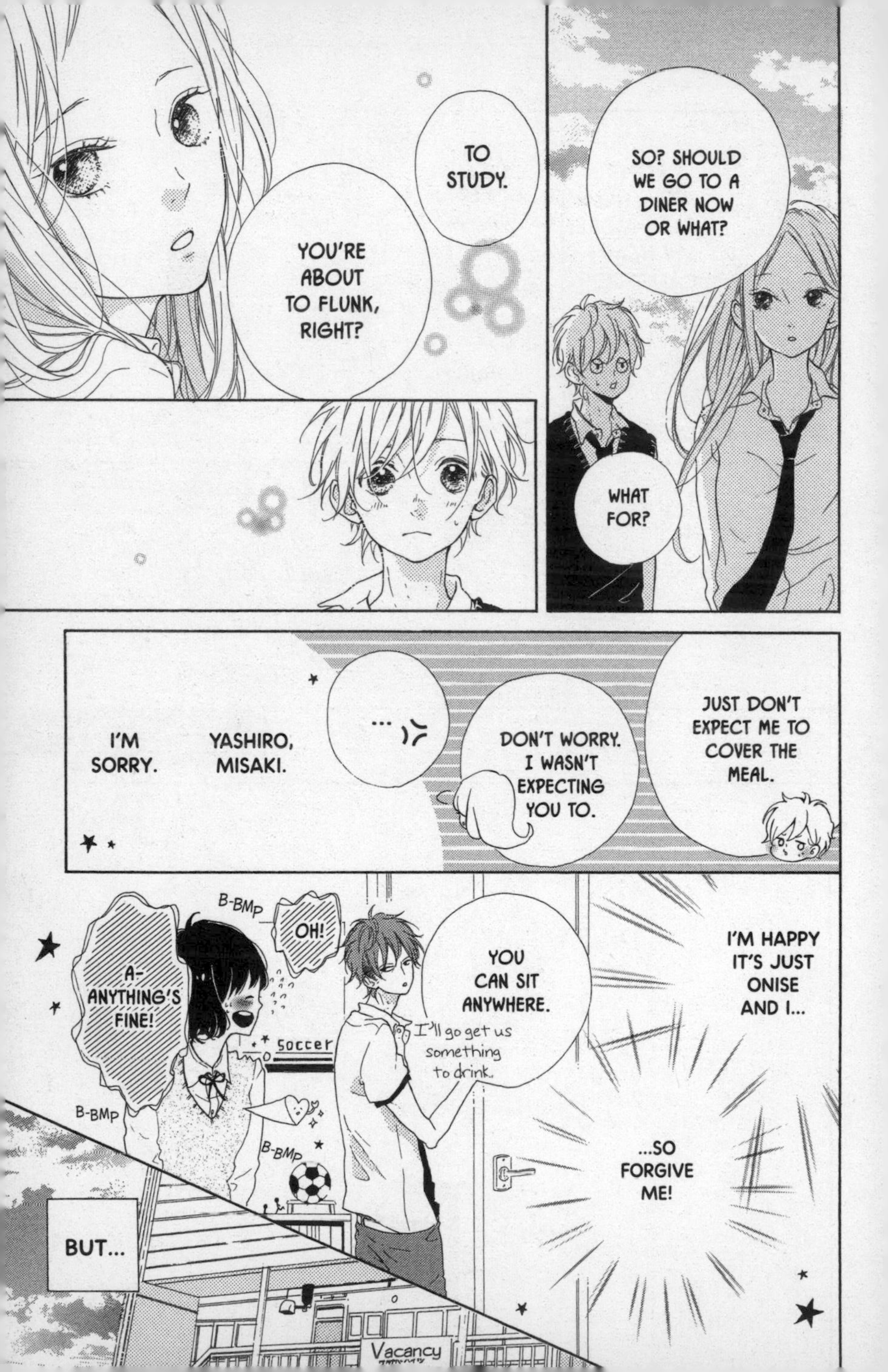
SO? SHOULD WE GO TO A DINER NOW OR WHAT?
WHAT FOR?
TO STUDY.
YOU'RE ABOUT TO FLUNK, RIGHT?
JUST DON'T EXPECT ME TO COVER THE MEAL.
DON'T WORRY. I WASN'T EXPECTING YOU TO.
...
YASHIRO, MISAKI.
I'M SORRY.
I'M HAPPY IT'S JUST ONISE AND I...
...SO FORGIVE ME!
YOU CAN SIT ANYWHERE.
I'll go get us something to drink.
OH!
B-BMP
A-ANYTHING'S FINE!
Soccer
B-BMP
B-BMP
BUT...
Vacancy

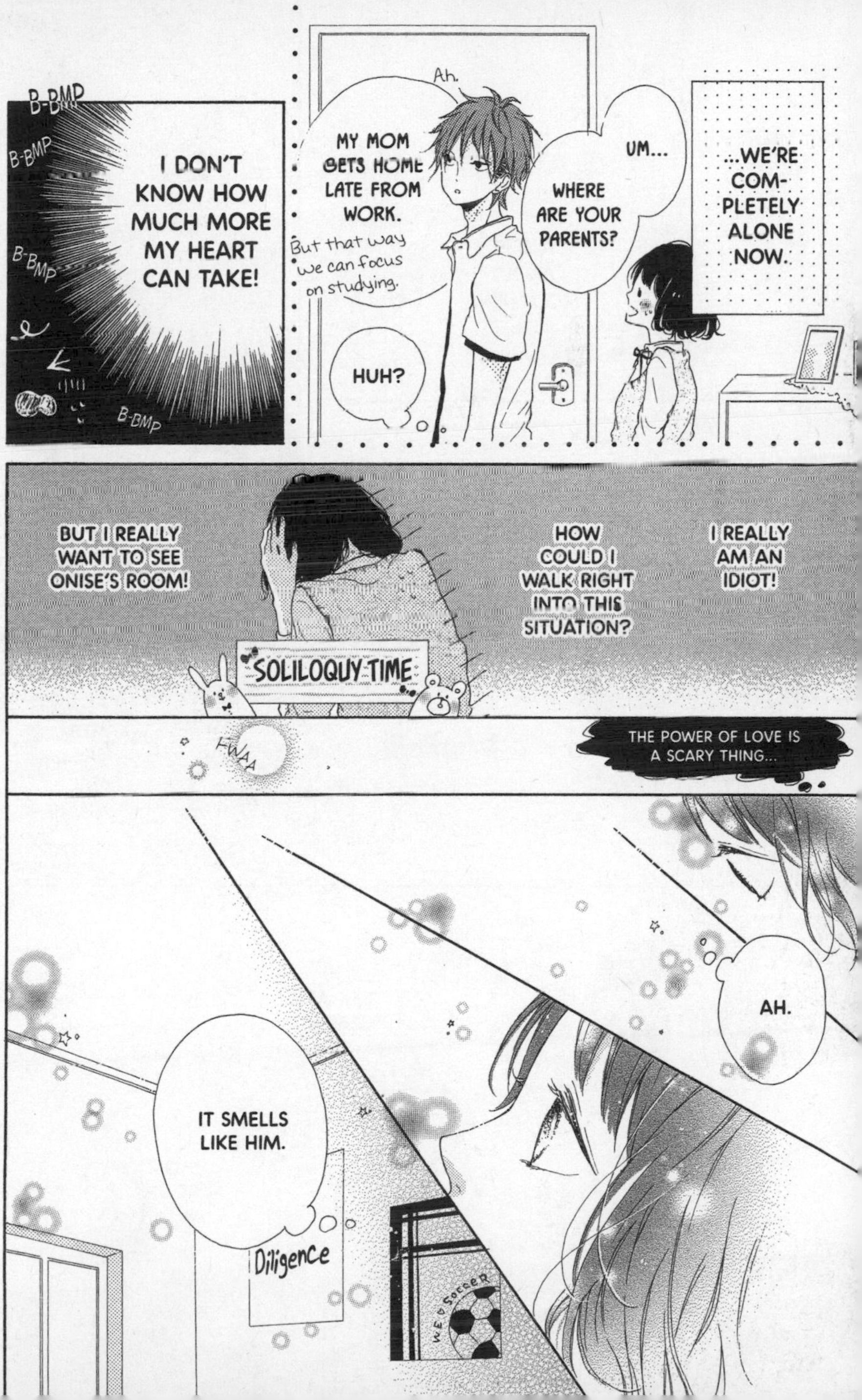
UM... WHERE ARE YOUR PARENTS?
Ah.
MY MOM GETS HOME LATE FROM WORK.
But that way we can focus on studying.
HUH?
...WE'RE COM-PLETELY ALONE NOW.
B-BMP
I DON'T KNOW HOW MUCH MORE MY HEART CAN TAKE!
B-BMP
B-BMP
B-BMP
I REALLY AM AN IDIOT!
HOW COULD I WALK RIGHT INTO THIS SITUATION?
BUT I REALLY WANT TO SEE ONISE'S ROOM!
SOLILOQUY TIME
THE POWER OF LOVE IS A SCARY THING...
FWAA
AH.
IT SMELLS LIKE HIM.
Diligence
WE ♡ Soccer

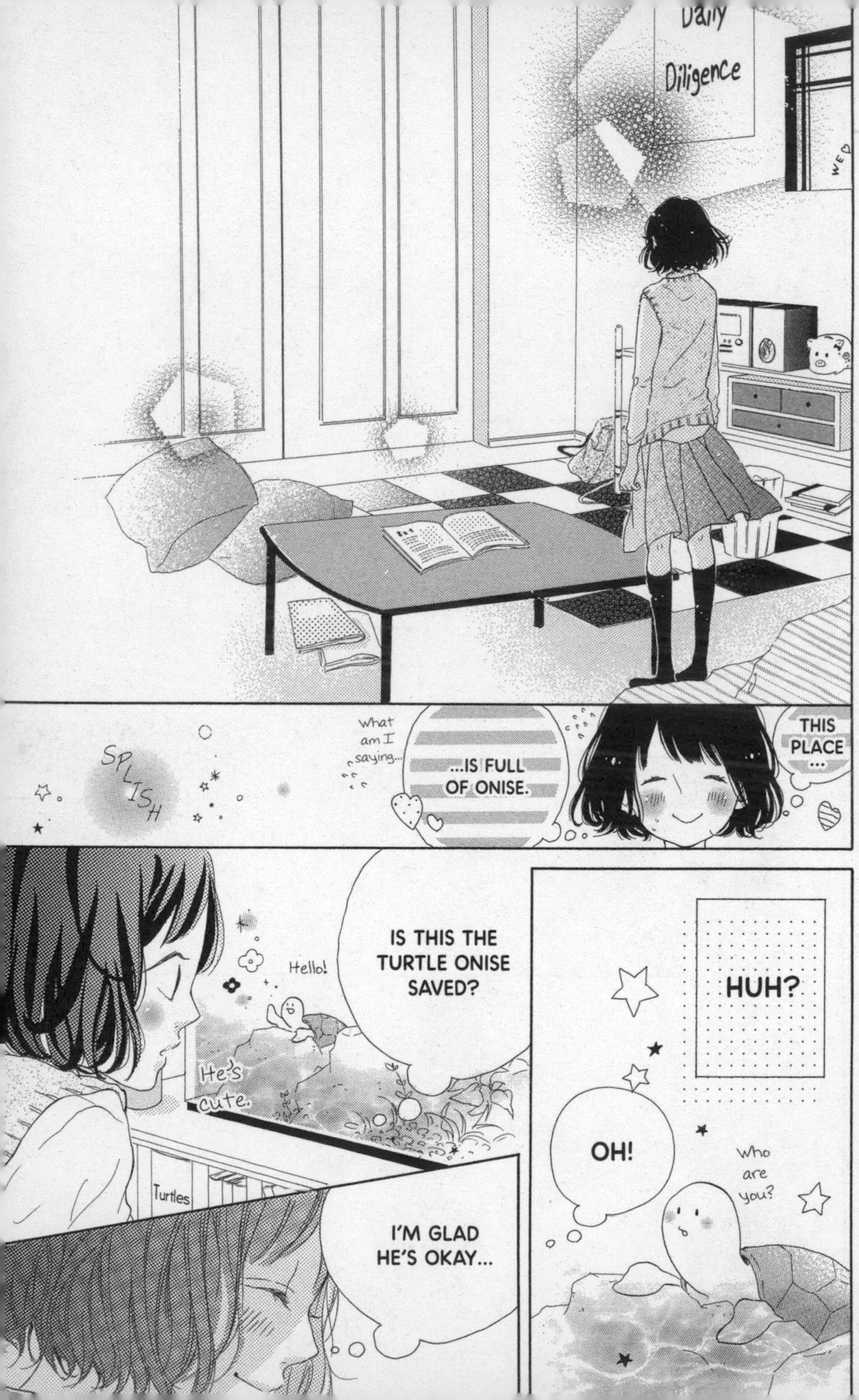
Daily
Diligence
THIS PLACE ...
...IS FULL OF ONISE.
What am I saying...
SPLISH
HUH?
OH!
Who are you?
IS THIS THE TURTLE ONISE SAVED?
Hello!
He's cute.
Turtles
I'M GLAD HE'S OKAY...

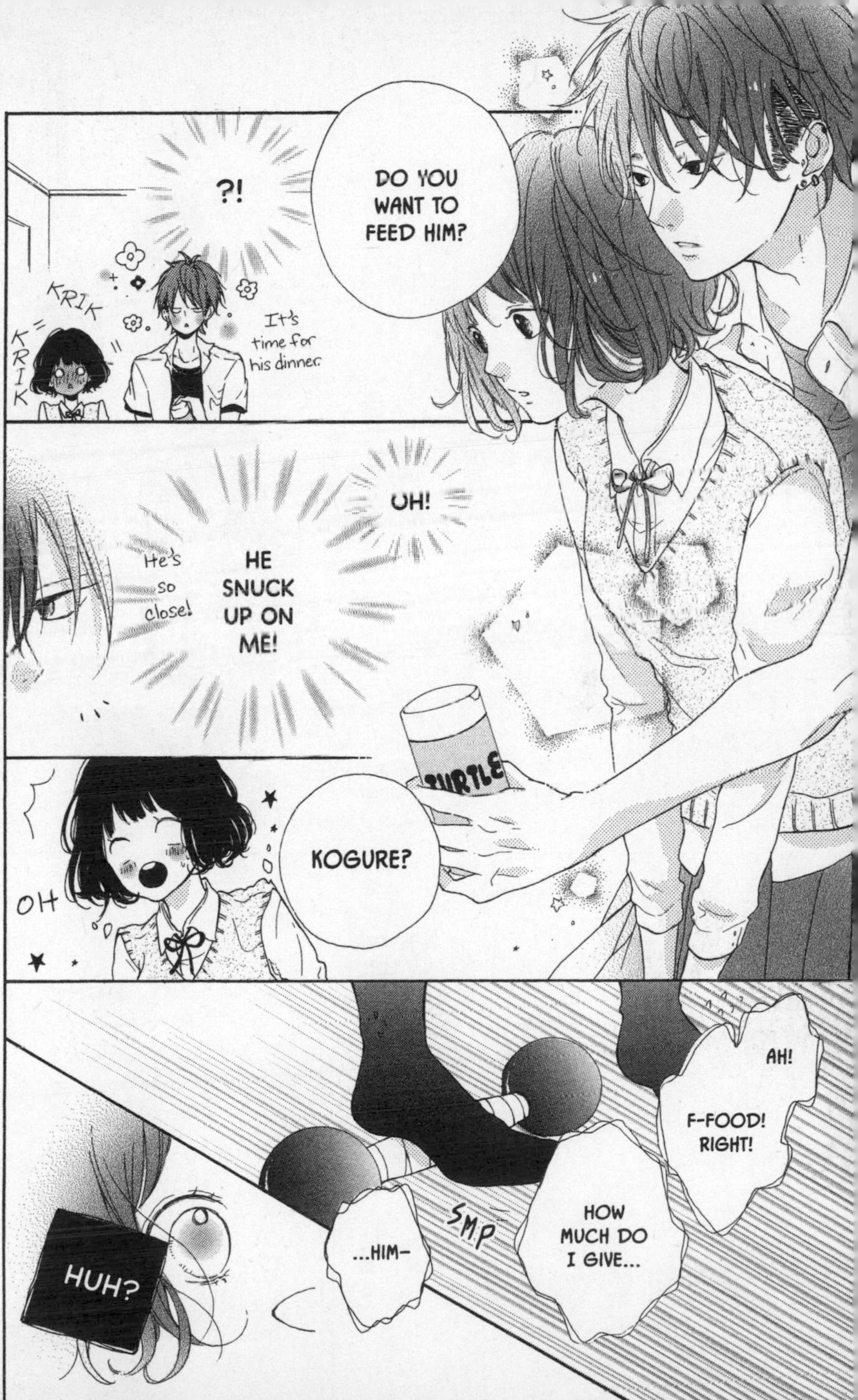
DO YOU WANT TO FEED HIM?
?!
KRIK
KRIK
It's time for his dinner.
OH!
HE SNUCK UP ON ME!
He's so close!
KOGURE?
OH
AH!
F-FOOD! RIGHT!
HOW MUCH DO I GIVE...
SMP
...HIM-
HUH?

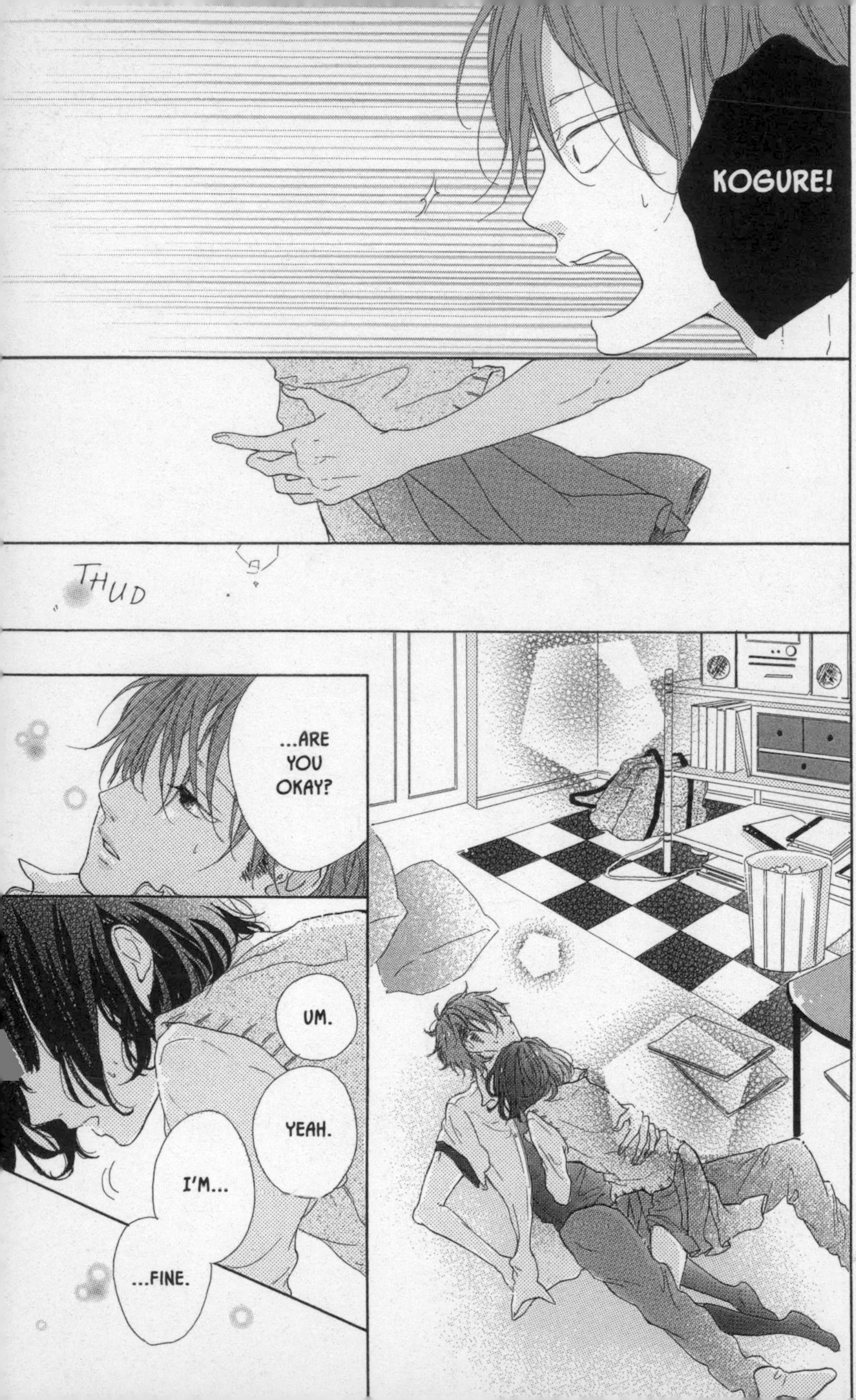
KOGURE!
THUD
...ARE YOU OKAY?
UM.
YEAH.
I'M...
...FINE.

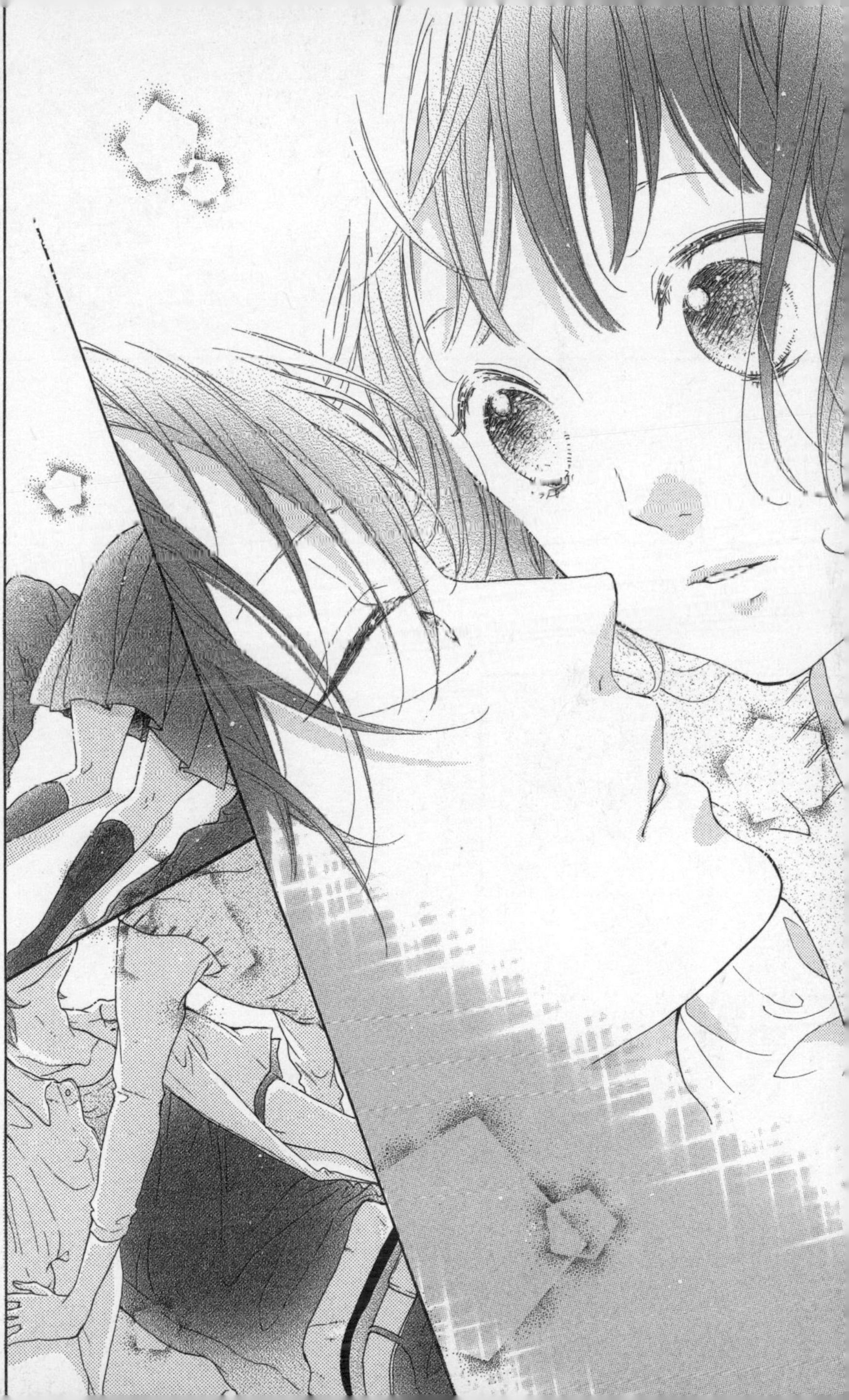

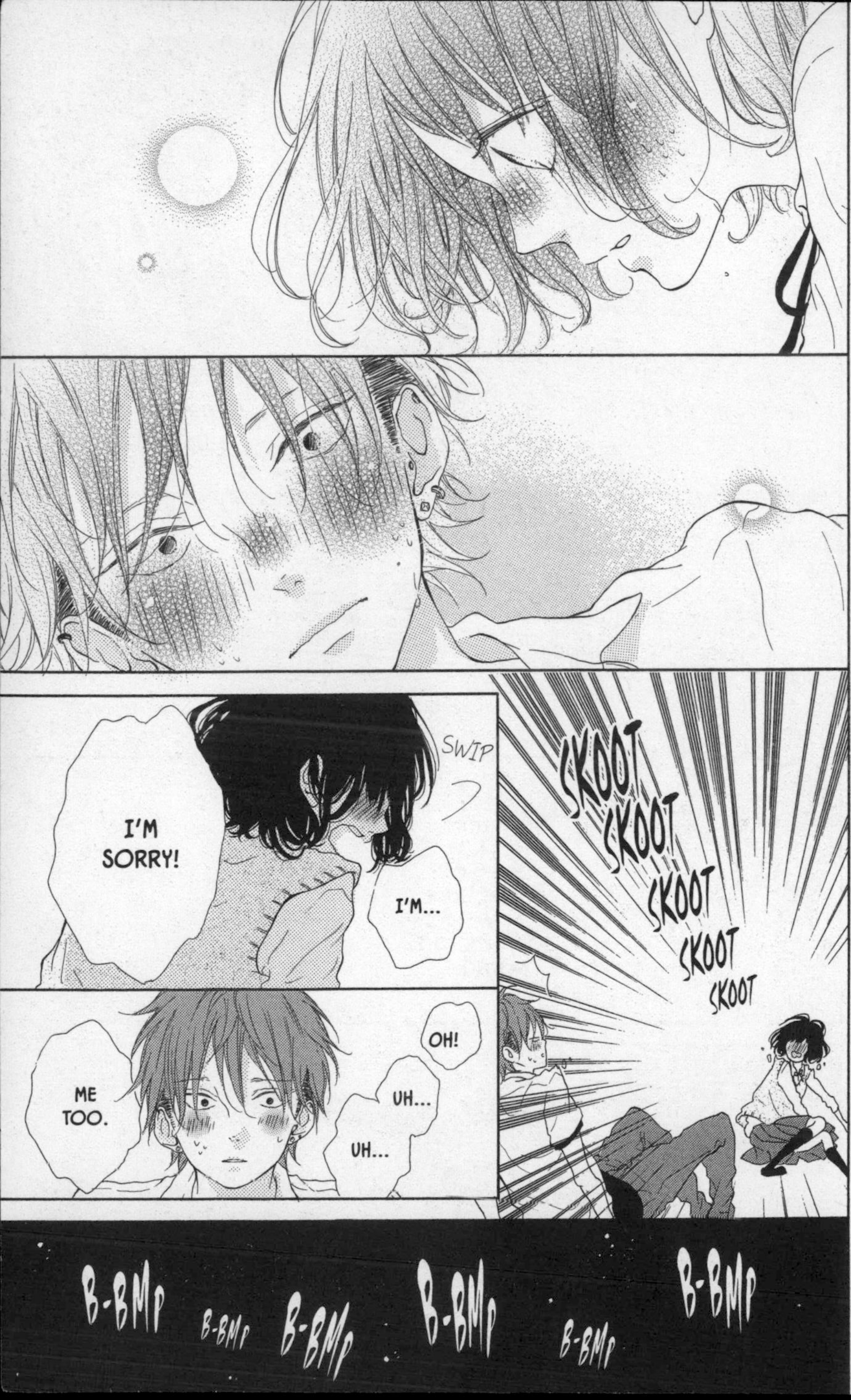
SKOOT
SKOOT
SKOOT
SKOOT
SKOOT
SWIP
I'M...
I'M SORRY!
OH!
UH...
UH...
ME TOO.
B-BMP
B-BMP
B-BMP
B-BMP
B-BMP
B-BMP

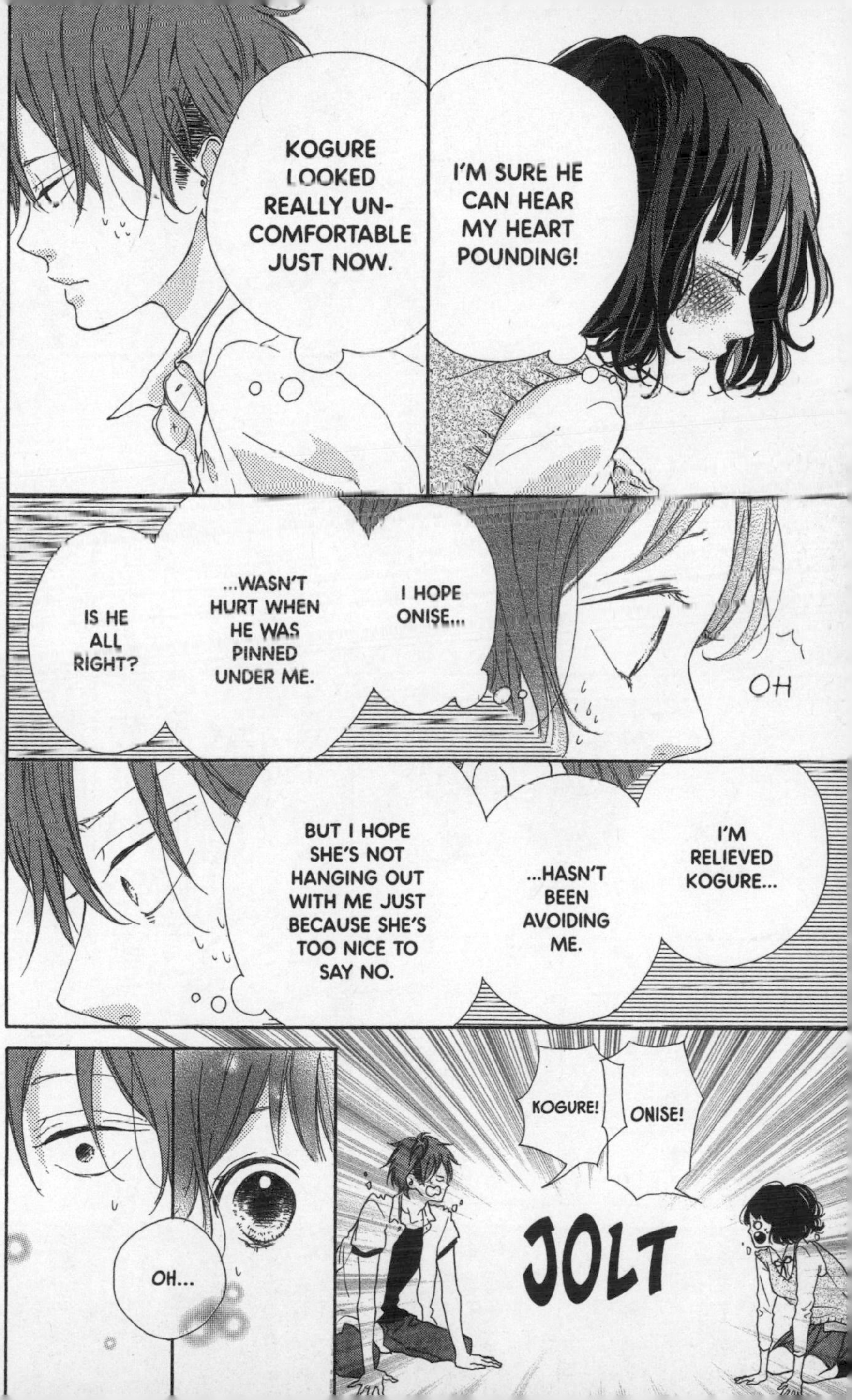
I'M SURE HE CAN HEAR MY HEART POUNDING!
KOGURE LOOKED REALLY UN-COMFORTABLE JUST NOW.
OH
I HOPE ONISE...
...WASN'T HURT WHEN HE WAS PINNED UNDER ME.
IS HE ALL RIGHT?
I'M RELIEVED KOGURE...
...HASN'T BEEN AVOIDING ME.
BUT I HOPE SHE'S NOT HANGING OUT WITH ME JUST BECAUSE SHE'S TOO NICE TO SAY NO.
ONISE!
KOGURE!
JOLT
OH...

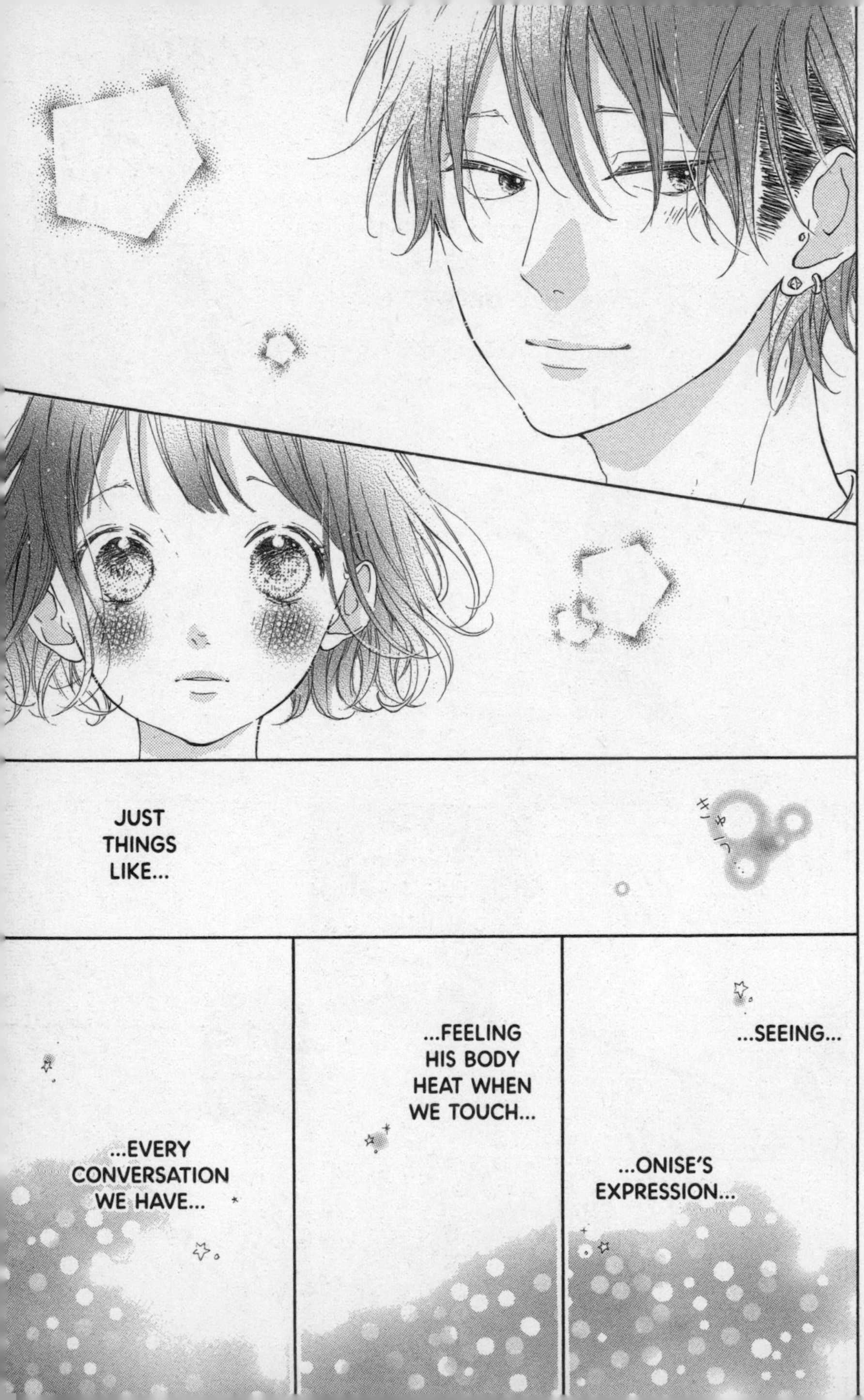
JUST THINGS LIKE...
...SEEING...
...ONISE'S EXPRESSION...
...FEELING HIS BODY HEAT WHEN WE TOUCH...
...EVERY CONVERSATION WE HAVE...

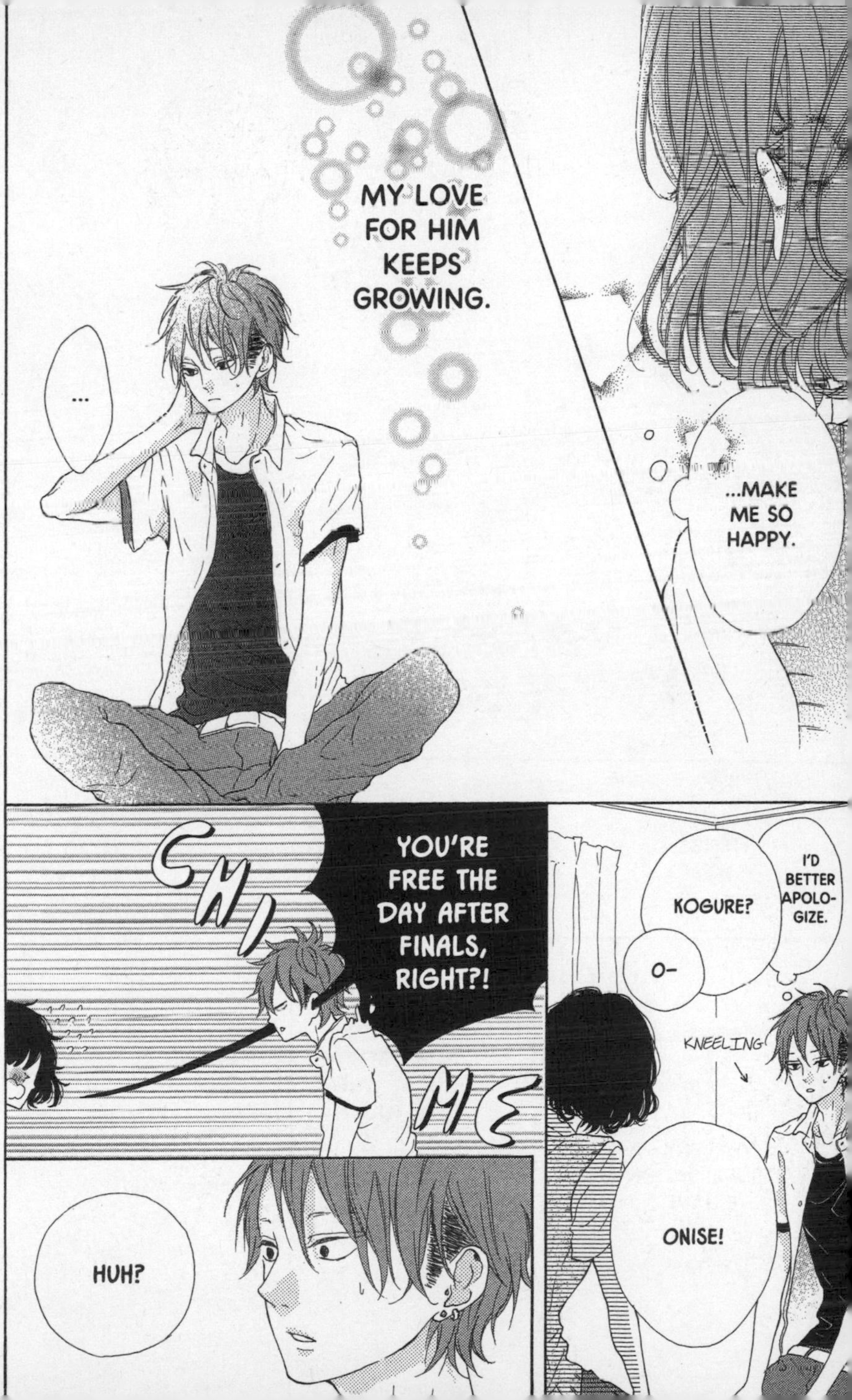

...MAKE ME SO HAPPY.
MY LOVE FOR HIM KEEPS GROWING.
...
I'D BETTER APOLOGIZE.
KOGURE?
O-
KNEELING
ONISE!
YOU'RE FREE THE DAY AFTER FINALS, RIGHT?!
CHIME
HUH?

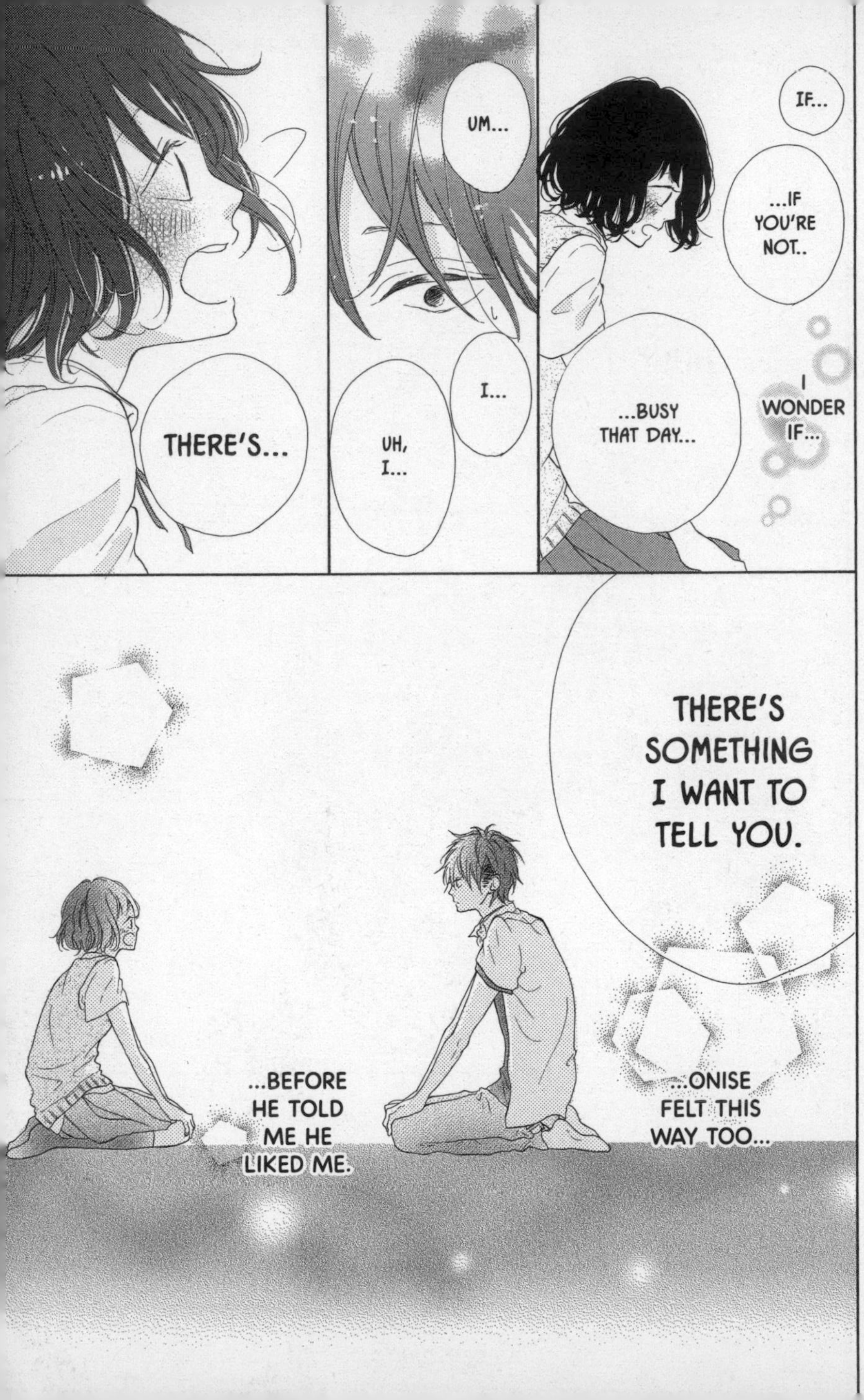
IF...
...IF YOU'RE NOT..
I WONDER IF...
...BUSY THAT DAY...
UM...
I...
UH, I...
THERE'S...
THERE'S SOMETHING I WANT TO TELL YOU.
...ONISE FELT THIS WAY TOO...
...BEFORE HE TOLD ME HE LIKED ME.

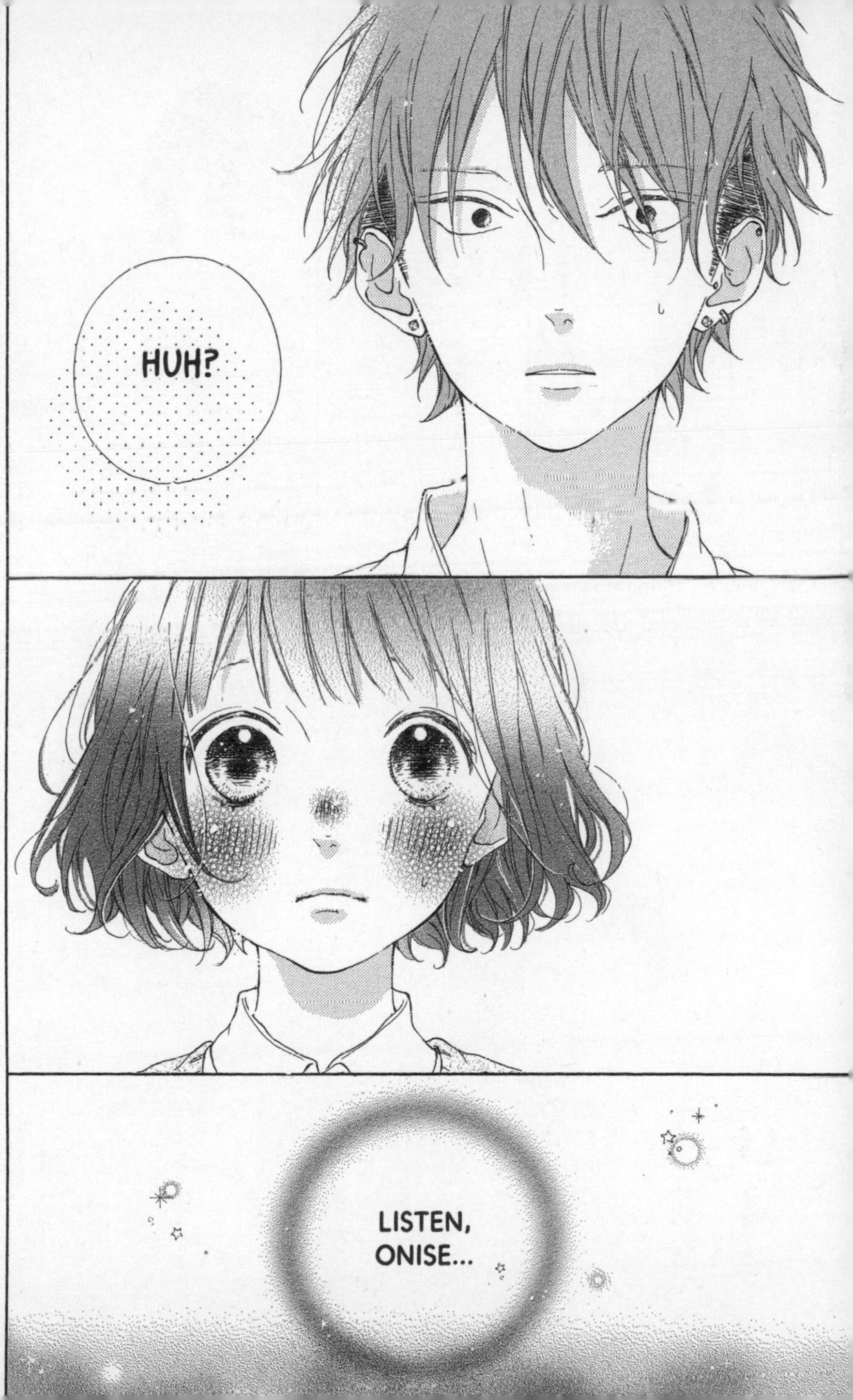
HUH?
LISTEN, ONISE...

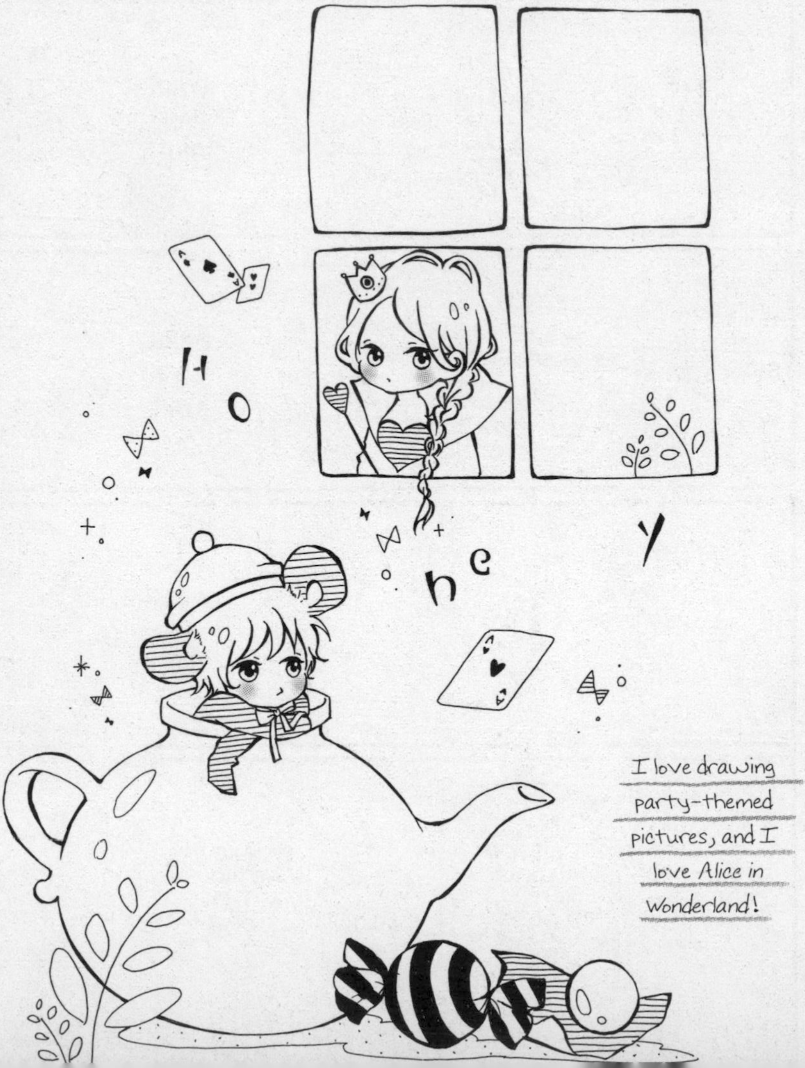
Honey
I love drawing party-themed pictures, and I love Alice in Wonderland!

Kyari Pamyu Pamyu

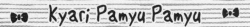

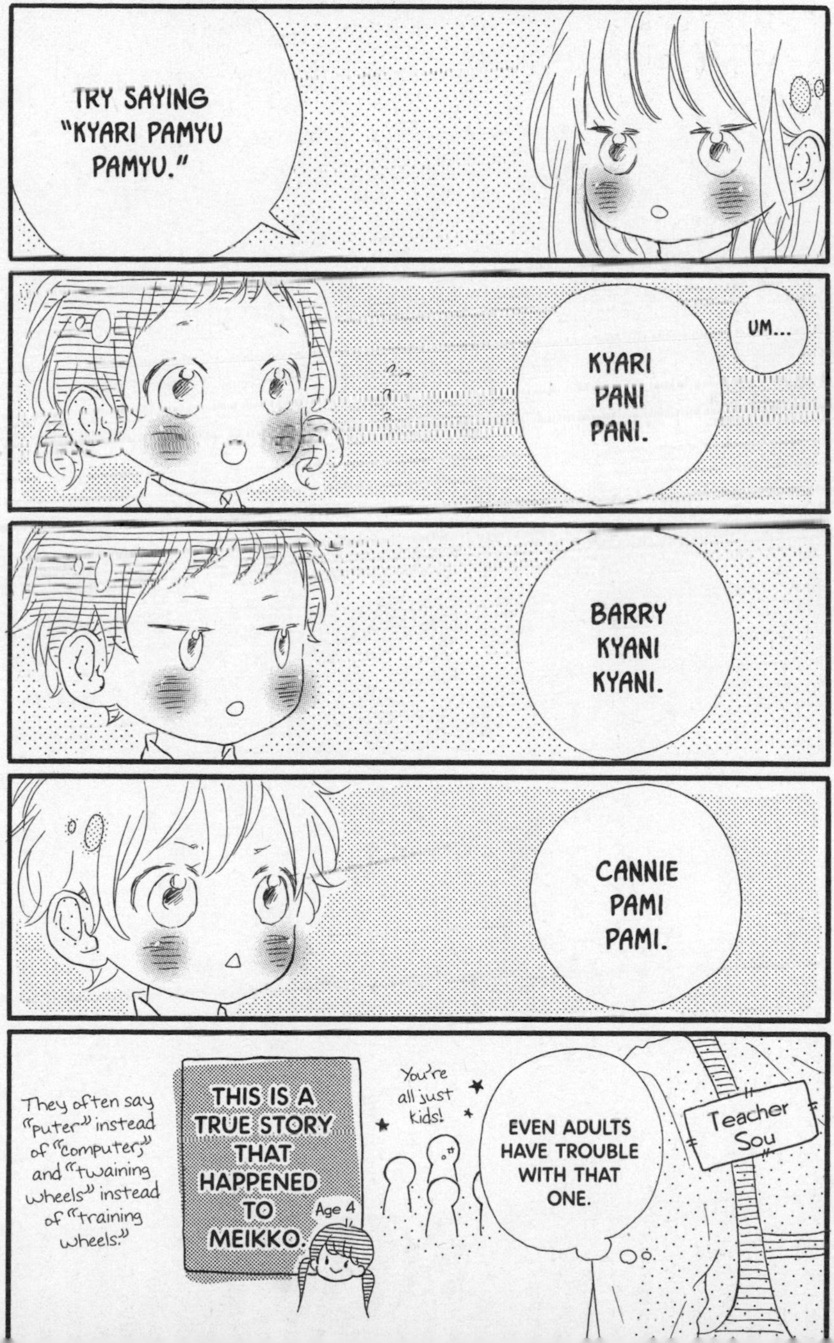
TRY SAYING "KYARI PAMYU PAMYU."
UM...
KYARI PANI PANI.
BARRY KYANI KYANI.
CANNIE PAMI PAMI.
Teacher Sou
EVEN ADULTS HAVE TROUBLE WITH THAT ONE.
You're all just kids!
THIS IS A TRUE STORY THAT HAPPENED TO MEIKKO.
Age 4
They often say "puter" instead of "computer," and "twaining wheels" instead of "training wheels."

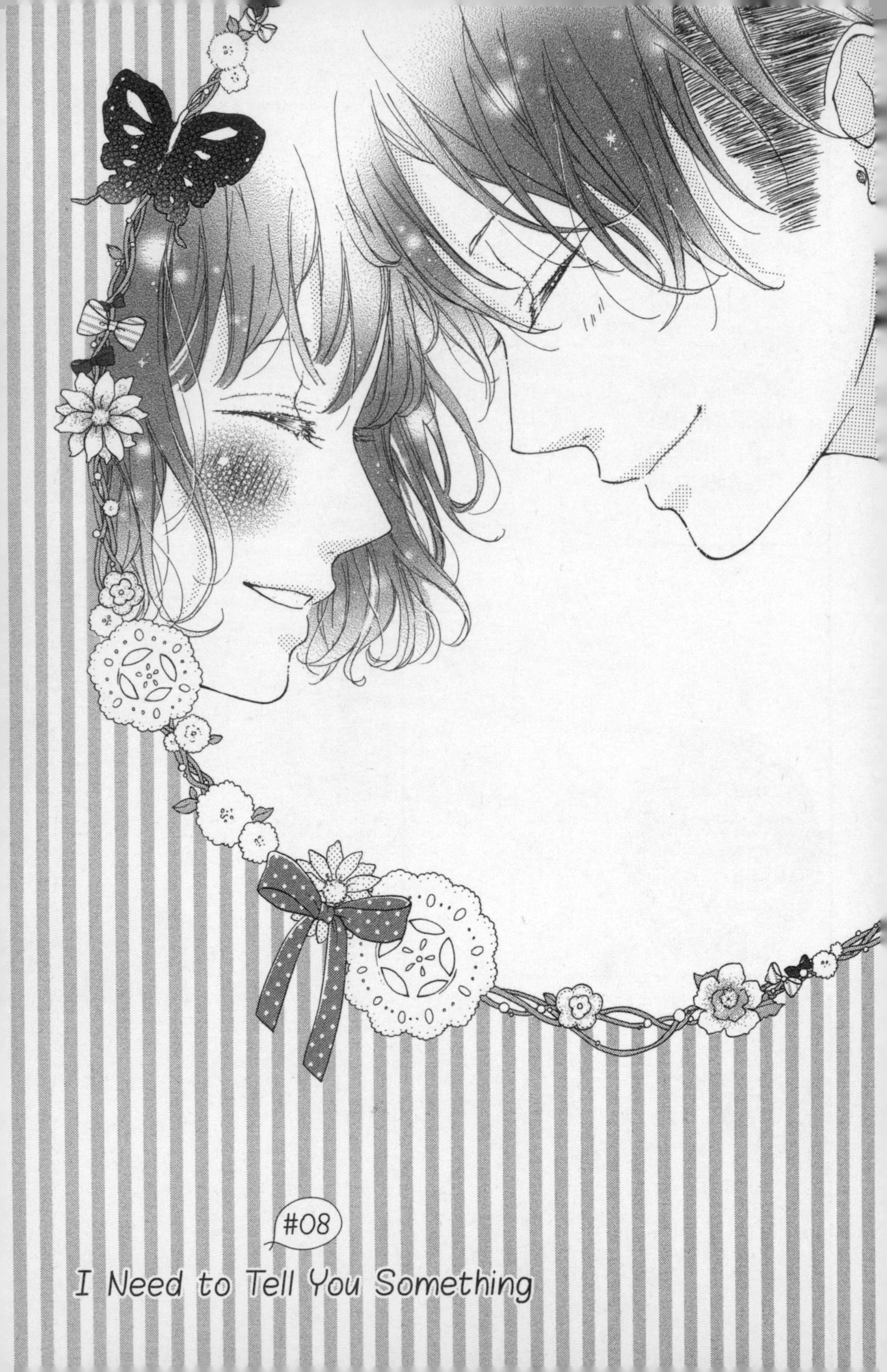
#08
I Need to Tell You Something

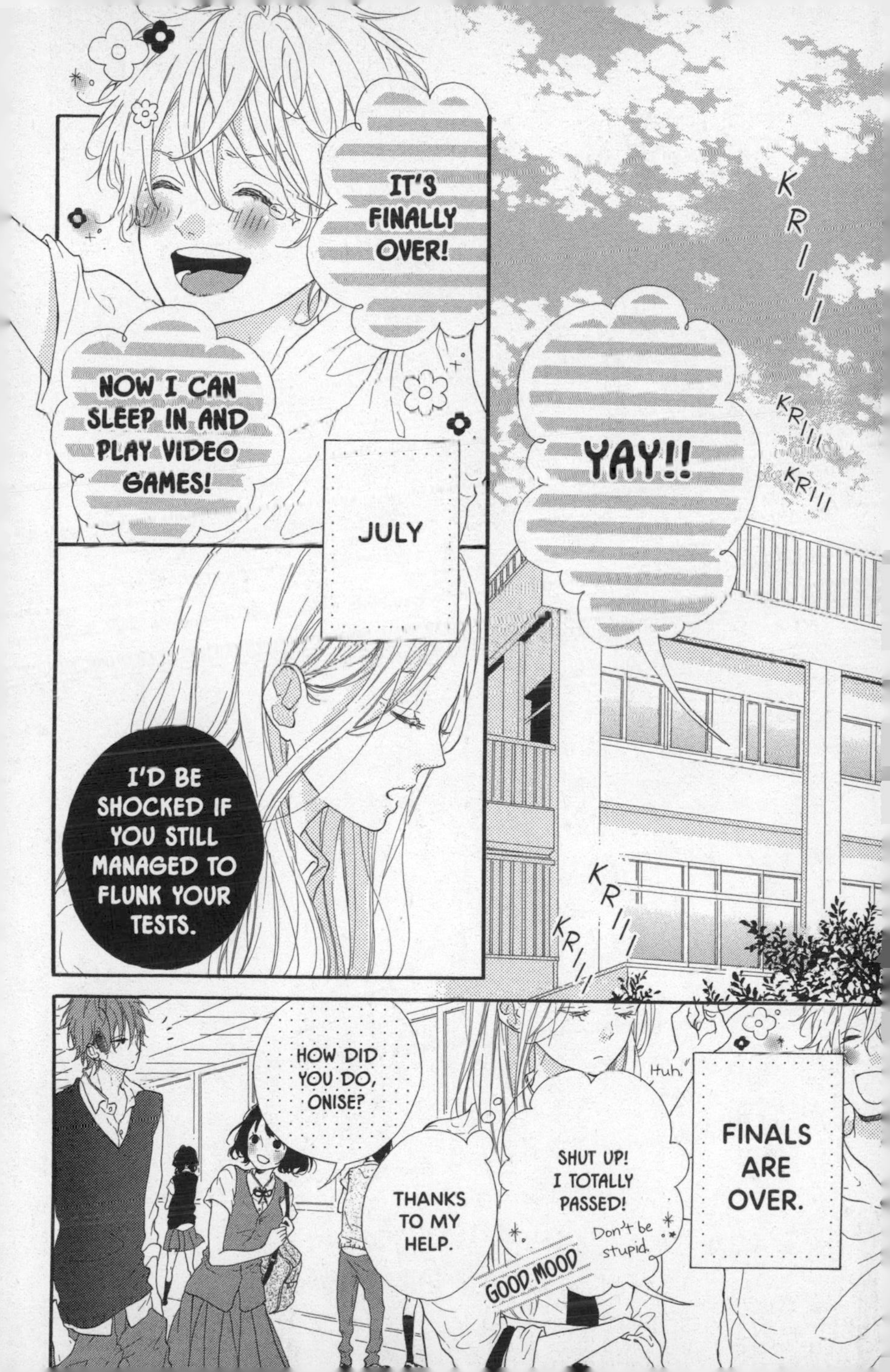
KRIII
KRIII KRIII
YAY!!
IT'S FINALLY OVER!
NOW I CAN SLEEP IN AND PLAY VIDEO GAMES!
JULY
I'D BE SHOCKED IF YOU STILL MANAGED TO FLUNK YOUR TESTS.
KRIII KRIII
FINALS ARE OVER.
HOW DID YOU DO, ONISE?
Huh.
SHUT UP! I TOTALLY PASSED!
Don't be stupid.
GOOD MOOD
THANKS TO MY HELP.

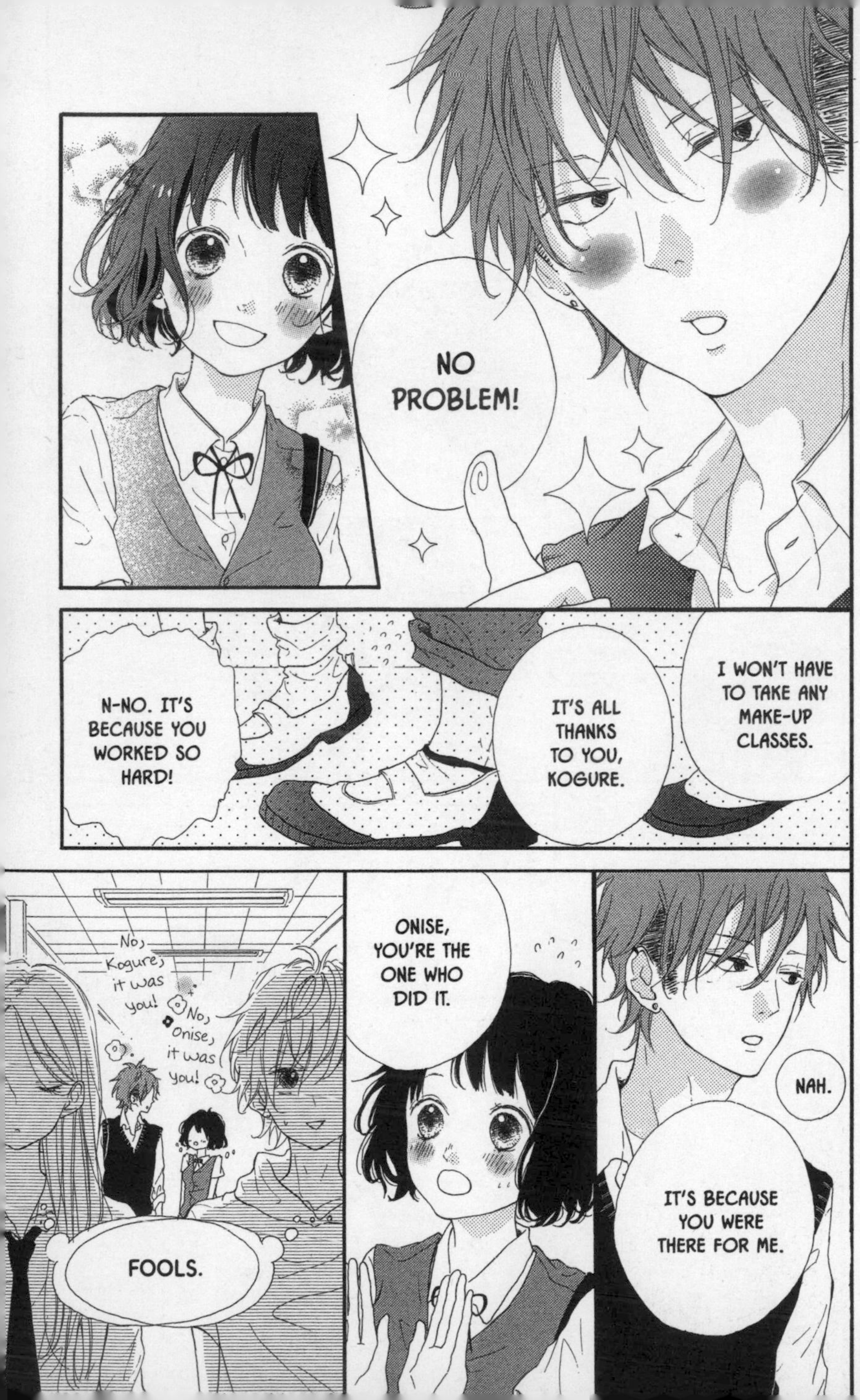
NO PROBLEM!
I WON'T HAVE TO TAKE ANY MAKE-UP CLASSES.
IT'S ALL THANKS TO YOU, KOGURE.
N-NO. IT'S BECAUSE YOU WORKED SO HARD!
NAH.
IT'S BECAUSE YOU WERE THERE FOR ME.
ONISE, YOU'RE THE ONE WHO DID IT.
No, Kogure, it was you!
No, Onise, it was you!
FOOLS.

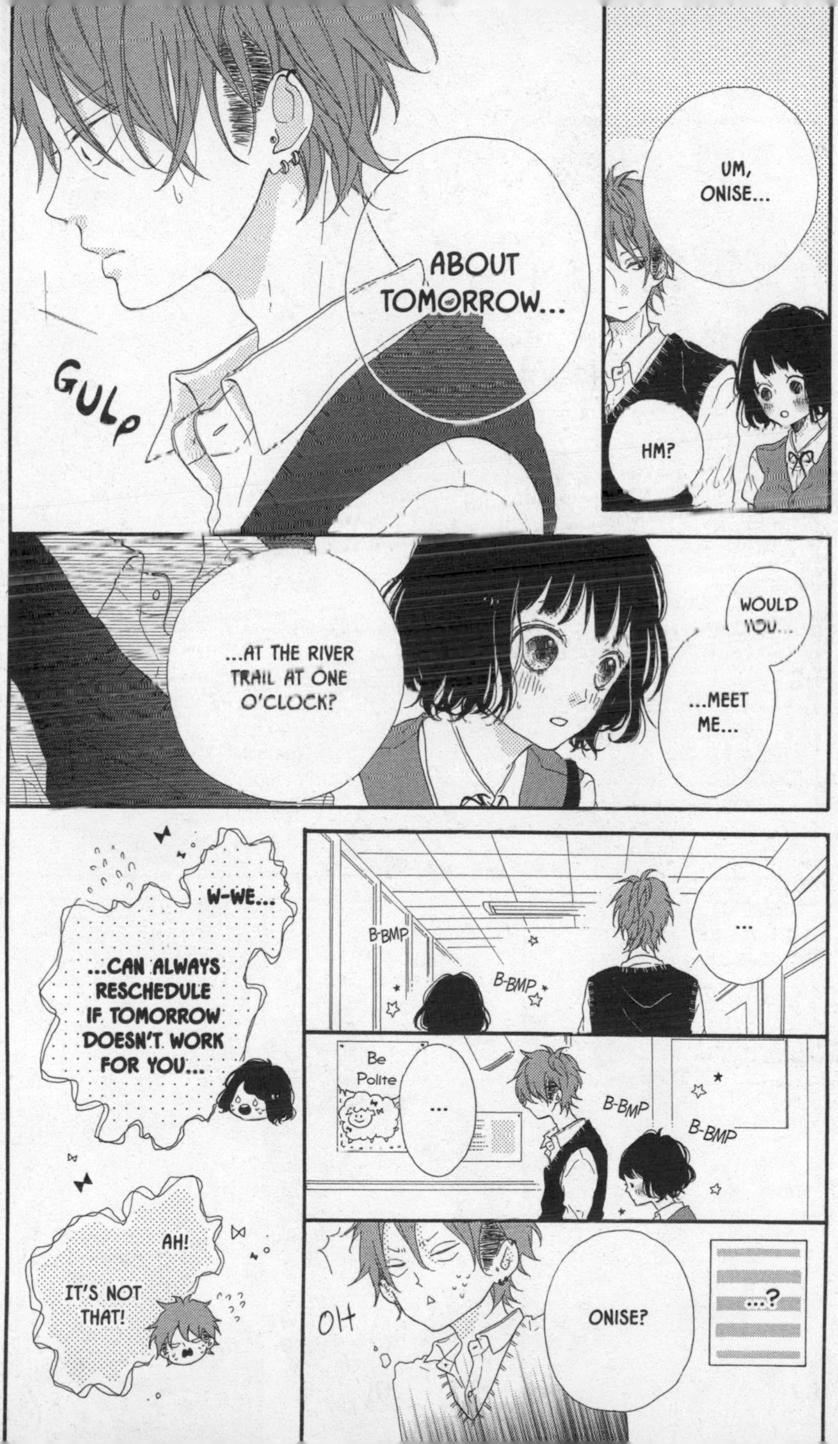
UM, ONISE...
HM?
ABOUT TOMORROW...
GULP
WOULD YOU...
...MEET ME...
...AT THE RIVER TRAIL AT ONE O'CLOCK?
...
B-BMP
B-BMP
Be Polite
...
B-BMP
B-BMP
...?
ONISE?
OH
W-WE...
...CAN ALWAYS RESCHEDULE IF TOMORROW DOESN'T WORK FOR YOU...
AH!
IT'S NOT THAT!

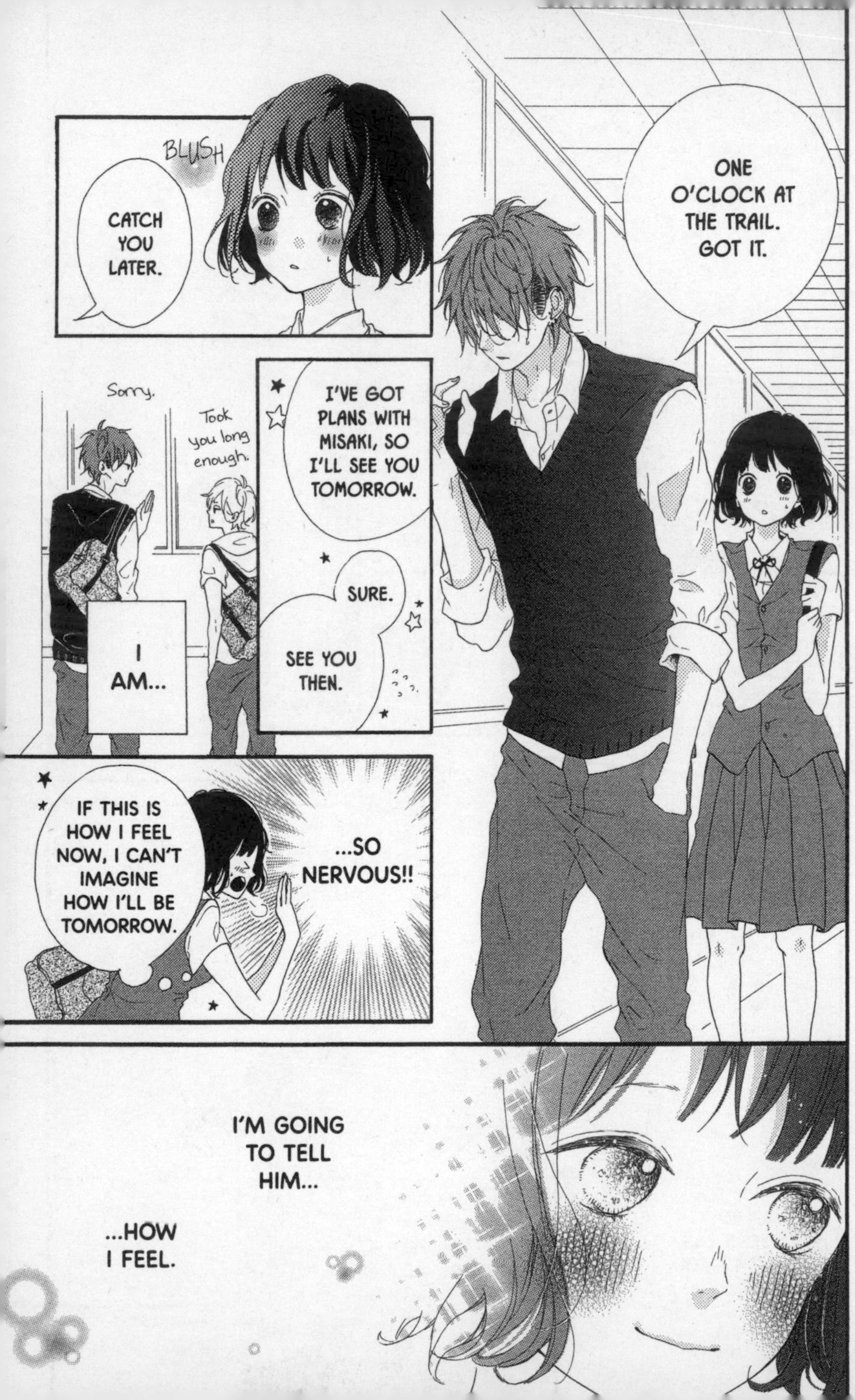
ONE O'CLOCK AT THE TRAIL. GOT IT.
BLUSH
CATCH YOU LATER.
I'VE GOT PLANS WITH MISAKI, SO I'LL SEE YOU TOMORROW.
SURE.
SEE YOU THEN.
Sorry.
Took you long enough.
I AM...
...SO NERVOUS!!
IF THIS IS HOW I FEEL NOW, I CAN'T IMAGINE HOW I'LL BE TOMORROW.
I'M GOING TO TELL HIM...
...HOW I FEEL.

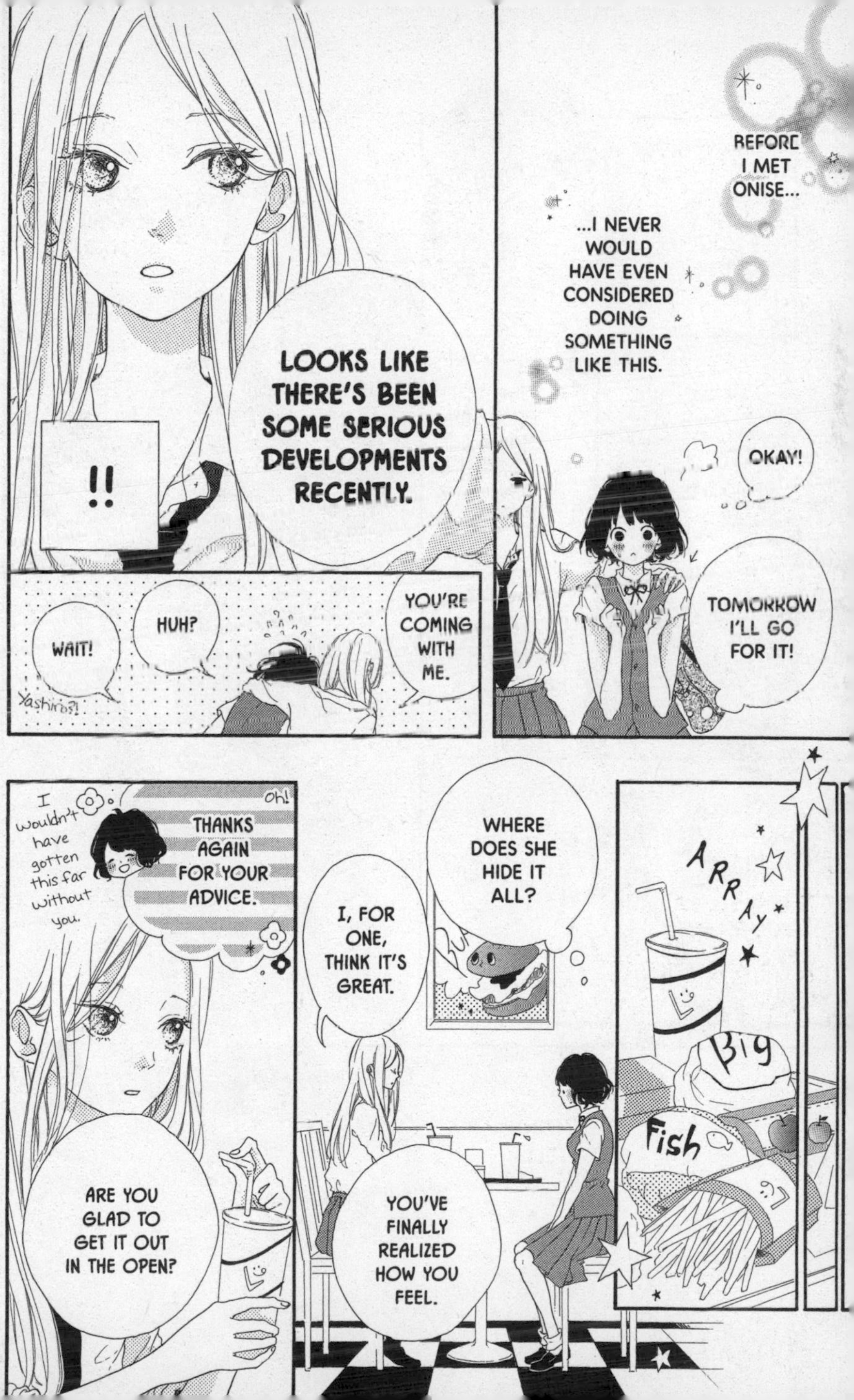
BEFORE I MET ONISE...
...I NEVER WOULD HAVE EVEN CONSIDERED DOING SOMETHING LIKE THIS.
OKAY!
TOMORROW I'LL GO FOR IT!
!!
LOOKS LIKE THERE'S BEEN SOME SERIOUS DEVELOPMENTS RECENTLY.
YOU'RE COMING WITH ME.
HUH?
WAIT!
Yashiro?!
ARRAY
Big
Fish
WHERE DOES SHE HIDE IT ALL?
I, FOR ONE, THINK IT'S GREAT.
YOU'VE FINALLY REALIZED HOW YOU FEEL.
Oh!
THANKS AGAIN FOR YOUR ADVICE.
I wouldn't have gotten this far without you.
ARE YOU GLAD TO GET IT OUT IN THE OPEN?

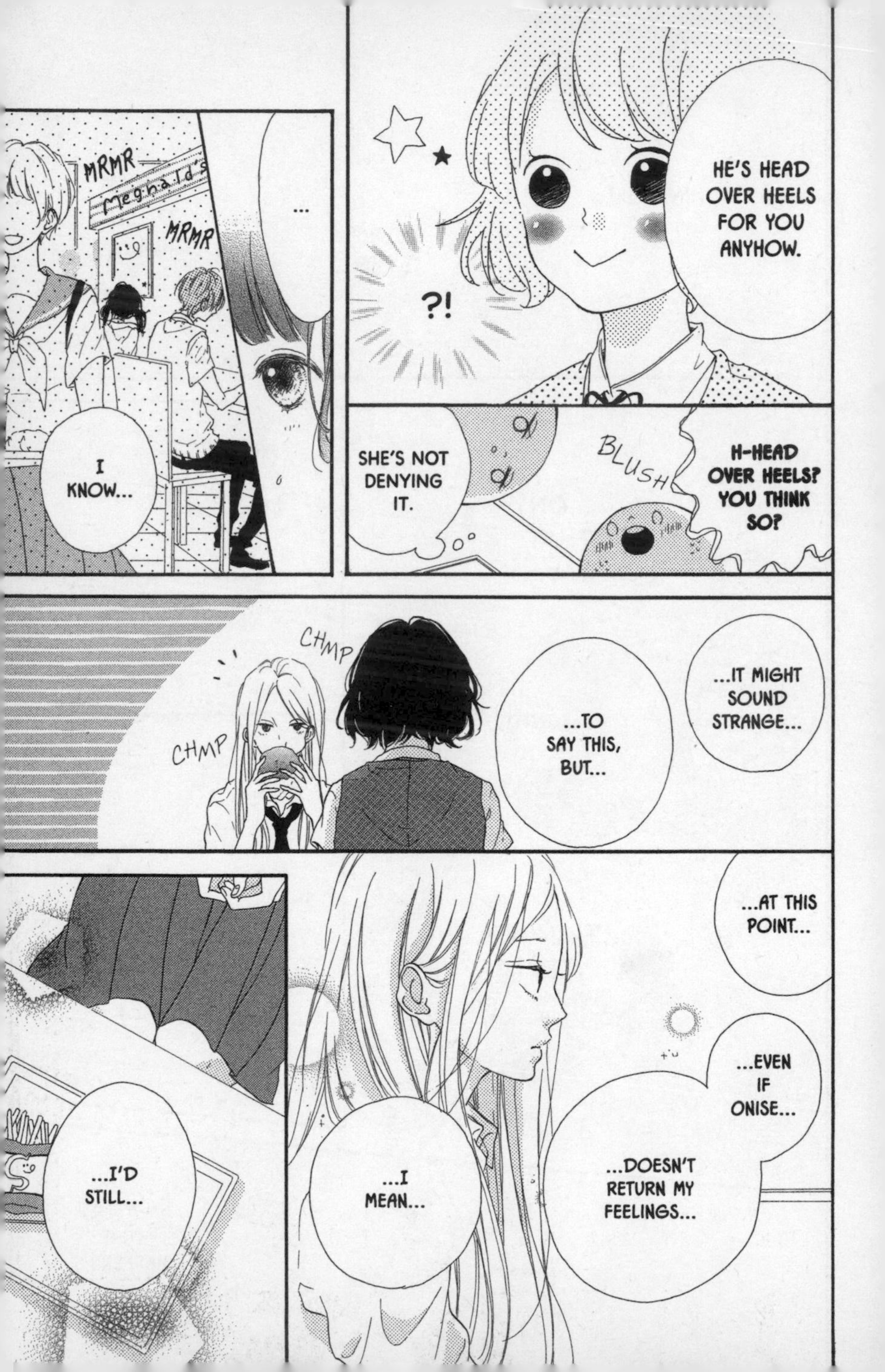
HE'S HEAD OVER HEELS FOR YOU ANYHOW.
?!
H-HEAD OVER HEELS? YOU THINK SO?
BLUSH
SHE'S NOT DENYING IT.
...
MRMR
MRMR
I KNOW...
...IT MIGHT SOUND STRANGE...
...TO SAY THIS, BUT...
CHMP
CHMP
...AT THIS POINT...
...EVEN IF ONISE...
...DOESN'T RETURN MY FEELINGS...
...I MEAN...
...I'D STILL...

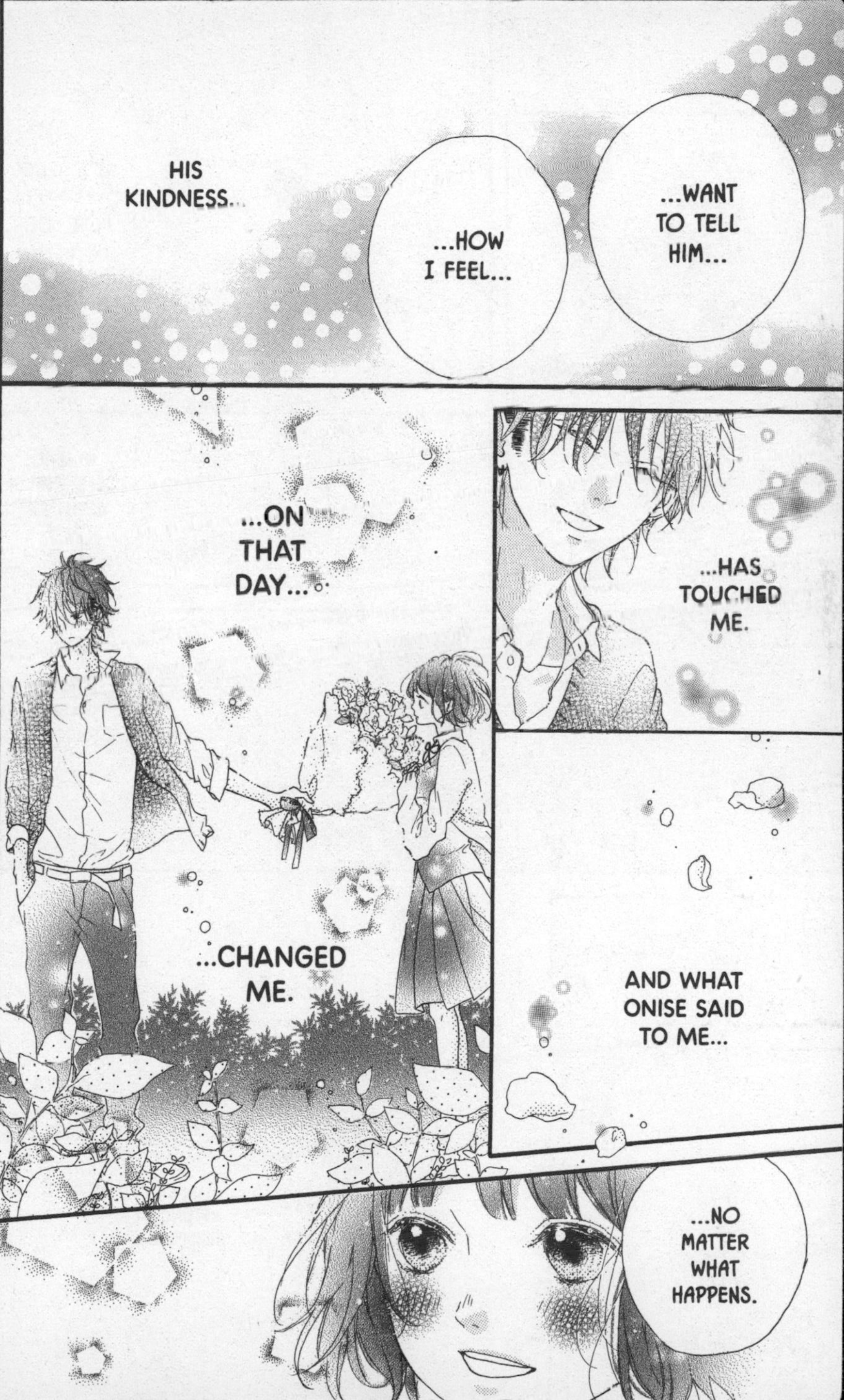
...WANT TO TELL HIM...
...HOW I FEEL...
HIS KINDNESS...
...HAS TOUCHED ME.
AND WHAT ONISE SAID TO ME...
...ON THAT DAY...
...CHANGED ME.
...NO MATTER WHAT HAPPENS.

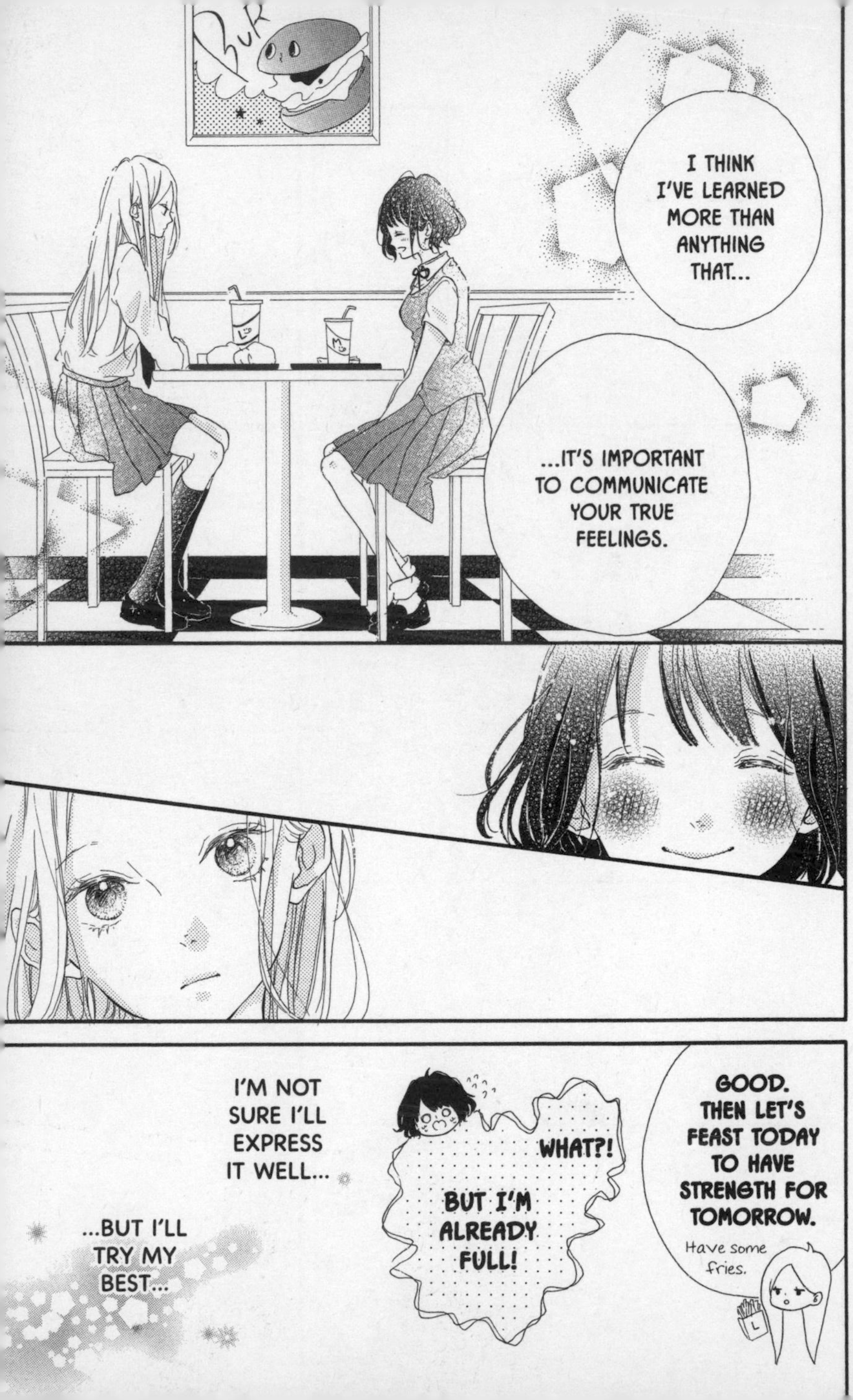
I THINK I'VE LEARNED MORE THAN ANYTHING THAT...
...IT'S IMPORTANT TO COMMUNICATE YOUR TRUE FEELINGS.
GOOD. THEN LET'S FEAST TODAY TO HAVE STRENGTH FOR TOMORROW.
Have some fries.
WHAT?!
BUT I'M ALREADY FULL!
I'M NOT SURE I'LL EXPRESS IT WELL...
...BUT I'LL TRY MY BEST...

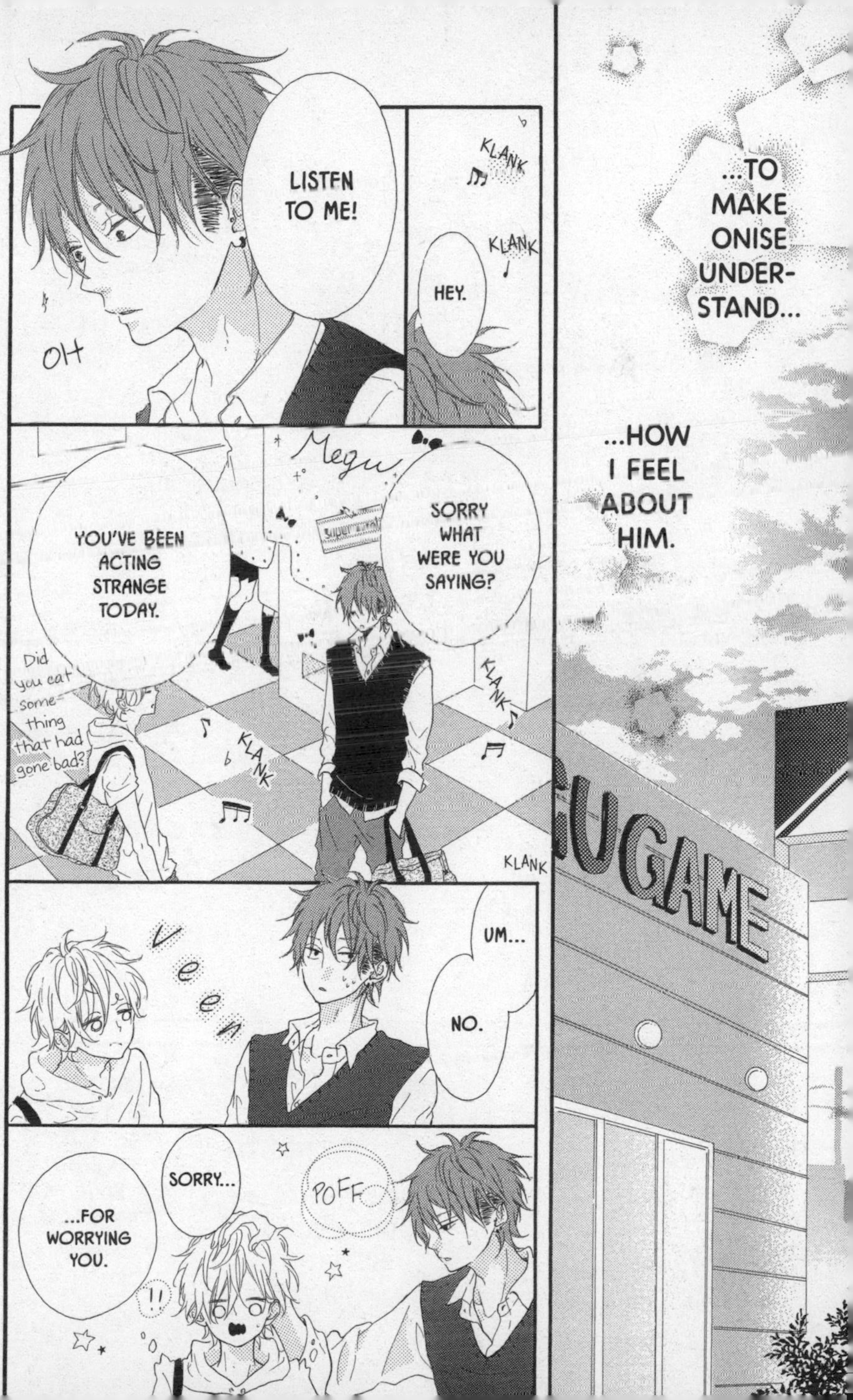
...TO MAKE ONISE UNDER-STAND...
...HOW I FEEL ABOUT HIM.
UGAME
KLANK
KLANK
HEY.
LISTEN TO ME!
OH
Megu
SORRY WHAT WERE YOU SAYING?
YOU'VE BEEN ACTING STRANGE TODAY.
Did you eat some-thing that had gone bad?
KLANK
KLANK
KLANK
UM...
NO.
veen
POFF
SORRY...
...FOR WORRYING YOU.
!!

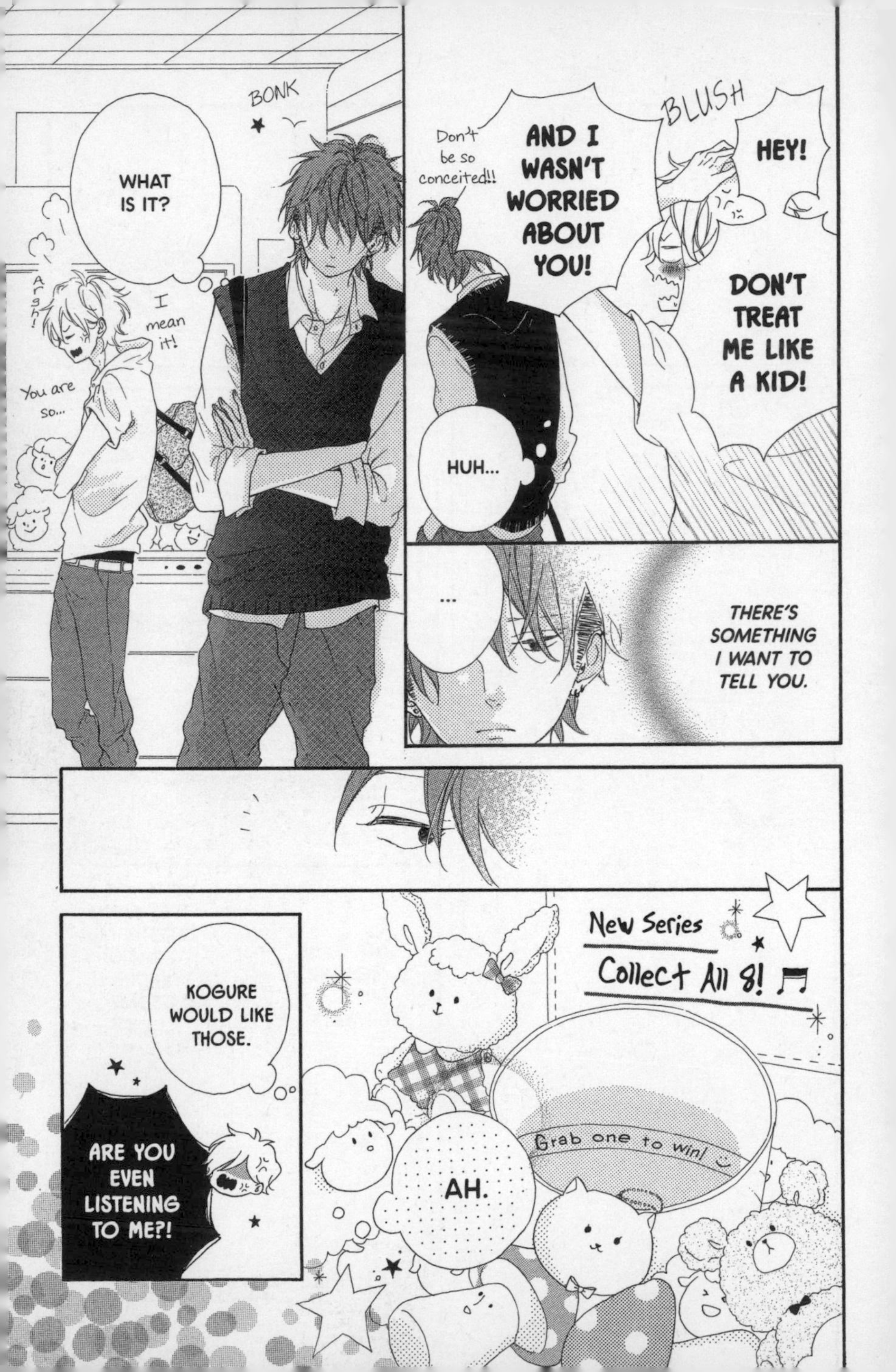
BLUSH
HEY!
DON'T TREAT ME LIKE A KID!
AND I WASN'T WORRIED ABOUT YOU!
Don't be so conceited!!
HUH...
THERE'S SOMETHING I WANT TO TELL YOU.
...
BONK
WHAT IS IT?
I mean it!
Argh!
You are so...
New Series
Collect All 8!
Grab one to win!
AH.
KOGURE WOULD LIKE THOSE.
ARE YOU EVEN LISTENING TO ME?!

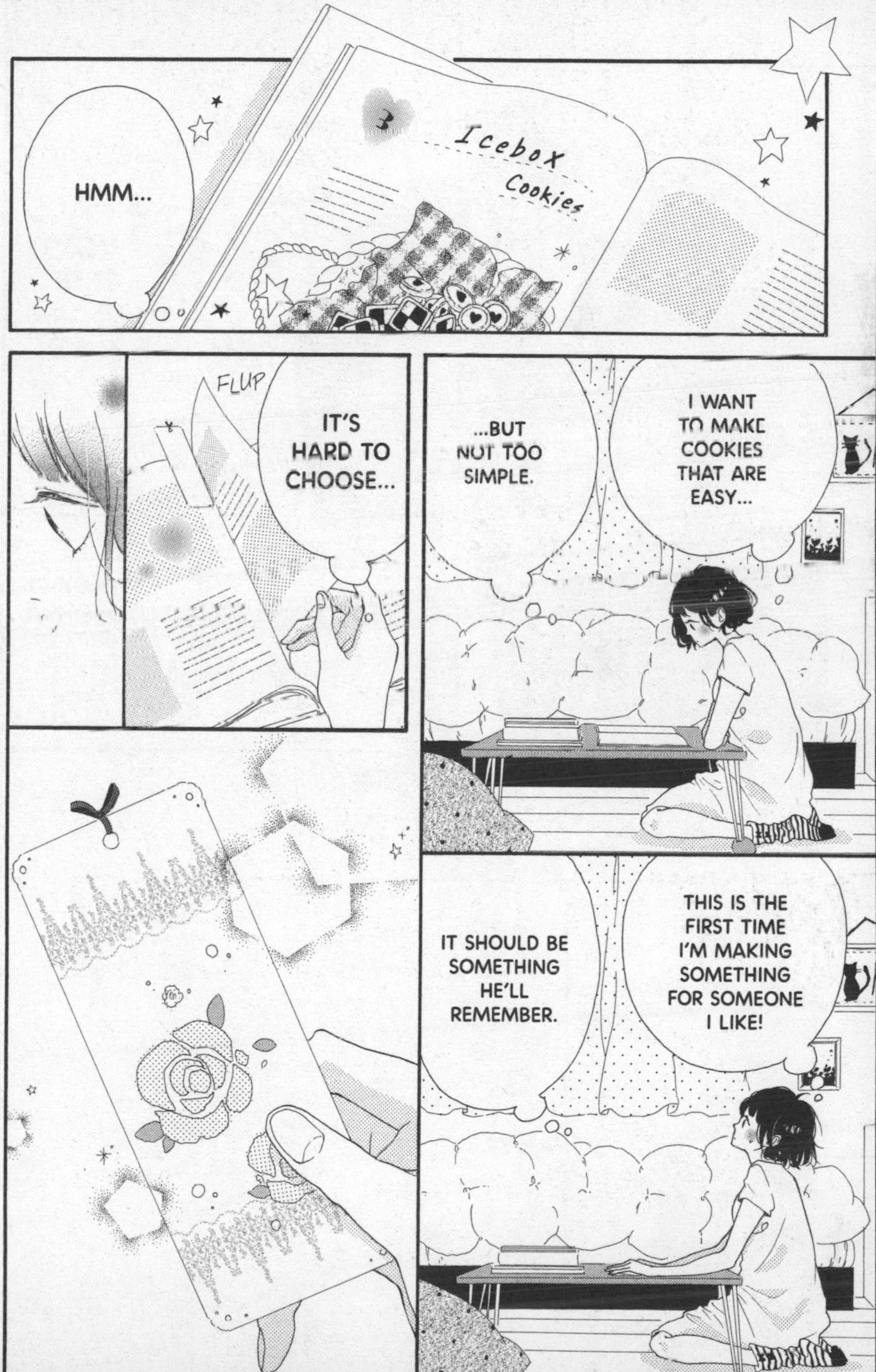
Icebox Cookies
HMM...
I WANT TO MAKE COOKIES THAT ARE EASY...
...BUT NOT TOO SIMPLE.
FLUP
IT'S HARD TO CHOOSE...
THIS IS THE FIRST TIME I'M MAKING SOMETHING FOR SOMEONE I LIKE!
IT SHOULD BE SOMETHING HE'LL REMEMBER.

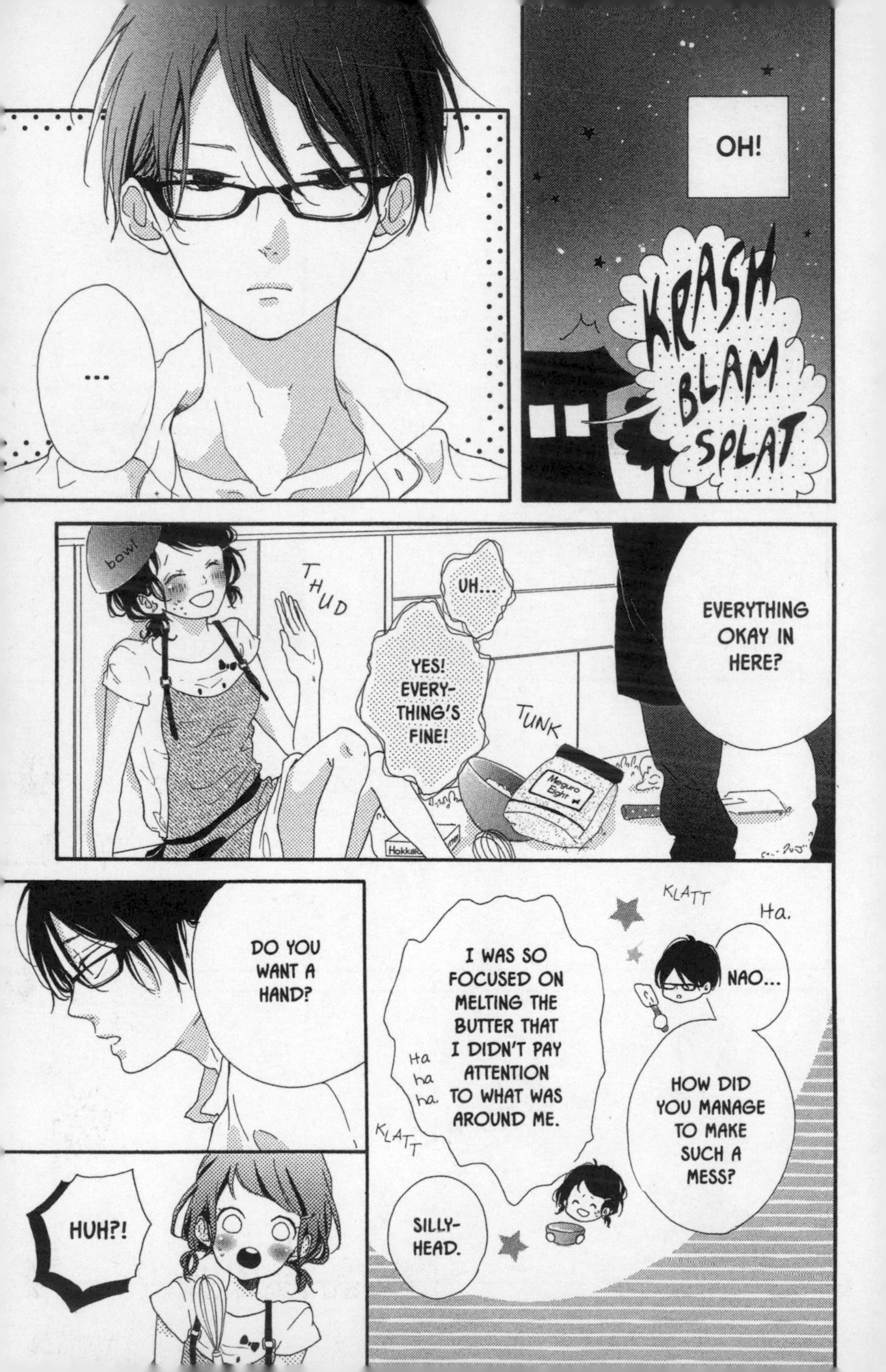
OH!
KRASH
BLAM
SPLAT
...
EVERYTHING OKAY IN HERE?
UH...
TUNK
YES! EVERY-THING'S FINE!
THUD
bowl
Meguro Eight
KLATT
Ha.
NAO...
HOW DID YOU MANAGE TO MAKE SUCH A MESS?
I WAS SO FOCUSED ON MELTING THE BUTTER THAT I DIDN'T PAY ATTENTION TO WHAT WAS AROUND ME.
Ha ha ha.
KLATT
SILLY-HEAD.
DO YOU WANT A HAND?
HUH?!

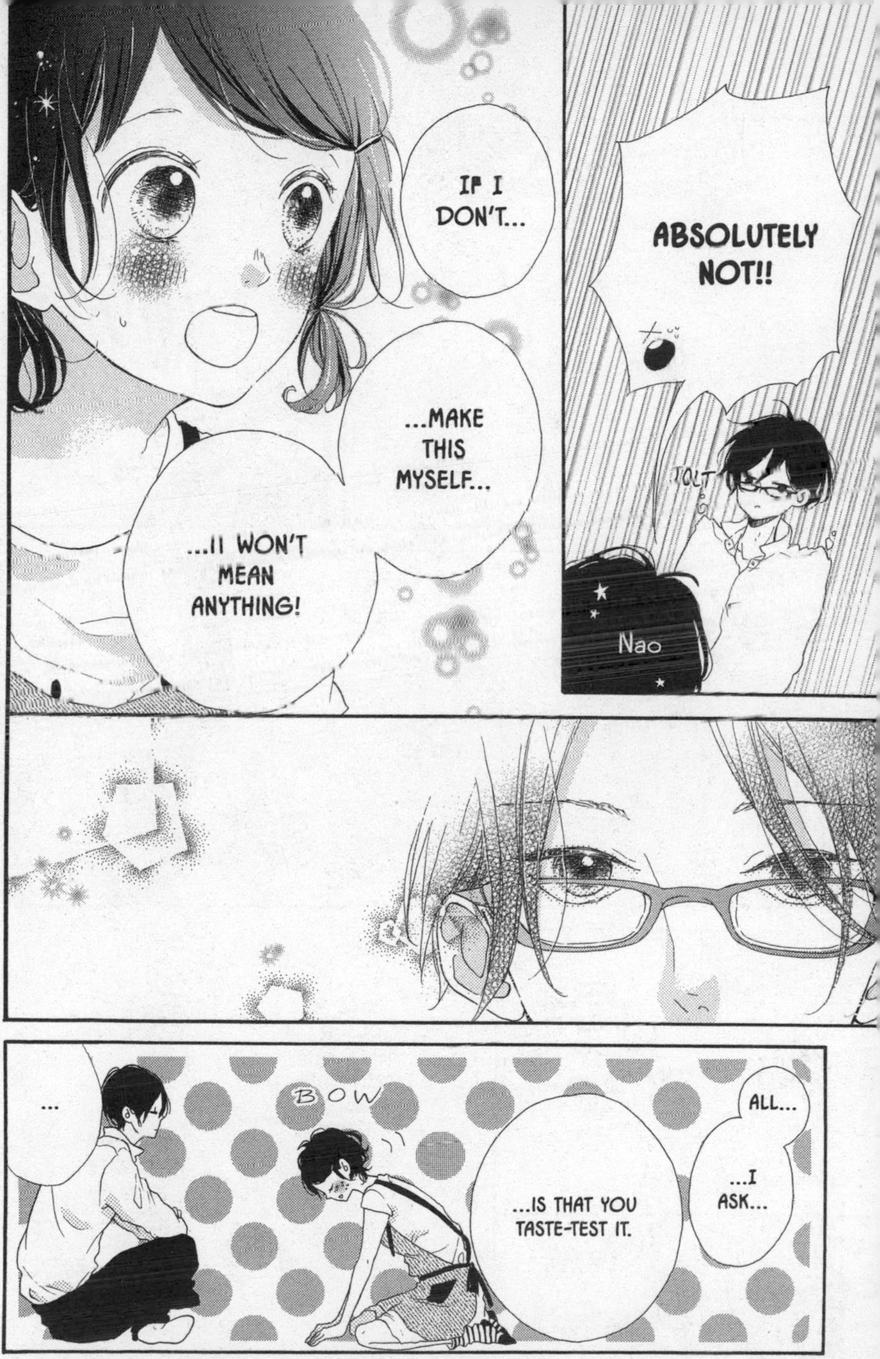
ABSOLUTELY NOT!!
JOLT
Nao
IF I DON'T...
...MAKE THIS MYSELF...
...IT WON'T MEAN ANYTHING!
ALL...
...I ASK...
...IS THAT YOU TASTE-TEST IT.
BOW
...

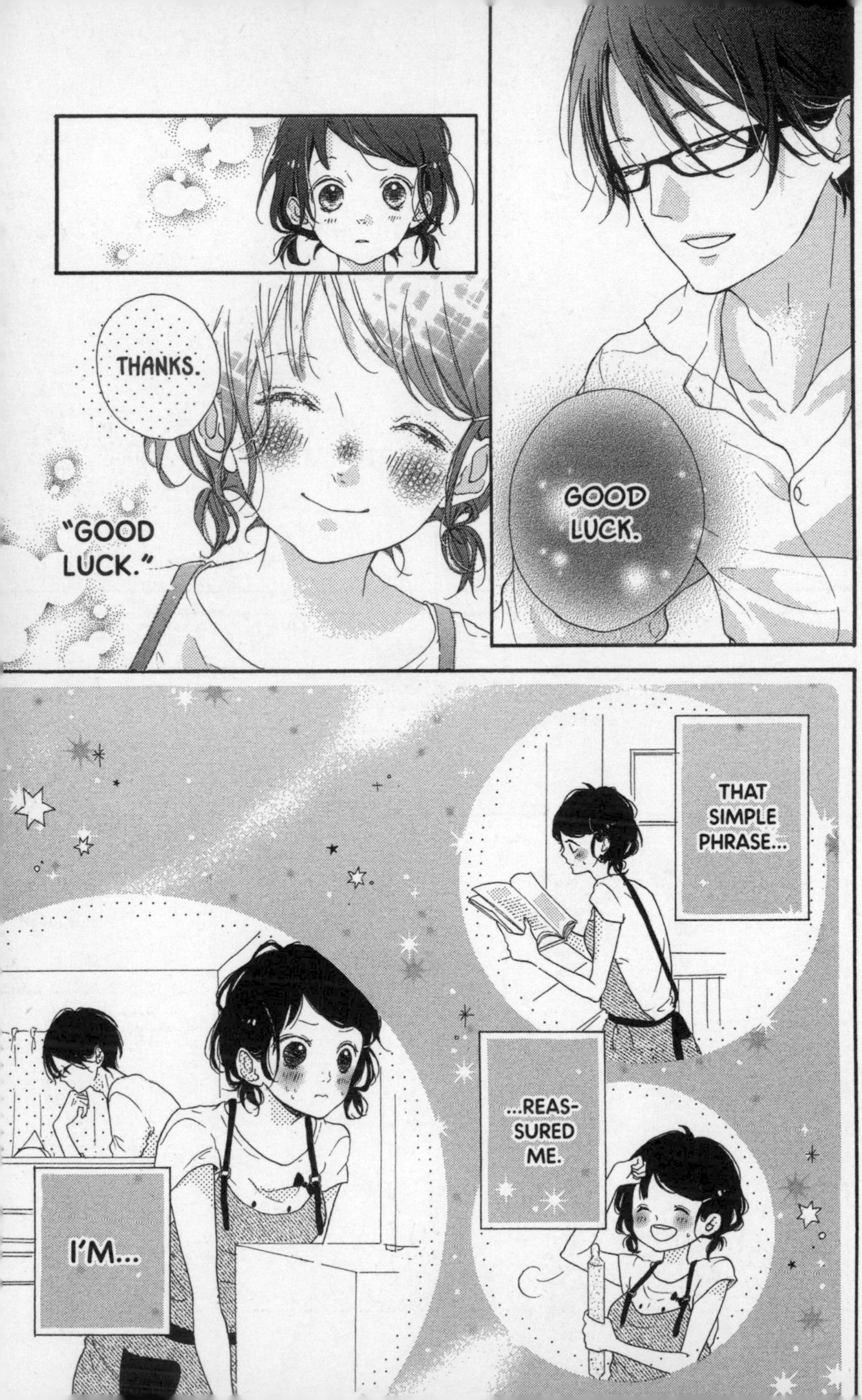
GOOD LUCK.
THANKS.
"GOOD LUCK."
THAT SIMPLE PHRASE...
...REAS-SURED ME.
I'M...

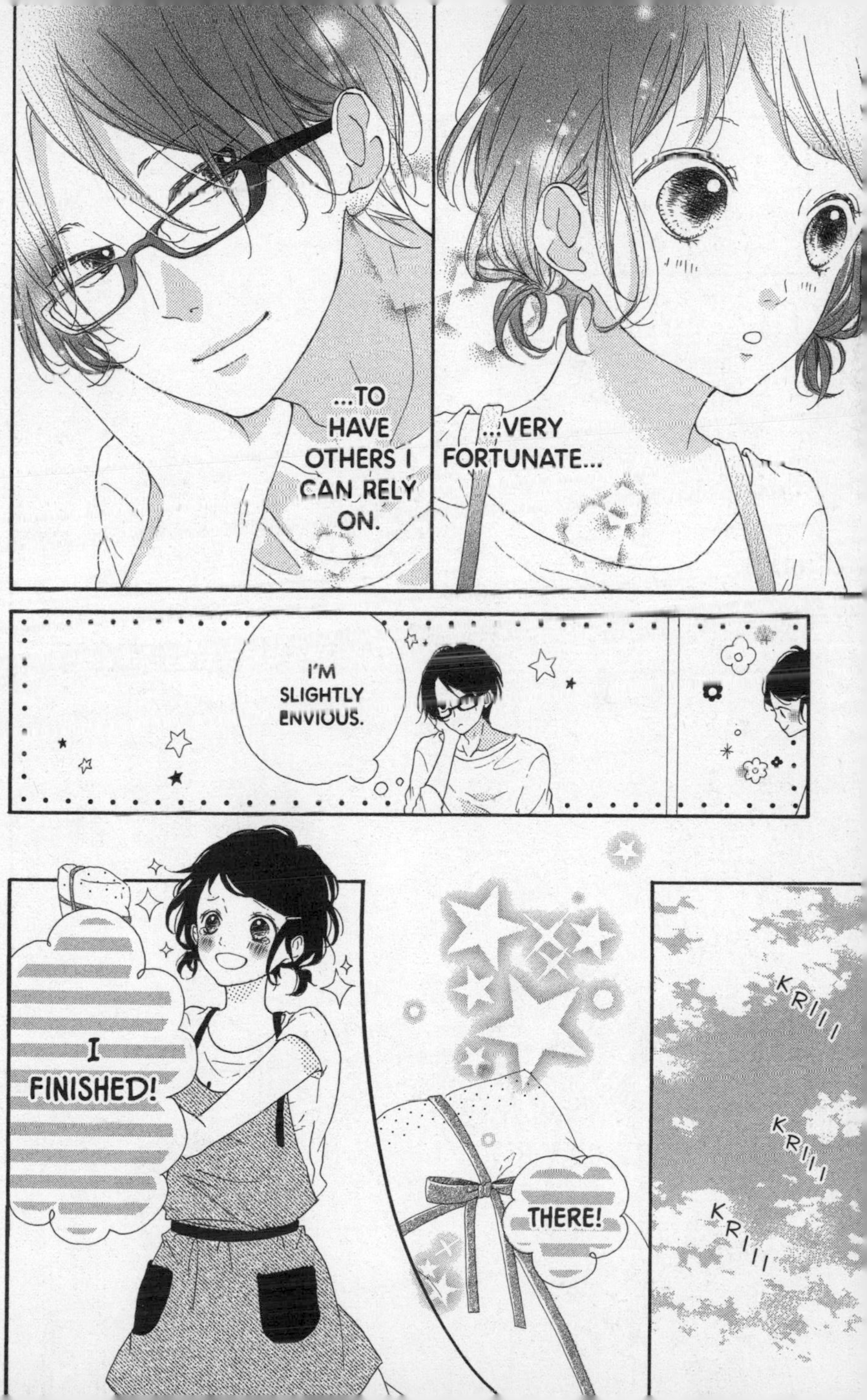
...VERY FORTUNATE...
...TO HAVE OTHERS I CAN RELY ON.
I'M SLIGHTLY ENVIOUS.
KRIII
KRIII
KRIII
THERE!
I FINISHED!

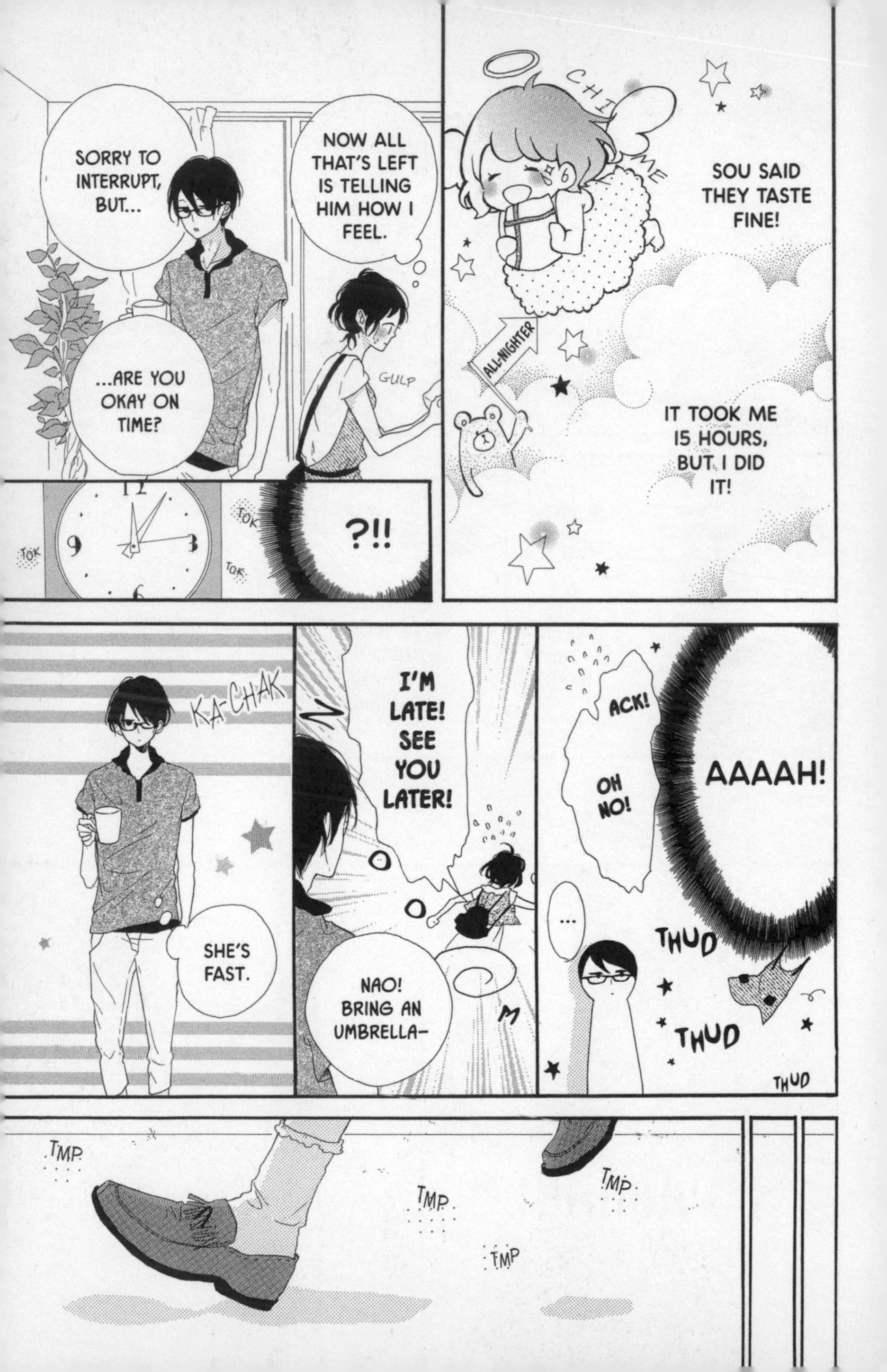
CHI ME
SOU SAID THEY TASTE FINE!
ALL-NIGHTER
IT TOOK ME 15 HOURS, BUT I DID IT!
NOW ALL THAT'S LEFT IS TELLING HIM HOW I FEEL.
SORRY TO INTERRUPT, BUT...
GULP
...ARE YOU OKAY ON TIME?
?!!
TOK
TOK
TOK
AAAAH!
ACK!
OH NO!
...
THUD
THUD
THUD
I'M LATE! SEE YOU LATER!
NAO! BRING AN UMBRELLA—
KA-CHAK
SHE'S FAST.
TMP
TMP
TMP
TMP

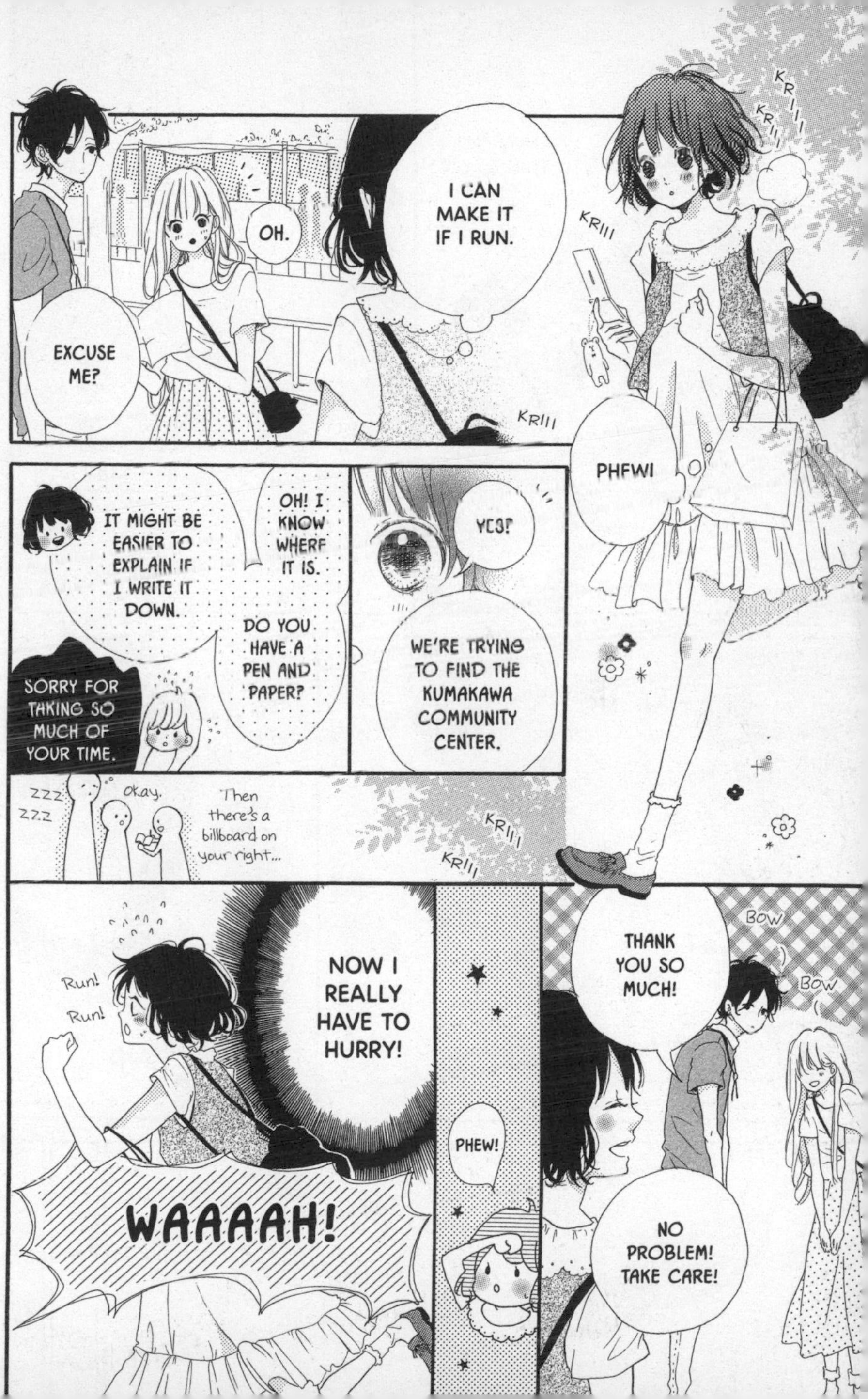
KRIII
KRIII
KRIII
PHEW!
I CAN MAKE IT IF I RUN.
OH.
EXCUSE ME?
KRIII
YES?
WE'RE TRYING TO FIND THE KUMAKAWA COMMUNITY CENTER.
OH! I KNOW WHERE IT IS.
DO YOU HAVE A PEN AND PAPER?
IT MIGHT BE EASIER TO EXPLAIN IF I WRITE IT DOWN.
SORRY FOR TAKING SO MUCH OF YOUR TIME.
KRIII
KRIII
Then there's a billboard on your right...
Okay.
ZZZ
ZZZ
THANK YOU SO MUCH!
BOW
BOW
NO PROBLEM! TAKE CARE!
PHEW!
NOW I REALLY HAVE TO HURRY!
Run!
Run!
WAAAAH!

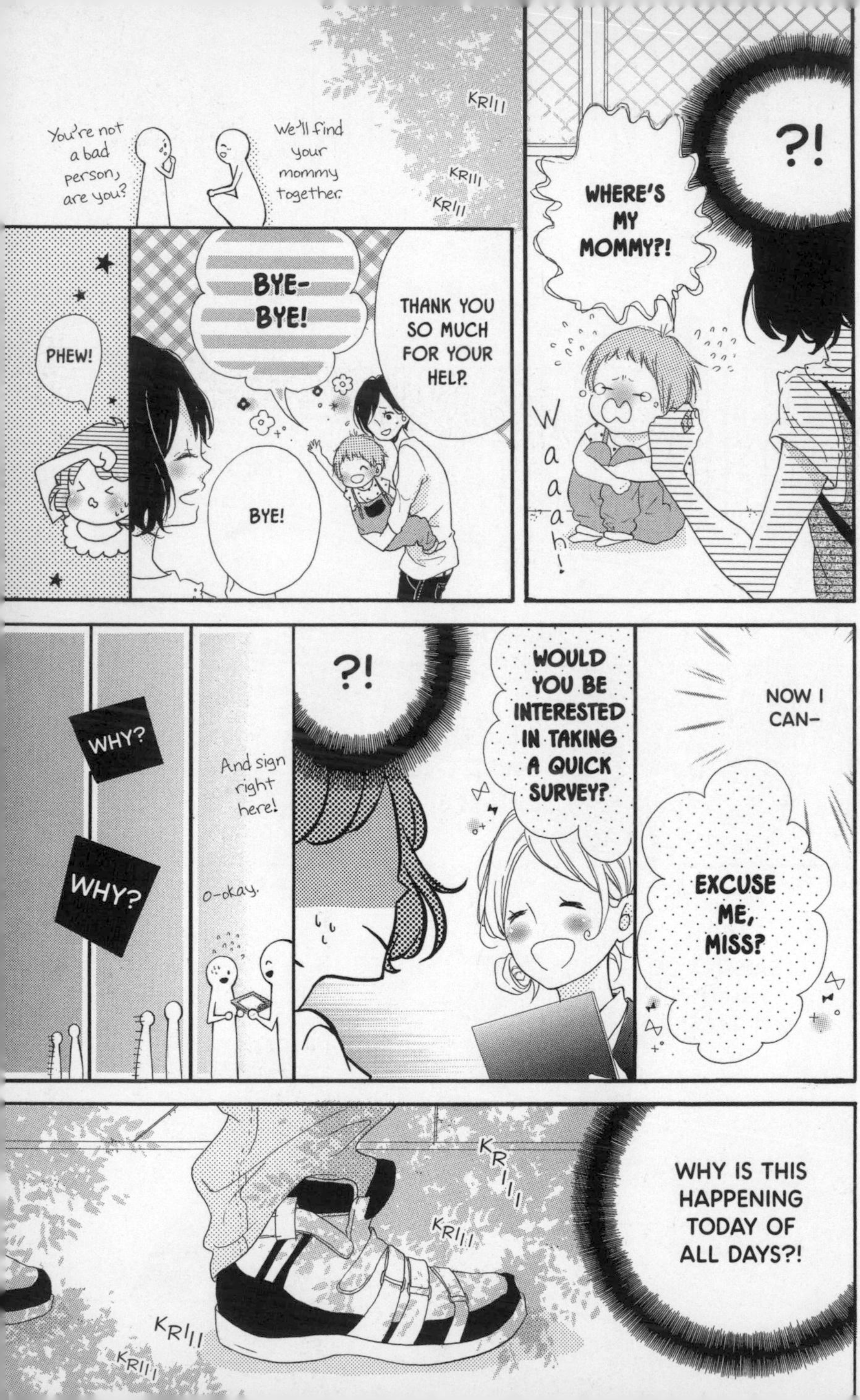
?!
WHERE'S MY MOMMY?!
Waaaah!
KRIII
We'll find your mommy together.
You're not a bad person, are you?
KRIII
KRIII
THANK YOU SO MUCH FOR YOUR HELP.
BYE-BYE!
BYE!
PHEW!
NOW I CAN—
EXCUSE ME, MISS?
WOULD YOU BE INTERESTED IN TAKING A QUICK SURVEY?
?!
And sign right here!
O-okay.
WHY?
WHY?
WHY IS THIS HAPPENING TODAY OF ALL DAYS?!
KRIII
KRIII
KRIII
KRIII

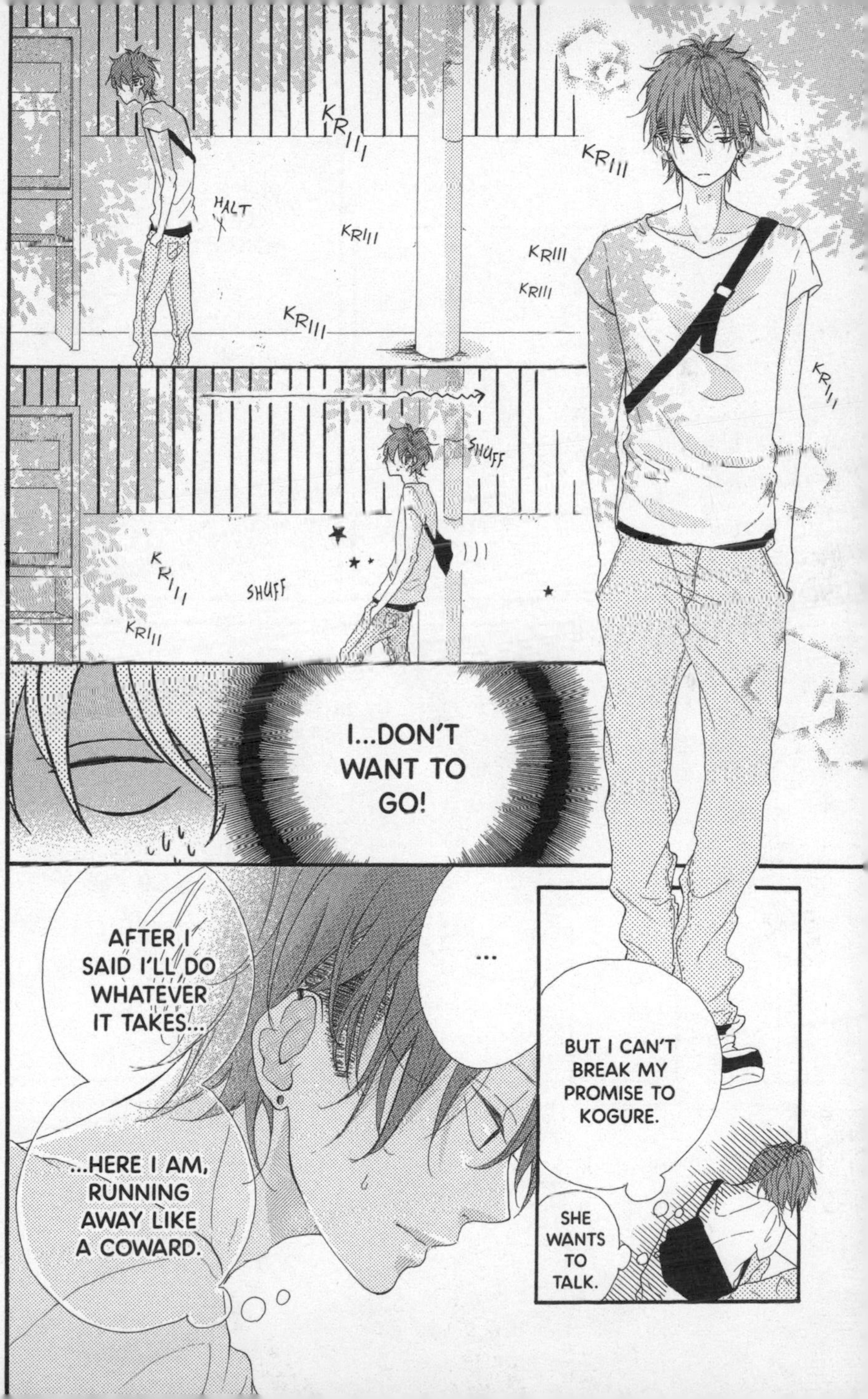
KRIII
KRIII
KRIII
KRIII
KRIII
HALT
KRIII
KRIII
SHUFF
SHUFF
KRIII
KRIII
I...DON'T WANT TO GO!
BUT I CAN'T BREAK MY PROMISE TO KOGURE.
SHE WANTS TO TALK.
...
AFTER I SAID I'LL DO WHATEVER IT TAKES...
...HERE I AM, RUNNING AWAY LIKE A COWARD.

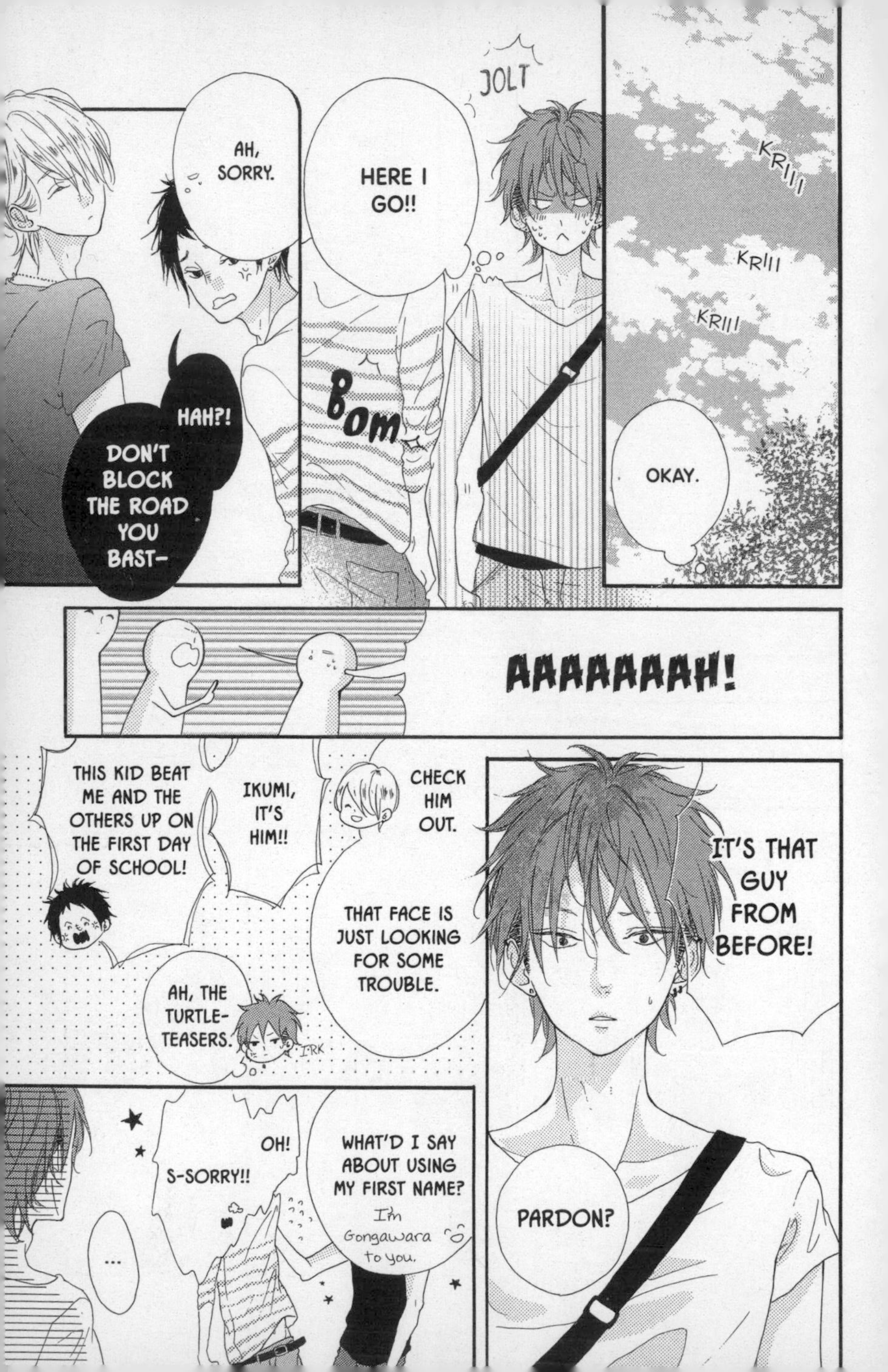
KRIII
KRIII
KRIII
OKAY.
JOLT
HERE I GO!!
BOM
AH, SORRY.
HAH?!
DON'T BLOCK THE ROAD YOU BAST-
AAAAAAAH!
IT'S THAT GUY FROM BEFORE!
PARDON?
CHECK HIM OUT.
THAT FACE IS JUST LOOKING FOR SOME TROUBLE.
IKUMI, IT'S HIM!!
THIS KID BEAT ME AND THE OTHERS UP ON THE FIRST DAY OF SCHOOL!
AH, THE TURTLE-TEASERS.
IRK
WHAT'D I SAY ABOUT USING MY FIRST NAME?
I'm Gongawara to you.
OH!
S-SORRY!!
...

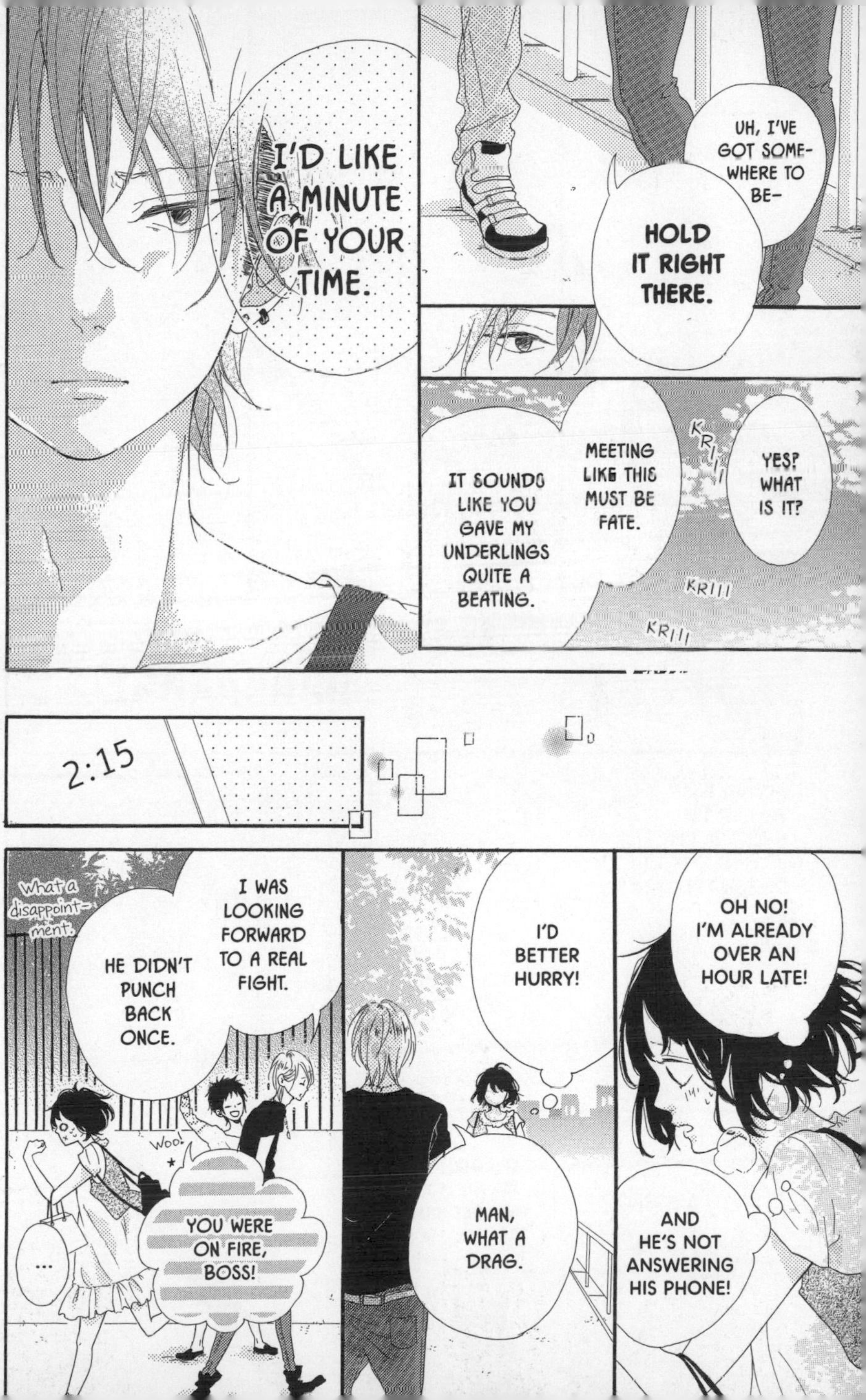
UH, I'VE GOT SOME-WHERE TO BE–
HOLD IT RIGHT THERE.
KRIII
YES? WHAT IS IT?
MEETING LIKE THIS MUST BE FATE.
IT SOUNDS LIKE YOU GAVE MY UNDERLINGS QUITE A BEATING.
KRIII
KRIII
I'D LIKE A MINUTE OF YOUR TIME.
2:15
OH NO! I'M ALREADY OVER AN HOUR LATE!
AND HE'S NOT ANSWERING HIS PHONE!
I'D BETTER HURRY!
MAN, WHAT A DRAG.
I WAS LOOKING FORWARD TO A REAL FIGHT.
HE DIDN'T PUNCH BACK ONCE.
What a disappoint-ment.
Woo!
YOU WERE ON FIRE, BOSS!
...

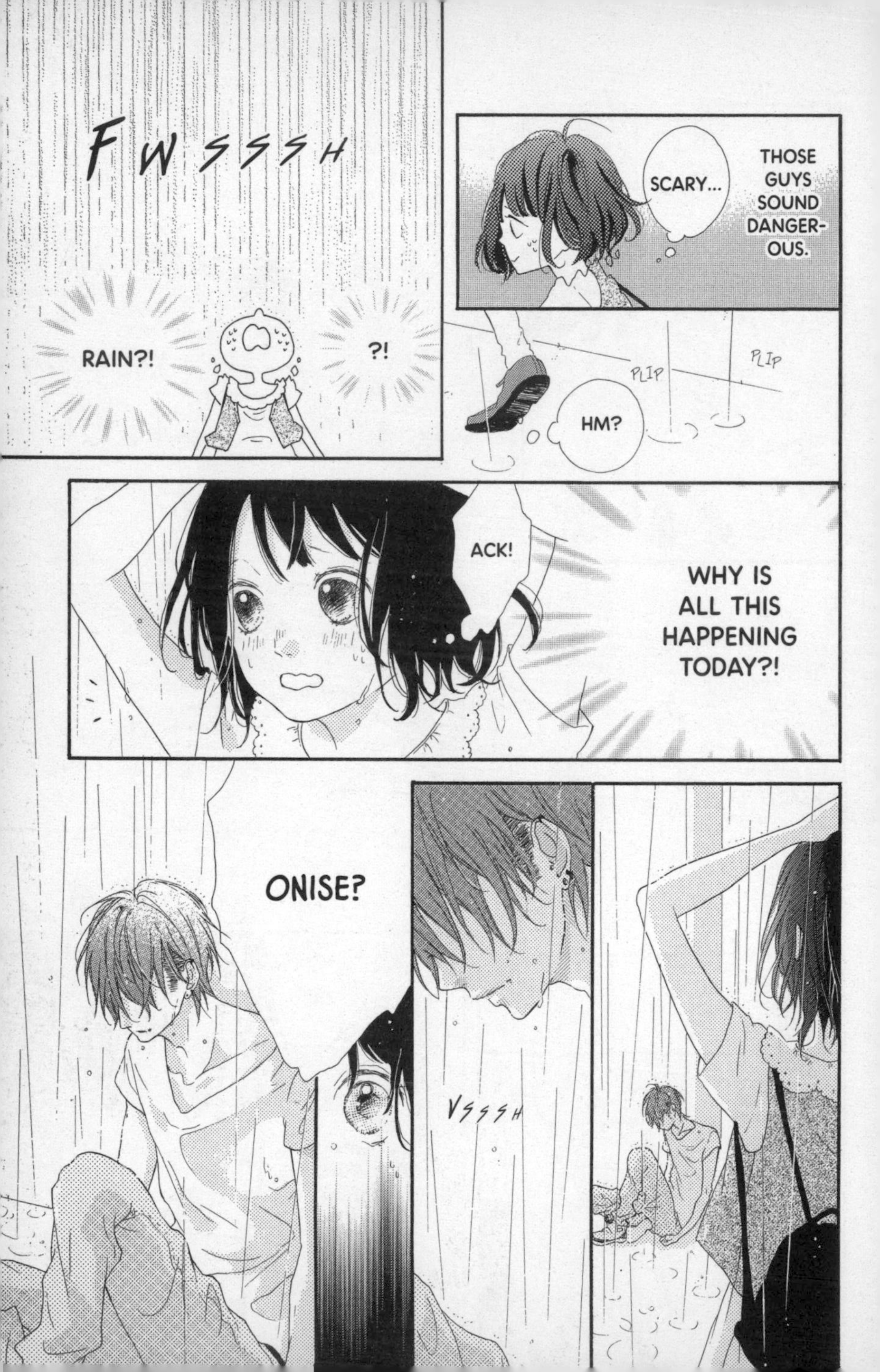
THOSE GUYS SOUND DANGER-OUS.
SCARY...
PLIP
PLIP
HM?
FWSSSH
?!
RAIN?!
WHY IS ALL THIS HAPPENING TODAY?!
ACK!
VSSSH
ONISE?

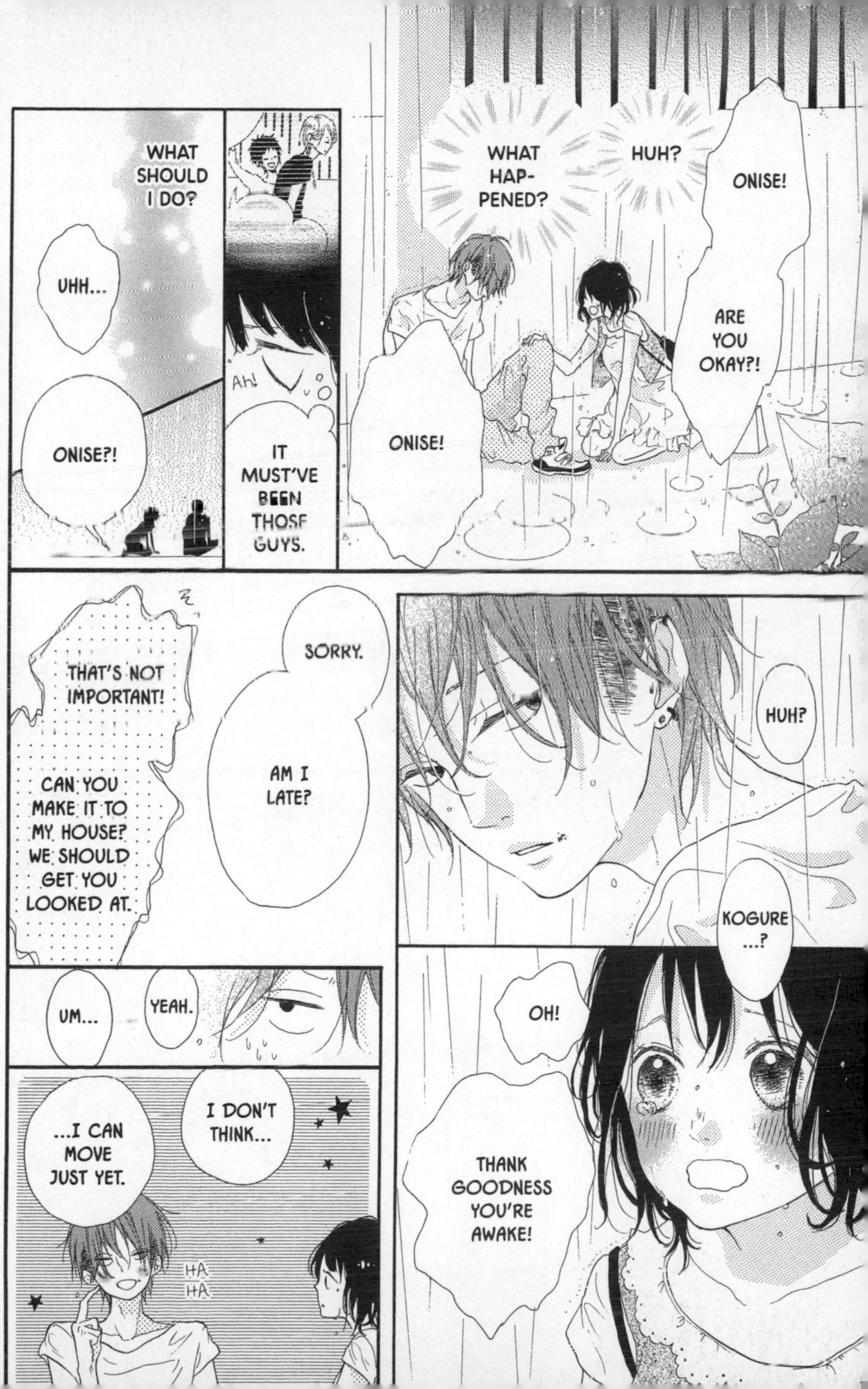
ONISE!
HUH?
WHAT HAP-PENED?
ARE YOU OKAY?!
ONISE!
Ah!
IT MUST'VE BEEN THOSE GUYS.
WHAT SHOULD I DO?
UHH...
ONISE?!
HUH?
KOGURE ...?
SORRY.
AM I LATE?
THAT'S NOT IMPORTANT!
CAN YOU MAKE IT TO MY HOUSE? WE SHOULD GET YOU LOOKED AT.
OH!
THANK GOODNESS YOU'RE AWAKE!
YEAH.
UM...
I DON'T THINK...
...I CAN MOVE JUST YET.
HA HA

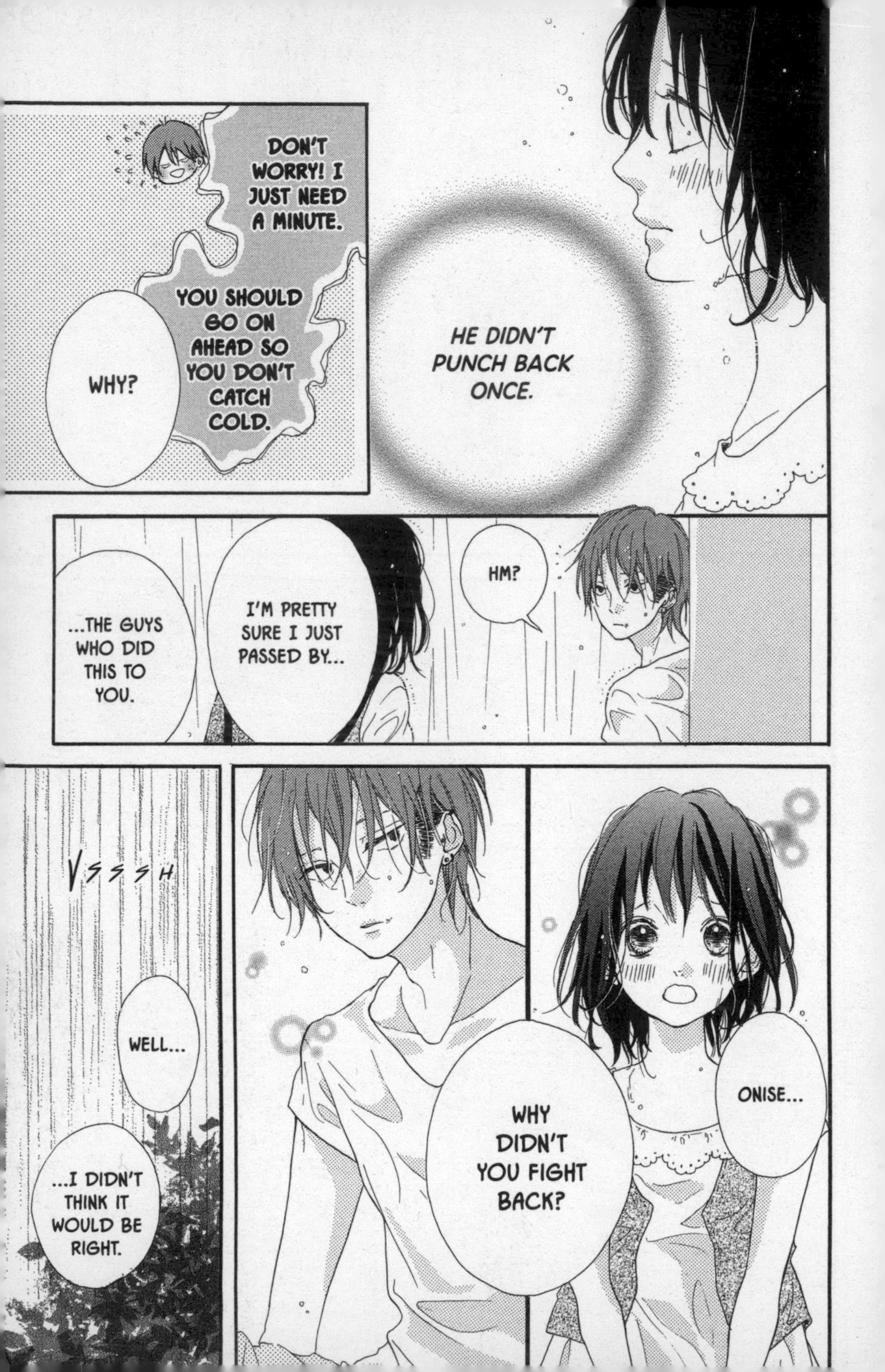
HE DIDN'T PUNCH BACK ONCE.
DON'T WORRY! I JUST NEED A MINUTE.
YOU SHOULD GO ON AHEAD SO YOU DON'T CATCH COLD.
WHY?
HM?
I'M PRETTY SURE I JUST PASSED BY...
...THE GUYS WHO DID THIS TO YOU.
ONISE...
WHY DIDN'T YOU FIGHT BACK?
VSSSH
WELL...
...I DIDN'T THINK IT WOULD BE RIGHT.

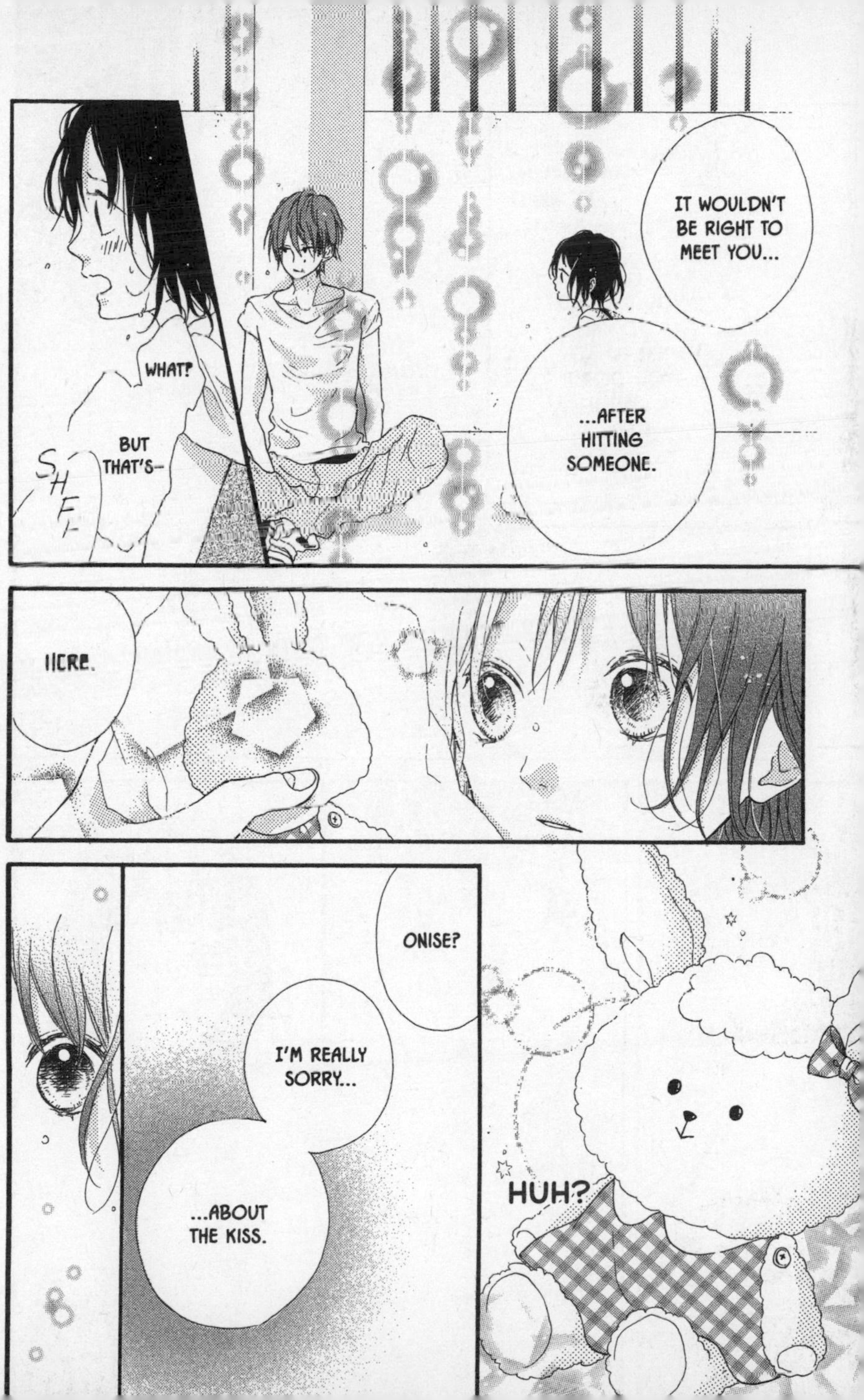
IT WOULDN'T BE RIGHT TO MEET YOU...
...AFTER HITTING SOMEONE.
WHAT?
BUT THAT'S—
SHF
HERE.
HUH?
ONISE?
I'M REALLY SORRY...
...ABOUT THE KISS.

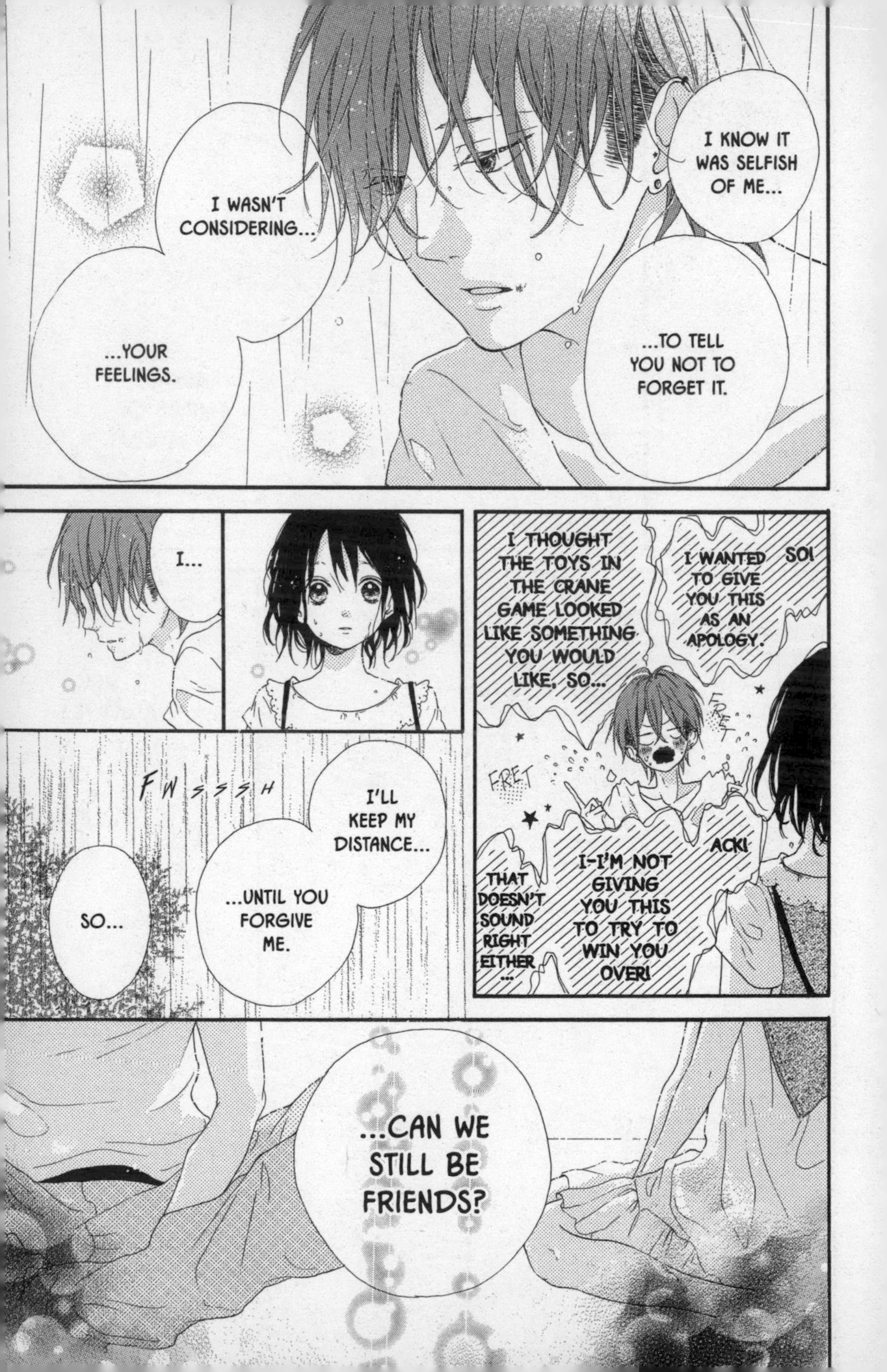
I KNOW IT WAS SELFISH OF ME...
...TO TELL YOU NOT TO FORGET IT.
I WASN'T CONSIDERING...
...YOUR FEELINGS.
SO!
I WANTED TO GIVE YOU THIS AS AN APOLOGY.
I THOUGHT THE TOYS IN THE CRANE GAME LOOKED LIKE SOMETHING YOU WOULD LIKE, SO...
FRET
FRET
ACK!
I-I'M NOT GIVING YOU THIS TO TRY TO WIN YOU OVER!
THAT DOESN'T SOUND RIGHT EITHER...
I...
FWSSSH
I'LL KEEP MY DISTANCE...
...UNTIL YOU FORGIVE ME.
SO...
...CAN WE STILL BE FRIENDS?

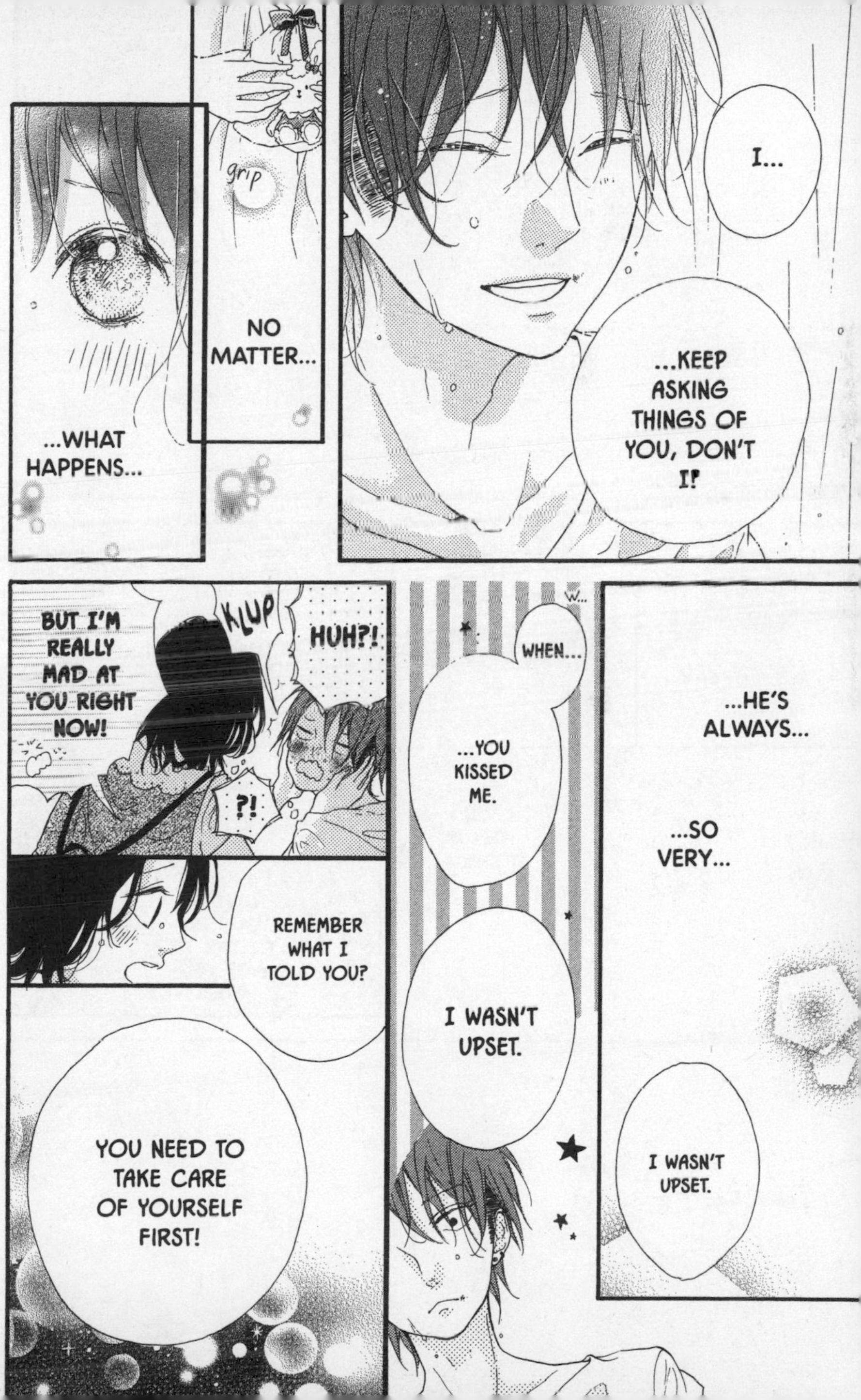

I...
...KEEP ASKING THINGS OF YOU, DON'T I?
grip
NO MATTER...
...WHAT HAPPENS...
...HE'S ALWAYS...
...SO VERY...
I WASN'T UPSET.
W...
WHEN...
...YOU KISSED ME.
I WASN'T UPSET.
HUH?!
KLUP
BUT I'M REALLY MAD AT YOU RIGHT NOW!
?!
REMEMBER WHAT I TOLD YOU?
YOU NEED TO TAKE CARE OF YOURSELF FIRST!

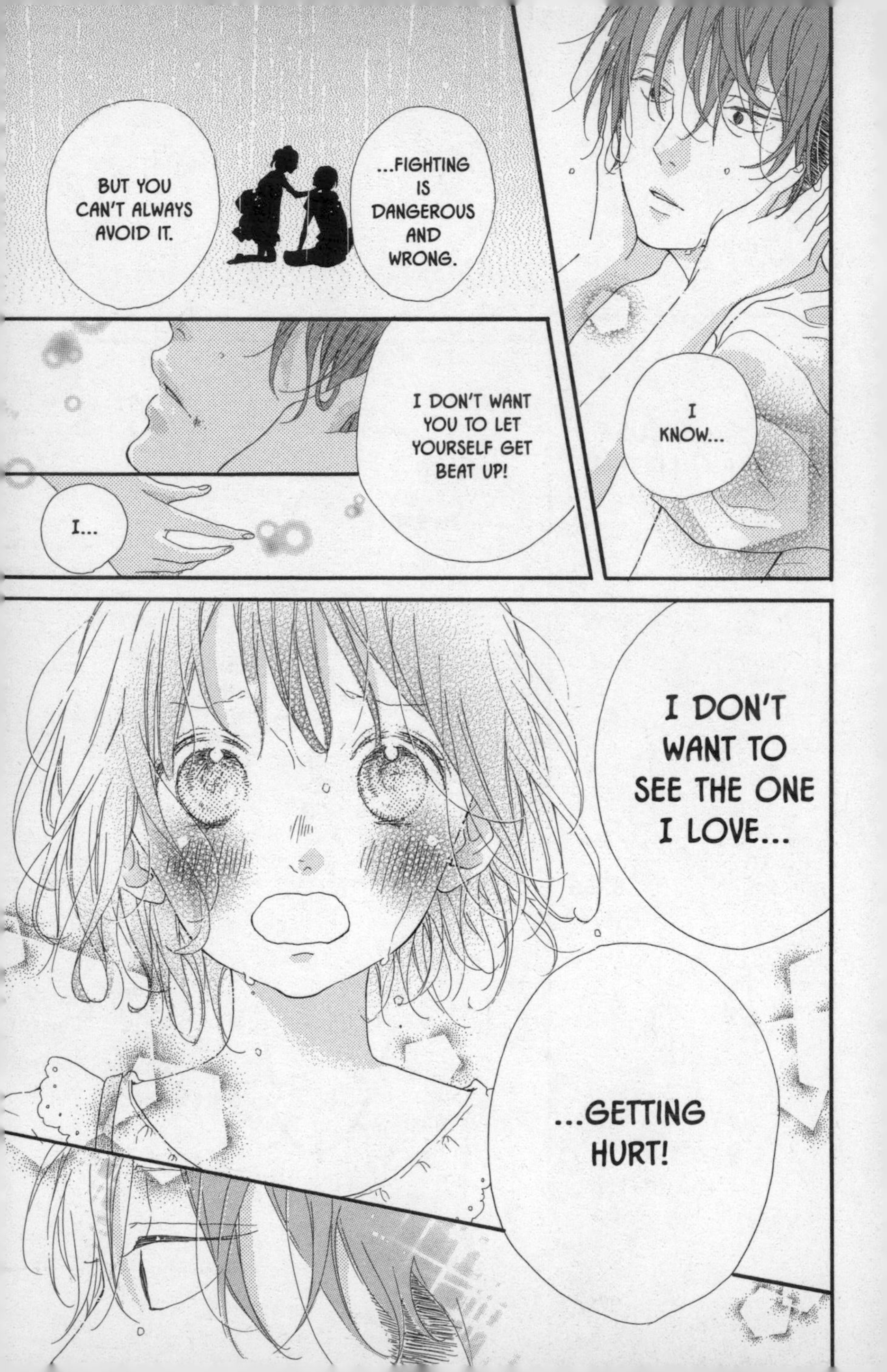
I KNOW...
...FIGHTING IS DANGEROUS AND WRONG.
BUT YOU CAN'T ALWAYS AVOID IT.
I DON'T WANT YOU TO LET YOURSELF GET BEAT UP!
I...
I DON'T WANT TO SEE THE ONE I LOVE...
...GETTING HURT!

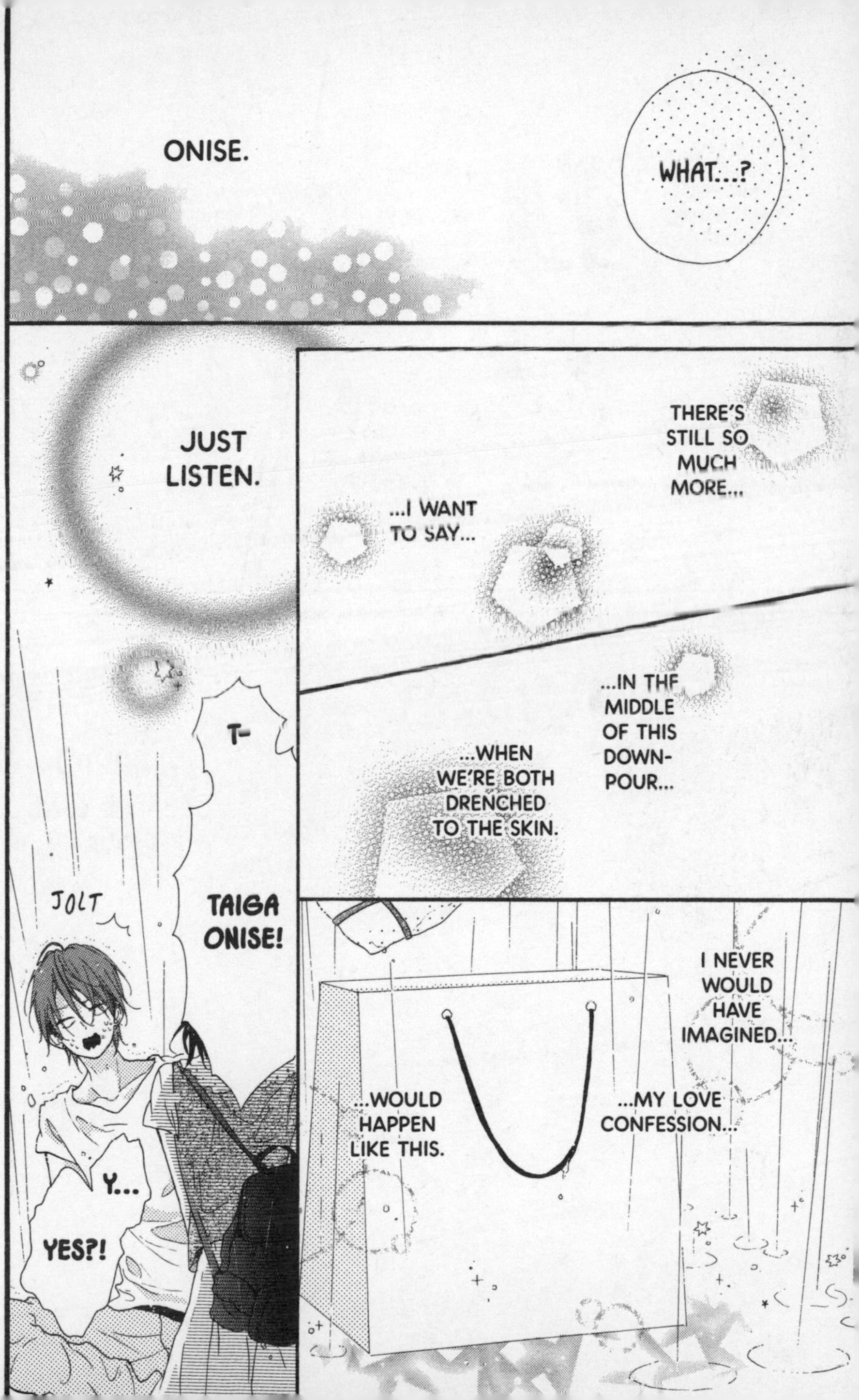
WHAT...?
ONISE.
THERE'S STILL SO MUCH MORE...
...I WANT TO SAY...
...IN THE MIDDLE OF THIS DOWNPOUR...
...WHEN WE'RE BOTH DRENCHED TO THE SKIN.
I NEVER WOULD HAVE IMAGINED...
...MY LOVE CONFESSION...
...WOULD HAPPEN LIKE THIS.
JUST LISTEN.
T-
TAIGA ONISE!
JOLT
Y...
YES?!

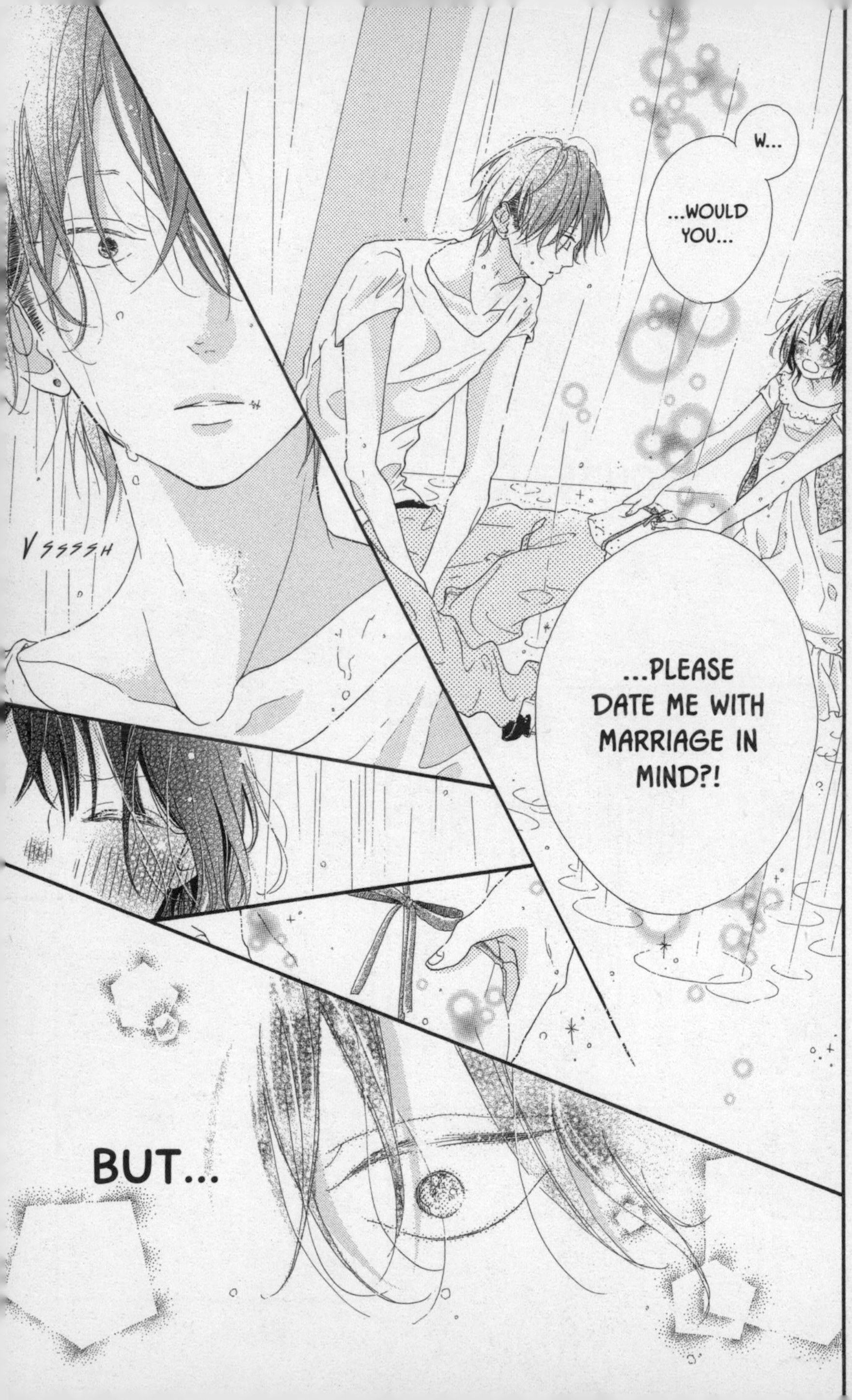
W...
...WOULD YOU...
...PLEASE DATE ME WITH MARRIAGE IN MIND?!
VSSSSH
BUT...

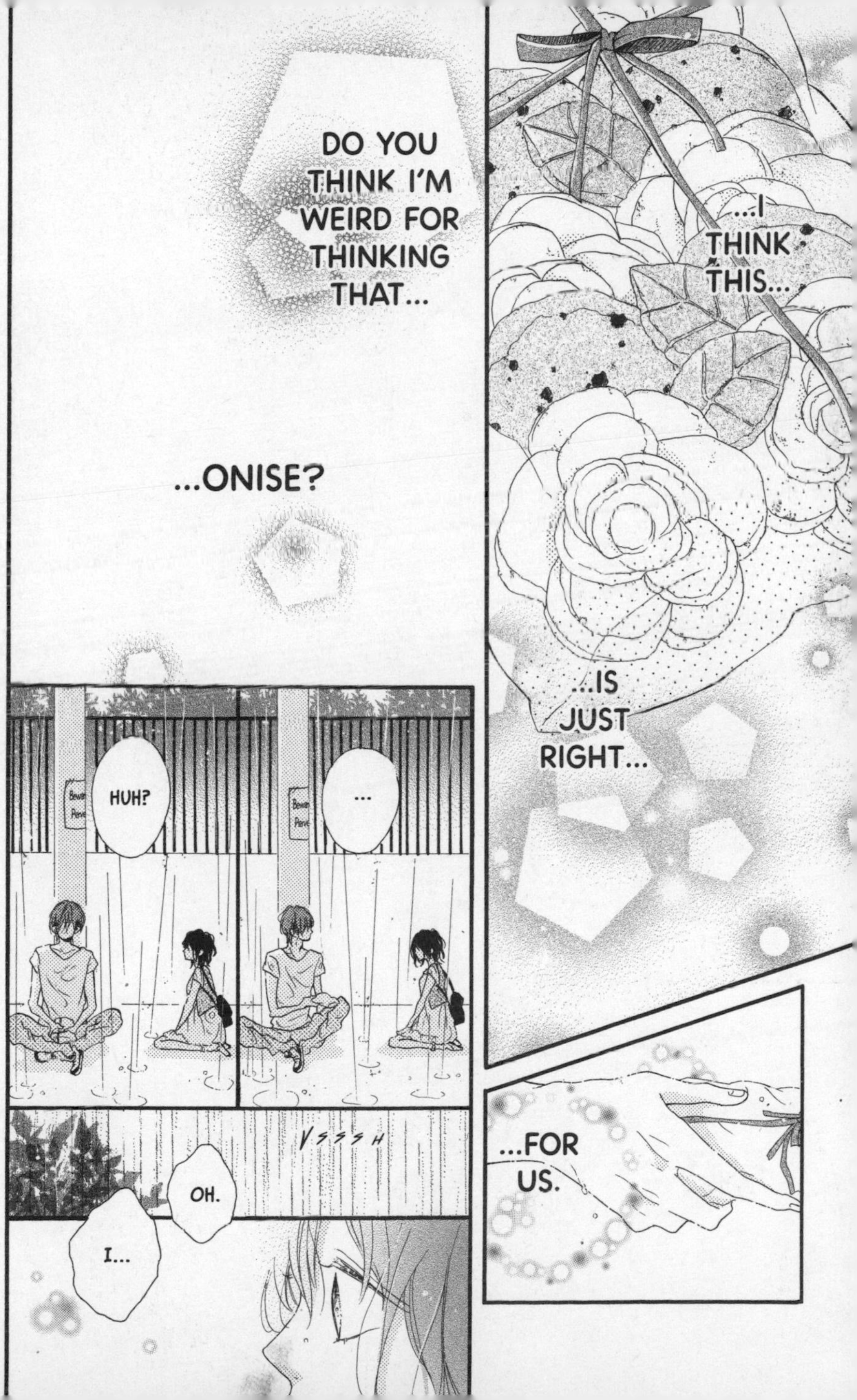
...I THINK THIS...
...IS JUST RIGHT...
...FOR US.
DO YOU THINK I'M WEIRD FOR THINKING THAT...
...ONISE?
...
HUH?
VSSSH
OH.
I...

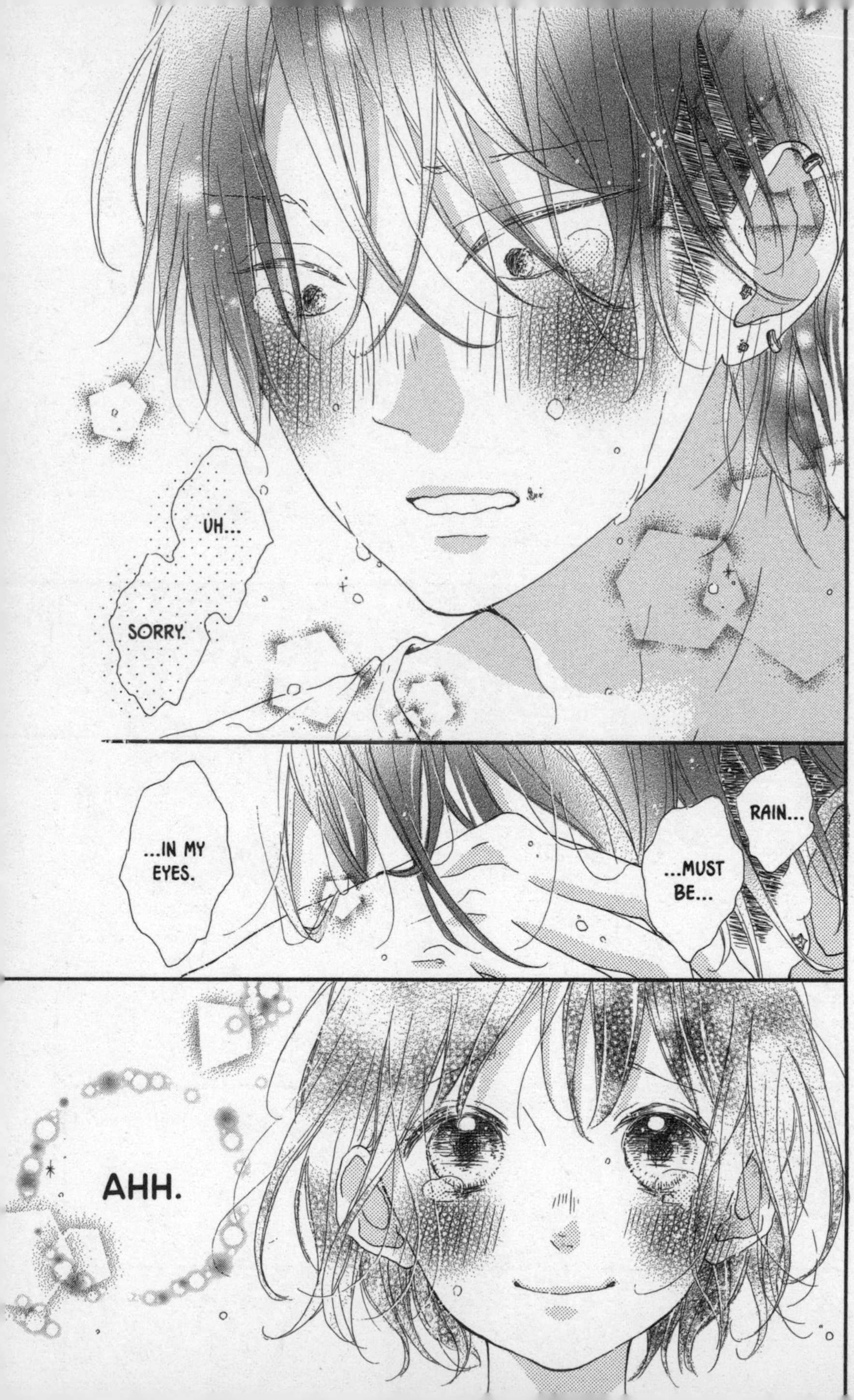
UH...
SORRY.
RAIN...
...MUST BE...
...IN MY EYES.
AHH.

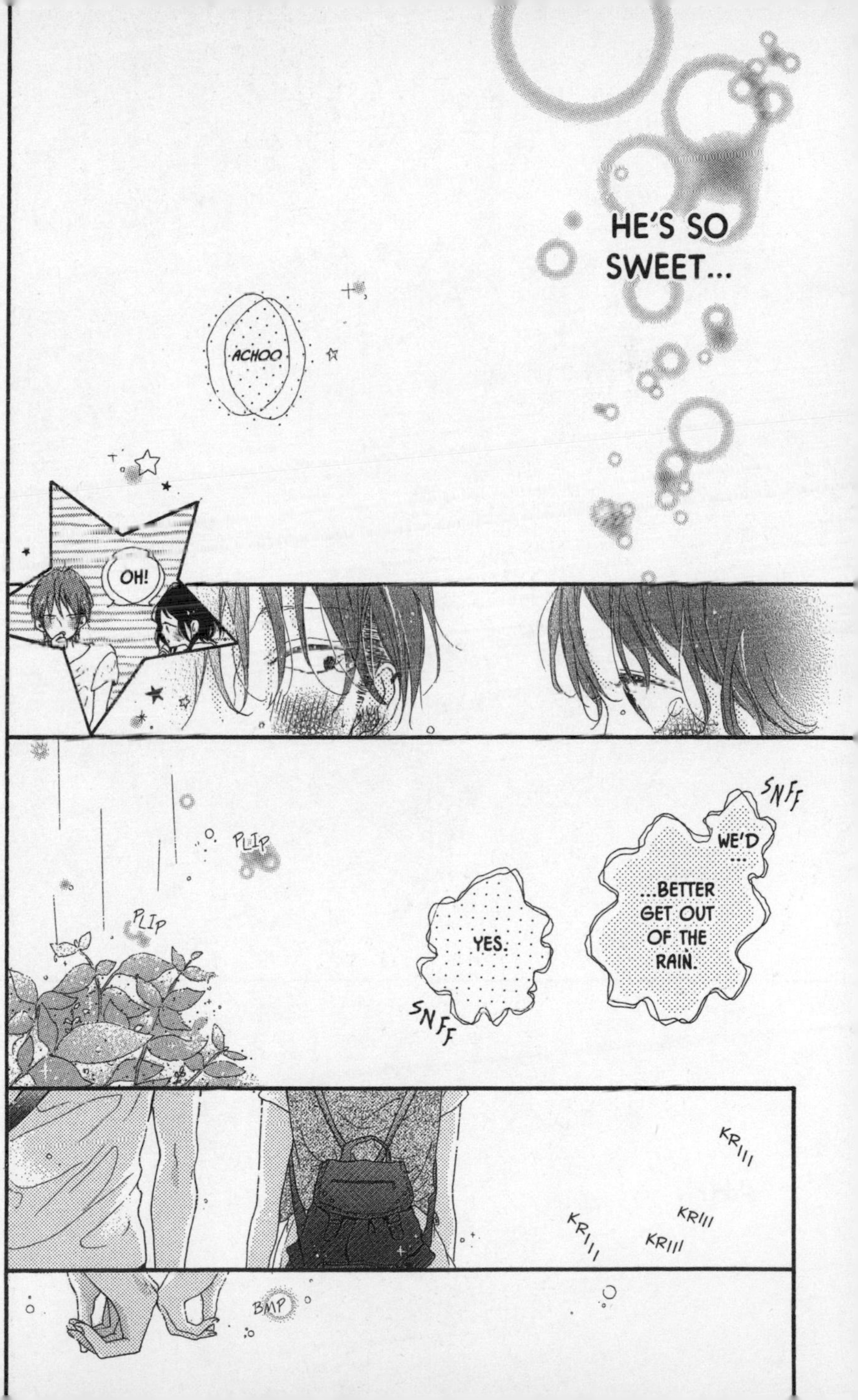
HE'S SO SWEET...
ACHOO
OH!
SNFF
WE'D...
...BETTER GET OUT OF THE RAIN.
YES.
SNFF
PLIP
PLIP
KRIII
KRIII
KRIII
KRIII
BMP

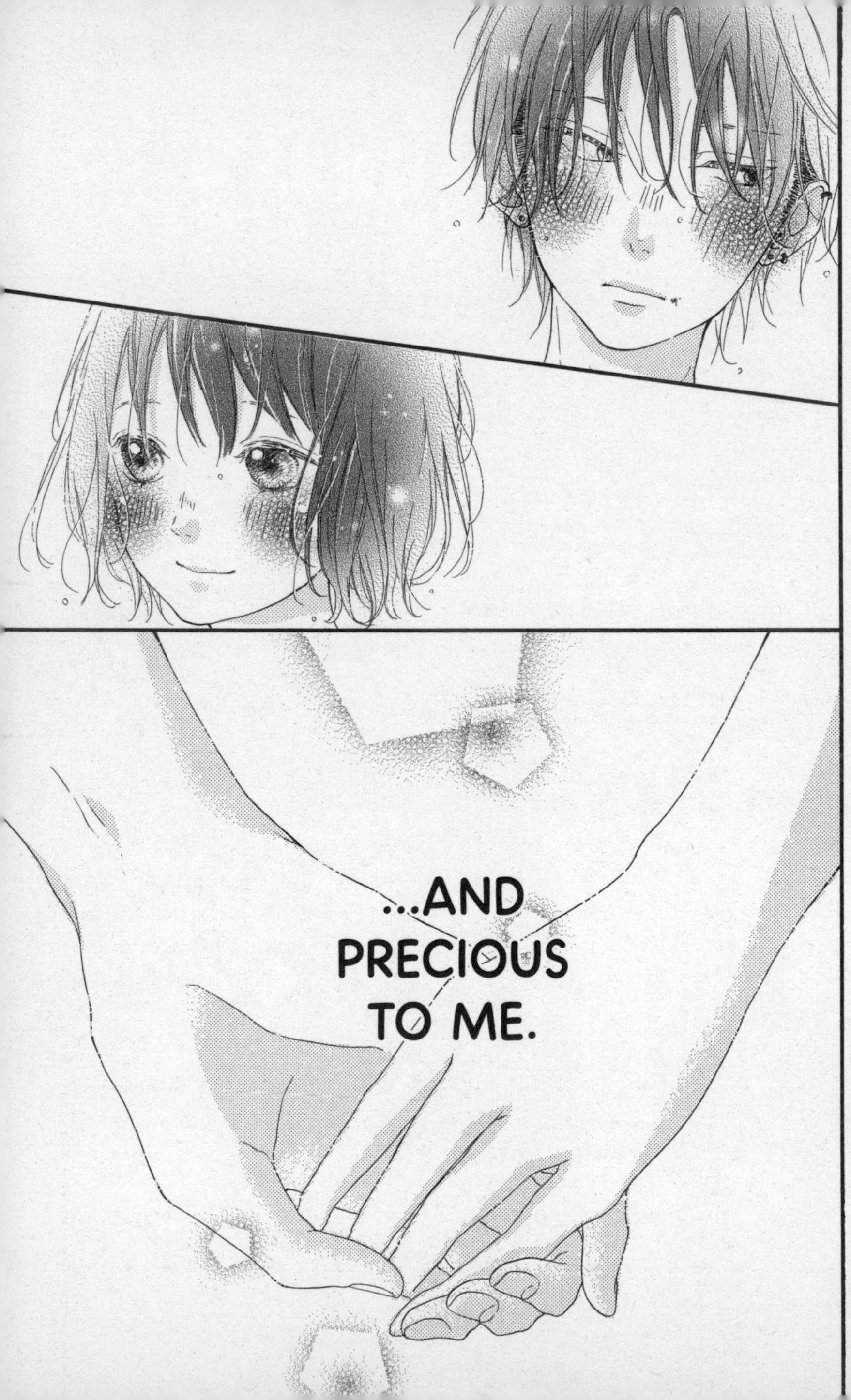

...AND PRECIOUS TO ME.

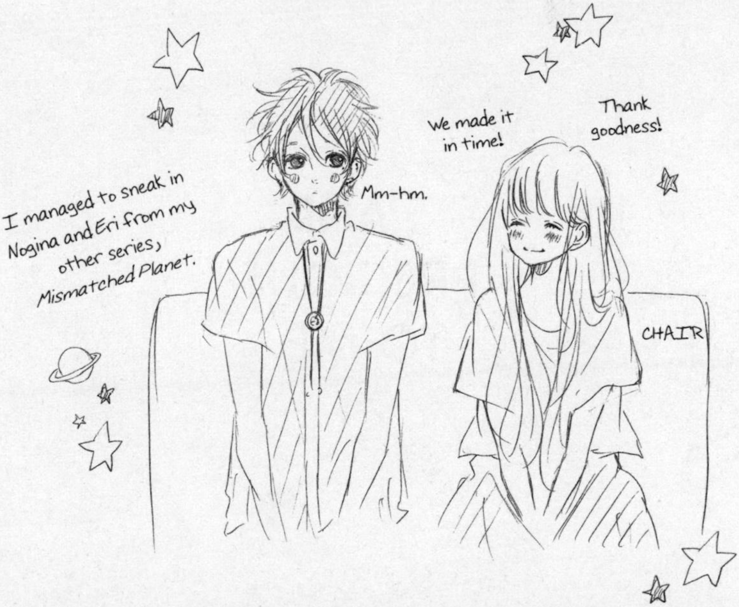
Thank goodness!
We made it in time!
Mm-hm.
I managed to sneak in Nogina and Eri from my other series, Mismatched Planet.
CHAIR

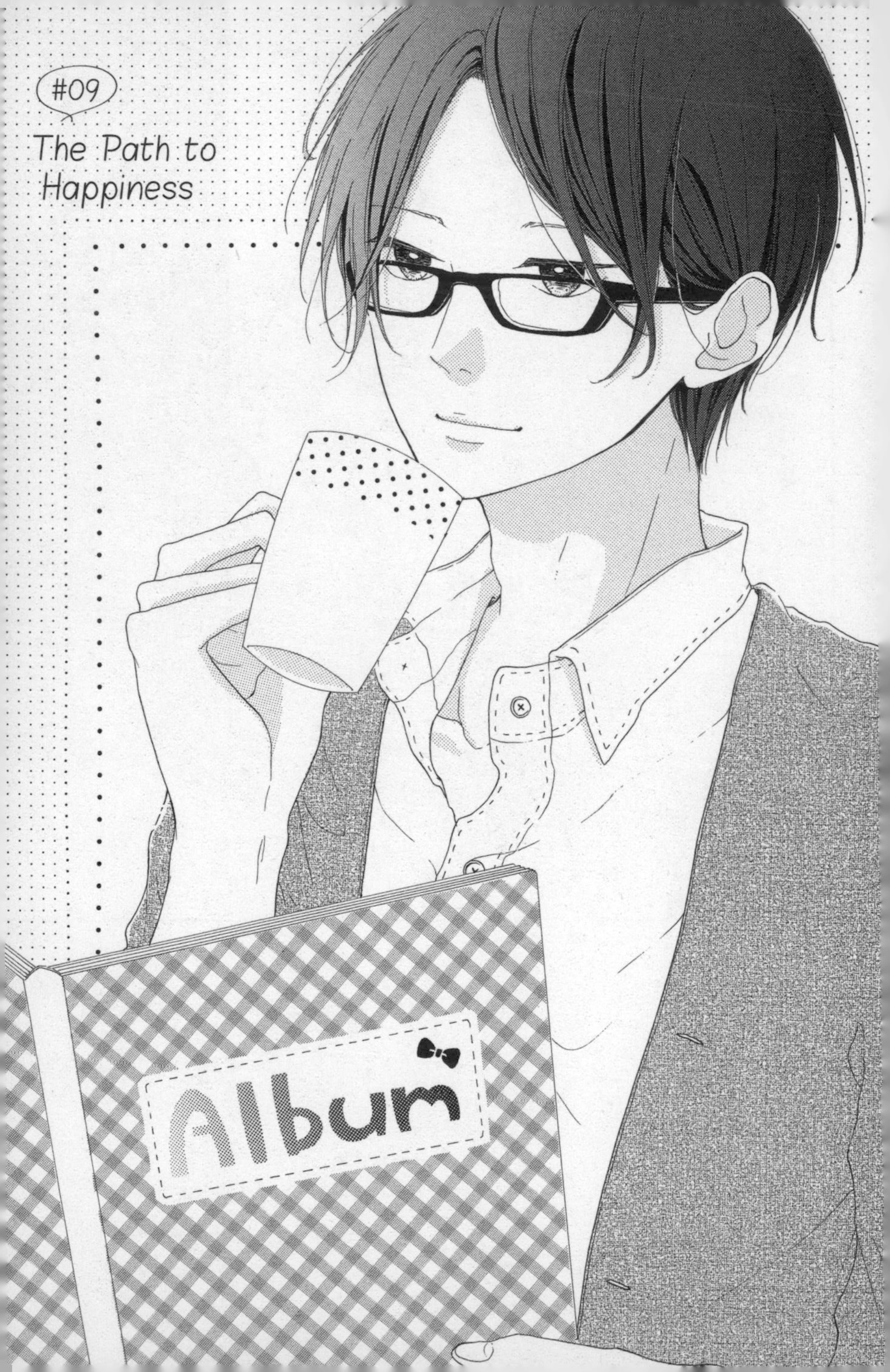
#09
The Path to Happiness
Album

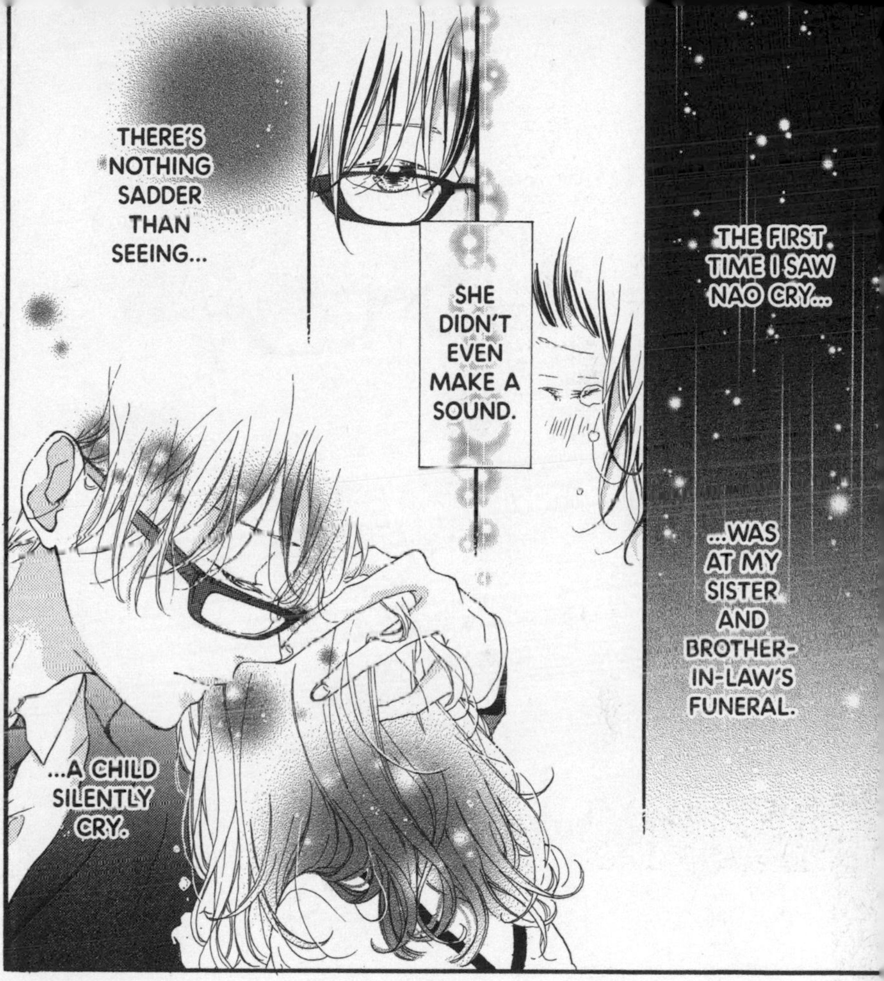
THE FIRST TIME I SAW NAO CRY...
...WAS AT MY SISTER AND BROTHER-IN-LAW'S FUNERAL.
SHE DIDN'T EVEN MAKE A SOUND.
THERE'S NOTHING SADDER THAN SEEING...
...A CHILD SILENTLY CRY.

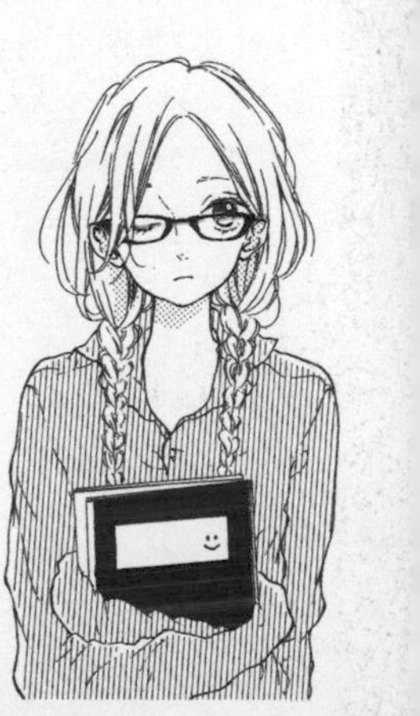

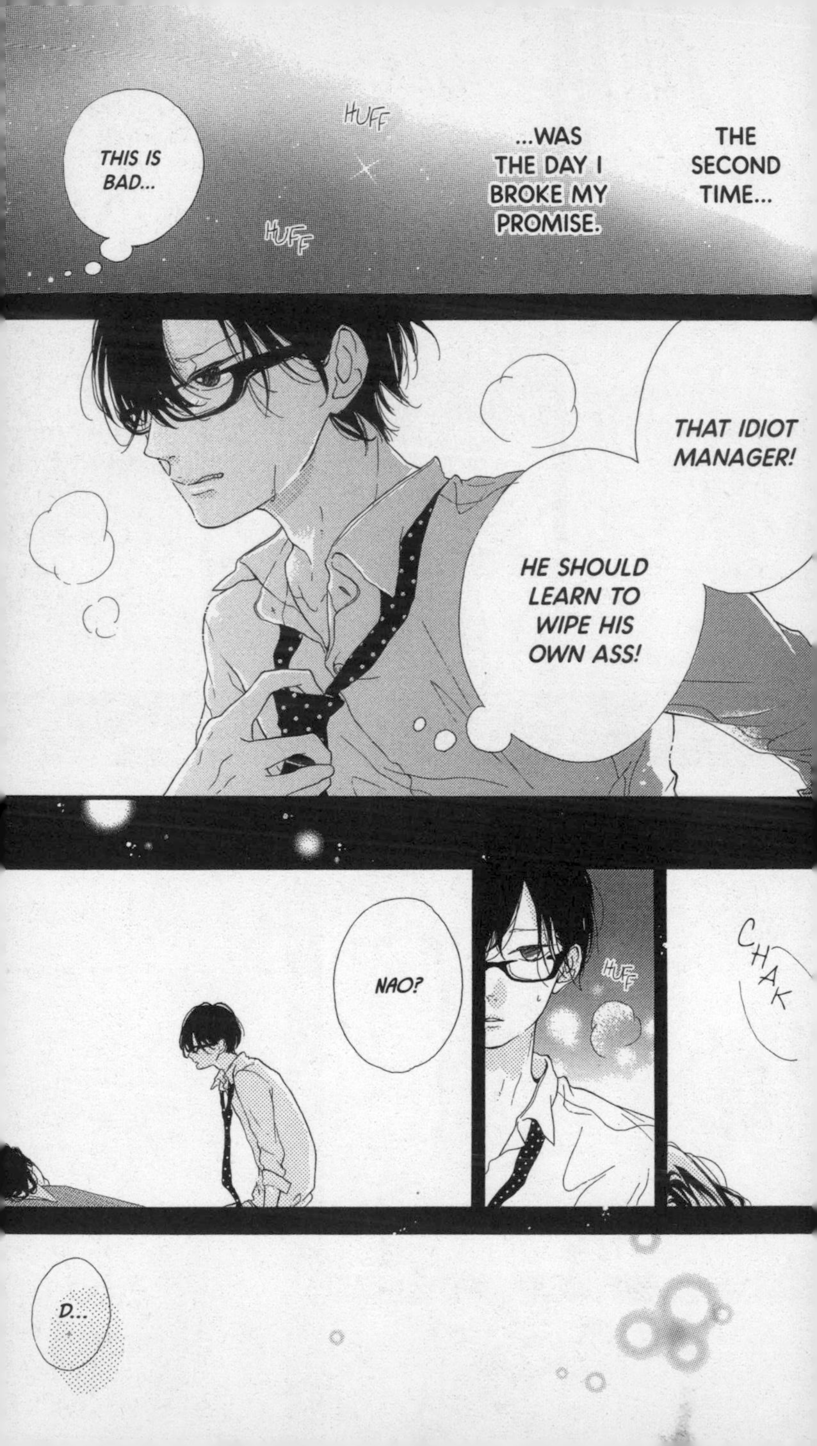
THE SECOND TIME...
...WAS THE DAY I BROKE MY PROMISE.
HUFF
HUFF
THIS IS BAD...
THAT IDIOT MANAGER!
HE SHOULD LEARN TO WIPE HIS OWN ASS!
CHAK
HUFF
NAO?
D...

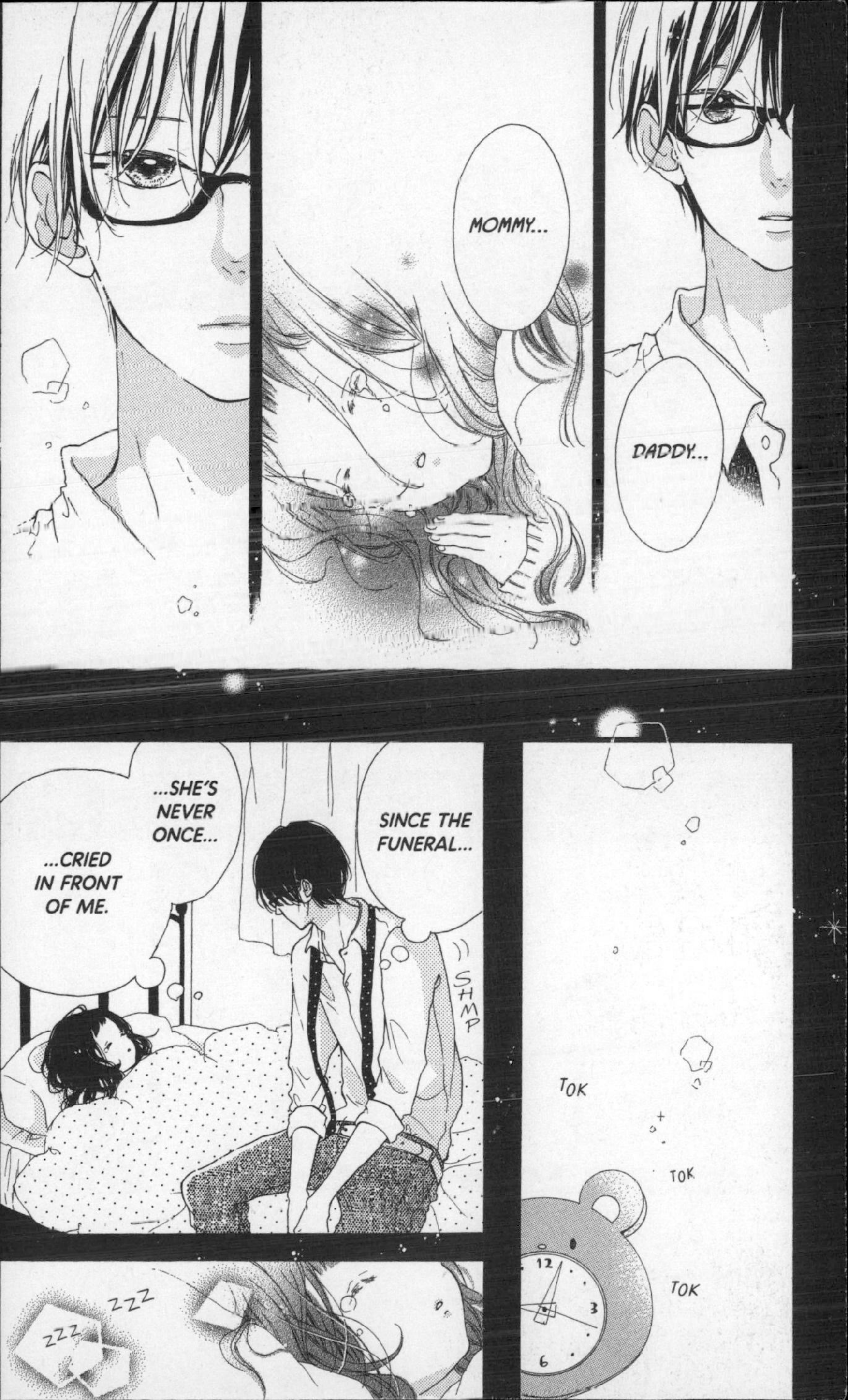
DADDY...
MOMMY...
TOK
TOK
TOK
SINCE THE FUNERAL...
SHMP
...SHE'S NEVER ONCE...
...CRIED IN FRONT OF ME.
ZZZ
ZZZ

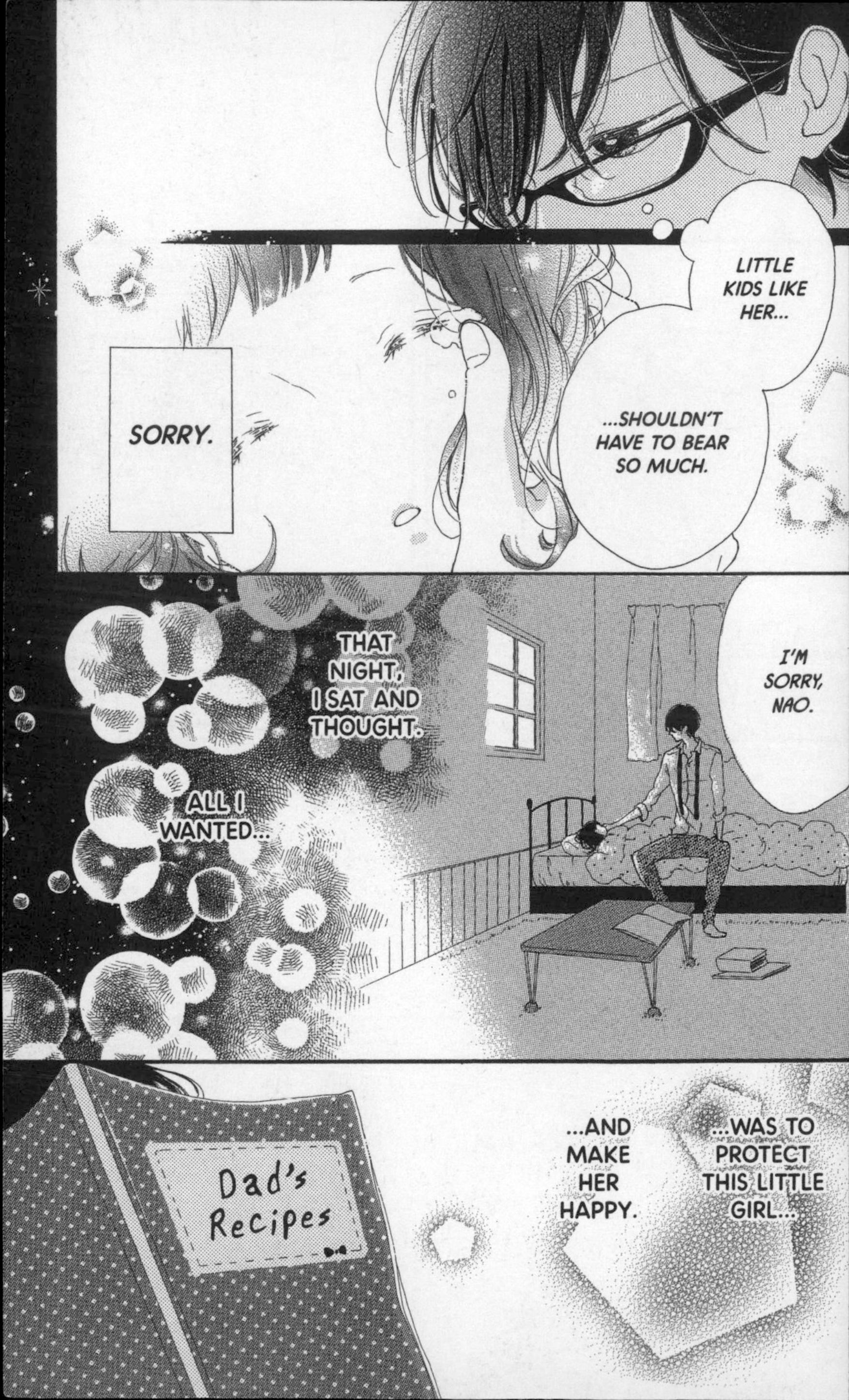
LITTLE KIDS LIKE HER...
...SHOULDN'T HAVE TO BEAR SO MUCH.
SORRY.
I'M SORRY, NAO.
THAT NIGHT, I SAT AND THOUGHT.
ALL I WANTED...
...WAS TO PROTECT THIS LITTLE GIRL...
...AND MAKE HER HAPPY.
Dad's Recipes

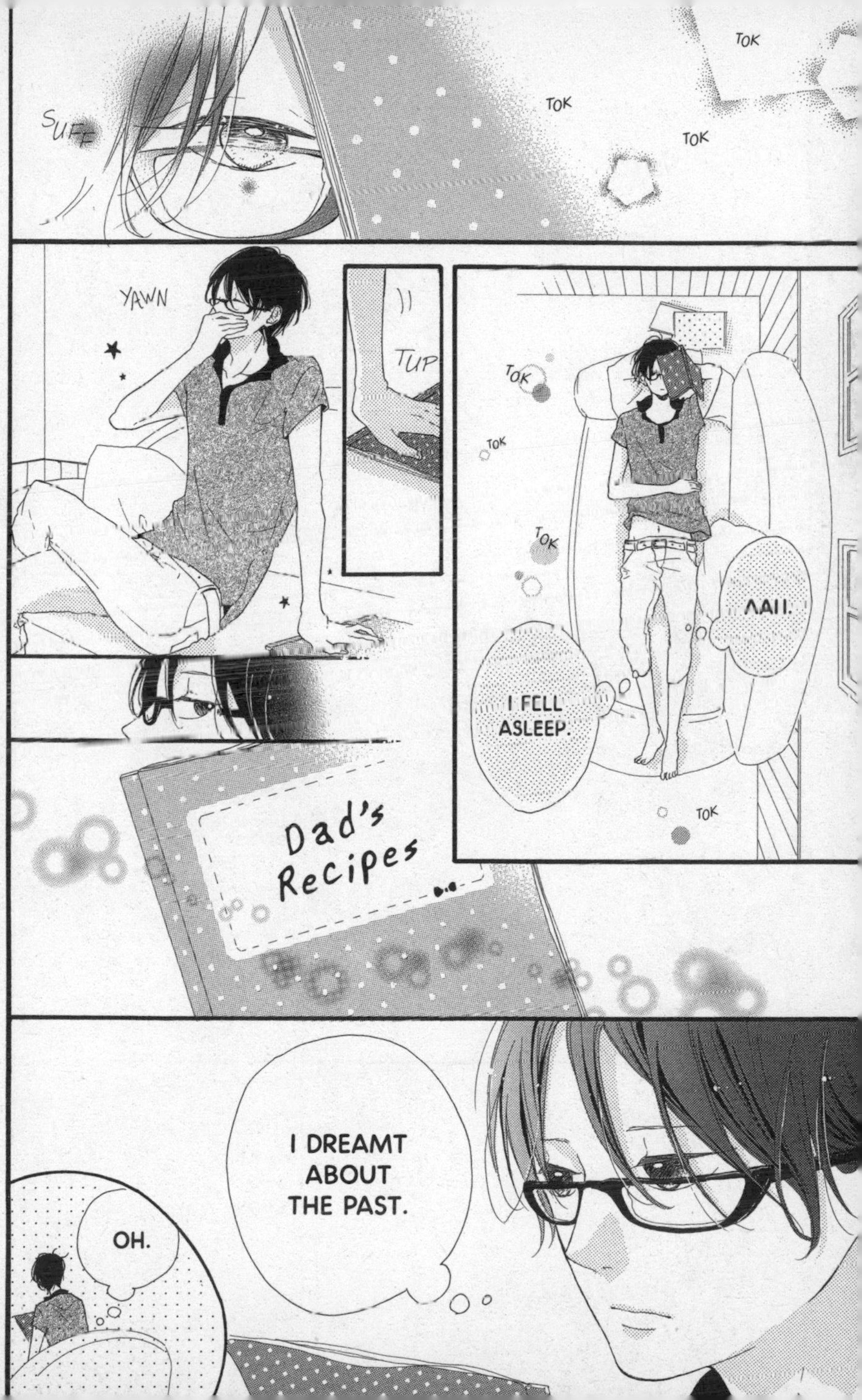
TOK
TOK
TOK
SUFF
TOK
TOK
AAH.
TOK
I FELL ASLEEP.
TOK
TUP
YAWN
Dad's Recipes
I DREAMT ABOUT THE PAST.
OH.

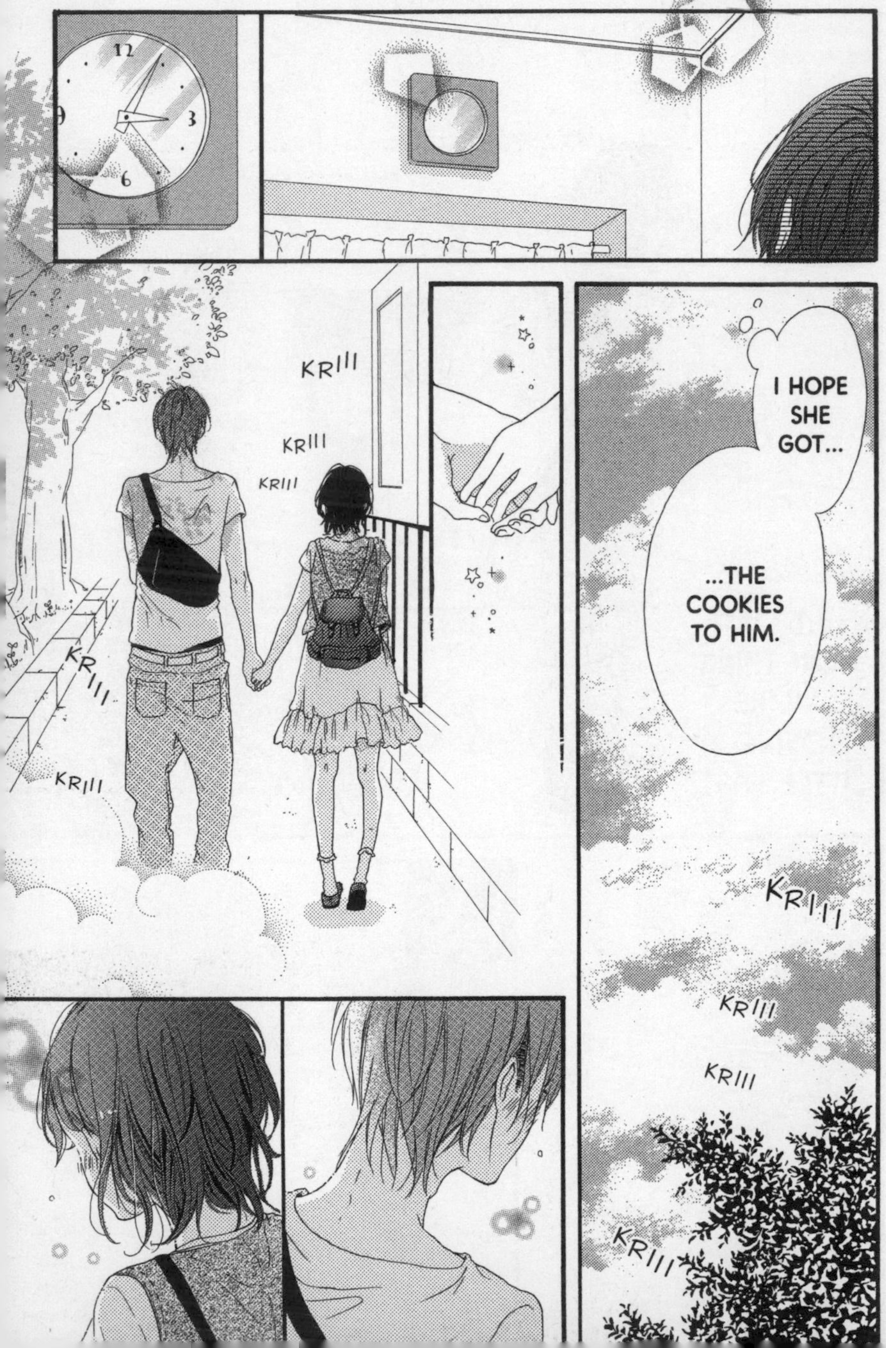
I HOPE SHE GOT...
...THE COOKIES TO HIM.
KRIII
KRIII
KRIII
KRIII
KRIII
KRIII
KRIII
KRIII
KRIII

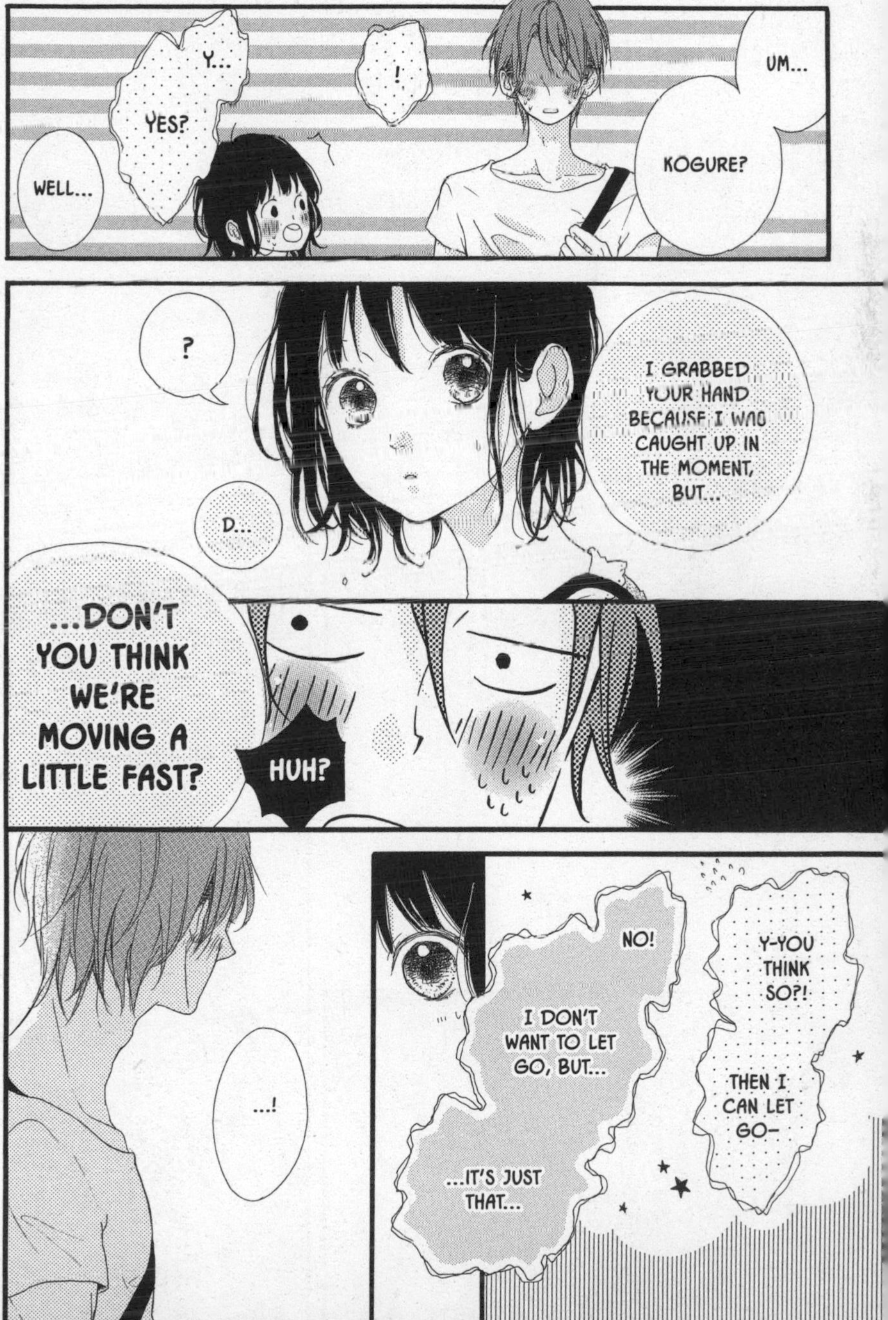
UM...
KOGURE?
!
Y...
YES?
WELL...
I GRABBED YOUR HAND BECAUSE I WAS CAUGHT UP IN THE MOMENT, BUT...
?
D...
...DON'T YOU THINK WE'RE MOVING A LITTLE FAST?
HUH?
Y-YOU THINK SO?!
THEN I CAN LET GO–
NO!
I DON'T WANT TO LET GO, BUT...
...IT'S JUST THAT...
...!

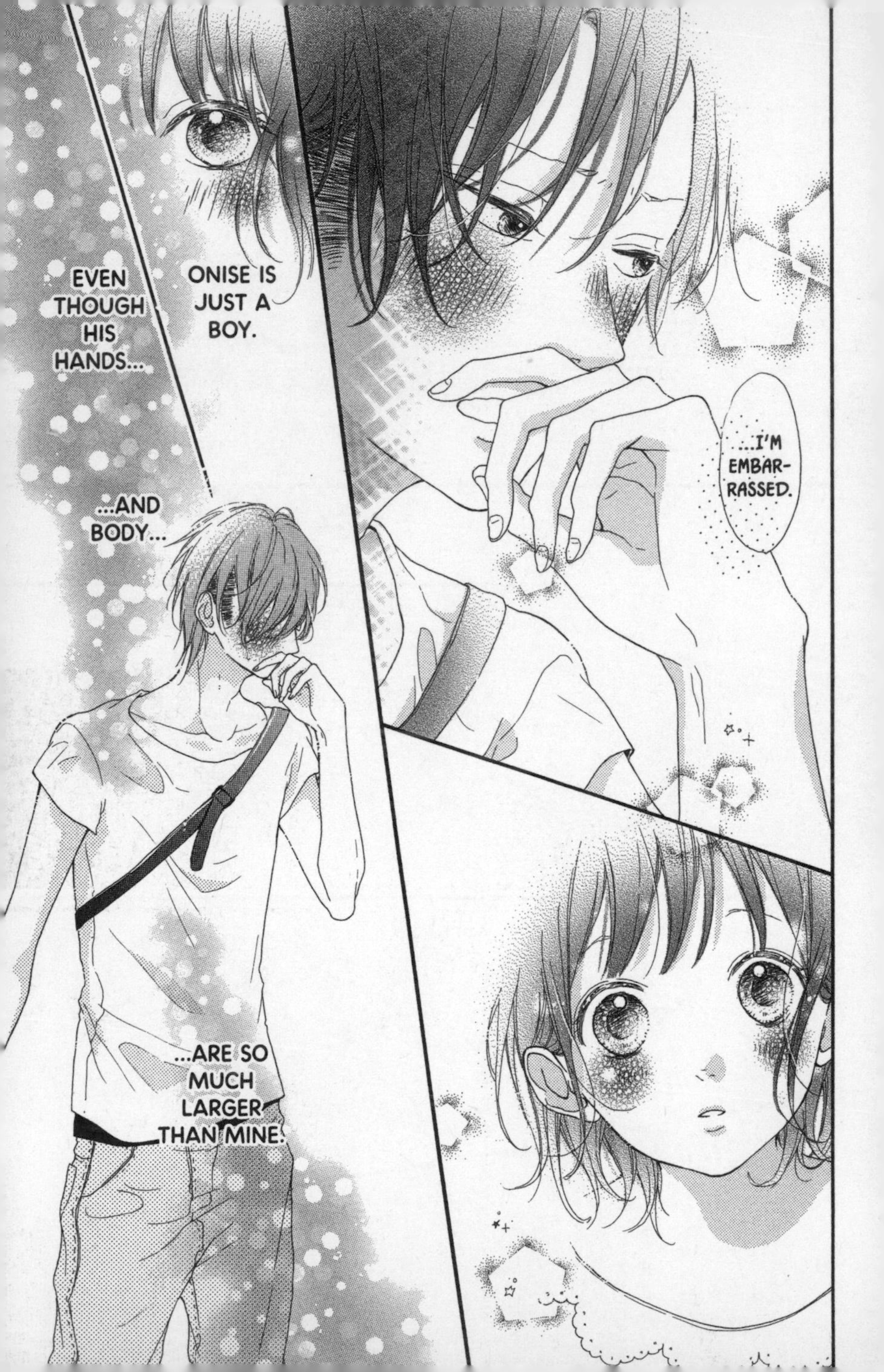
...I'M EMBARRASSED.
ONISE IS JUST A BOY.
EVEN THOUGH HIS HANDS...
...AND BODY...
...ARE SO MUCH LARGER THAN MINE.

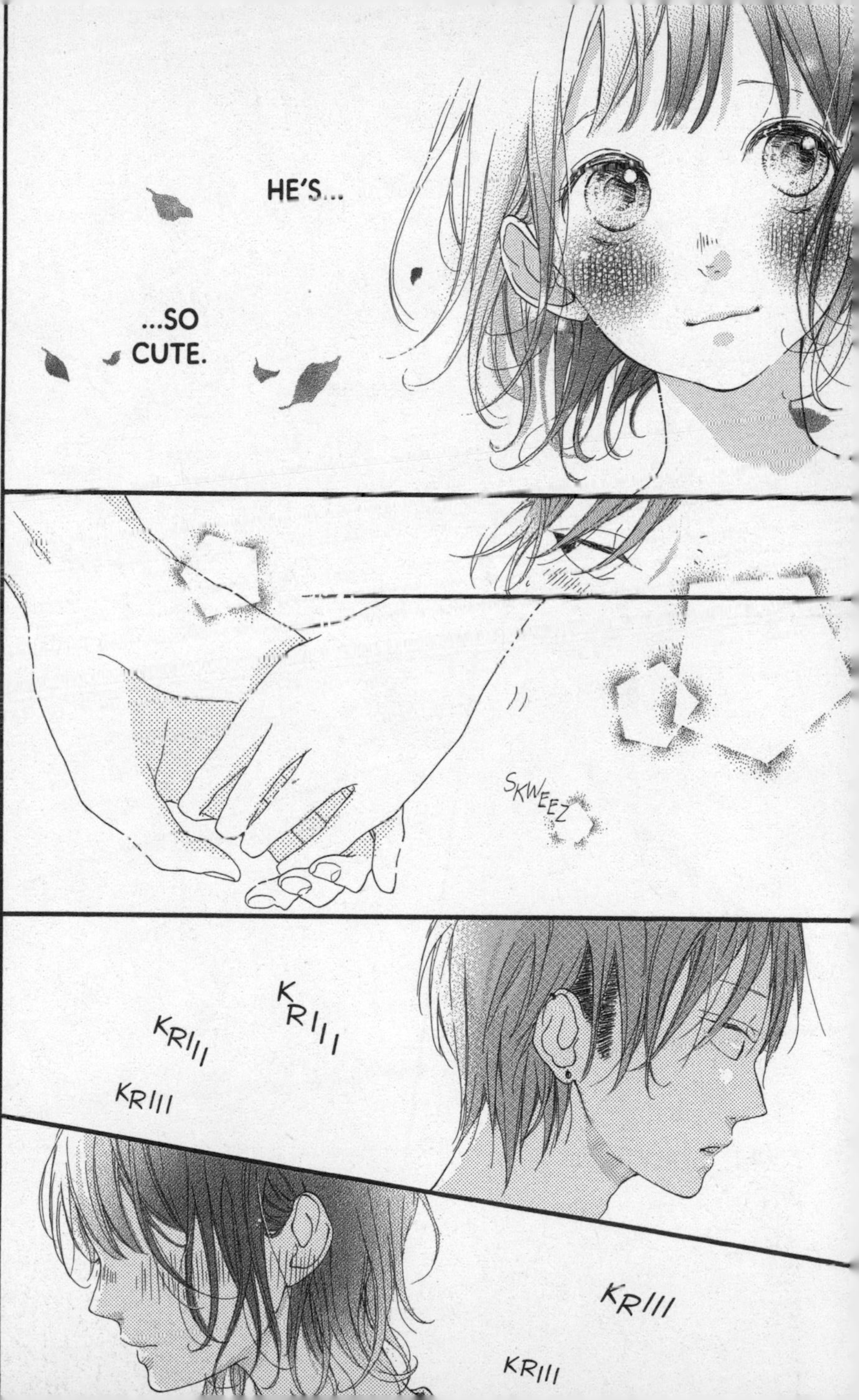
HE'S...
...SO CUTE.
SKWEEZ
KRIII
KRIII
KRIII
KRIII
KRIII

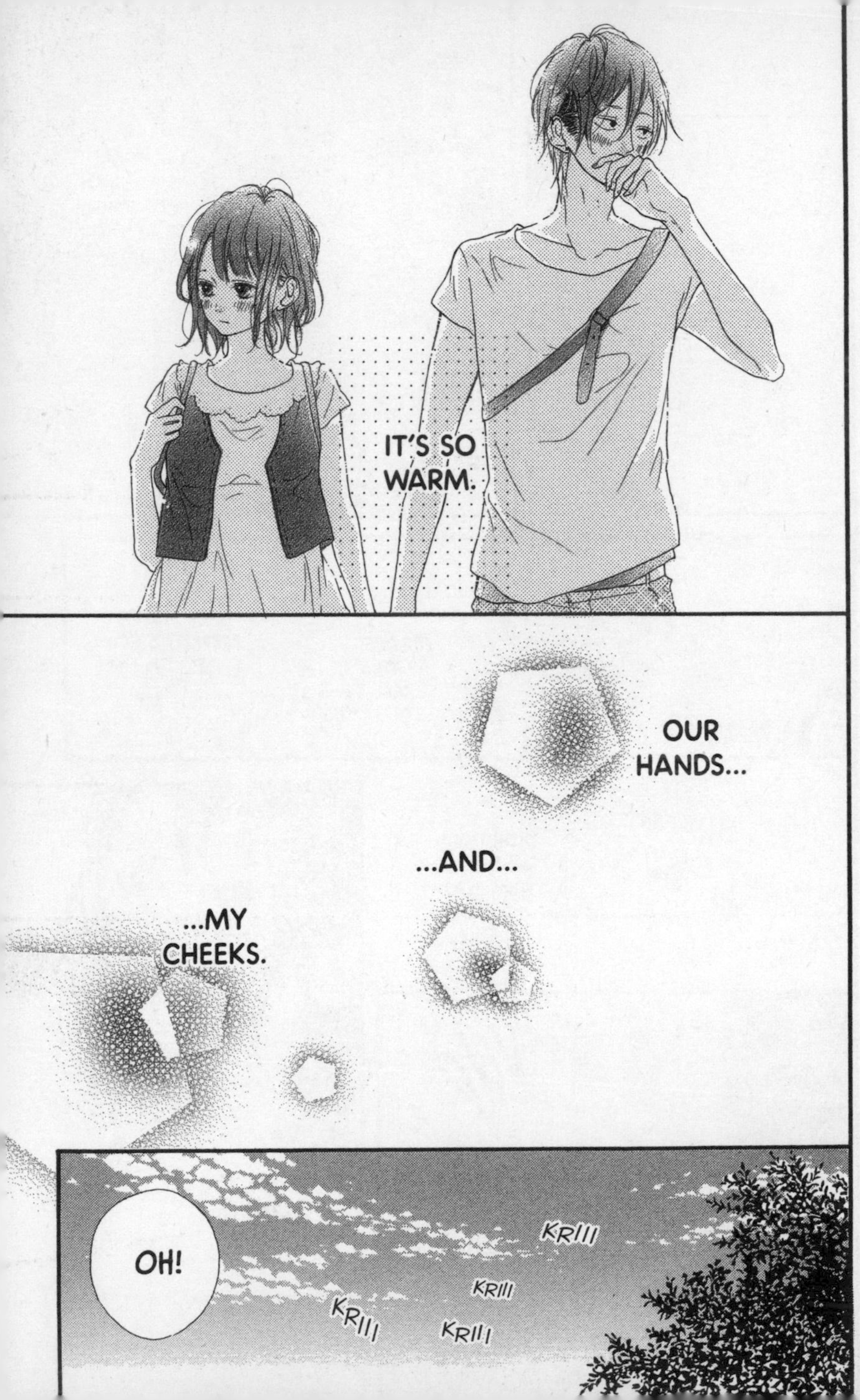
IT'S SO WARM.
OUR HANDS...
...AND...
...MY CHEEKS.
KRIII
KRIII
KRIII
KRIII
OH!

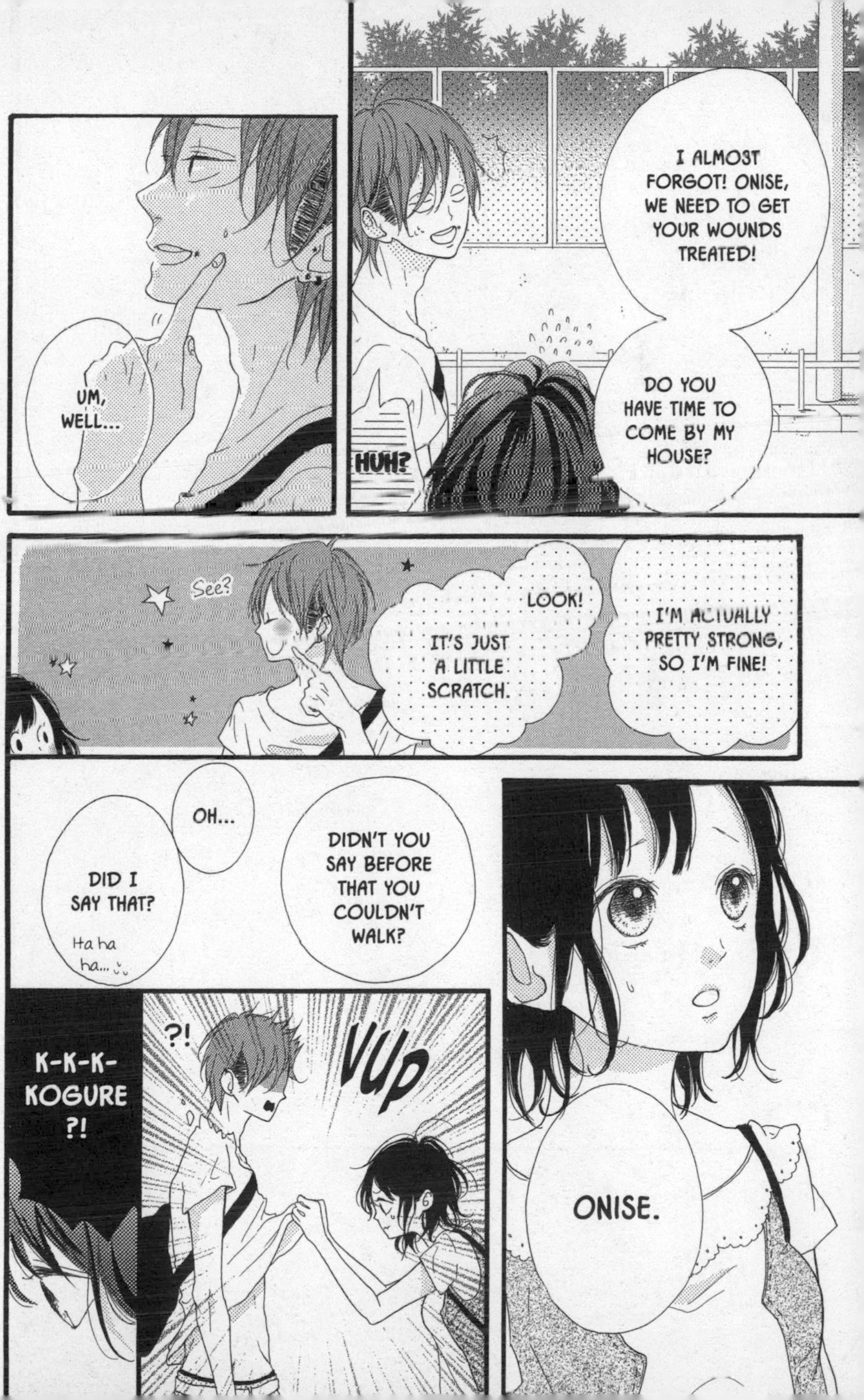
I ALMOST FORGOT! ONISE, WE NEED TO GET YOUR WOUNDS TREATED!
DO YOU HAVE TIME TO COME BY MY HOUSE?
HUH?
UM, WELL...
I'M ACTUALLY PRETTY STRONG, SO I'M FINE!
LOOK!
IT'S JUST A LITTLE SCRATCH.
See?
ONISE.
DIDN'T YOU SAY BEFORE THAT YOU COULDN'T WALK?
OH...
DID I SAY THAT?
Ha ha ha...
VUP
?!
K-K-K-KOGURE ?!

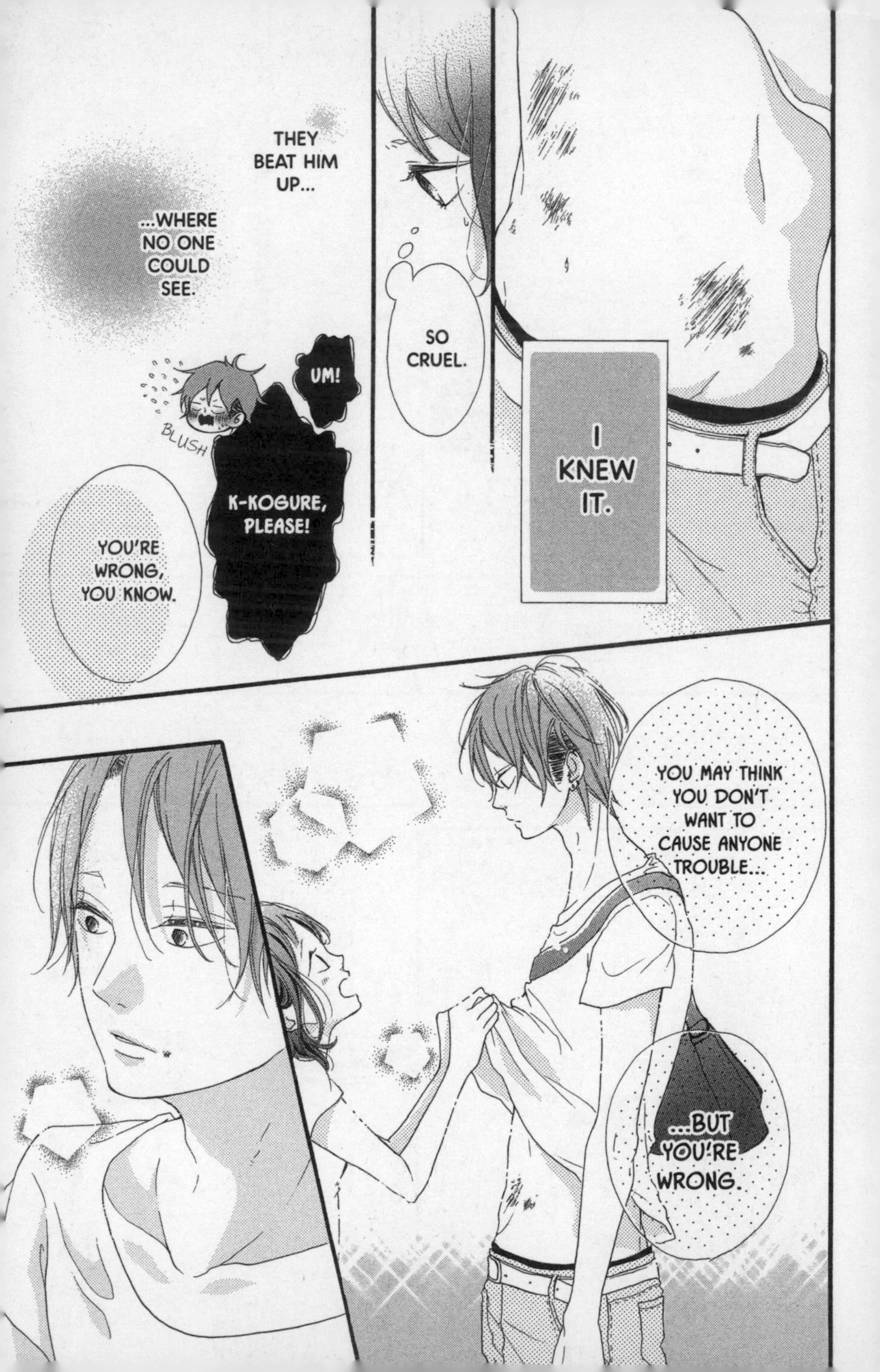
I KNEW IT.
SO CRUEL.
THEY BEAT HIM UP...
...WHERE NO ONE COULD SEE.
UM!
K-KOGURE, PLEASE!
BLUSH
YOU'RE WRONG, YOU KNOW.
YOU MAY THINK YOU DON'T WANT TO CAUSE ANYONE TROUBLE...
...BUT YOU'RE WRONG.

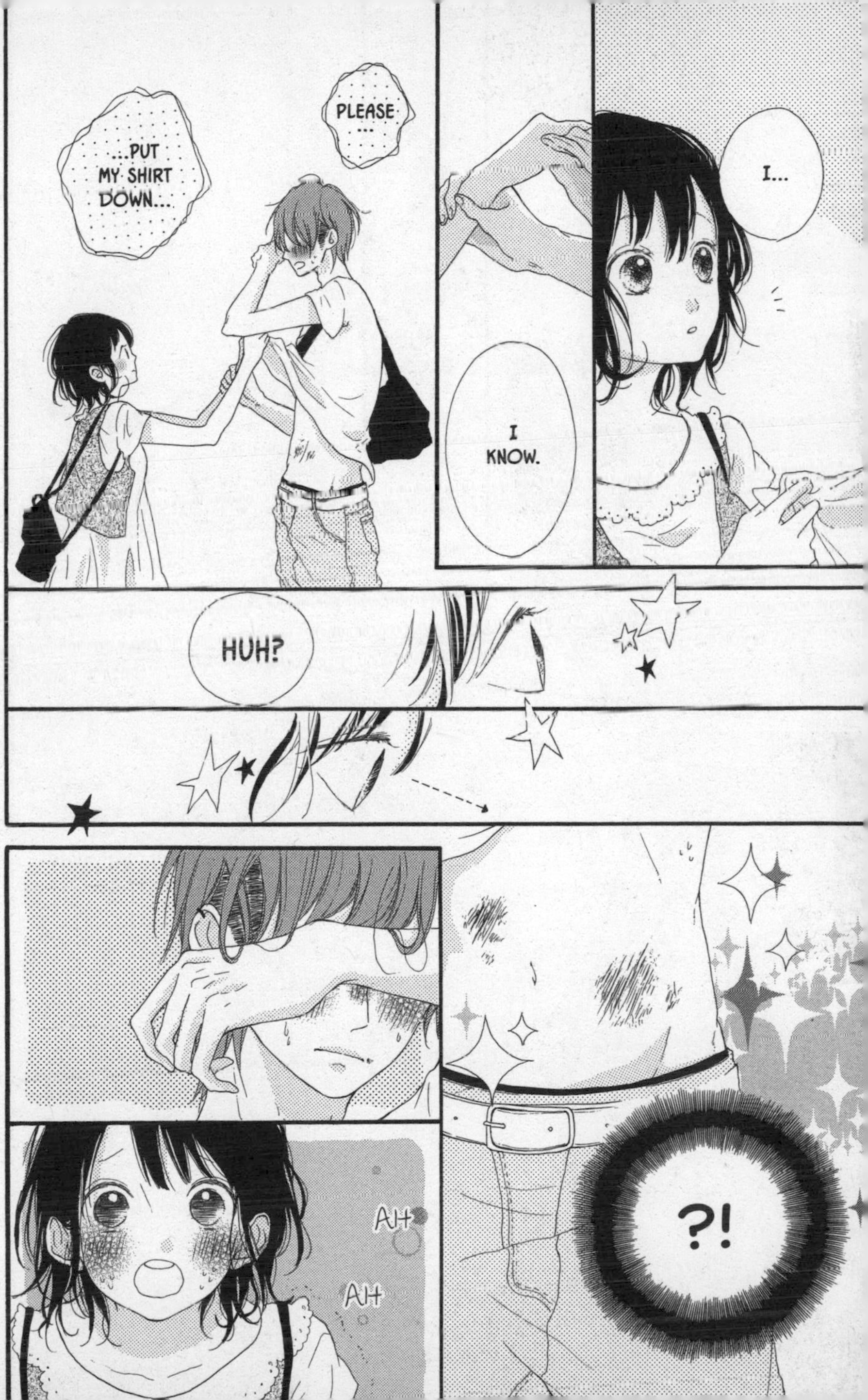

I...
I KNOW.
PLEASE...
...PUT MY SHIRT DOWN...
HUH?
?!
AH
AH

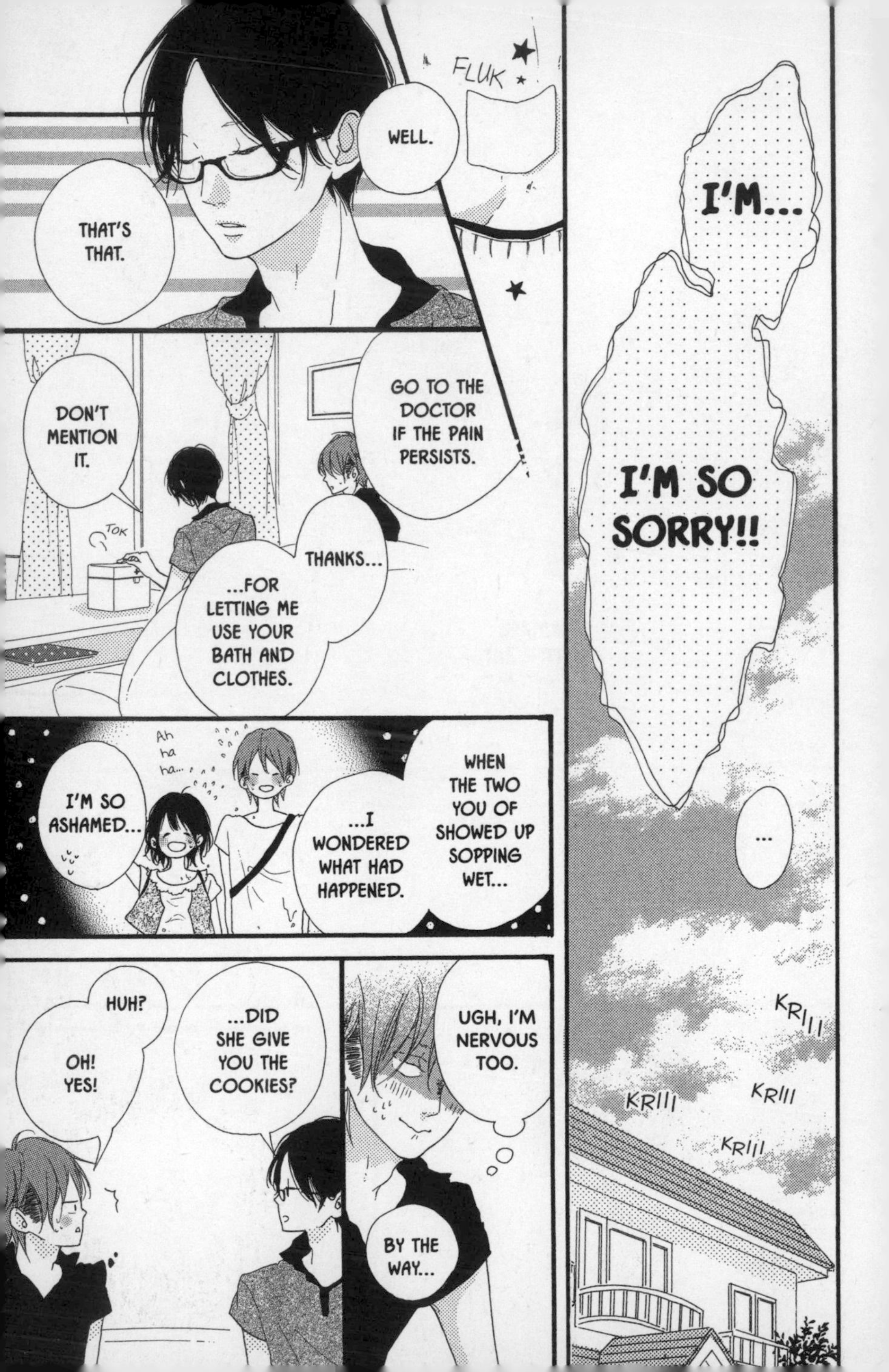
I'M...
I'M SO SORRY!!
...
KRIII
KRIII
KRIII
KRIII
FLUK
WELL.
THAT'S THAT.
GO TO THE DOCTOR IF THE PAIN PERSISTS.
THANKS...
...FOR LETTING ME USE YOUR BATH AND CLOTHES.
DON'T MENTION IT.
TOK
WHEN THE TWO YOU OF SHOWED UP SOPPING WET...
...I WONDERED WHAT HAD HAPPENED.
Ah ha ha...
I'M SO ASHAMED...
UGH, I'M NERVOUS TOO.
BY THE WAY...
...DID SHE GIVE YOU THE COOKIES?
HUH?
OH! YES!

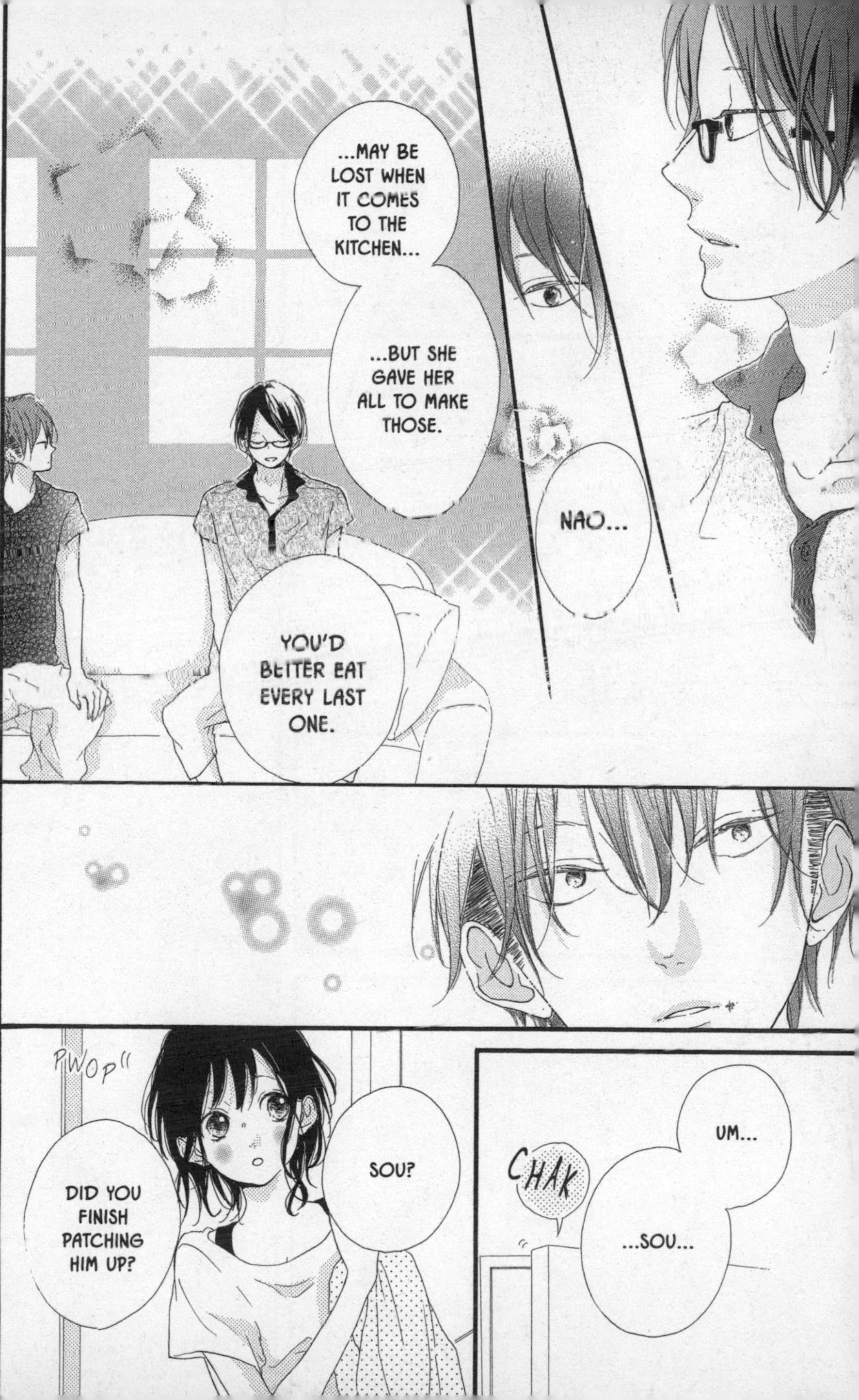
...MAY BE LOST WHEN IT COMES TO THE KITCHEN...
...BUT SHE GAVE HER ALL TO MAKE THOSE.
YOU'D BETTER EAT EVERY LAST ONE.
NAO...
CHAK
UM...
...SOU...
PWOP
SOU?
DID YOU FINISH PATCHING HIM UP?

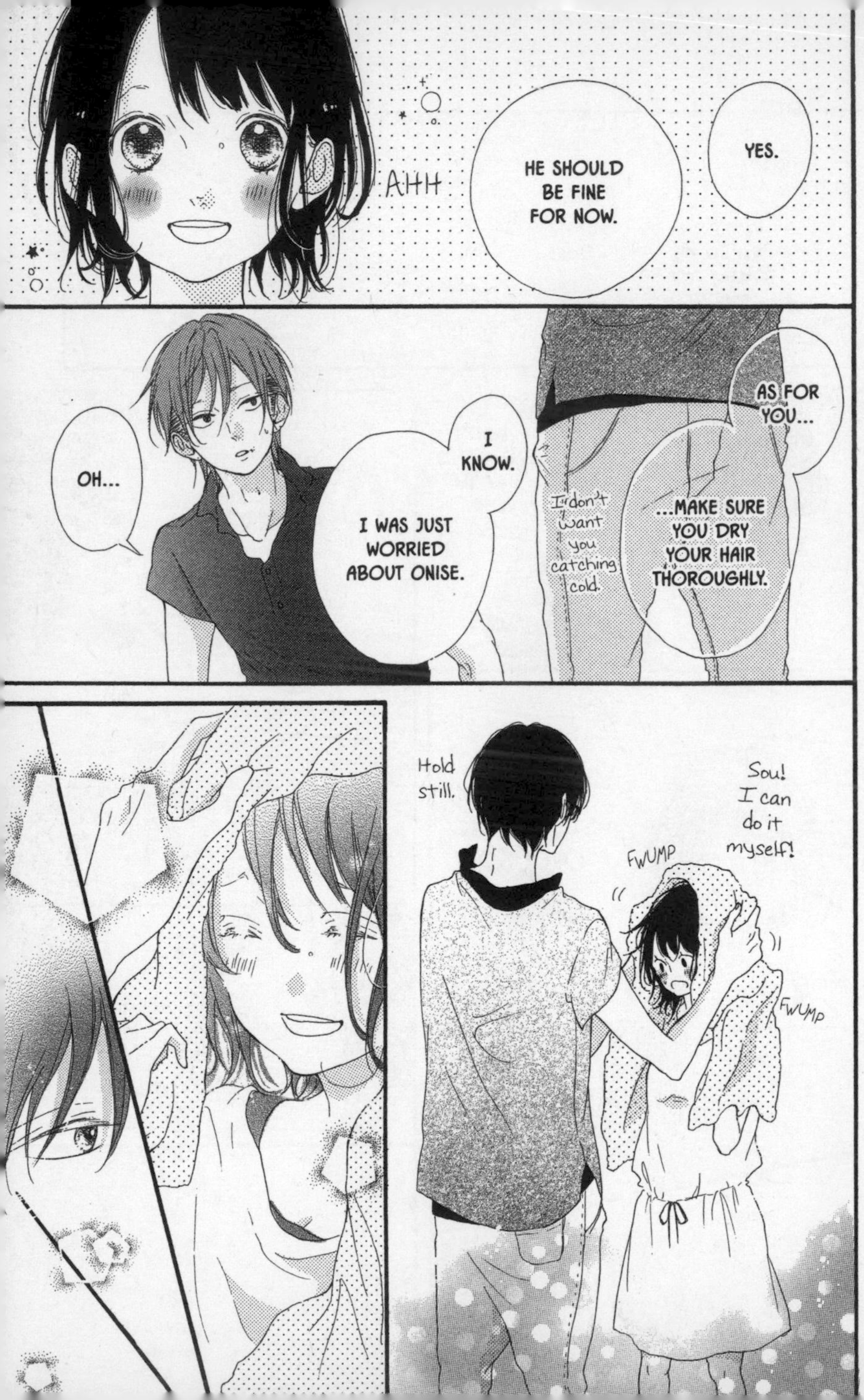
YES.
HE SHOULD BE FINE FOR NOW.
AHH
AS FOR YOU...
...MAKE SURE YOU DRY YOUR HAIR THOROUGHLY.
I don't want you catching cold.
I KNOW.
I WAS JUST WORRIED ABOUT ONISE.
OH...
Sou! I can do it myself!
FWUMP
FWUMP
Hold still.

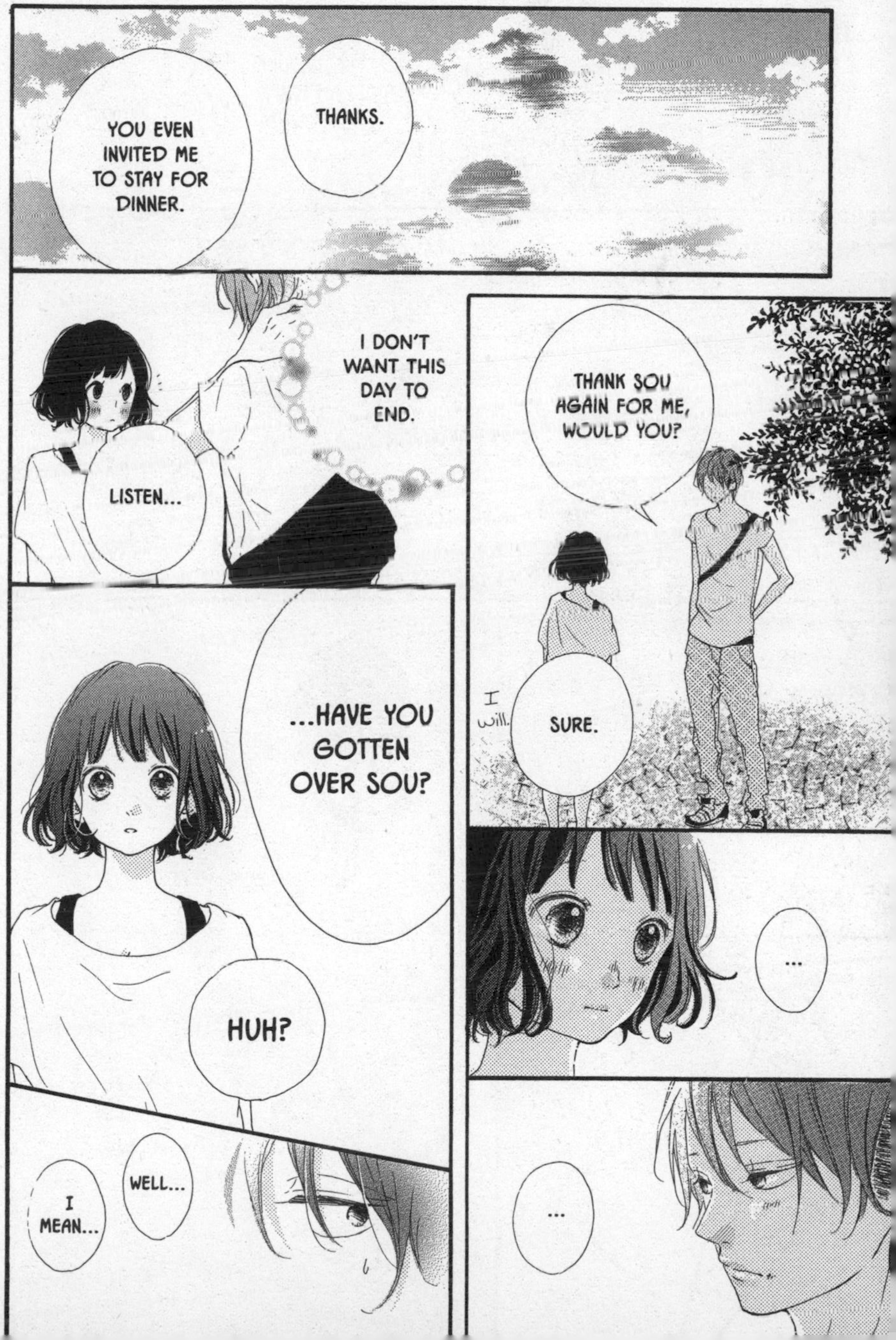
THANKS.
YOU EVEN INVITED ME TO STAY FOR DINNER.
THANK SOU AGAIN FOR ME, WOULD YOU?
SURE.
I will.
...
...
I DON'T WANT THIS DAY TO END.
LISTEN...
...HAVE YOU GOTTEN OVER SOU?
HUH?
WELL...
I MEAN...

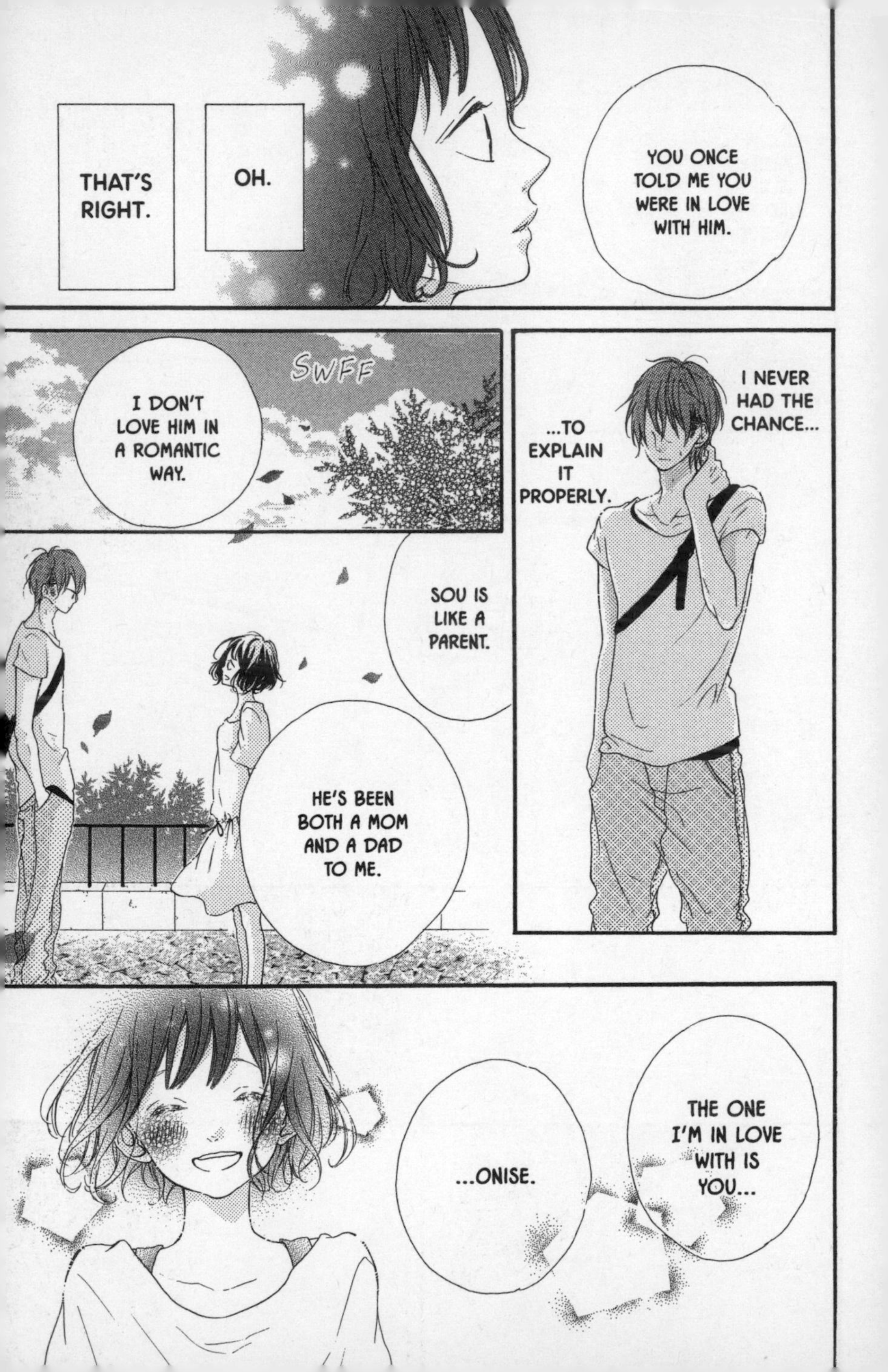
YOU ONCE TOLD ME YOU WERE IN LOVE WITH HIM.
OH.
THAT'S RIGHT.
I NEVER HAD THE CHANCE...
...TO EXPLAIN IT PROPERLY.
SWFF
I DON'T LOVE HIM IN A ROMANTIC WAY.
SOU IS LIKE A PARENT.
HE'S BEEN BOTH A MOM AND A DAD TO ME.
THE ONE I'M IN LOVE WITH IS YOU...
...ONISE.

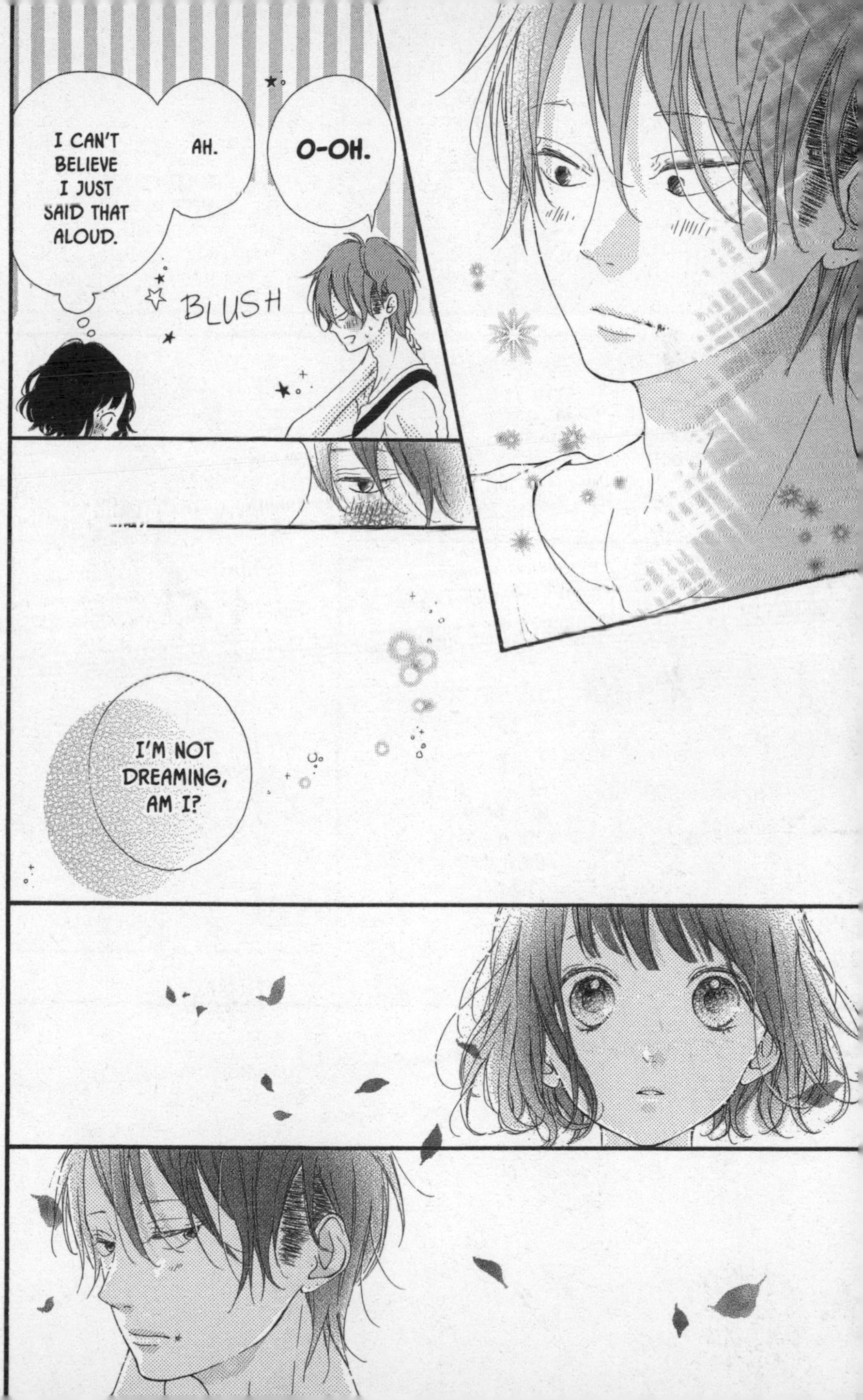
O-OH.
AH.
I CAN'T BELIEVE I JUST SAID THAT ALOUD.
BLUSH
I'M NOT DREAMING, AM I?

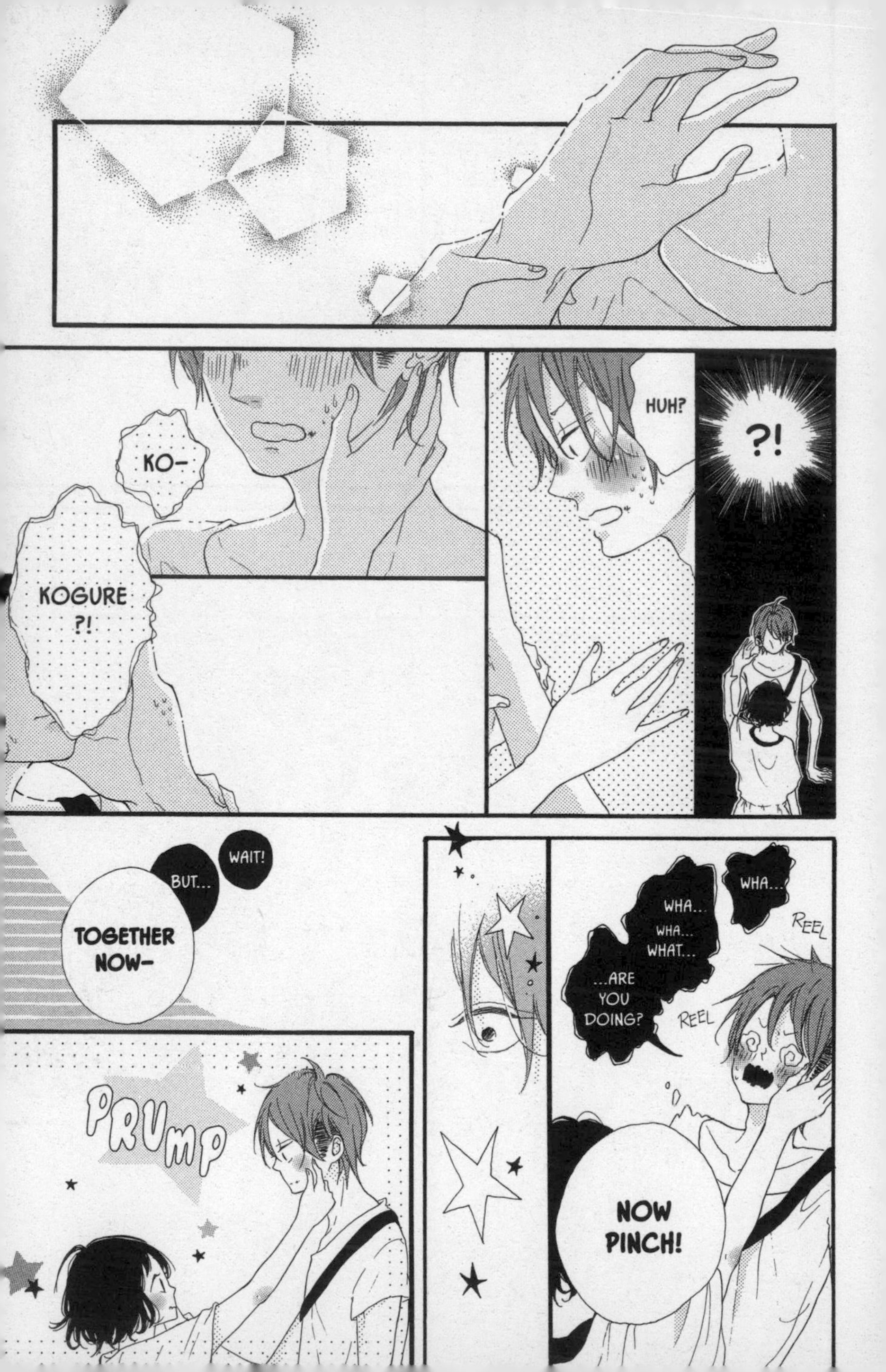
?!
HUH?
KO-
KOGURE ?!
WHA...
WHA... WHA... WHAT... ...ARE YOU DOING?
REEL
REEL
NOW PINCH!
WAIT!
BUT...
TOGETHER NOW-
PRUMP

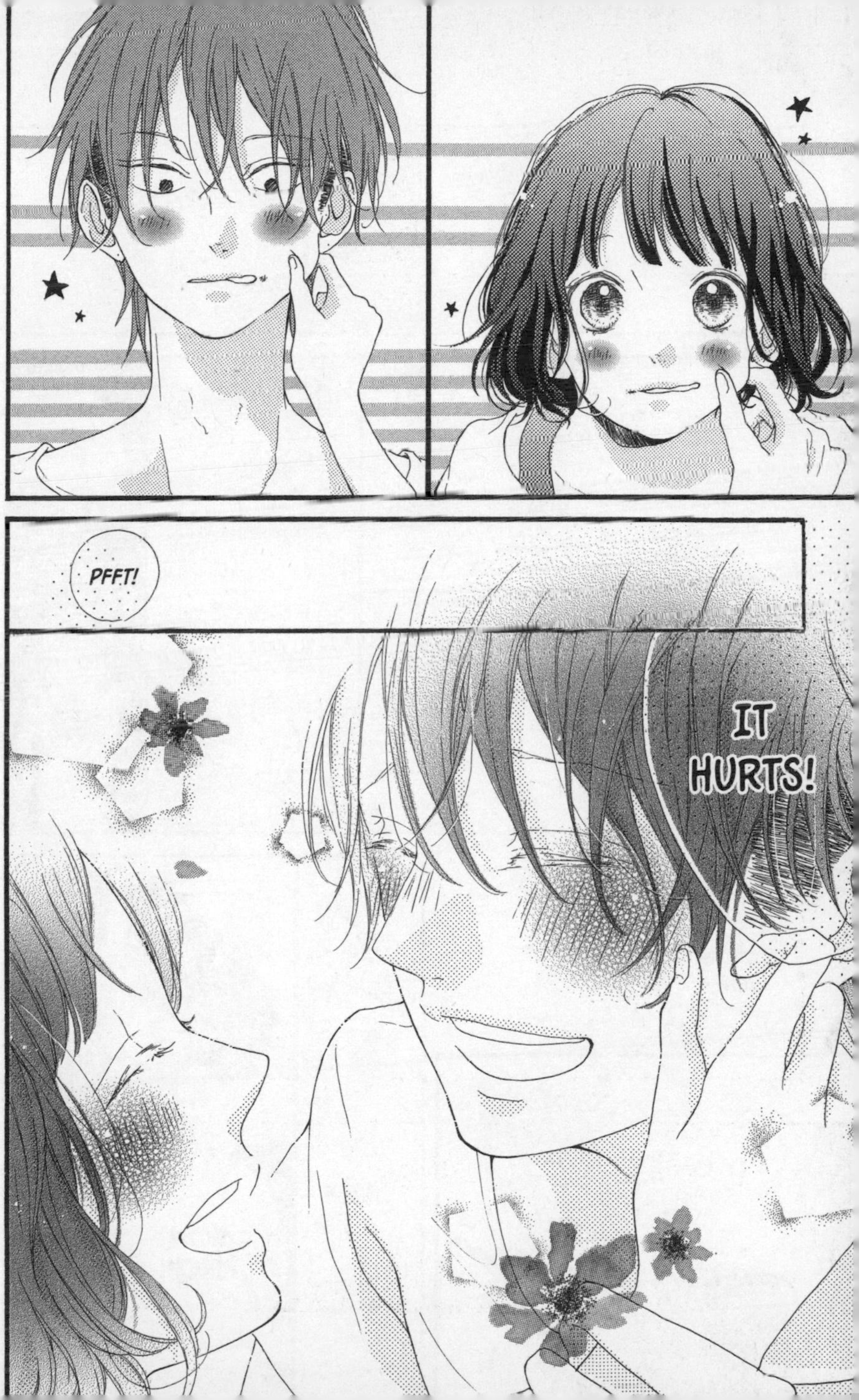
PFFT!
IT HURTS!

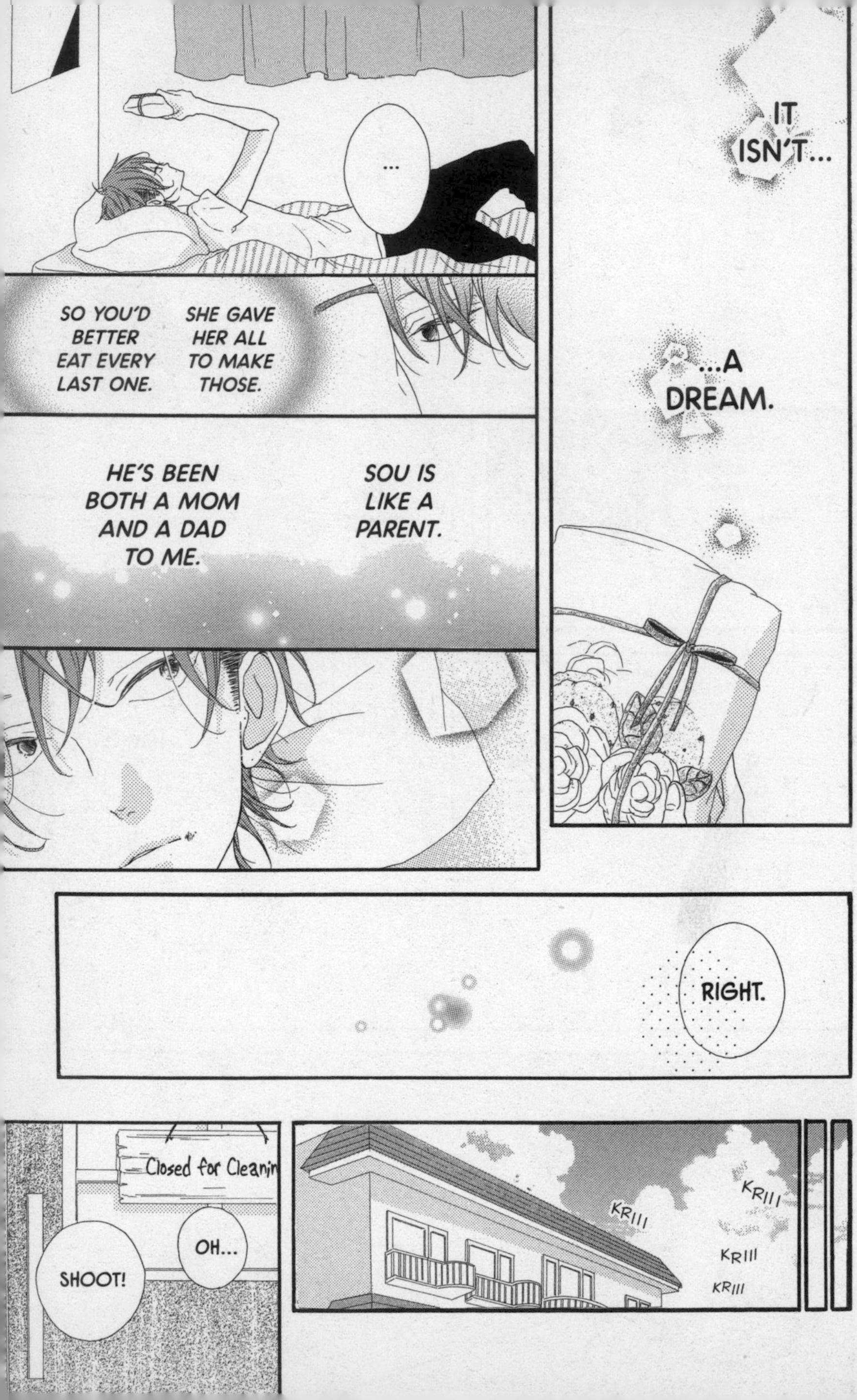
IT ISN'T...
...A DREAM.
...
SHE GAVE HER ALL TO MAKE THOSE.
SO YOU'D BETTER EAT EVERY LAST ONE.
SOU IS LIKE A PARENT.
HE'S BEEN BOTH A MOM AND A DAD TO ME.
RIGHT.
KRIII
KRIII
KRIII
KRIII
Closed for Cleanin
OH...
SHOOT!

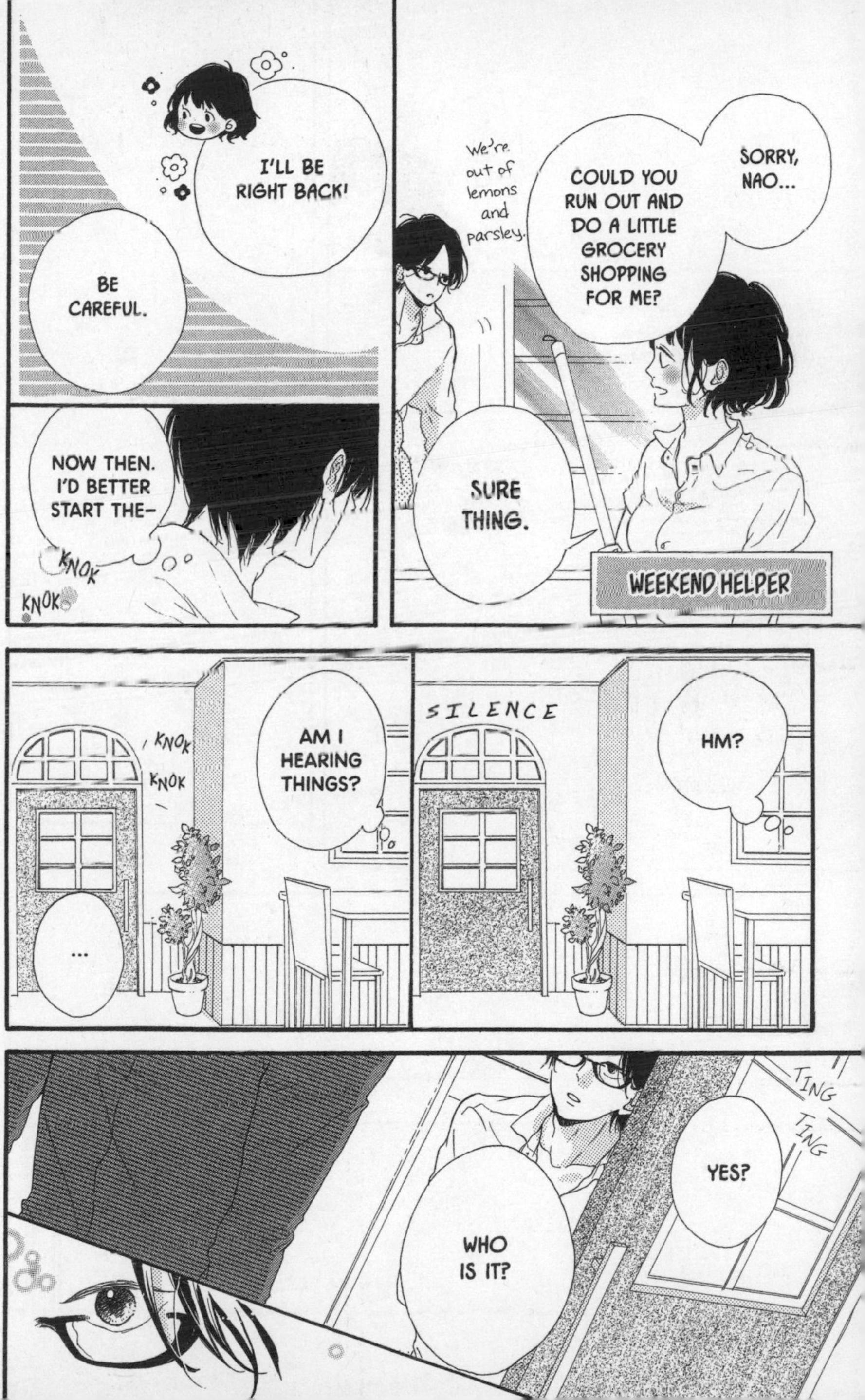
SORRY, NAO...
COULD YOU RUN OUT AND DO A LITTLE GROCERY SHOPPING FOR ME?
We're out of lemons and parsley.
SURE THING.
WEEKEND HELPER
I'LL BE RIGHT BACK!
BE CAREFUL.
NOW THEN. I'D BETTER START THE—
KNOK
KNOK
HM?
SILENCE
AM I HEARING THINGS?
KNOK
KNOK
...
TING
TING
YES?
WHO IS IT?

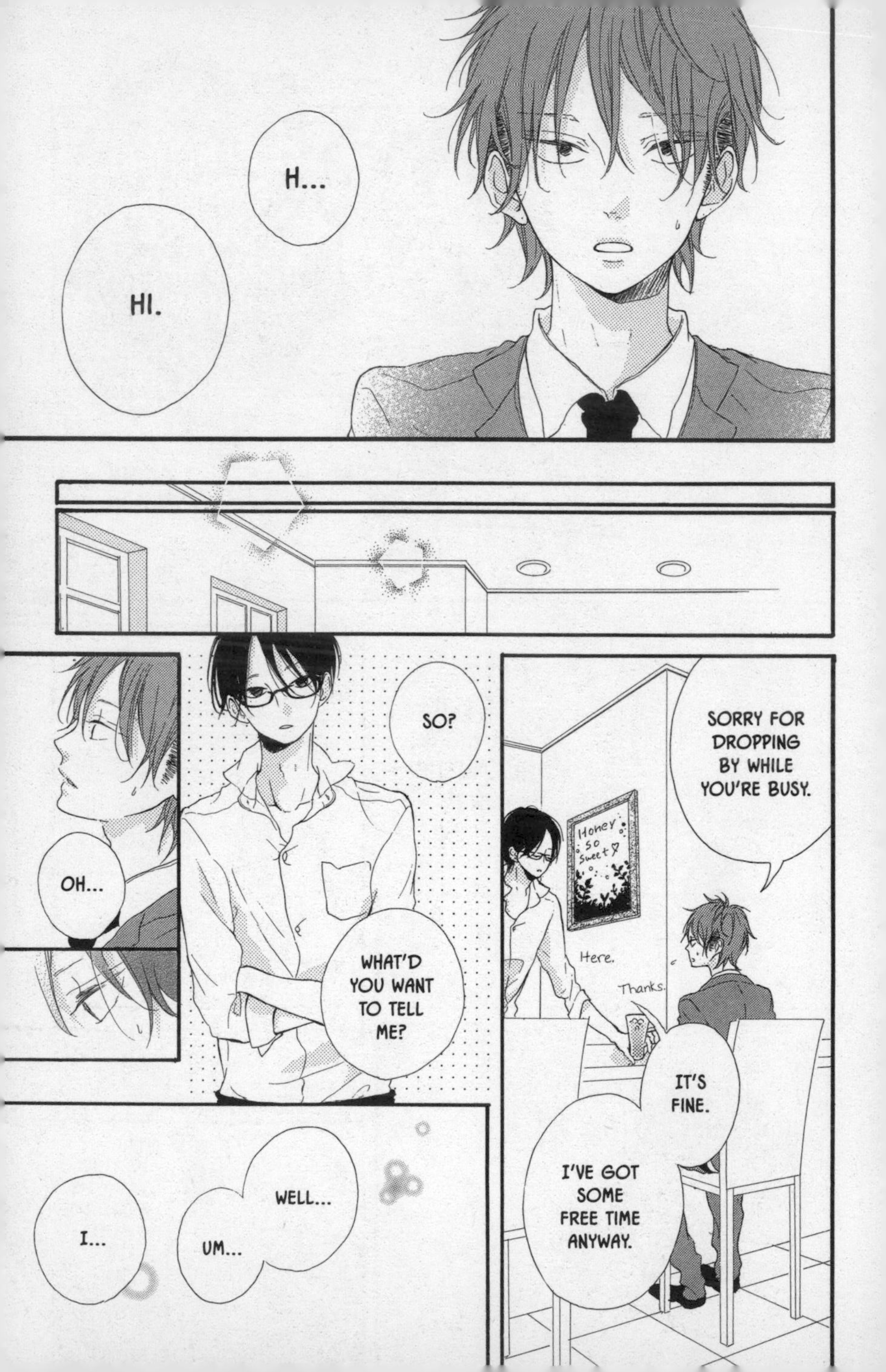
H...
HI.
SORRY FOR DROPPING BY WHILE YOU'RE BUSY.
Here.
Thanks.
IT'S FINE.
I'VE GOT SOME FREE TIME ANYWAY.
SO?
WHAT'D YOU WANT TO TELL ME?
OH...
WELL...
UM...
I...

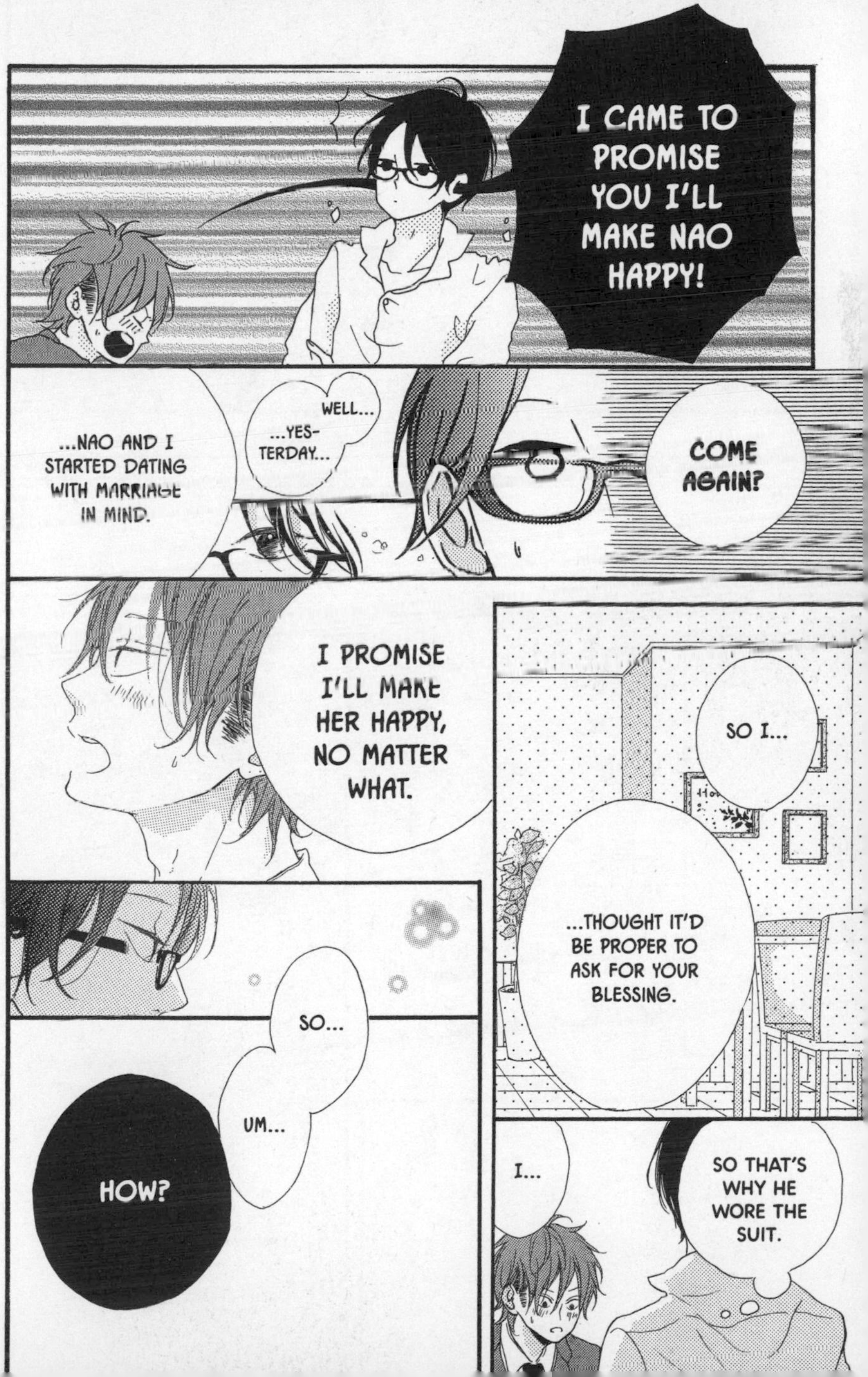
I CAME TO PROMISE YOU I'LL MAKE NAO HAPPY!
COME AGAIN?
WELL...
...YES-TERDAY...
...NAO AND I STARTED DATING WITH MARRIAGE IN MIND.
SO I...
...THOUGHT IT'D BE PROPER TO ASK FOR YOUR BLESSING.
I PROMISE I'LL MAKE HER HAPPY, NO MATTER WHAT.
SO...
UM...
HOW?
I...
SO THAT'S WHY HE WORE THE SUIT.

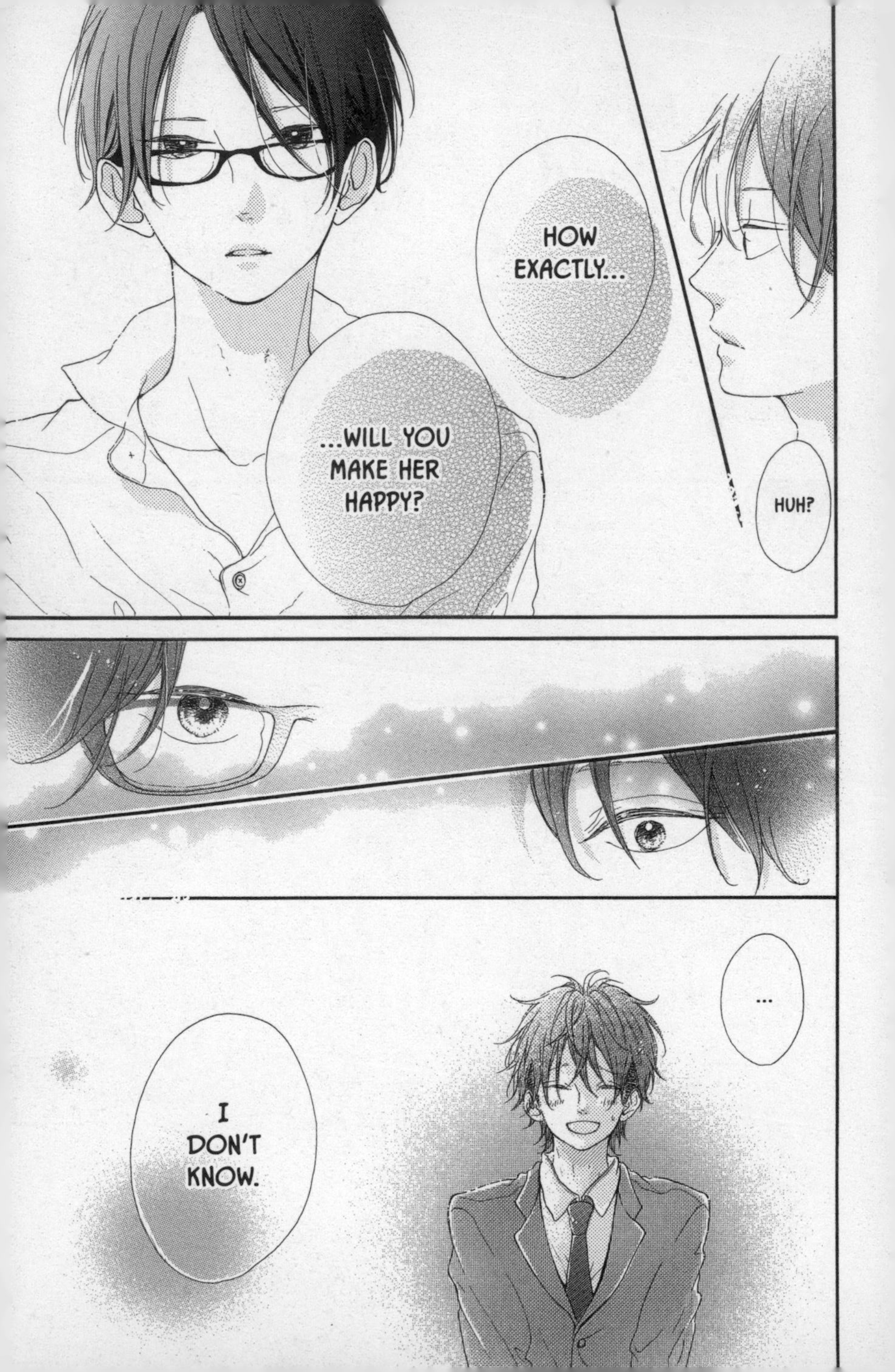
HUH?
HOW EXACTLY...
...WILL YOU MAKE HER HAPPY?
...
I DON'T KNOW.

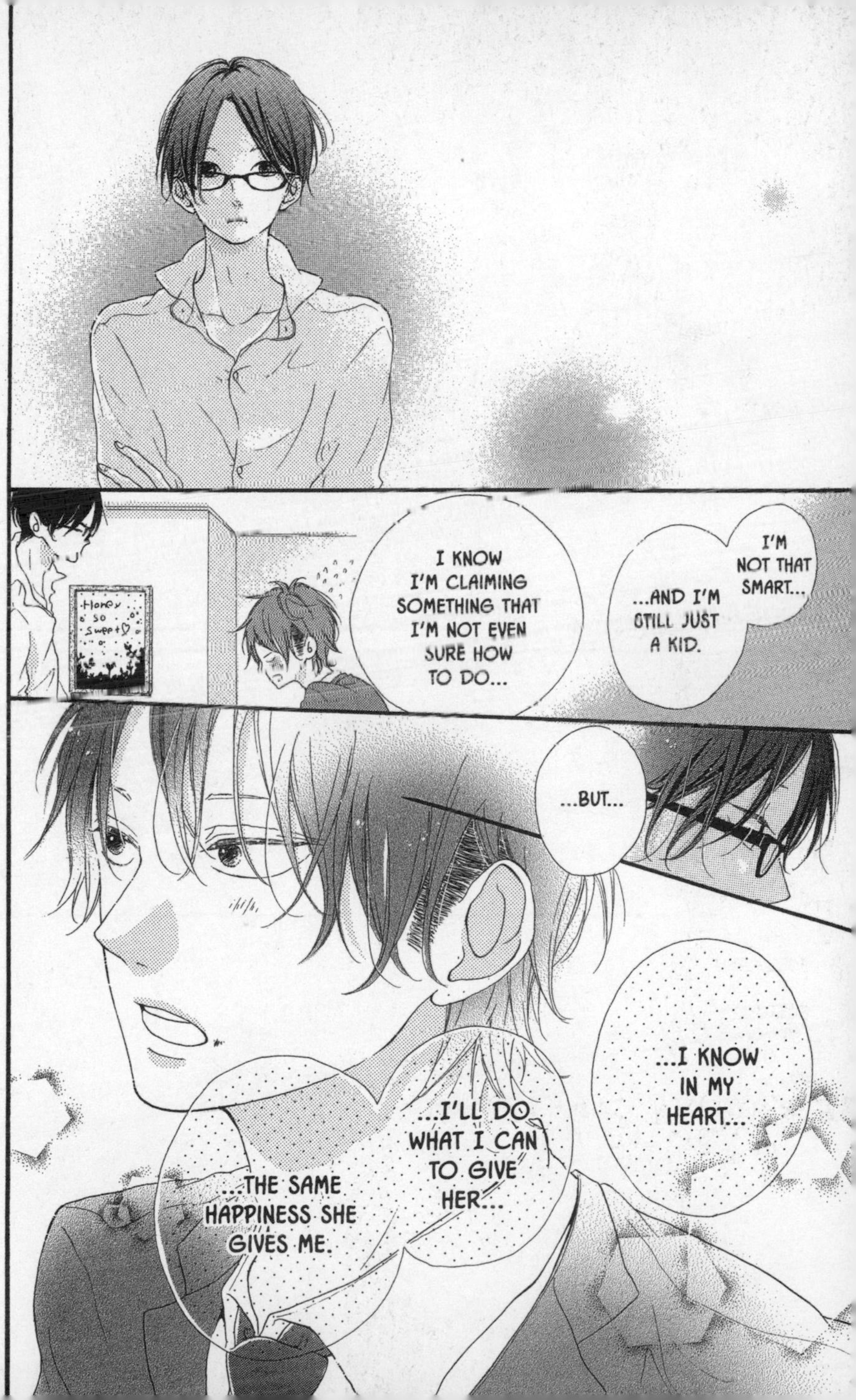
I'M NOT THAT SMART...
...AND I'M STILL JUST A KID.
I KNOW I'M CLAIMING SOMETHING THAT I'M NOT EVEN SURE HOW TO DO...
Honey so sweet♡
...BUT...
...I KNOW IN MY HEART...
...I'LL DO WHAT I CAN TO GIVE HER...
...THE SAME HAPPINESS SHE GIVES ME.

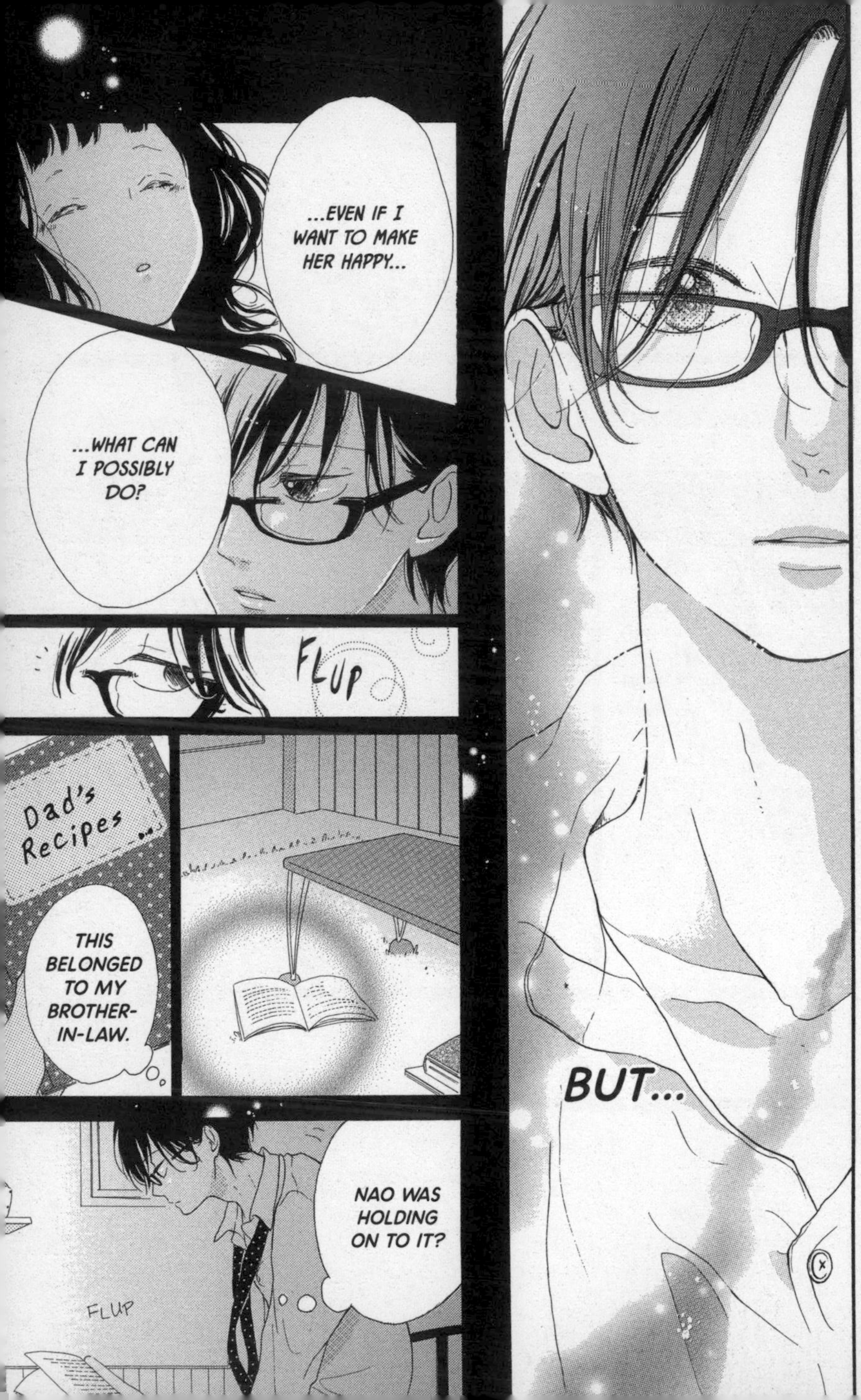
BUT...
...EVEN IF I WANT TO MAKE HER HAPPY...
...WHAT CAN I POSSIBLY DO?
FLUP
Dad's Recipes
THIS BELONGED TO MY BROTHER-IN-LAW.
NAO WAS HOLDING ON TO IT?
FLUP

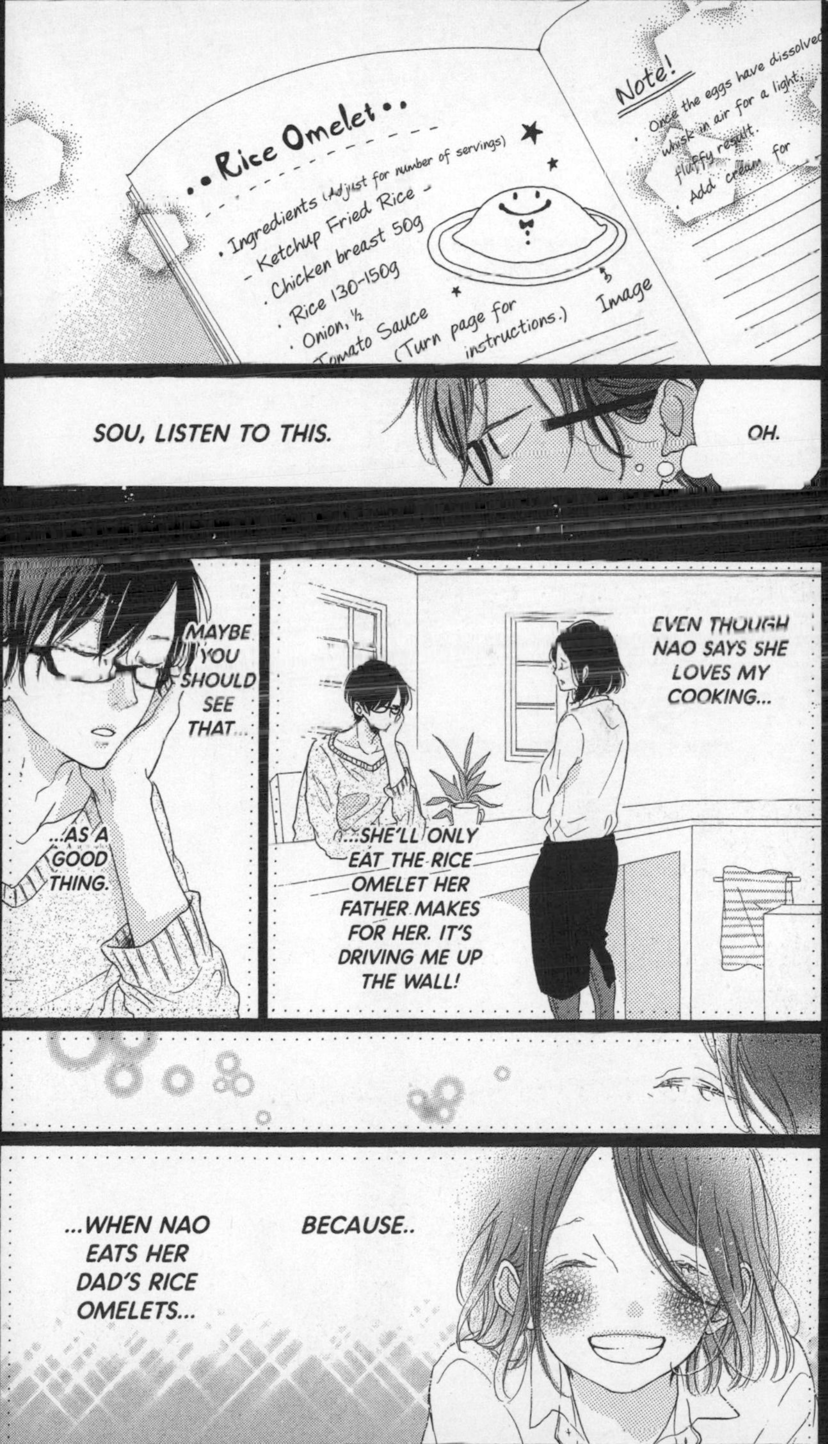
Rice Omelet
Ingredients (Adjust for number of servings)
Ketchup Fried Rice
Chicken breast 50g
Rice 130-150g
Onion, ½
Tomato Sauce
(Turn page for instructions.)
Image
Note!
Once the eggs have dissolved whisk in air for a light, fluffy result.
Add cream for
OH.
SOU, LISTEN TO THIS.
EVEN THOUGH NAO SAYS SHE LOVES MY COOKING...
...SHE'LL ONLY EAT THE RICE OMELET HER FATHER MAKES FOR HER. IT'S DRIVING ME UP THE WALL!
MAYBE YOU SHOULD SEE THAT...
...AS A GOOD THING.
BECAUSE..
...WHEN NAO EATS HER DAD'S RICE OMELETS...

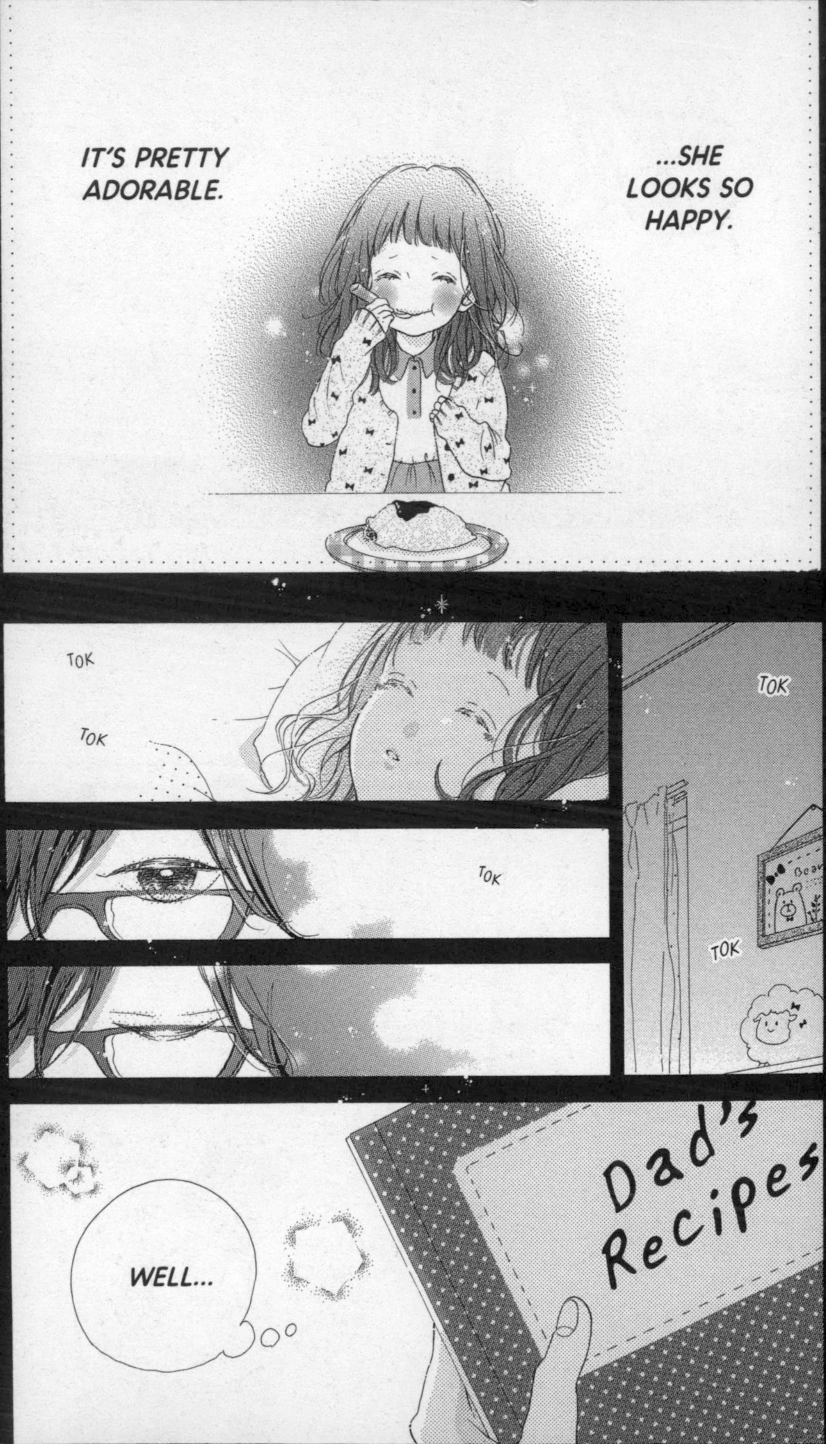
...SHE LOOKS SO HAPPY.
IT'S PRETTY ADORABLE.
TOK
TOK
TOK
TOK
TOK
Dad's Recipes
WELL...

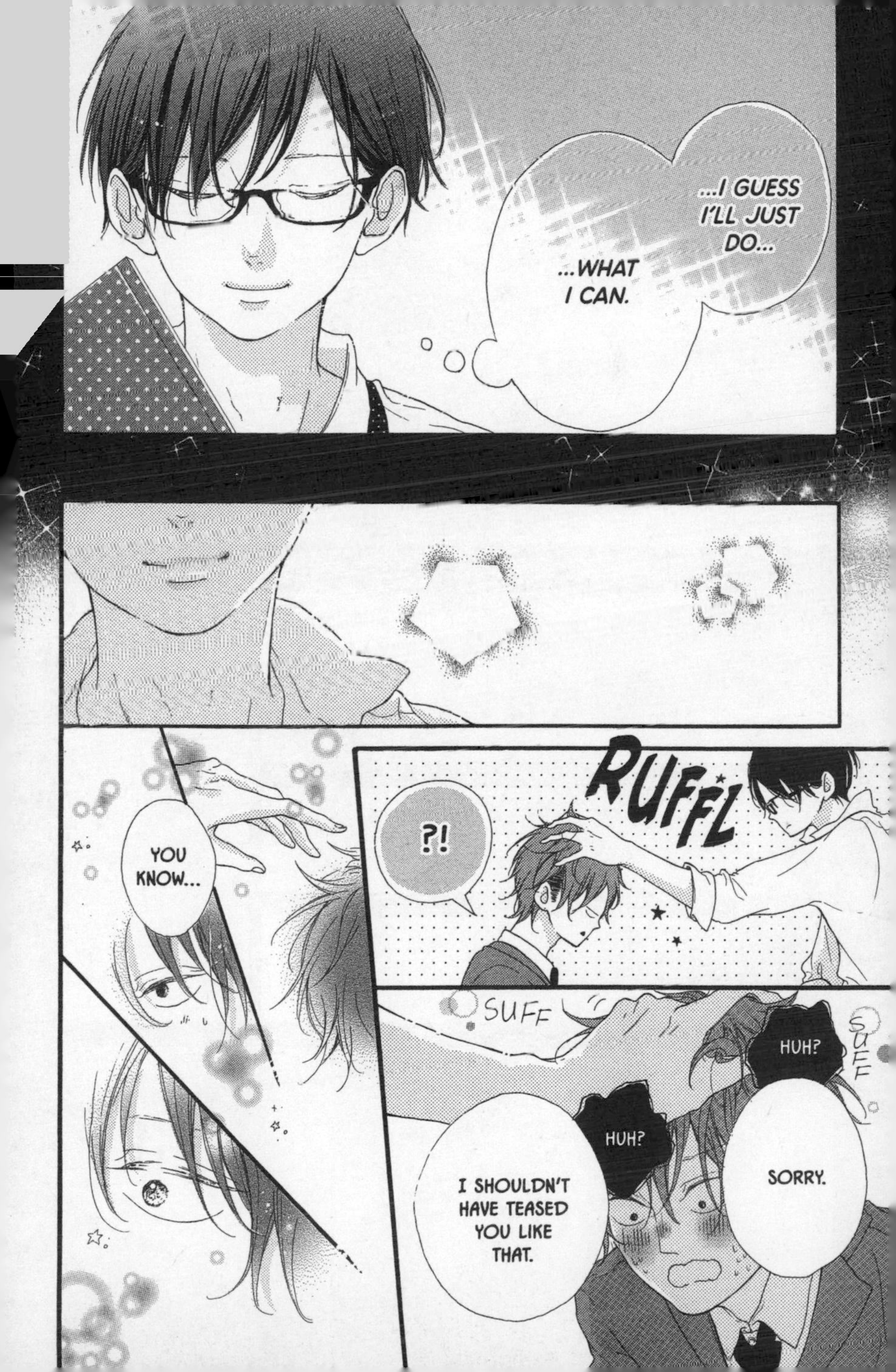
...I GUESS I'LL JUST DO...
...WHAT I CAN.
RUFFL
?!
SUFF
HUH?
SORRY.
HUH?
I SHOULDN'T HAVE TEASED YOU LIKE THAT.
SUFF
YOU KNOW...

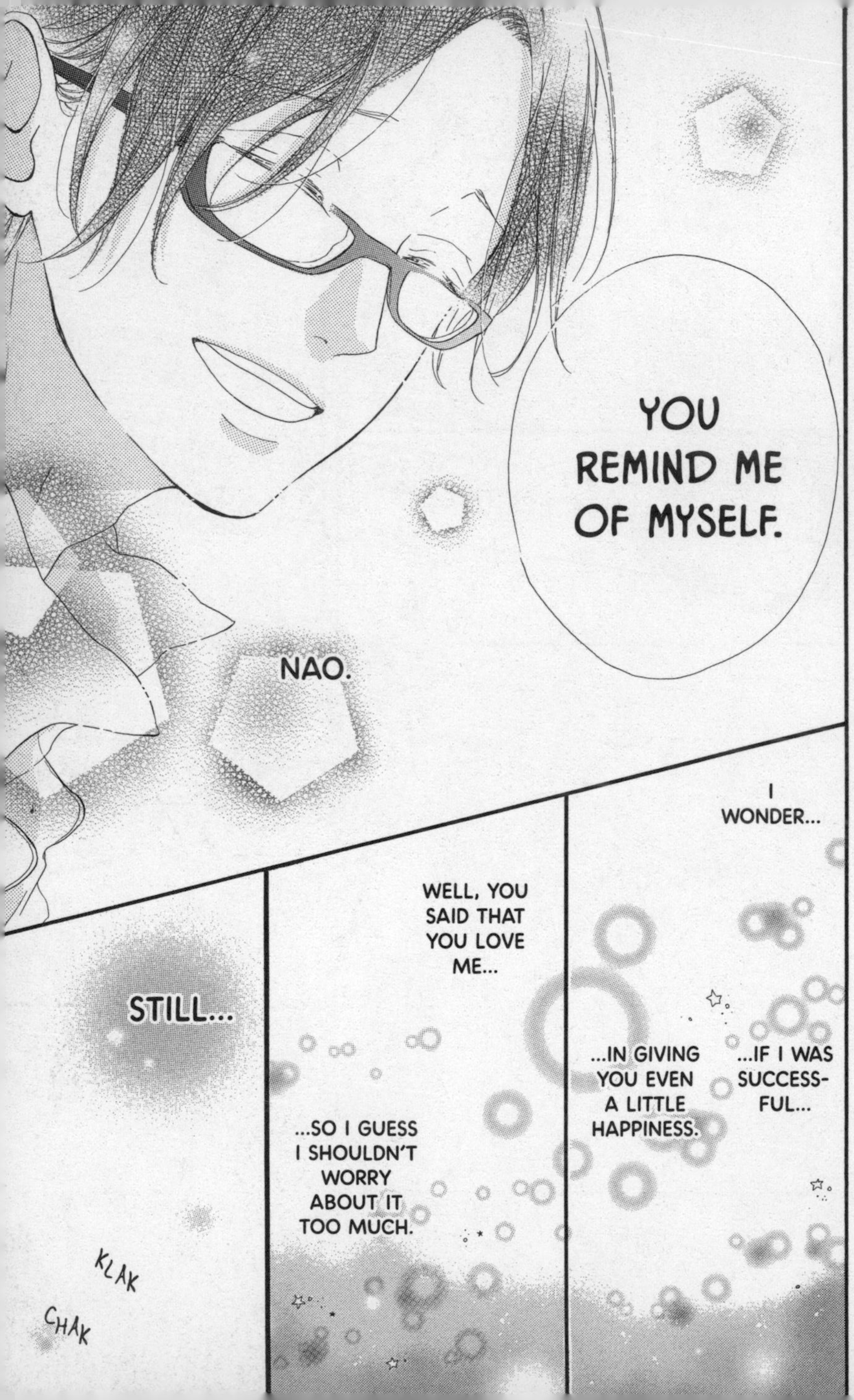
YOU REMIND ME OF MYSELF.
NAO.
I WONDER...
...IF I WAS SUCCESSFUL...
...IN GIVING YOU EVEN A LITTLE HAPPINESS.
WELL, YOU SAID THAT YOU LOVE ME...
...SO I GUESS I SHOULDN'T WORRY ABOUT IT TOO MUCH.
STILL...
KLAK
CHAK

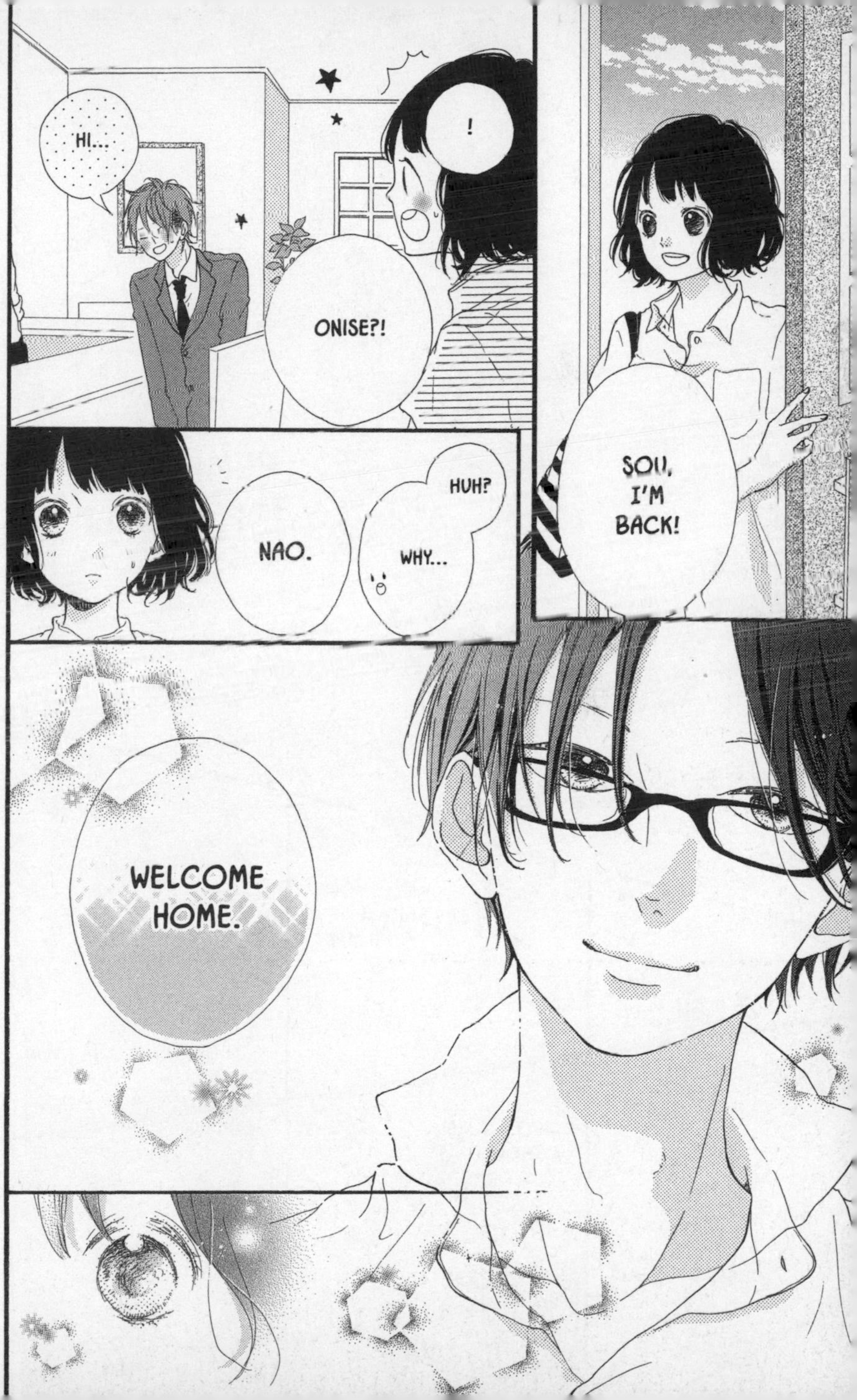
SOU, I'M BACK!
!
ONISE?!
HI...
HUH?
WHY...
NAO.
WELCOME HOME.

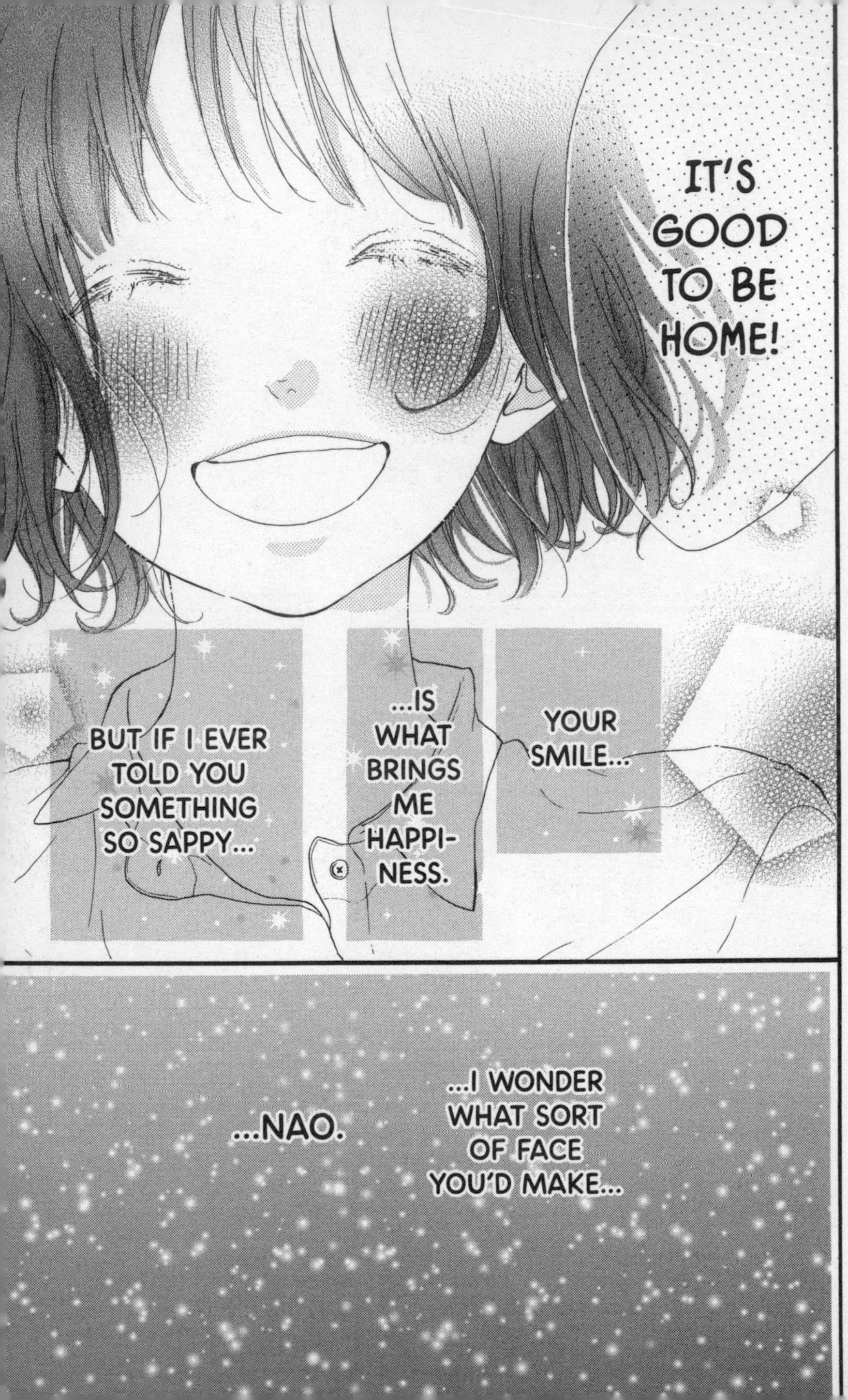
IT'S GOOD TO BE HOME!
YOUR SMILE...
...IS WHAT BRINGS ME HAPPINESS.
BUT IF I EVER TOLD YOU SOMETHING SO SAPPY...
...I WONDER WHAT SORT OF FACE YOU'D MAKE...
...NAO.

The Proposal

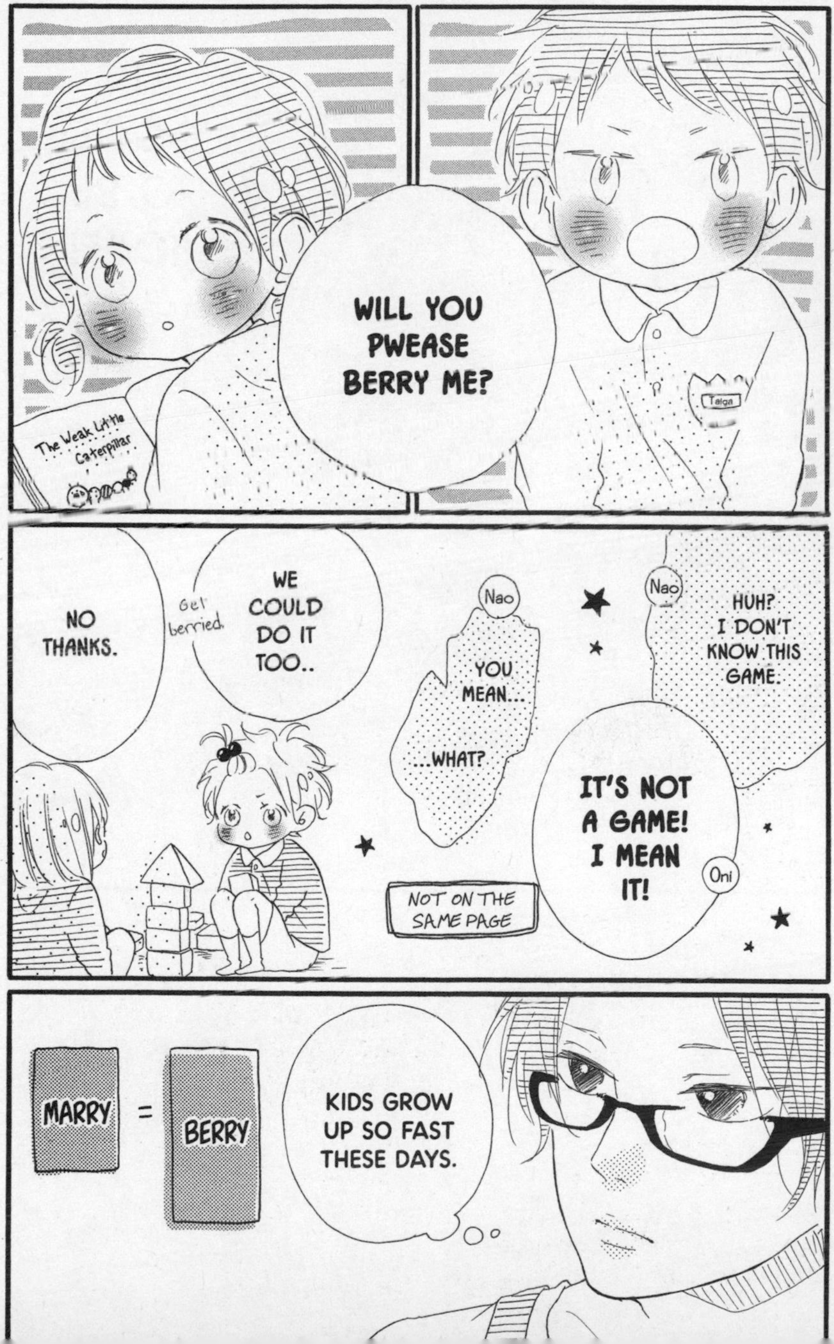
WILL YOU PWEASE BERRY ME?
Taiga
The Weak Little Caterpillar
Nao
HUH? I DON'T KNOW THIS GAME.
Oni
IT'S NOT A GAME! I MEAN IT!
Nao
YOU MEAN...
...WHAT?
NOT ON THE SAME PAGE
WE COULD DO IT TOO..
Get berried.
NO THANKS.
KIDS GROW UP SO FAST THESE DAYS.
MARRY
=
BERRY

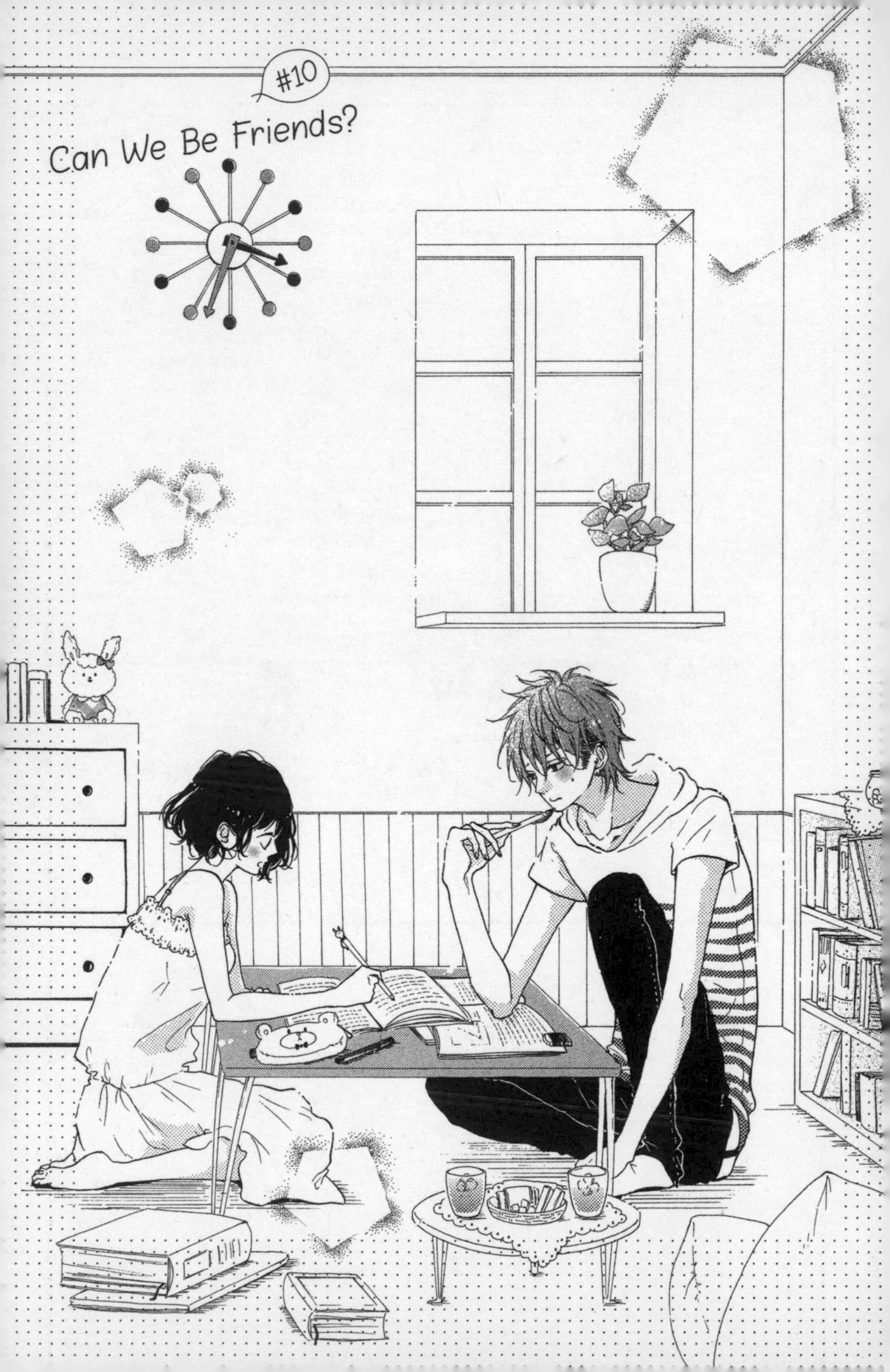
#10
Can We Be Friends?

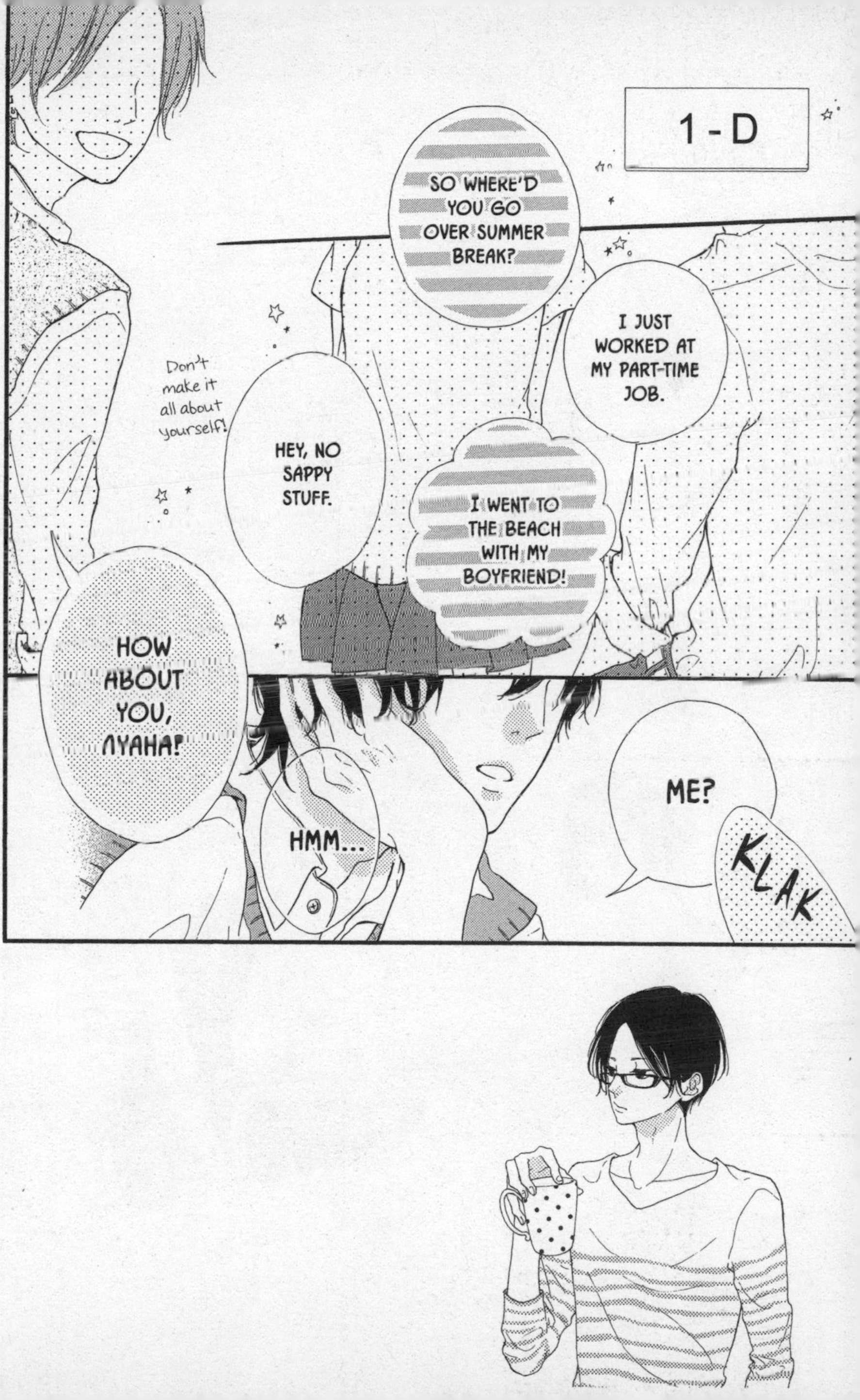
1 - D
SO WHERE'D YOU GO OVER SUMMER BREAK?
I JUST WORKED AT MY PART-TIME JOB.
I WENT TO THE BEACH WITH MY BOYFRIEND!
HEY, NO SAPPY STUFF.
Don't make it all about yourself!
HOW ABOUT YOU, AYAHA?
ME?
KLAK
HMM...

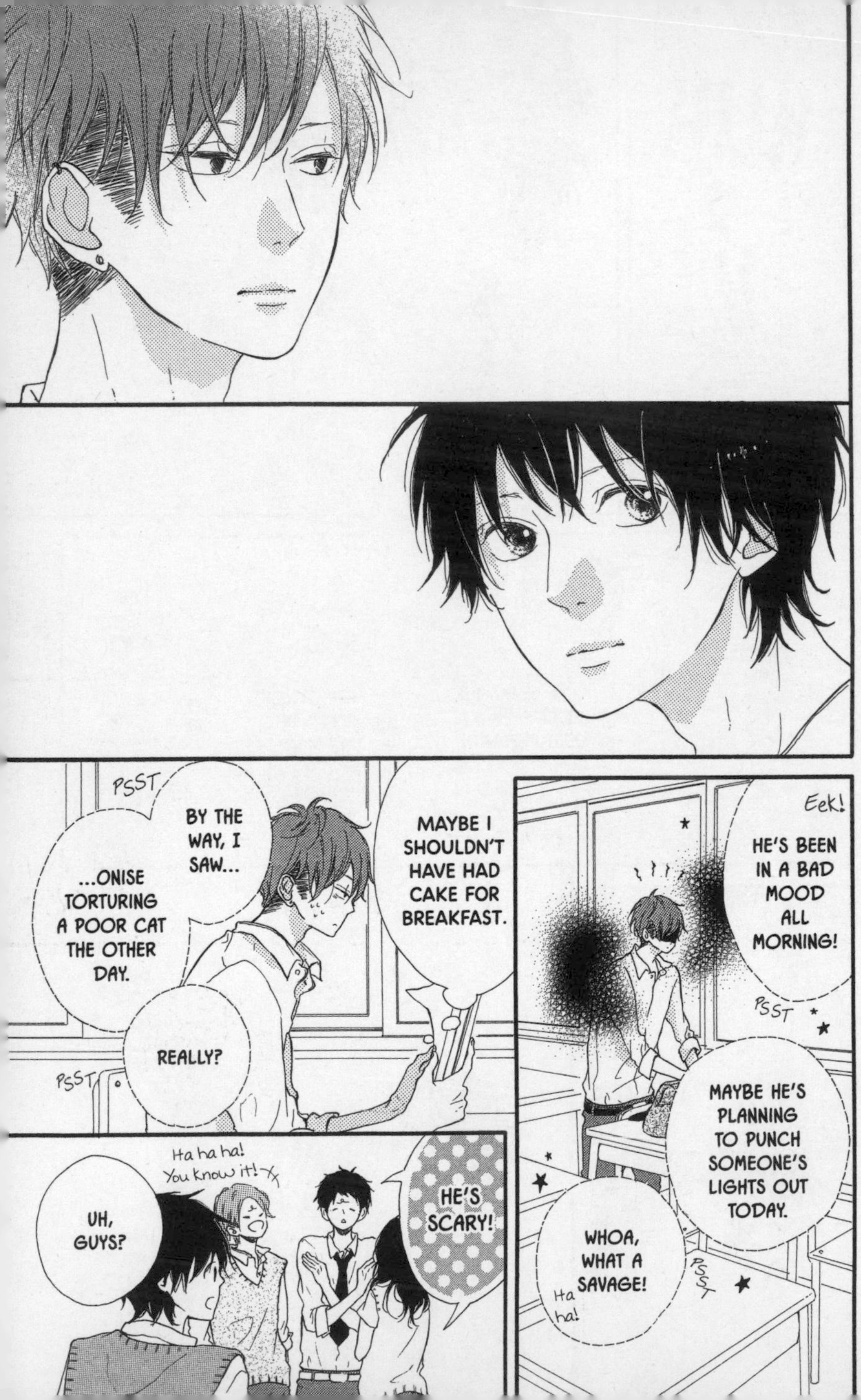
Eek!
HE'S BEEN IN A BAD MOOD ALL MORNING!
PSST
MAYBE HE'S PLANNING TO PUNCH SOMEONE'S LIGHTS OUT TODAY.
WHOA, WHAT A SAVAGE!
PSST
Ha ha!
MAYBE I SHOULDN'T HAVE HAD CAKE FOR BREAKFAST.
PSST
BY THE WAY, I SAW...
...ONISE TORTURING A POOR CAT THE OTHER DAY.
PSST
REALLY?
HE'S SCARY!
Ha ha ha! You know it!
UH, GUYS?

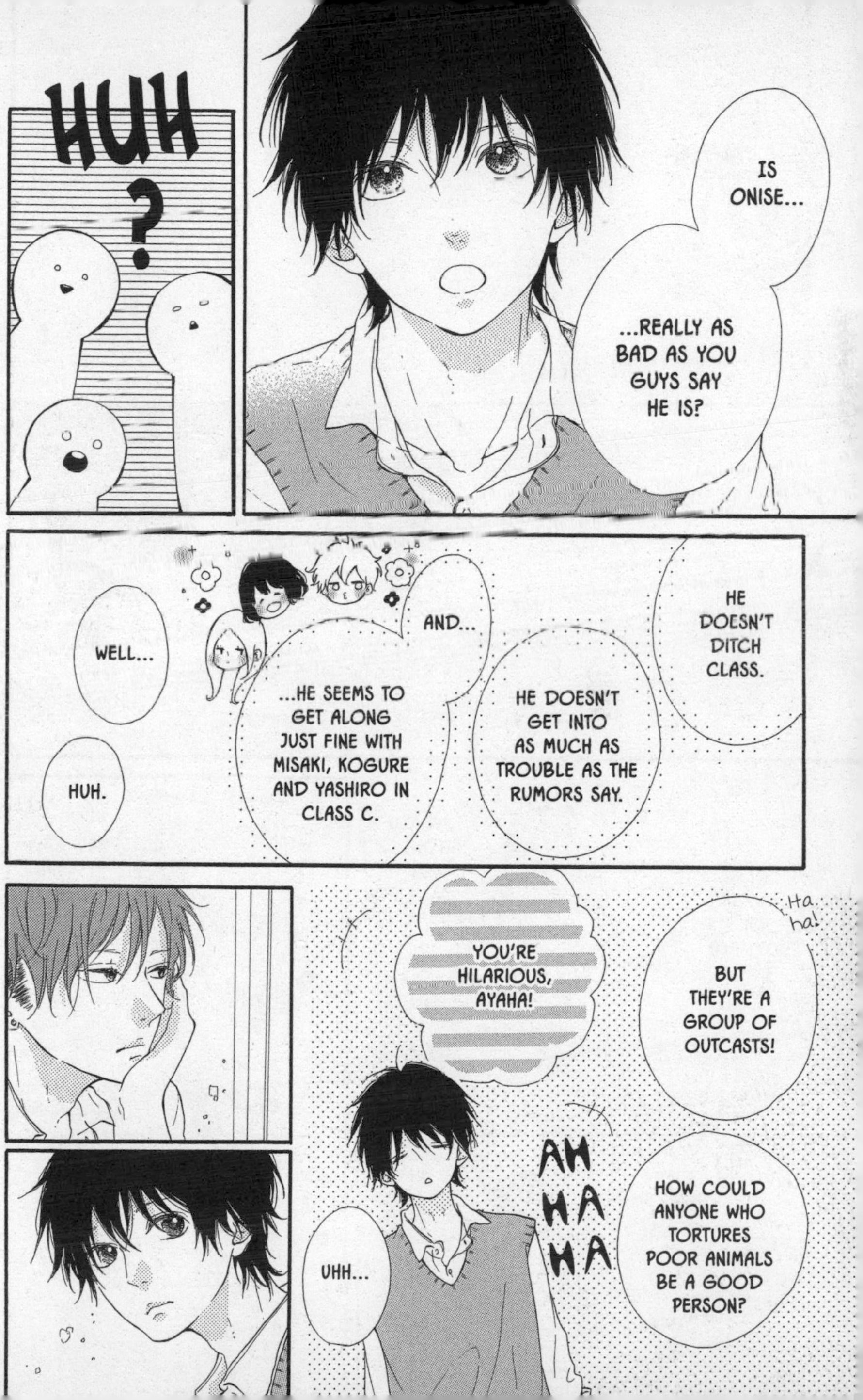
IS ONISE...
...REALLY AS BAD AS YOU GUYS SAY HE IS?
HUH ?
HE DOESN'T DITCH CLASS.
HE DOESN'T GET INTO AS MUCH AS TROUBLE AS THE RUMORS SAY.
AND...
...HE SEEMS TO GET ALONG JUST FINE WITH MISAKI, KOGURE AND YASHIRO IN CLASS C.
WELL...
HUH.
Ha ha!
BUT THEY'RE A GROUP OF OUTCASTS!
YOU'RE HILARIOUS, AYAHA!
HOW COULD ANYONE WHO TORTURES POOR ANIMALS BE A GOOD PERSON?
AH HA HA
UHH...

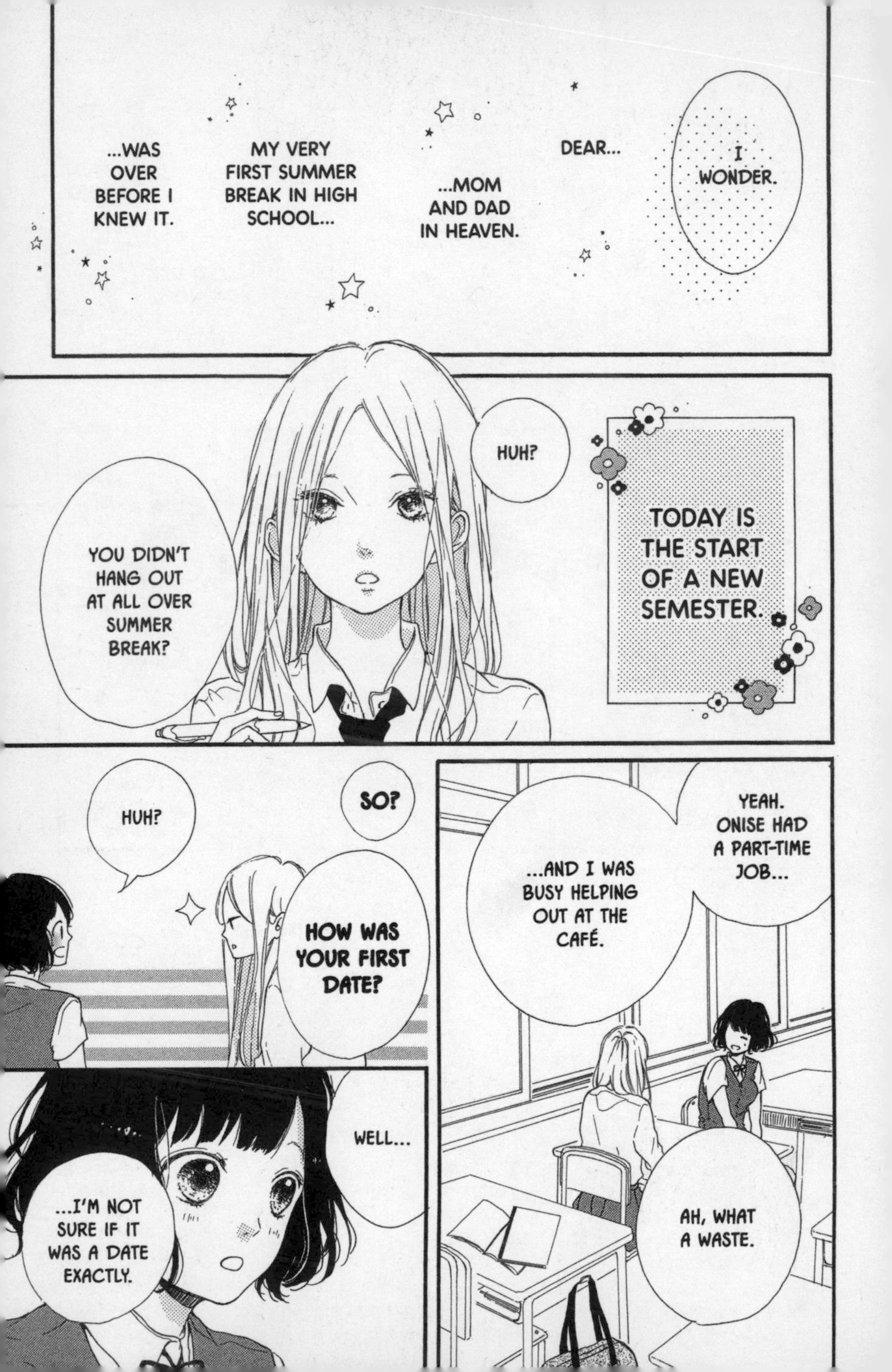
I WONDER.
DEAR...
...MOM AND DAD IN HEAVEN.
MY VERY FIRST SUMMER BREAK IN HIGH SCHOOL...
...WAS OVER BEFORE I KNEW IT.
TODAY IS THE START OF A NEW SEMESTER.
HUH?
YOU DIDN'T HANG OUT AT ALL OVER SUMMER BREAK?
YEAH. ONISE HAD A PART-TIME JOB...
...AND I WAS BUSY HELPING OUT AT THE CAFÉ.
AH, WHAT A WASTE.
SO?
HUH?
HOW WAS YOUR FIRST DATE?
WELL...
...I'M NOT SURE IF IT WAS A DATE EXACTLY.

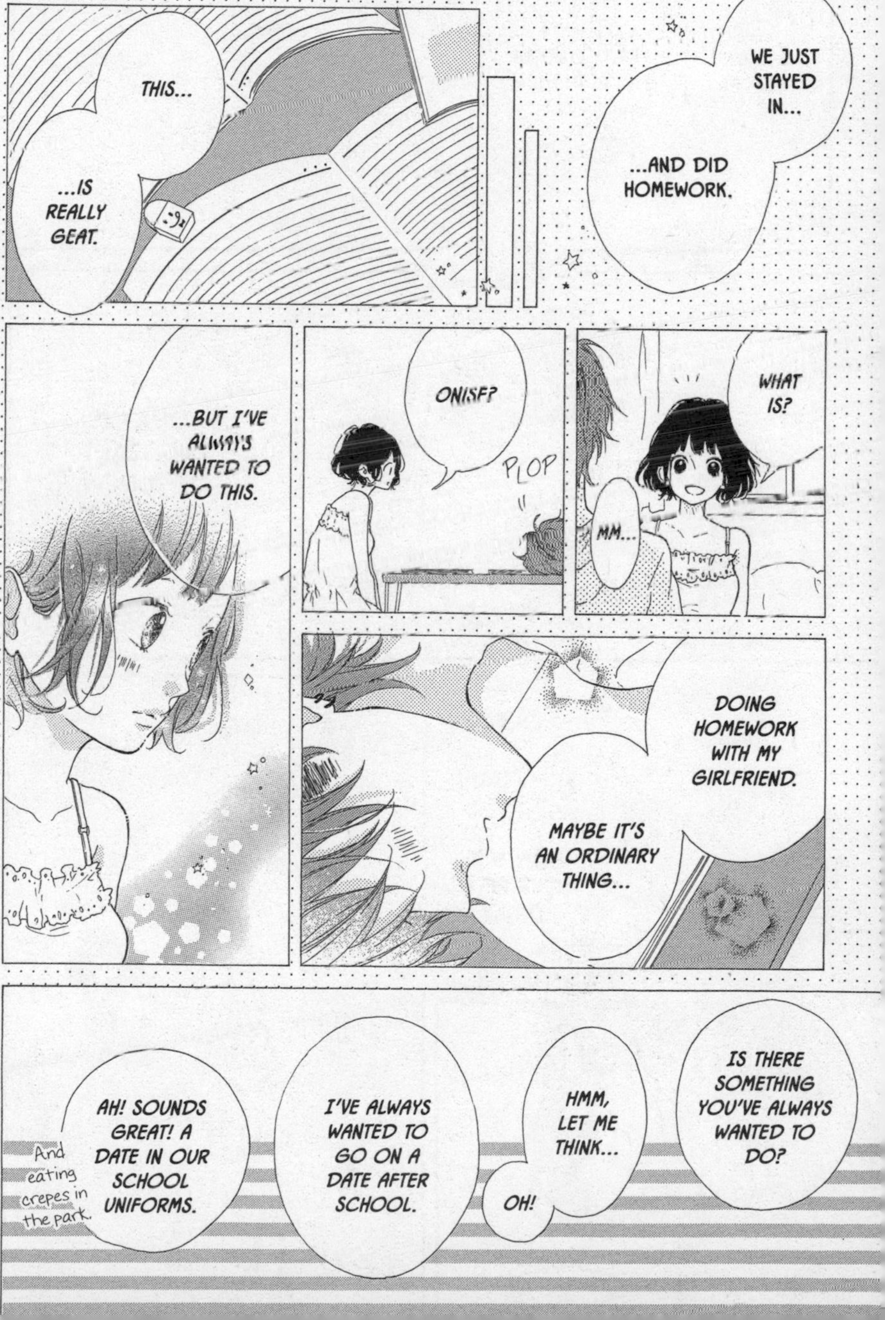
WE JUST STAYED IN...
...AND DID HOMEWORK.
THIS...
...IS REALLY GEAT.
WHAT IS?
MM...
ONISF?
PLOP
DOING HOMEWORK WITH MY GIRLFRIEND.
MAYBE IT'S AN ORDINARY THING...
...BUT I'VE ALWAYS WANTED TO DO THIS.
IS THERE SOMETHING YOU'VE ALWAYS WANTED TO DO?
HMM, LET ME THINK...
OH!
I'VE ALWAYS WANTED TO GO ON A DATE AFTER SCHOOL.
AH! SOUNDS GREAT! A DATE IN OUR SCHOOL UNIFORMS.
And eating crepes in the park.

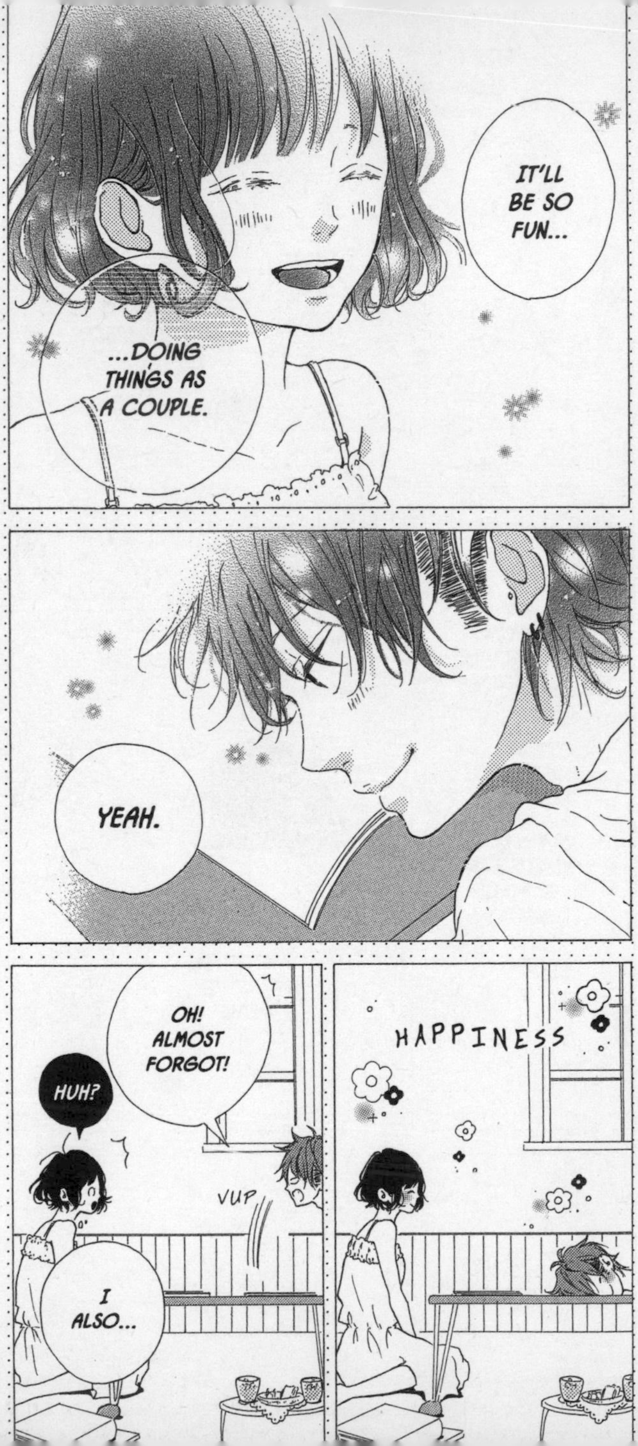
IT'LL BE SO FUN...
...DOING THINGS AS A COUPLE.
YEAH.
HAPPINESS
OH! ALMOST FORGOT!
HUH?
VUP
I ALSO...

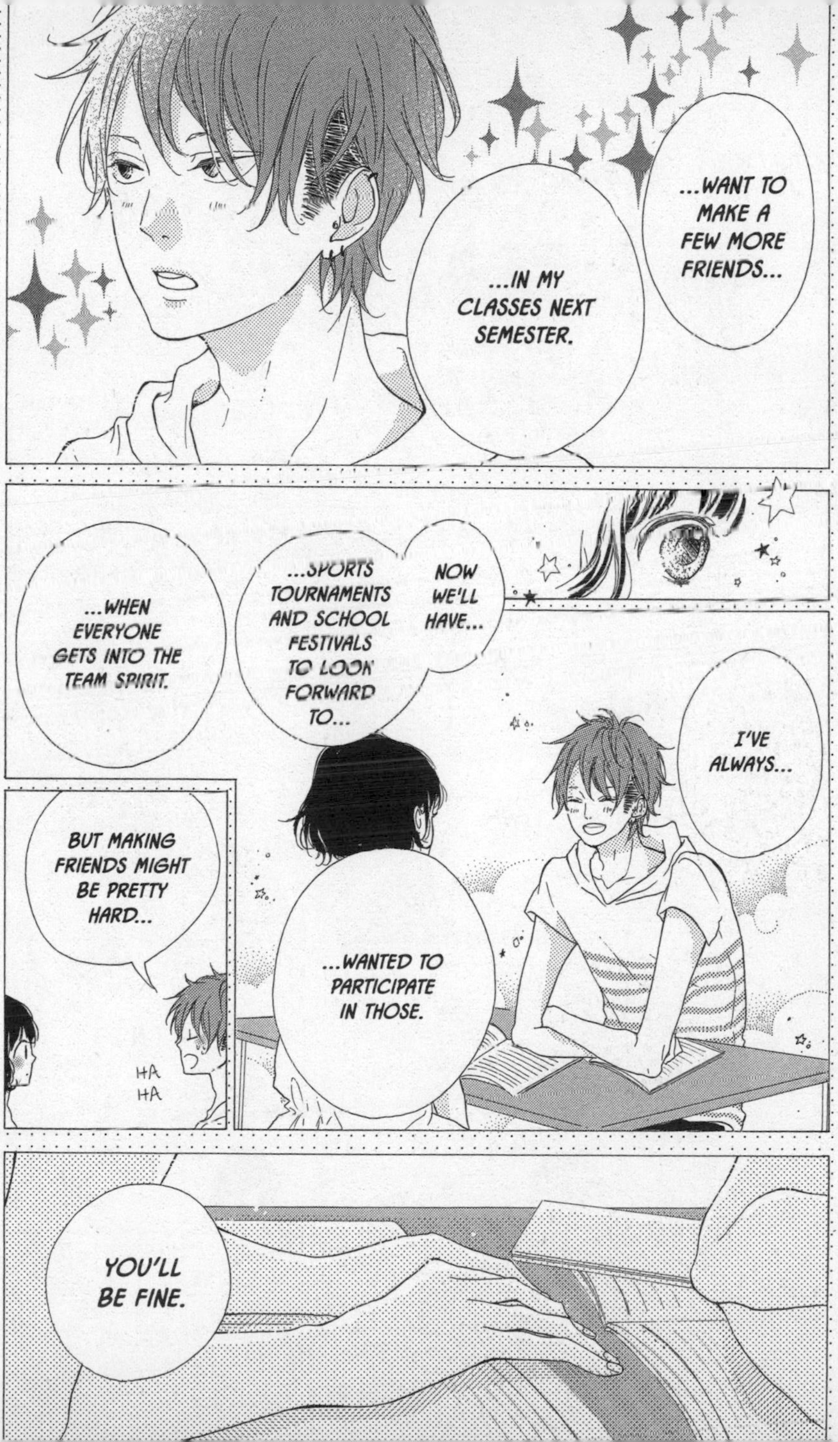
...WANT TO MAKE A FEW MORE FRIENDS...
...IN MY CLASSES NEXT SEMESTER.
NOW WE'LL HAVE...
...SPORTS TOURNAMENTS AND SCHOOL FESTIVALS TO LOOK FORWARD TO...
...WHEN EVERYONE GETS INTO THE TEAM SPIRIT.
I'VE ALWAYS...
...WANTED TO PARTICIPATE IN THOSE.
BUT MAKING FRIENDS MIGHT BE PRETTY HARD...
HA HA
YOU'LL BE FINE.

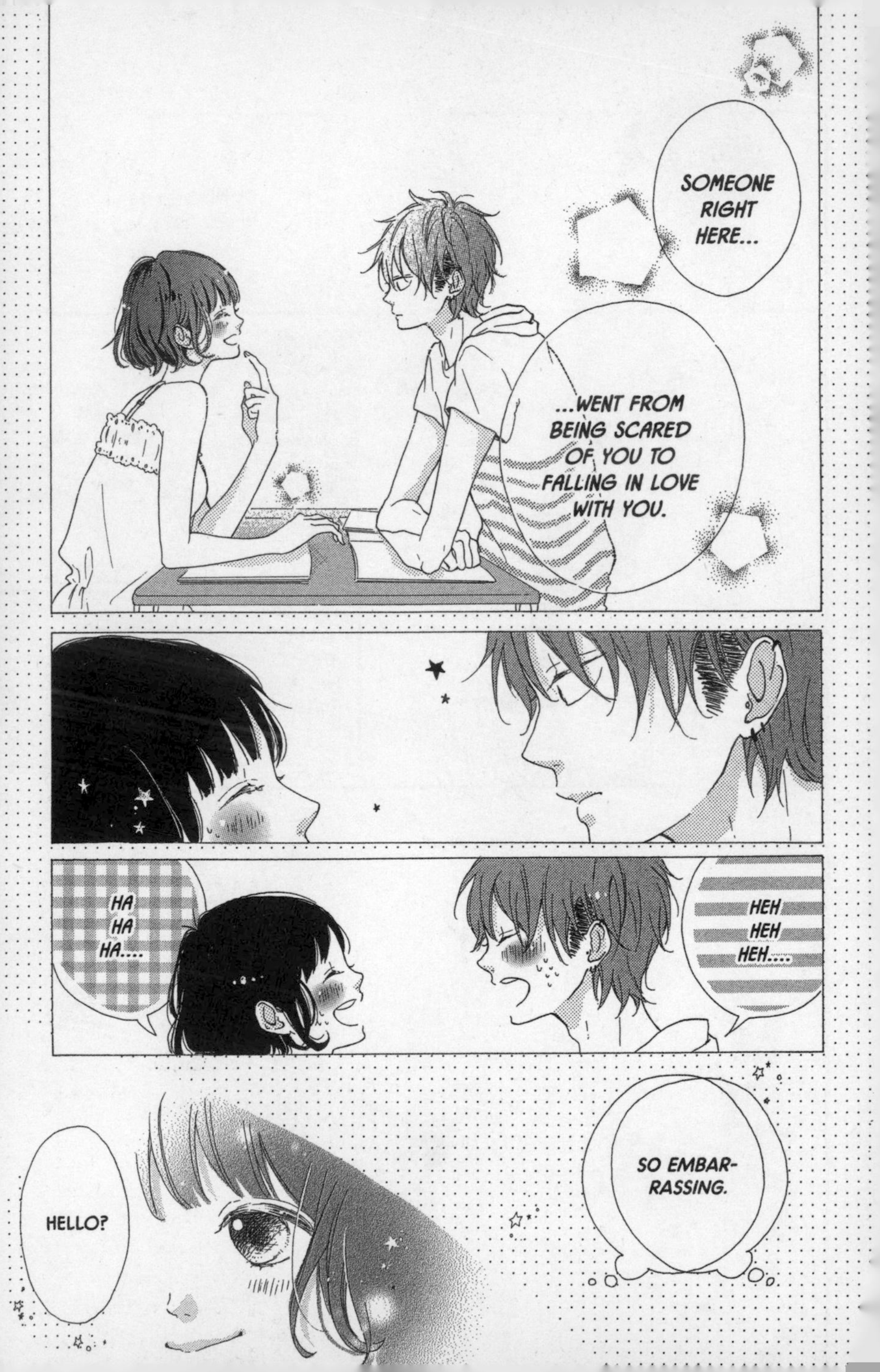
SOMEONE RIGHT HERE...
...WENT FROM BEING SCARED OF YOU TO FALLING IN LOVE WITH YOU.
HEH HEH HEH....
HA HA HA....
SO EMBAR-RASSING.
HELLO?

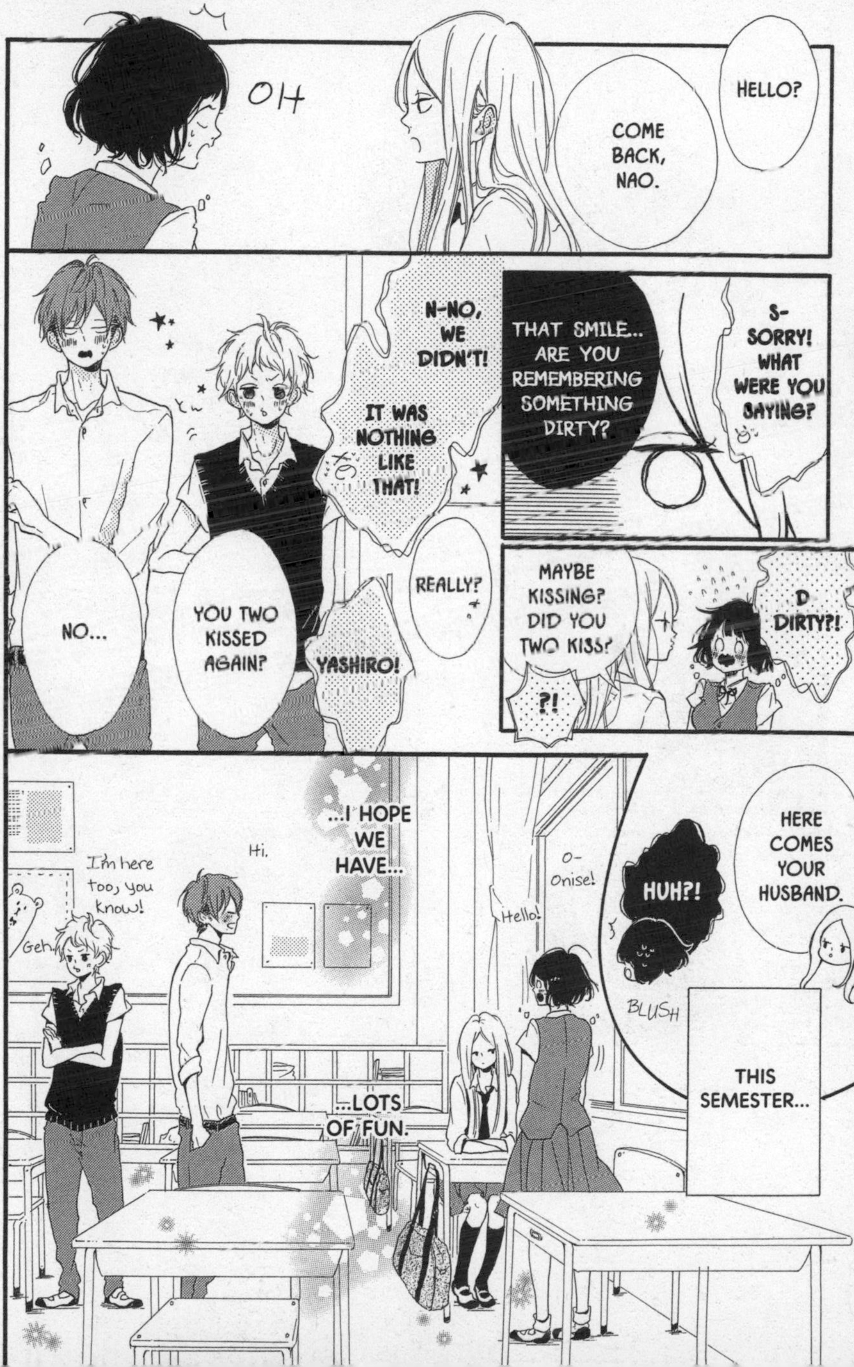
HELLO?
COME BACK, NAO.
OH
S-SORRY! WHAT WERE YOU SAYING?
THAT SMILE... ARE YOU REMEMBERING SOMETHING DIRTY?
D-DIRTY?!
MAYBE KISSING? DID YOU TWO KISS?
?!
N-NO, WE DIDN'T!
IT WAS NOTHING LIKE THAT!
REALLY?
YASHIRO!
YOU TWO KISSED AGAIN?
NO...
HERE COMES YOUR HUSBAND.
HUH?!
BLUSH
O-Onise!
Hello!
THIS SEMESTER...
...I HOPE WE HAVE...
...LOTS OF FUN.
Hi.
I'm here too, you know!
Geh.

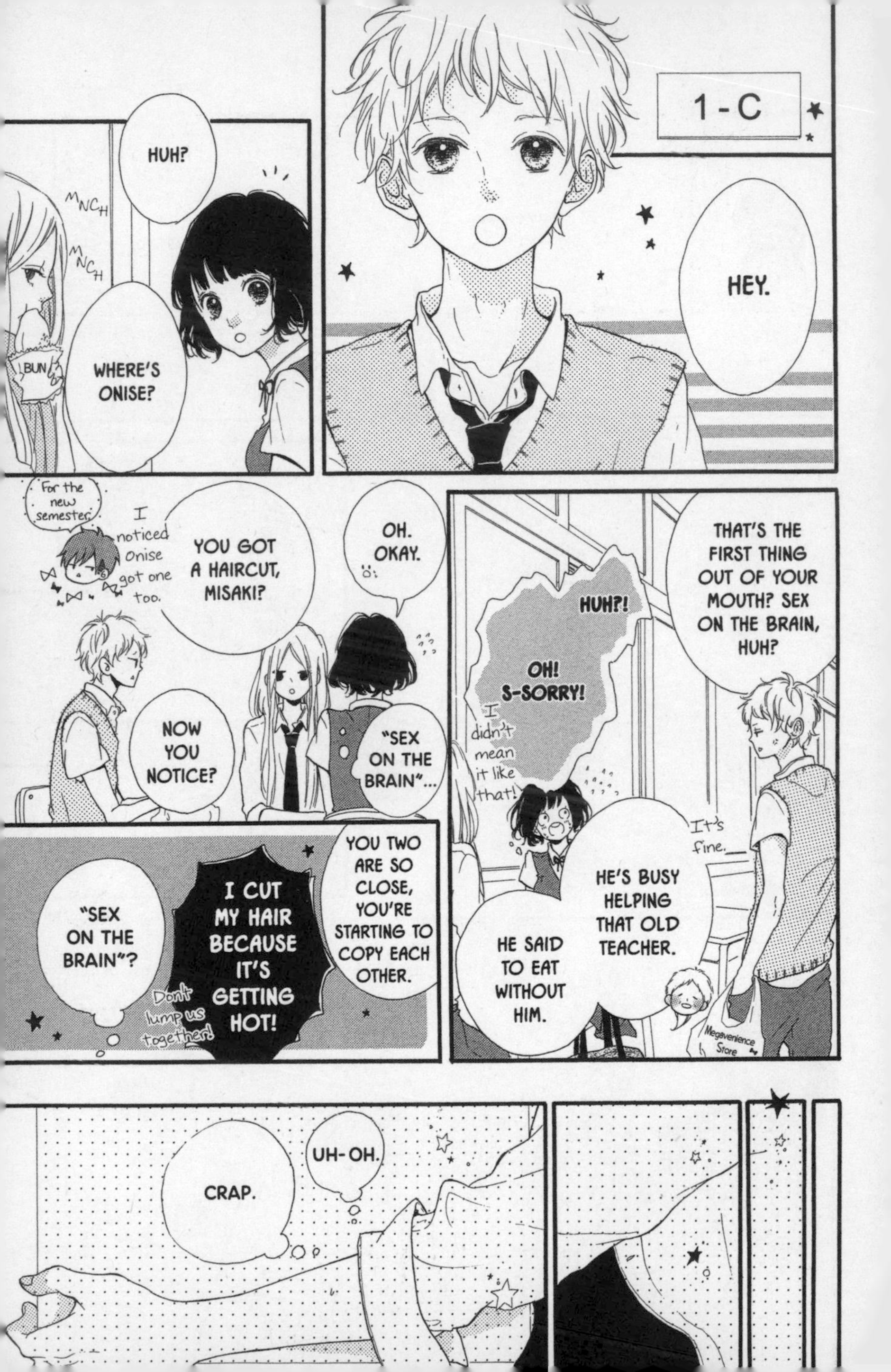
1 - C
HEY.
HUH?
MNCH
MNCH
WHERE'S ONISE?
BUN
THAT'S THE FIRST THING OUT OF YOUR MOUTH? SEX ON THE BRAIN, HUH?
HUH?!
OH! S-SORRY!
I didn't mean it like that!
It's fine.
HE'S BUSY HELPING THAT OLD TEACHER.
HE SAID TO EAT WITHOUT HIM.
Megavenience Store
OH. OKAY.
YOU GOT A HAIRCUT, MISAKI?
For the new semester
I noticed Onise got one too.
"SEX ON THE BRAIN"...
NOW YOU NOTICE?
YOU TWO ARE SO CLOSE, YOU'RE STARTING TO COPY EACH OTHER.
I CUT MY HAIR BECAUSE IT'S GETTING HOT!
Don't lump us together!
"SEX ON THE BRAIN"?
UH-OH.
CRAP.

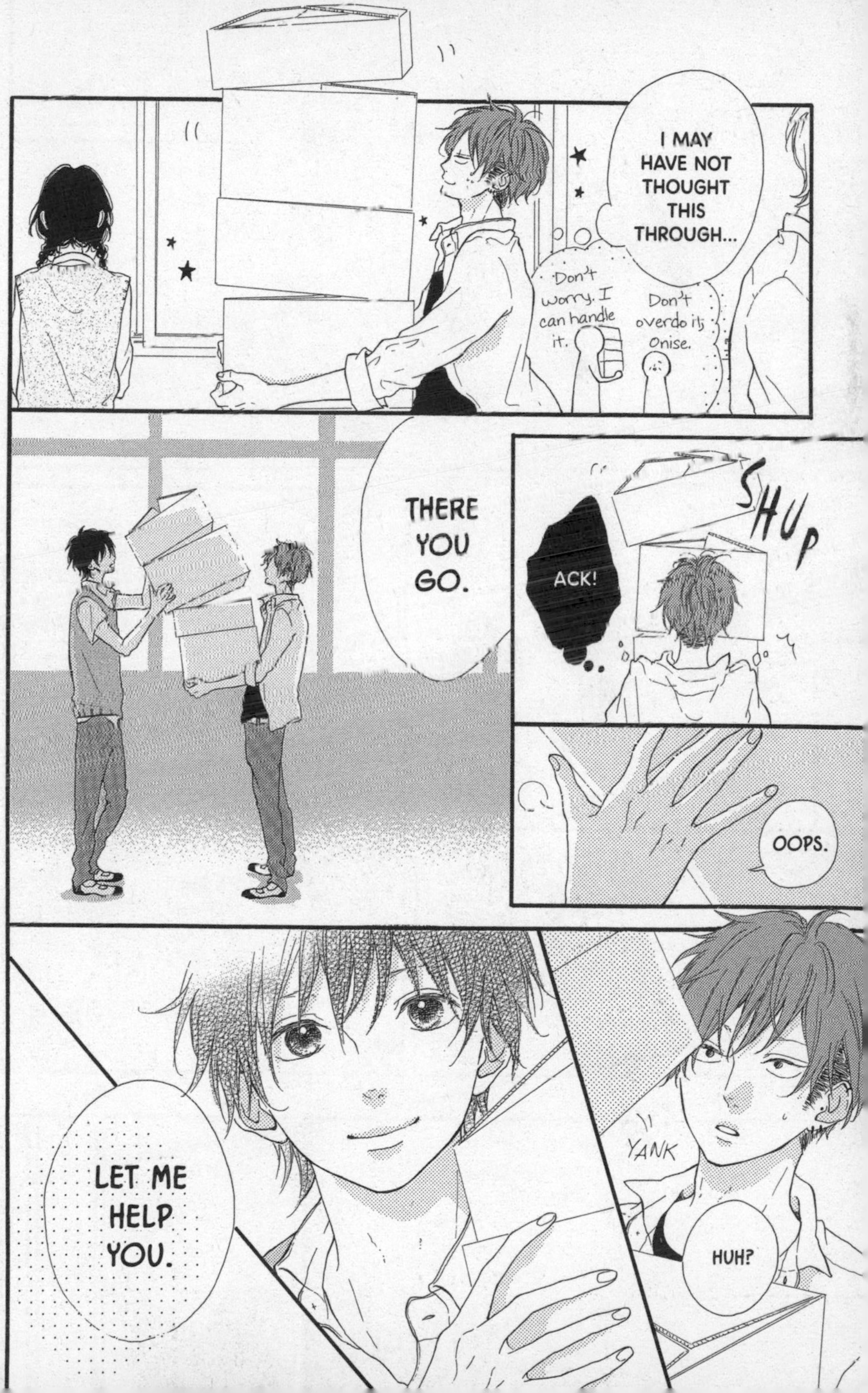
I MAY HAVE NOT THOUGHT THIS THROUGH...
Don't overdo it, Onise.
Don't worry. I can handle it.
SHUP
ACK!
OOPS.
THERE YOU GO.
HUH?
YANK
LET ME HELP YOU.

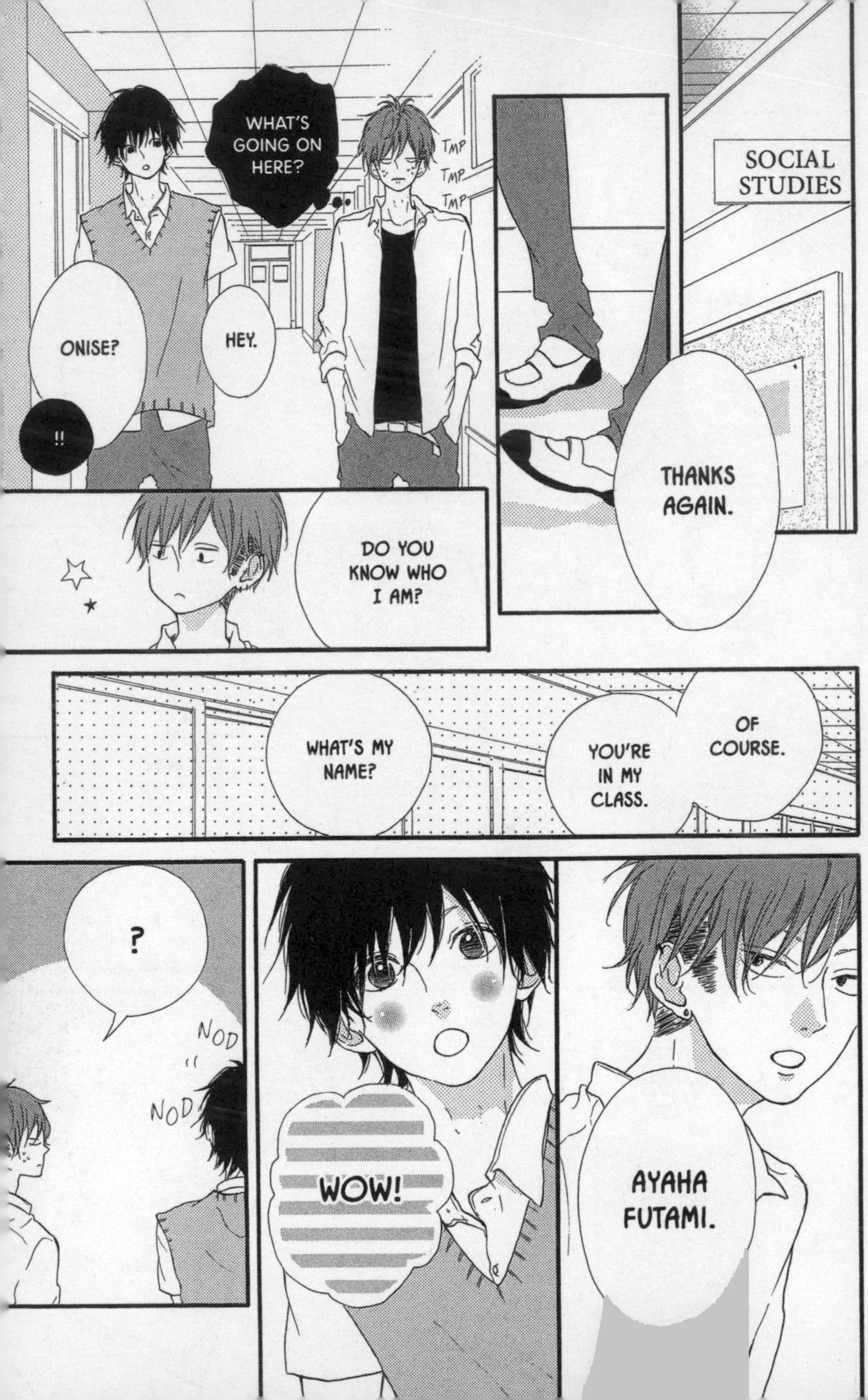
SOCIAL STUDIES
THANKS AGAIN.
TMP TMP TMP
WHAT'S GOING ON HERE?
HEY.
ONISE?
!!
DO YOU KNOW WHO I AM?
OF COURSE.
YOU'RE IN MY CLASS.
WHAT'S MY NAME?
AYAHA FUTAMI.
WOW!
?
NOD
NOD

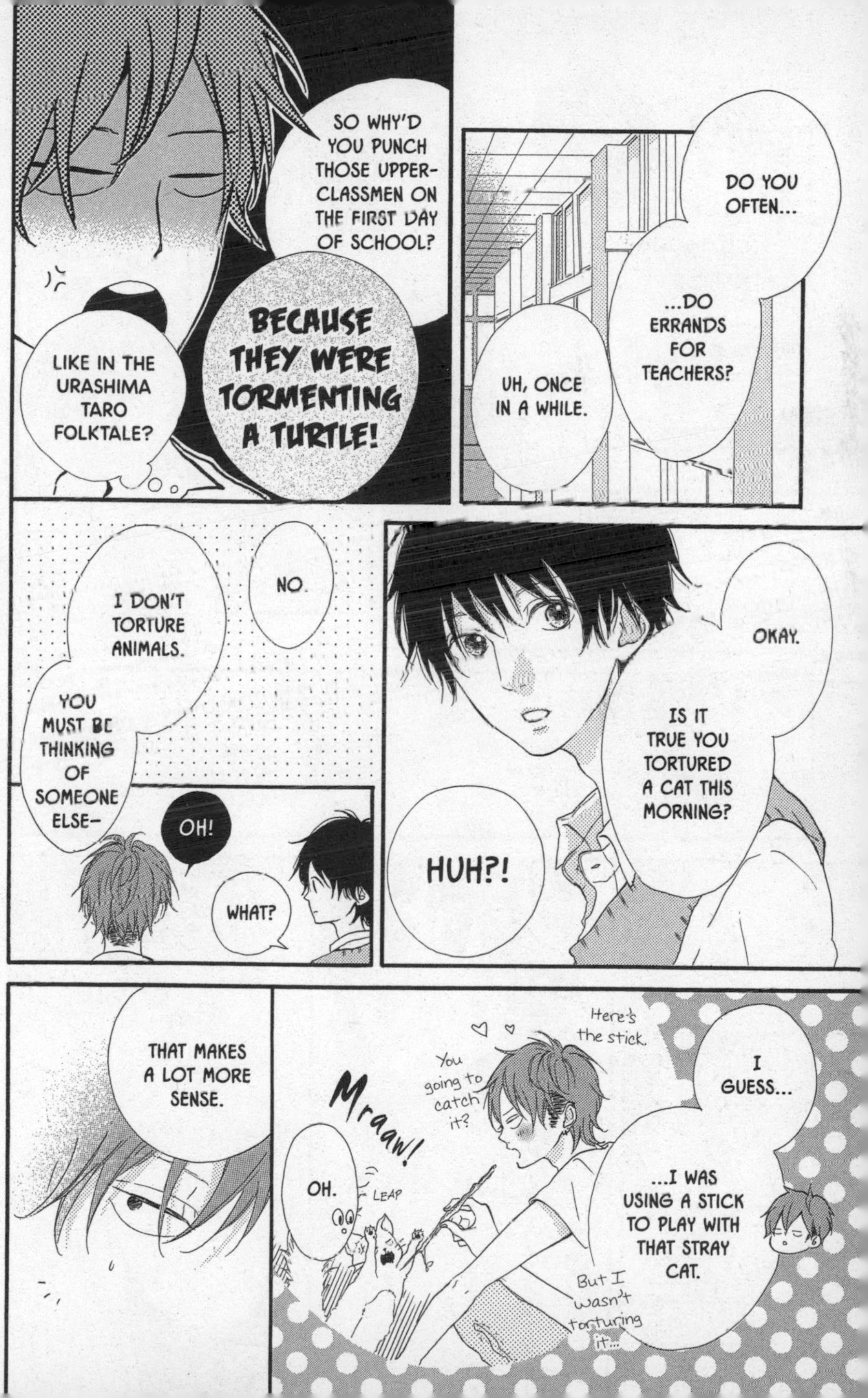
DO YOU OFTEN...
...DO ERRANDS FOR TEACHERS?
UH, ONCE IN A WHILE.
SO WHY'D YOU PUNCH THOSE UPPER-CLASSMEN ON THE FIRST DAY OF SCHOOL?
BECAUSE THEY WERE TORMENTING A TURTLE!
LIKE IN THE URASHIMA TARO FOLKTALE?
OKAY.
IS IT TRUE YOU TORTURED A CAT THIS MORNING?
HUH?!
NO.
I DON'T TORTURE ANIMALS.
YOU MUST BE THINKING OF SOMEONE ELSE-
OH!
WHAT?
I GUESS...
...I WAS USING A STICK TO PLAY WITH THAT STRAY CAT.
Here's the stick.
You going to catch it?
Mraaw!
LEAP
OH.
But I wasn't torturing it...
THAT MAKES A LOT MORE SENSE.

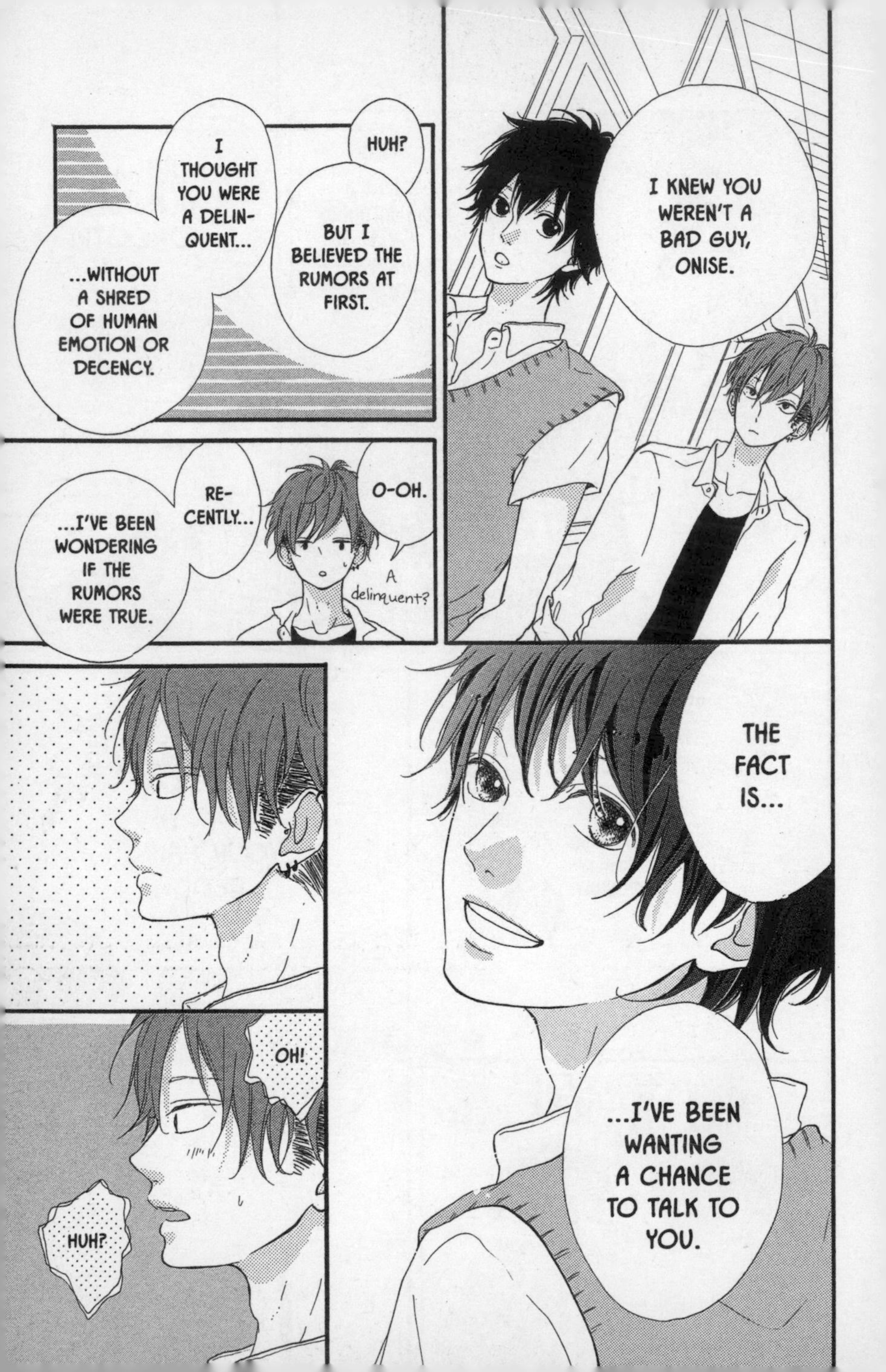
I KNEW YOU WEREN'T A BAD GUY, ONISE.
HUH?
BUT I BELIEVED THE RUMORS AT FIRST.
I THOUGHT YOU WERE A DELINQUENT...
...WITHOUT A SHRED OF HUMAN EMOTION OR DECENCY.
O-OH.
A delinquent?
RECENTLY...
...I'VE BEEN WONDERING IF THE RUMORS WERE TRUE.
THE FACT IS...
...I'VE BEEN WANTING A CHANCE TO TALK TO YOU.
OH!
HUH?

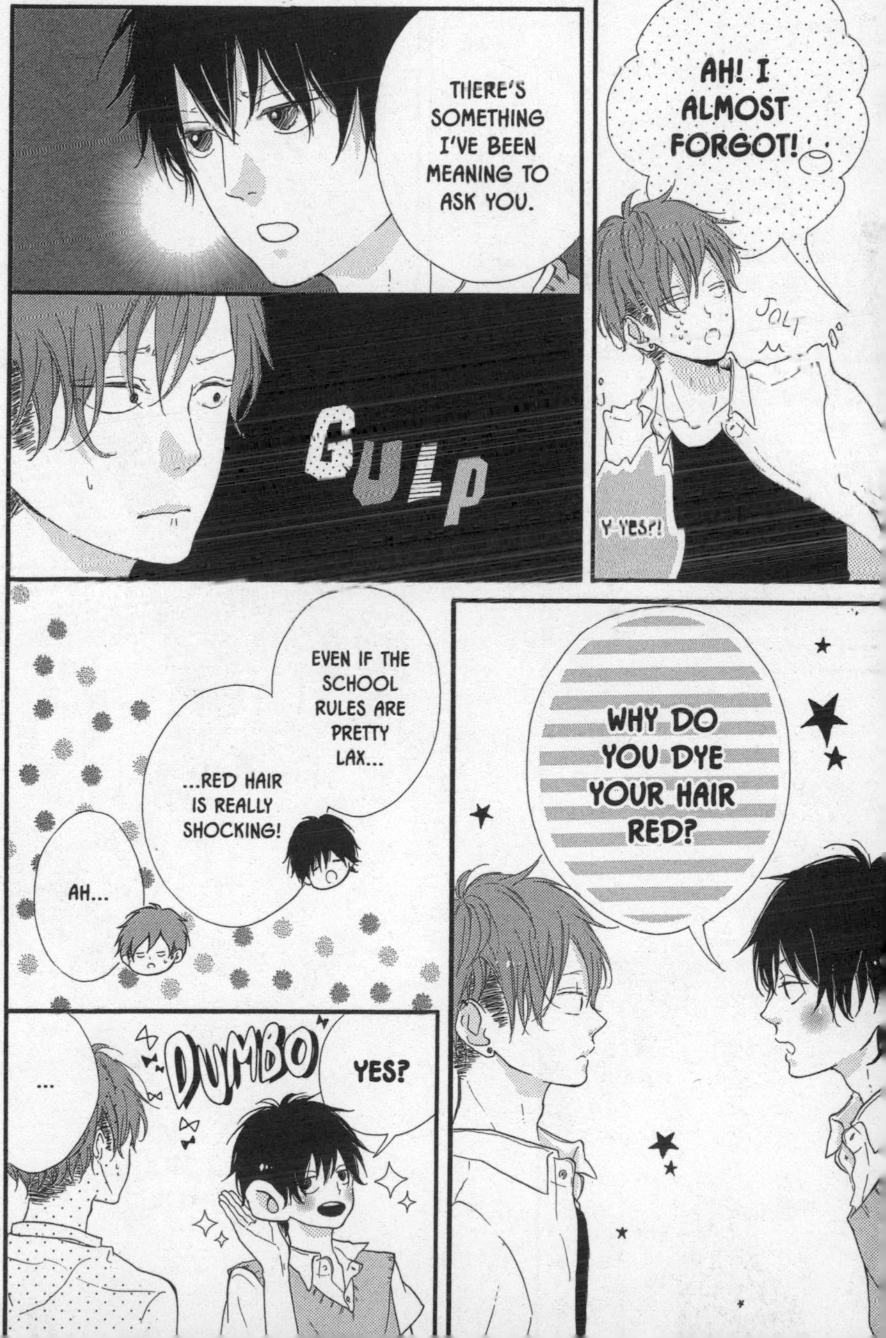
AH! I ALMOST FORGOT!
JOLT
Y-YES?!
THERE'S SOMETHING I'VE BEEN MEANING TO ASK YOU.
GULP
WHY DO YOU DYE YOUR HAIR RED?
EVEN IF THE SCHOOL RULES ARE PRETTY LAX...
...RED HAIR IS REALLY SHOCKING!
AH...
YES?
DUMBO
...

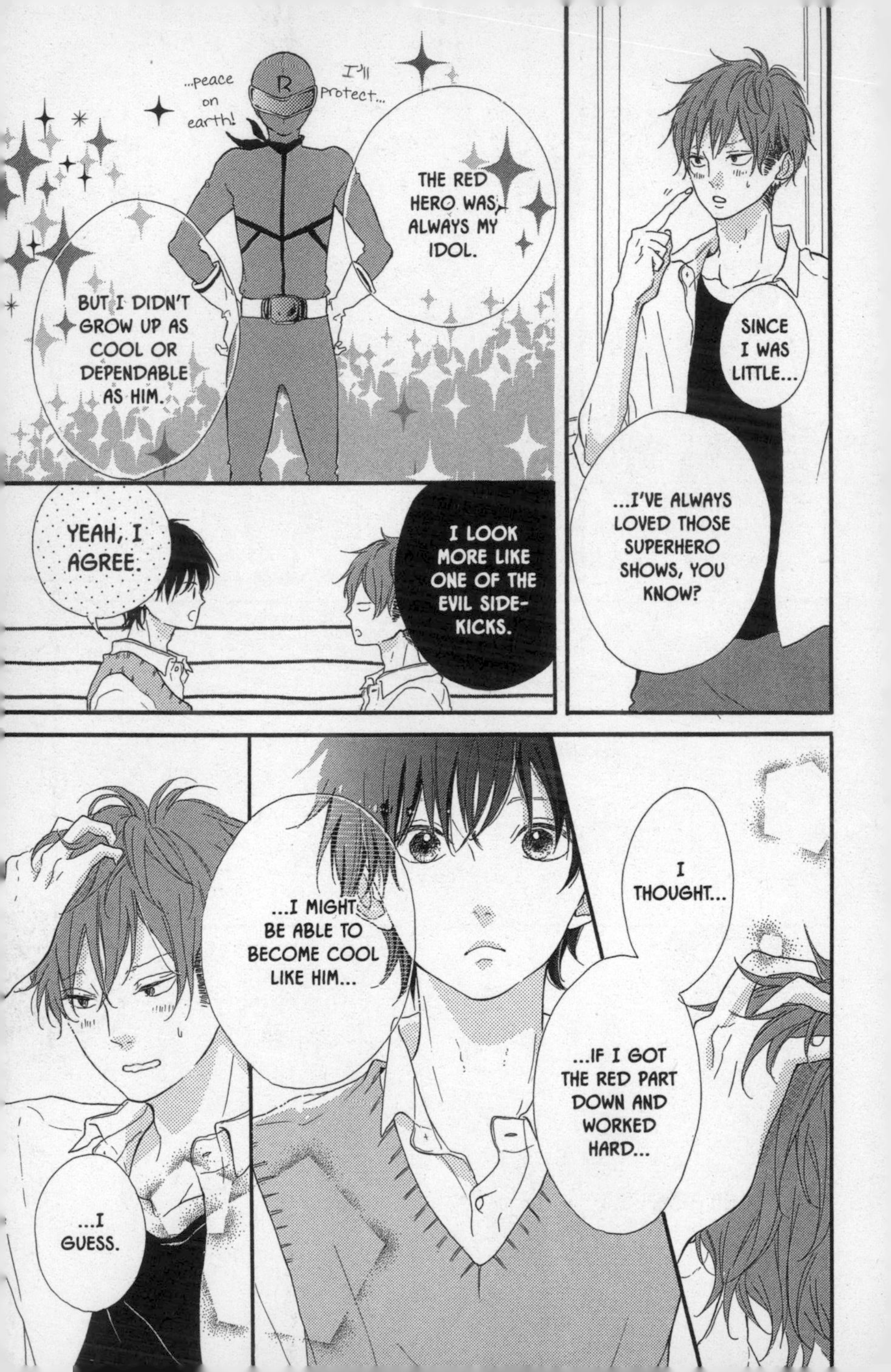
SINCE I WAS LITTLE...
...I'VE ALWAYS LOVED THOSE SUPERHERO SHOWS, YOU KNOW?
I'll protect...
...peace on earth!
THE RED HERO WAS ALWAYS MY IDOL.
BUT I DIDN'T GROW UP AS COOL OR DEPENDABLE AS HIM.
I LOOK MORE LIKE ONE OF THE EVIL SIDE-KICKS.
YEAH, I AGREE.
I THOUGHT...
...IF I GOT THE RED PART DOWN AND WORKED HARD...
...I MIGHT BE ABLE TO BECOME COOL LIKE HIM...
...I GUESS.

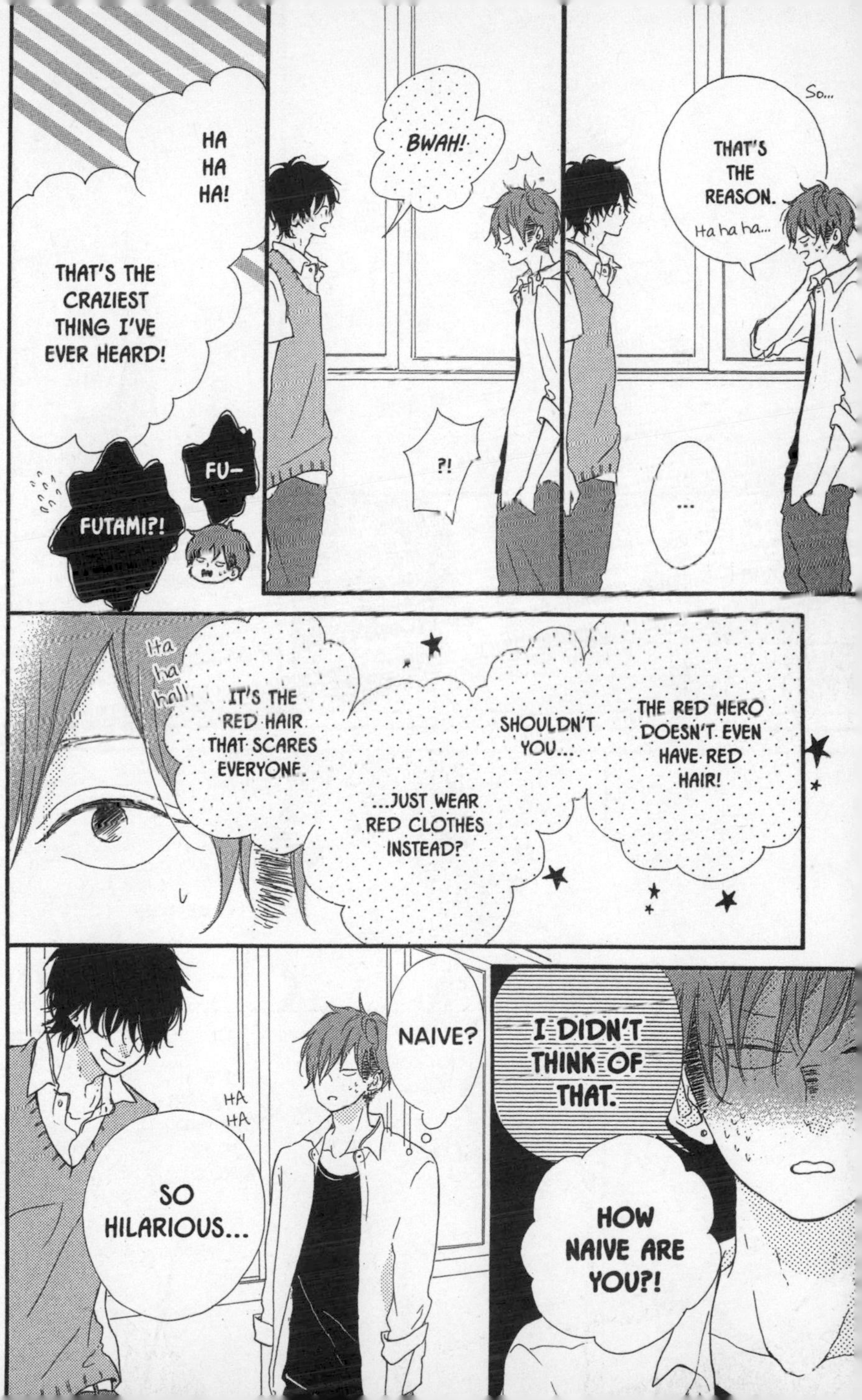
So...
THAT'S THE REASON.
Ha ha ha...
...
BWAH!
?!
HA HA HA!
THAT'S THE CRAZIEST THING I'VE EVER HEARD!
FU—
FUTAMI?!
THE RED HERO DOESN'T EVEN HAVE RED HAIR!
SHOULDN'T YOU...
...JUST WEAR RED CLOTHES INSTEAD?
IT'S THE RED HAIR THAT SCARES EVERYONE.
Ha ha ha!!
I DIDN'T THINK OF THAT.
HOW NAIVE ARE YOU?!
NAIVE?
HA HA
SO HILARIOUS...

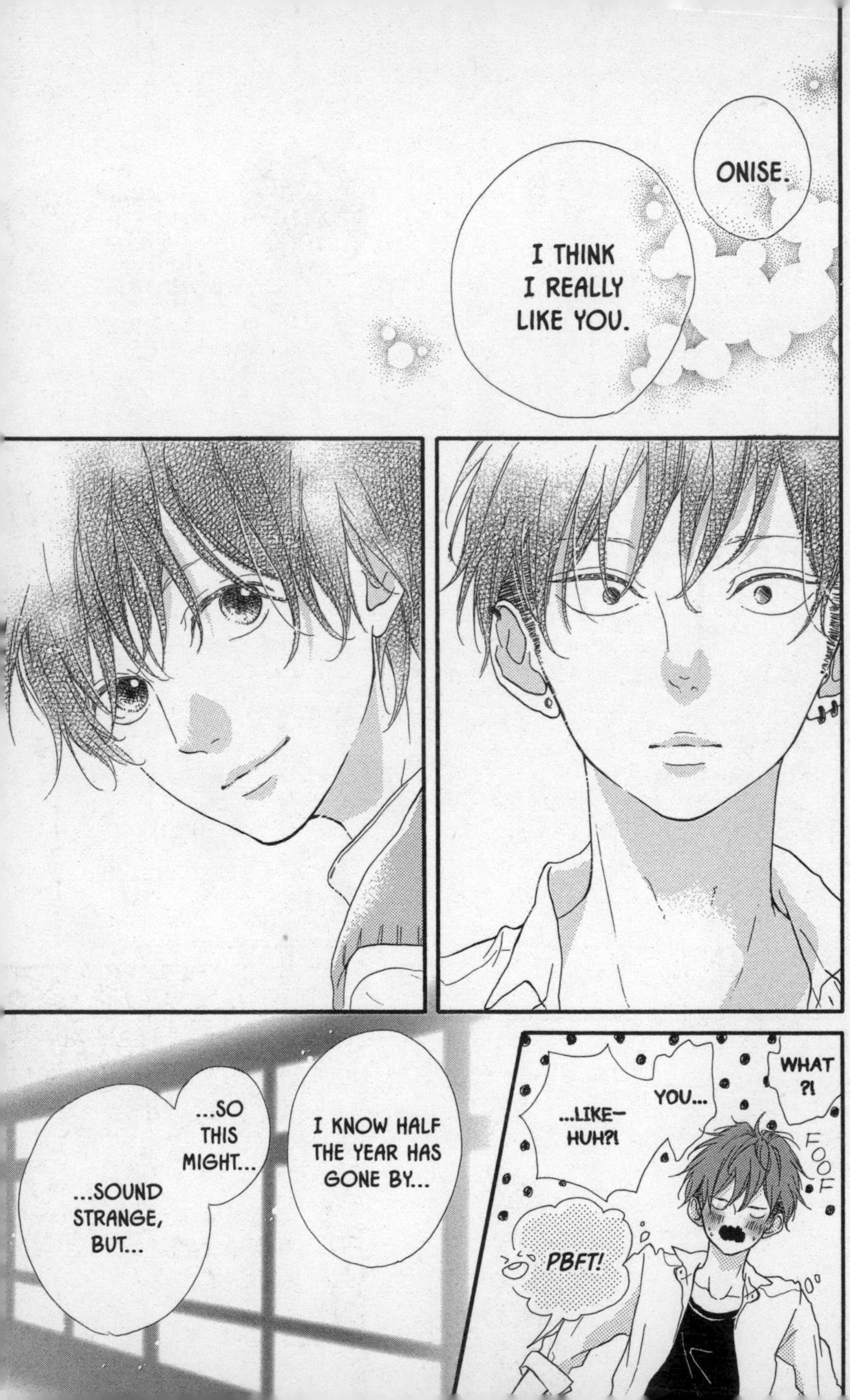
ONISE.
I THINK I REALLY LIKE YOU.
WHAT ?!
YOU...
...LIKE—HUH?!
FOOF
PBFT!
I KNOW HALF THE YEAR HAS GONE BY...
...SO THIS MIGHT...
...SOUND STRANGE, BUT...

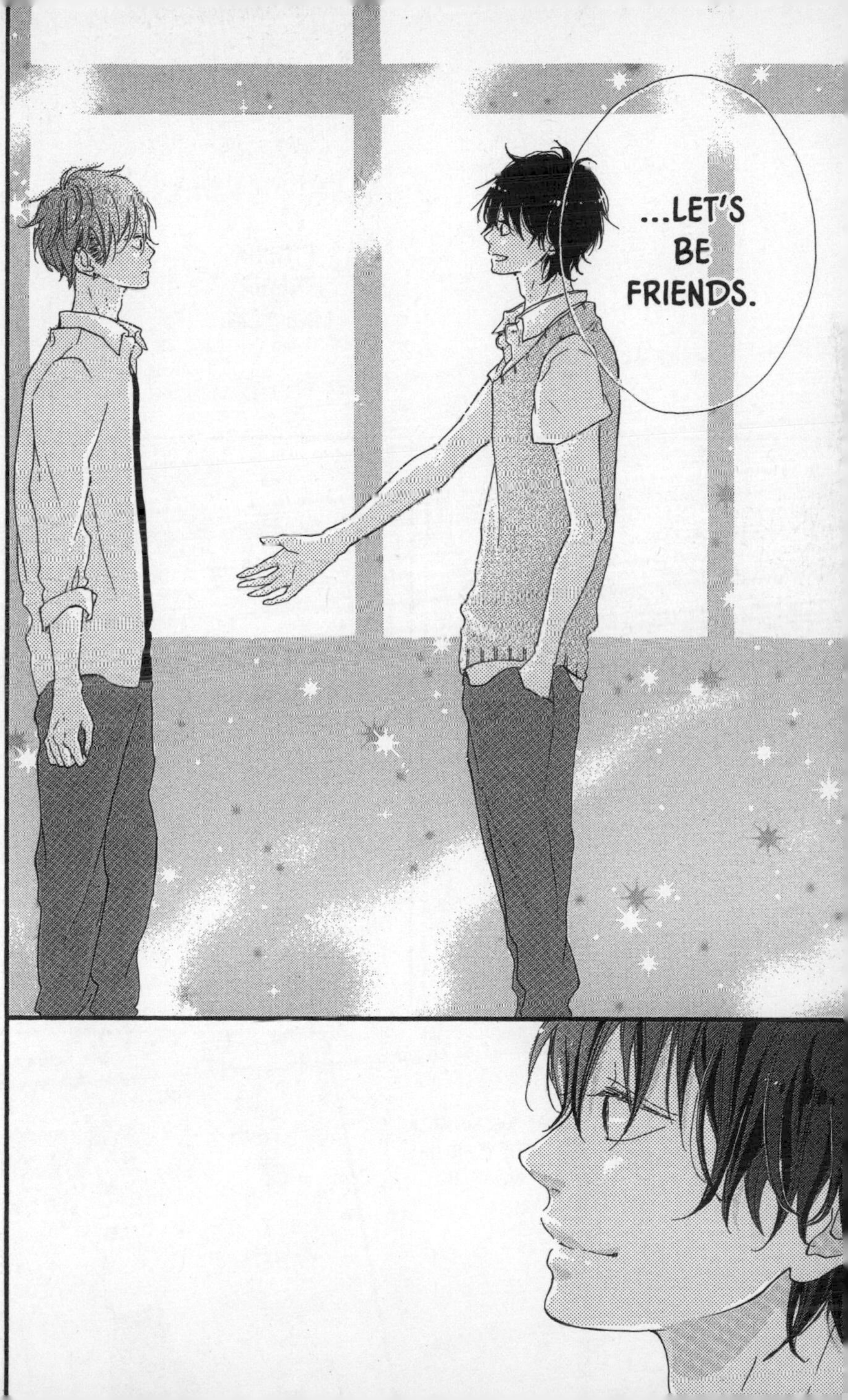
...LET'S BE FRIENDS.

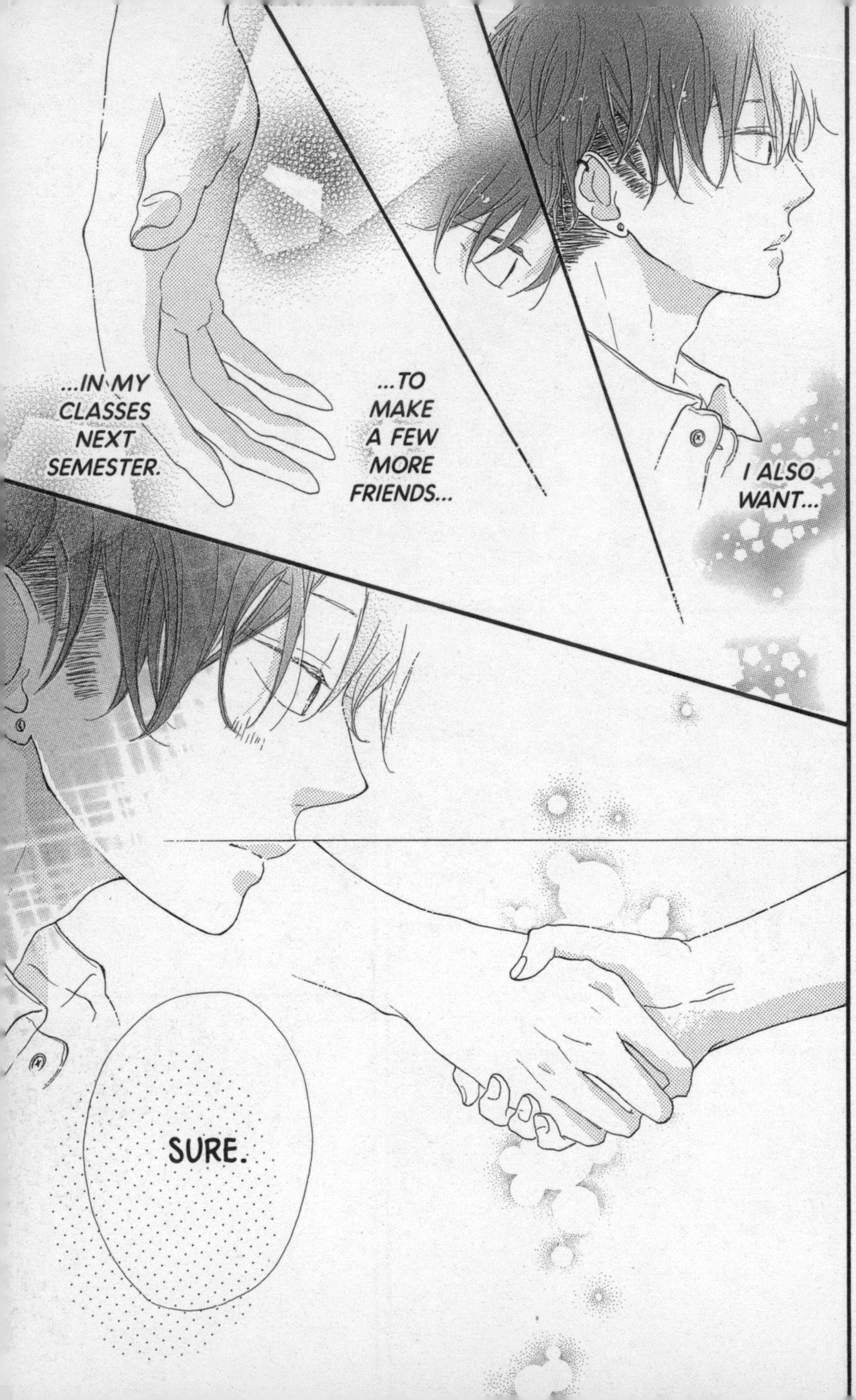
I ALSO WANT...
...TO MAKE A FEW MORE FRIENDS...
...IN MY CLASSES NEXT SEMESTER.
SURE.

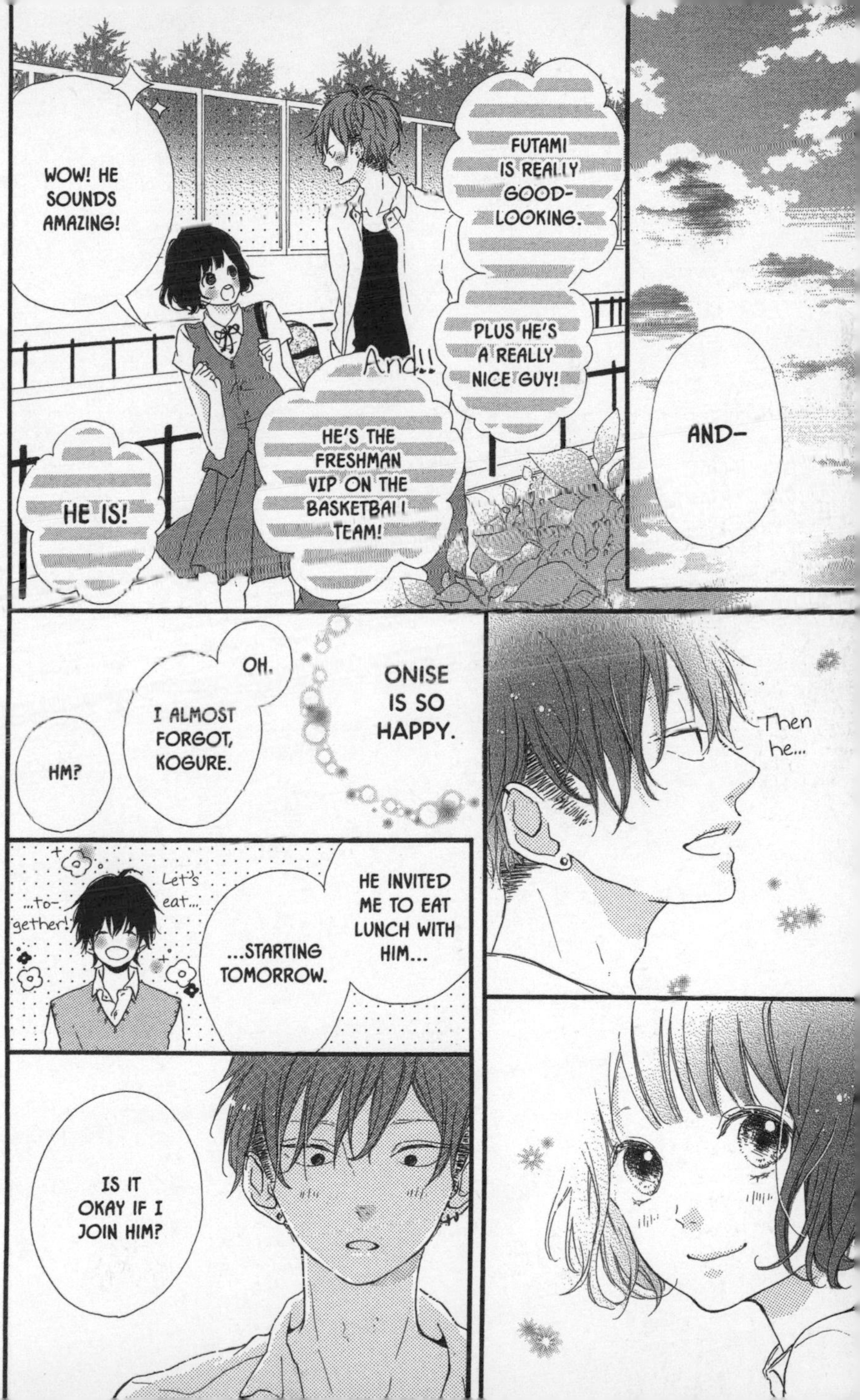
AND-
FUTAMI IS REALLY GOOD-LOOKING.
PLUS HE'S A REALLY NICE GUY!
WOW! HE SOUNDS AMAZING!
And!!
HE'S THE FRESHMAN VIP ON THE BASKETBALL TEAM!
HE IS!
Then he...
ONISE IS SO HAPPY.
OH.
I ALMOST FORGOT, KOGURE.
HM?
HE INVITED ME TO EAT LUNCH WITH HIM...
...STARTING TOMORROW.
Let's eat...
...to-gether!
IS IT OKAY IF I JOIN HIM?

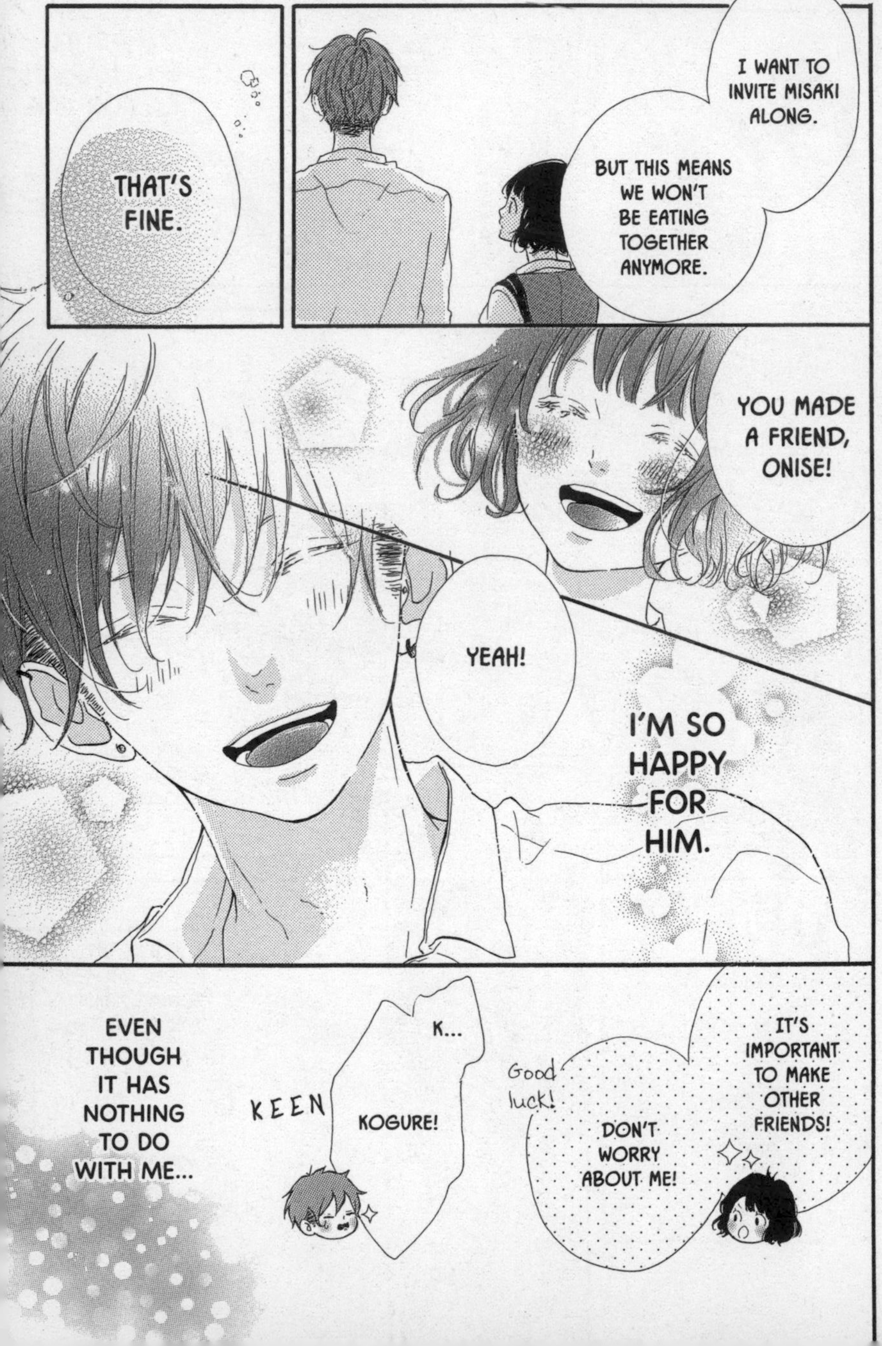
I WANT TO INVITE MISAKI ALONG.
BUT THIS MEANS WE WON'T BE EATING TOGETHER ANYMORE.
THAT'S FINE.
YOU MADE A FRIEND, ONISE!
YEAH!
I'M SO HAPPY FOR HIM.
IT'S IMPORTANT TO MAKE OTHER FRIENDS!
DON'T WORRY ABOUT ME!
Good luck!
K... KOGURE!
KEEN
EVEN THOUGH IT HAS NOTHING TO DO WITH ME...

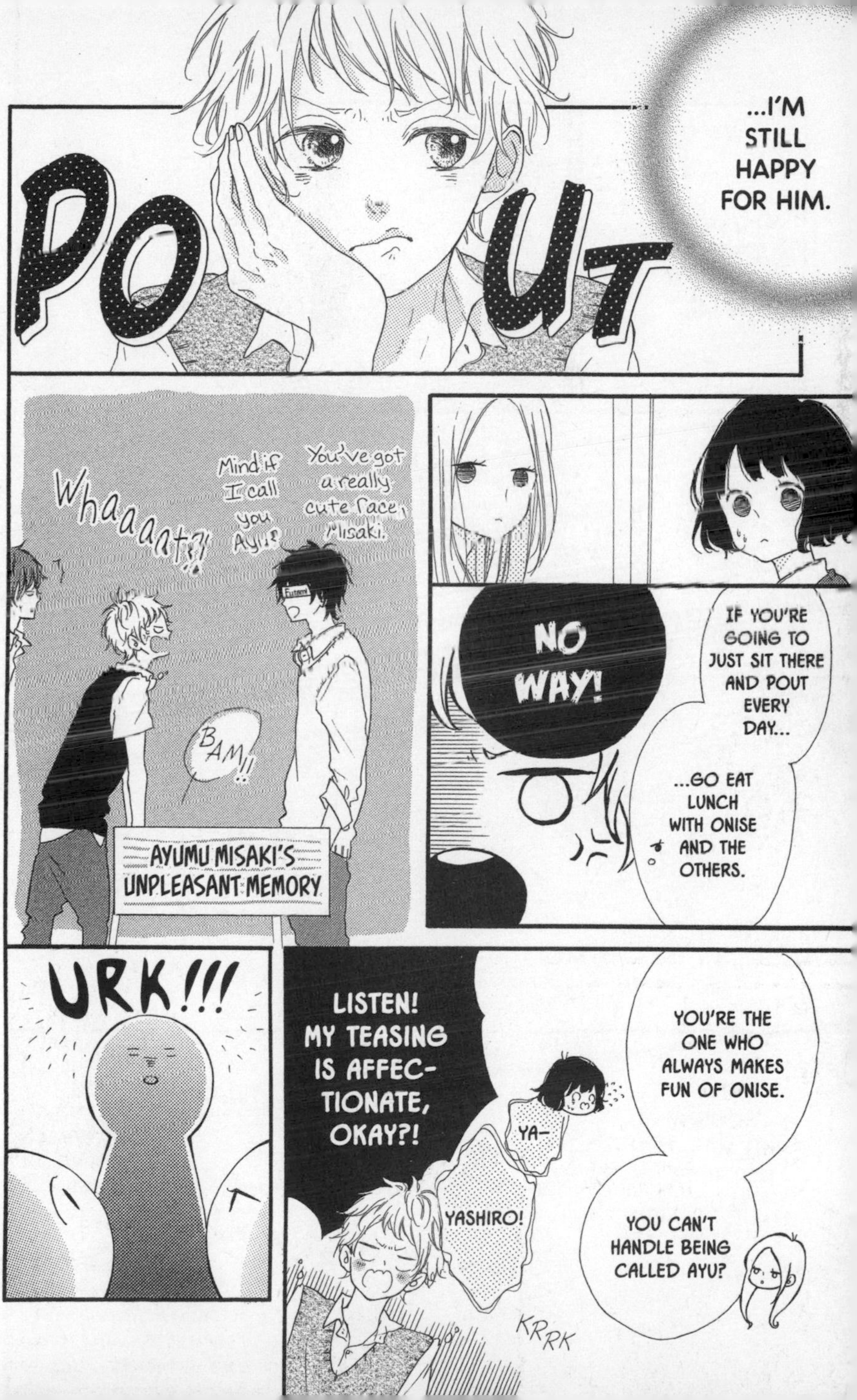
...I'M STILL HAPPY FOR HIM.
POUT
IF YOU'RE GOING TO JUST SIT THERE AND POUT EVERY DAY...
NO WAY!
...GO EAT LUNCH WITH ONISE AND THE OTHERS.
You've got a really cute face, Misaki.
Mind if I call you Ayu!?
Whaaaat?!
BAM!!
AYUMU MISAKI'S UNPLEASANT MEMORY
YOU'RE THE ONE WHO ALWAYS MAKES FUN OF ONISE.
LISTEN! MY TEASING IS AFFEC-TIONATE, OKAY?!
YA-
YASHIRO!
YOU CAN'T HANDLE BEING CALLED AYU?
KRRK
URK!!!

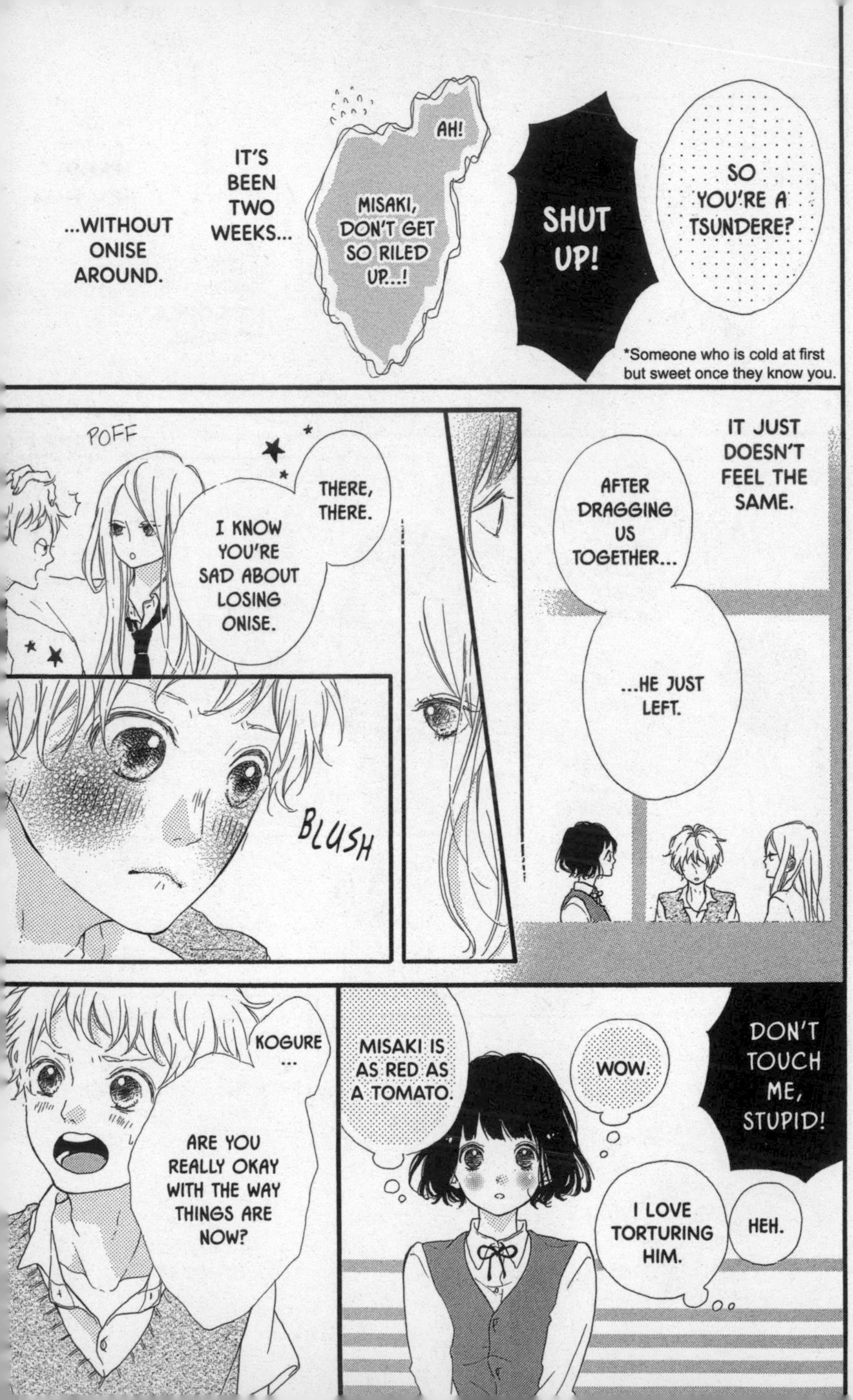
SO YOU'RE A TSUNDERE?
SHUT UP!
AH!
MISAKI, DON'T GET SO RILED UP...!
IT'S BEEN TWO WEEKS...
...WITHOUT ONISE AROUND.
*Someone who is cold at first but sweet once they know you.
IT JUST DOESN'T FEEL THE SAME.
AFTER DRAGGING US TOGETHER...
...HE JUST LEFT.
POFF
THERE, THERE.
I KNOW YOU'RE SAD ABOUT LOSING ONISE.
BLUSH
DON'T TOUCH ME, STUPID!
WOW.
HEH.
I LOVE TORTURING HIM.
MISAKI IS AS RED AS A TOMATO.
KOGURE ...
ARE YOU REALLY OKAY WITH THE WAY THINGS ARE NOW?

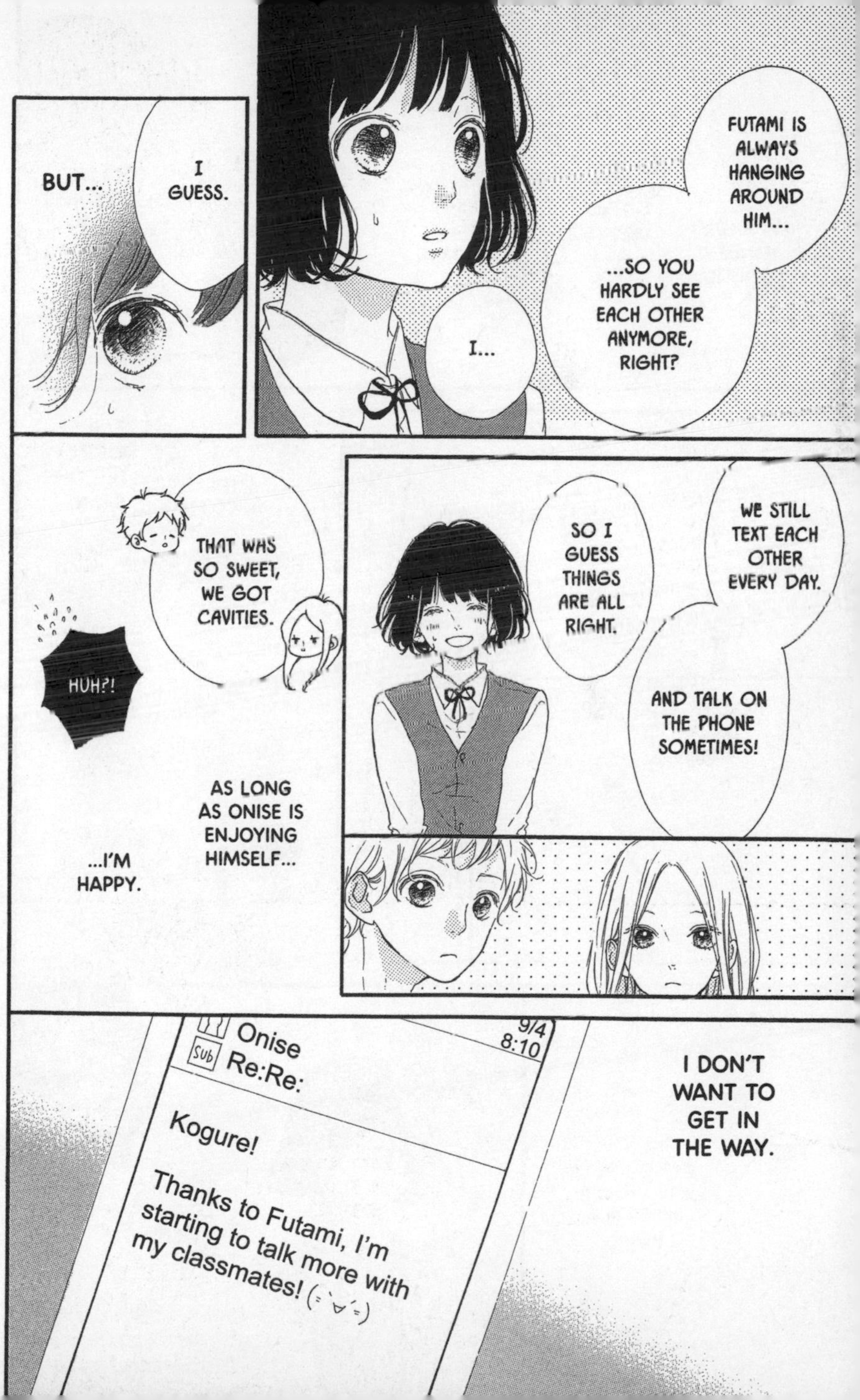
FUTAMI IS ALWAYS HANGING AROUND HIM...
...SO YOU HARDLY SEE EACH OTHER ANYMORE, RIGHT?
I...
I GUESS.
BUT...
WE STILL TEXT EACH OTHER EVERY DAY.
AND TALK ON THE PHONE SOMETIMES!
SO I GUESS THINGS ARE ALL RIGHT.
THAT WAS SO SWEET, WE GOT CAVITIES.
HUH?!
AS LONG AS ONISE IS ENJOYING HIMSELF...
...I'M HAPPY.
Onise
9/4 8:10
Sub Re:Re:
Kogure!
Thanks to Futami, I'm starting to talk more with my classmates! (=´∀`=)
I DON'T WANT TO GET IN THE WAY.

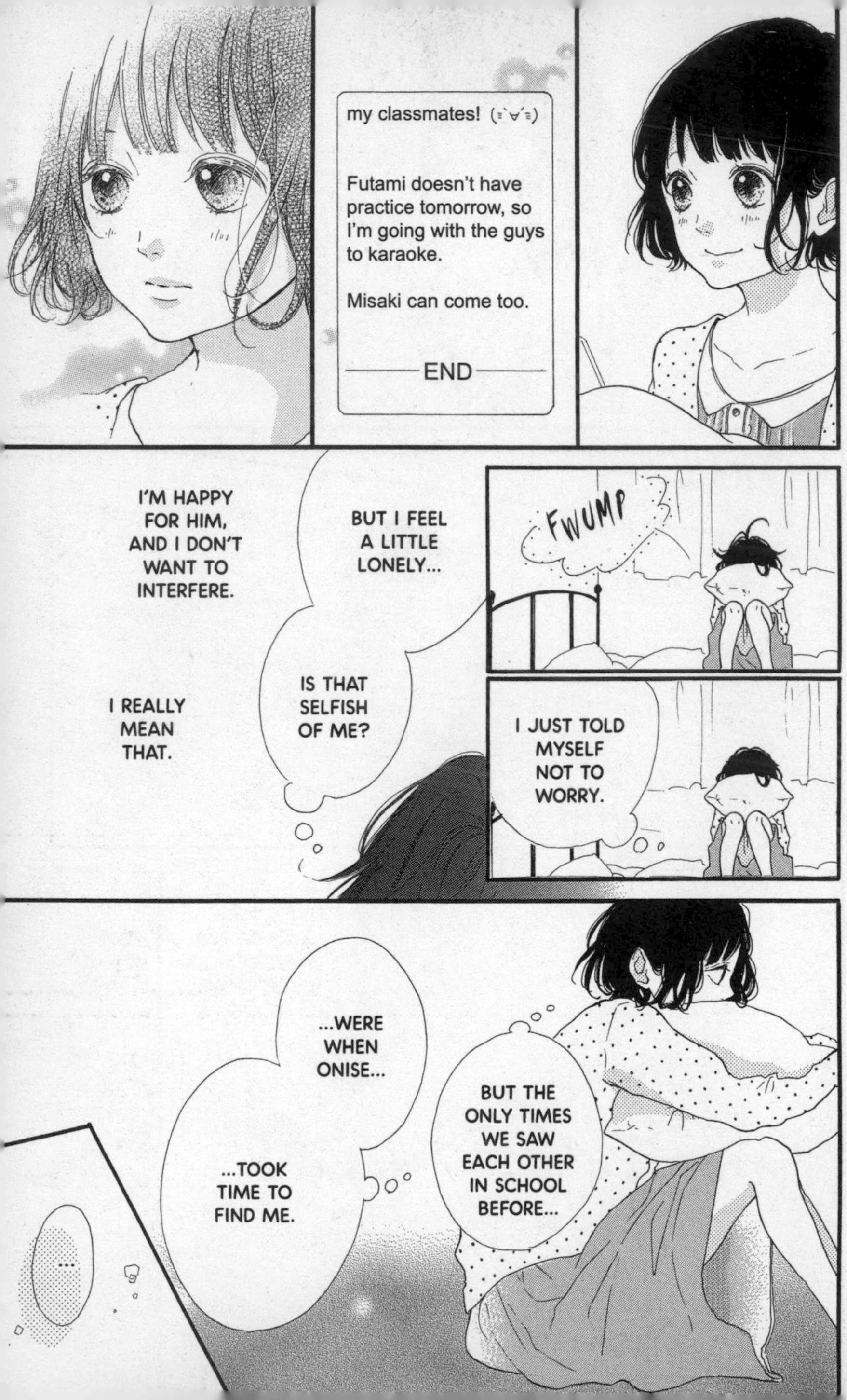
my classmates! (≧∀≦)
Futami doesn't have practice tomorrow, so I'm going with the guys to karaoke.
Misaki can come too.
END
FWUMP
I JUST TOLD MYSELF NOT TO WORRY.
BUT I FEEL A LITTLE LONELY...
IS THAT SELFISH OF ME?
I'M HAPPY FOR HIM, AND I DON'T WANT TO INTERFERE.
I REALLY MEAN THAT.
BUT THE ONLY TIMES WE SAW EACH OTHER IN SCHOOL BEFORE...
...WERE WHEN ONISE...
...TOOK TIME TO FIND ME.
...

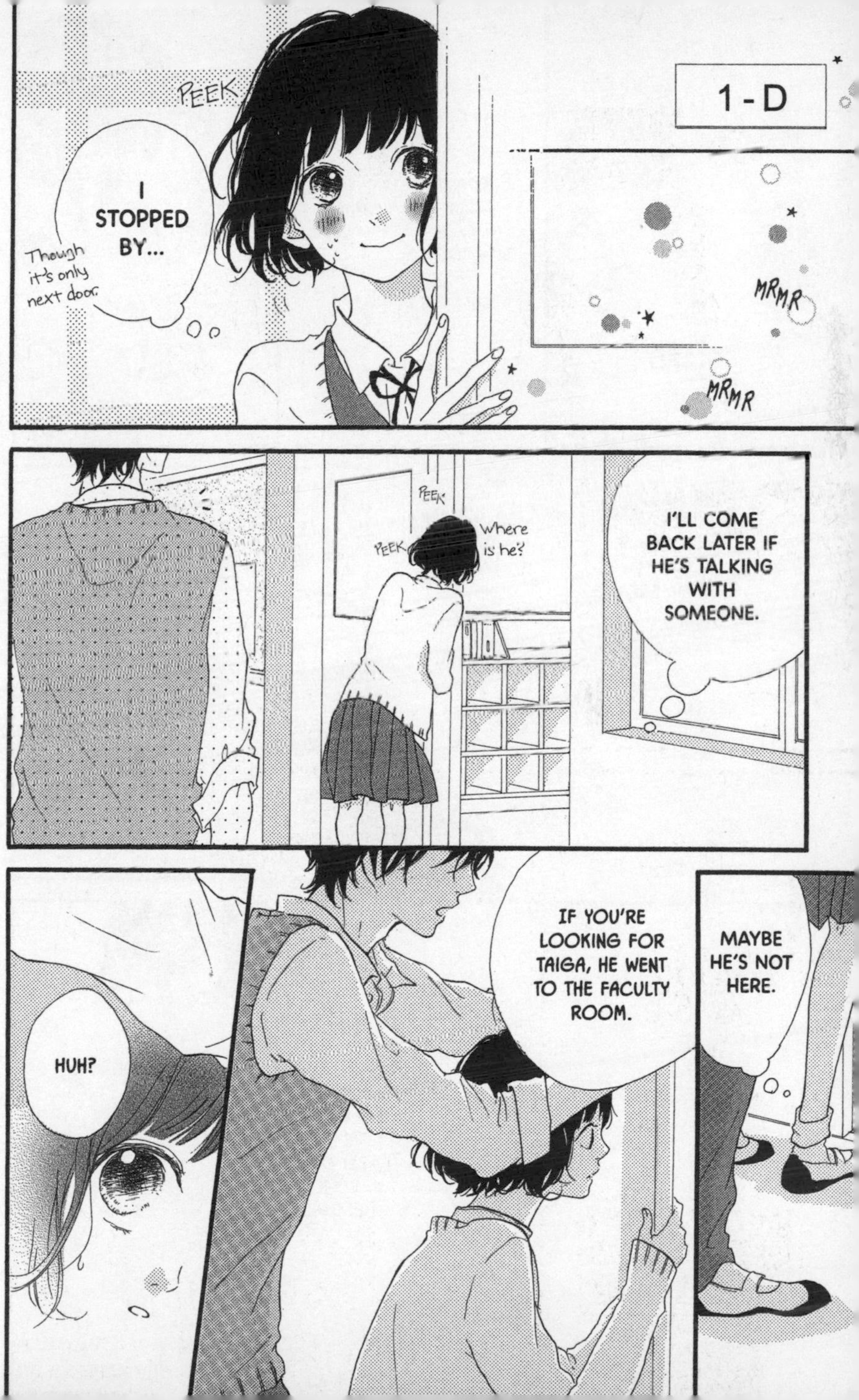
1 - D
MRMR
MRMR
PEEK
I STOPPED BY...
Though it's only next door.
I'LL COME BACK LATER IF HE'S TALKING WITH SOMEONE.
PEEK
Where is he?
PEEK
MAYBE HE'S NOT HERE.
IF YOU'RE LOOKING FOR TAIGA, HE WENT TO THE FACULTY ROOM.
HUH?

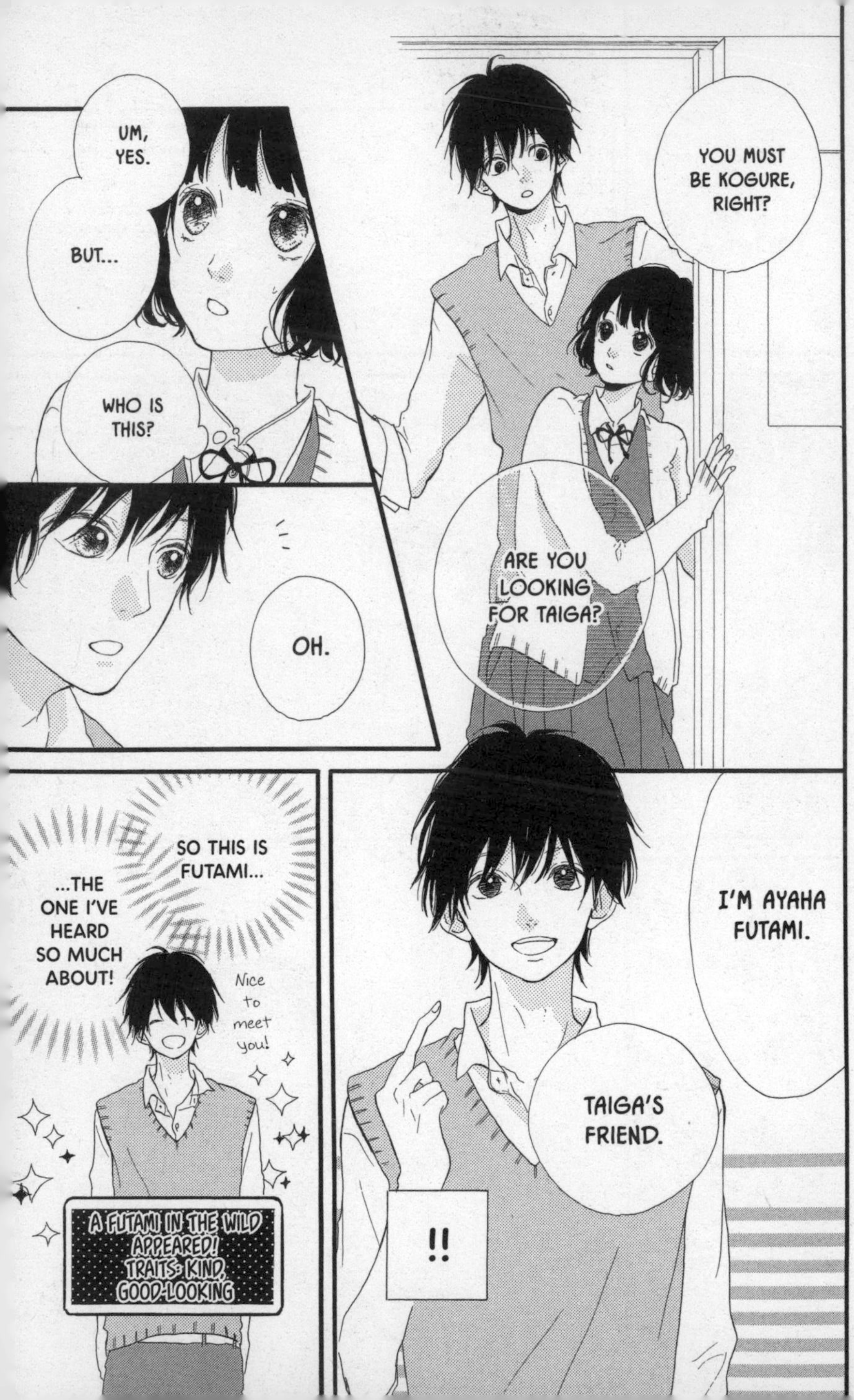
YOU MUST BE KOGURE, RIGHT?
ARE YOU LOOKING FOR TAIGA?
UM, YES.
BUT...
WHO IS THIS?
OH.
I'M AYAHA FUTAMI.
TAIGA'S FRIEND.
!!
SO THIS IS FUTAMI...
...THE ONE I'VE HEARD SO MUCH ABOUT!
Nice to meet you!
A FUTAMI IN THE WILD APPEARED! TRAITS: KIND, GOOD-LOOKING

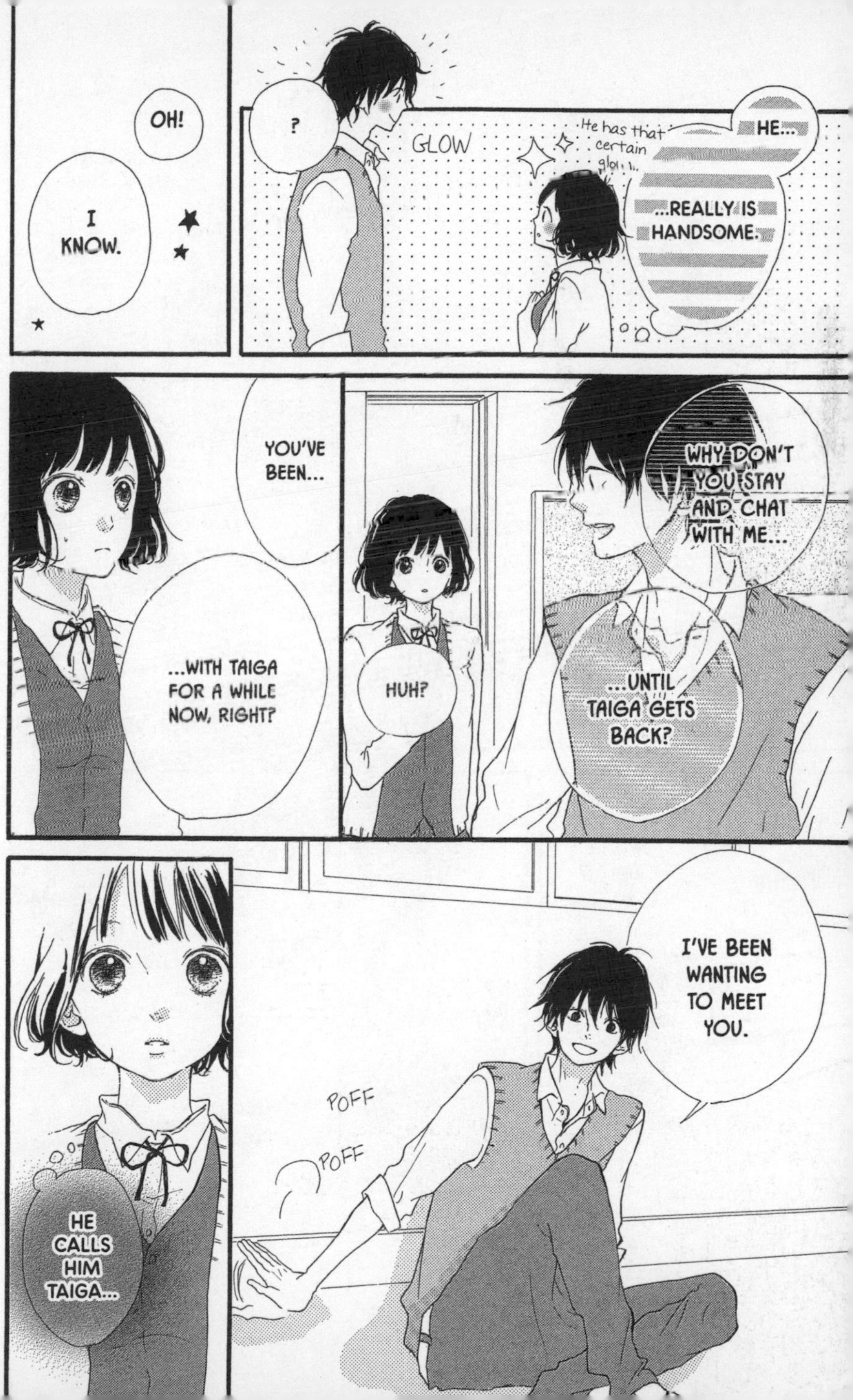
HE... ...REALLY IS HANDSOME.
He has that certain glow...
GLOW
?
OH!
I KNOW.
WHY DON'T YOU STAY AND CHAT WITH ME...
...UNTIL TAIGA GETS BACK?
HUH?
YOU'VE BEEN...
...WITH TAIGA FOR A WHILE NOW, RIGHT?
I'VE BEEN WANTING TO MEET YOU.
POFF
POFF
HE CALLS HIM TAIGA...

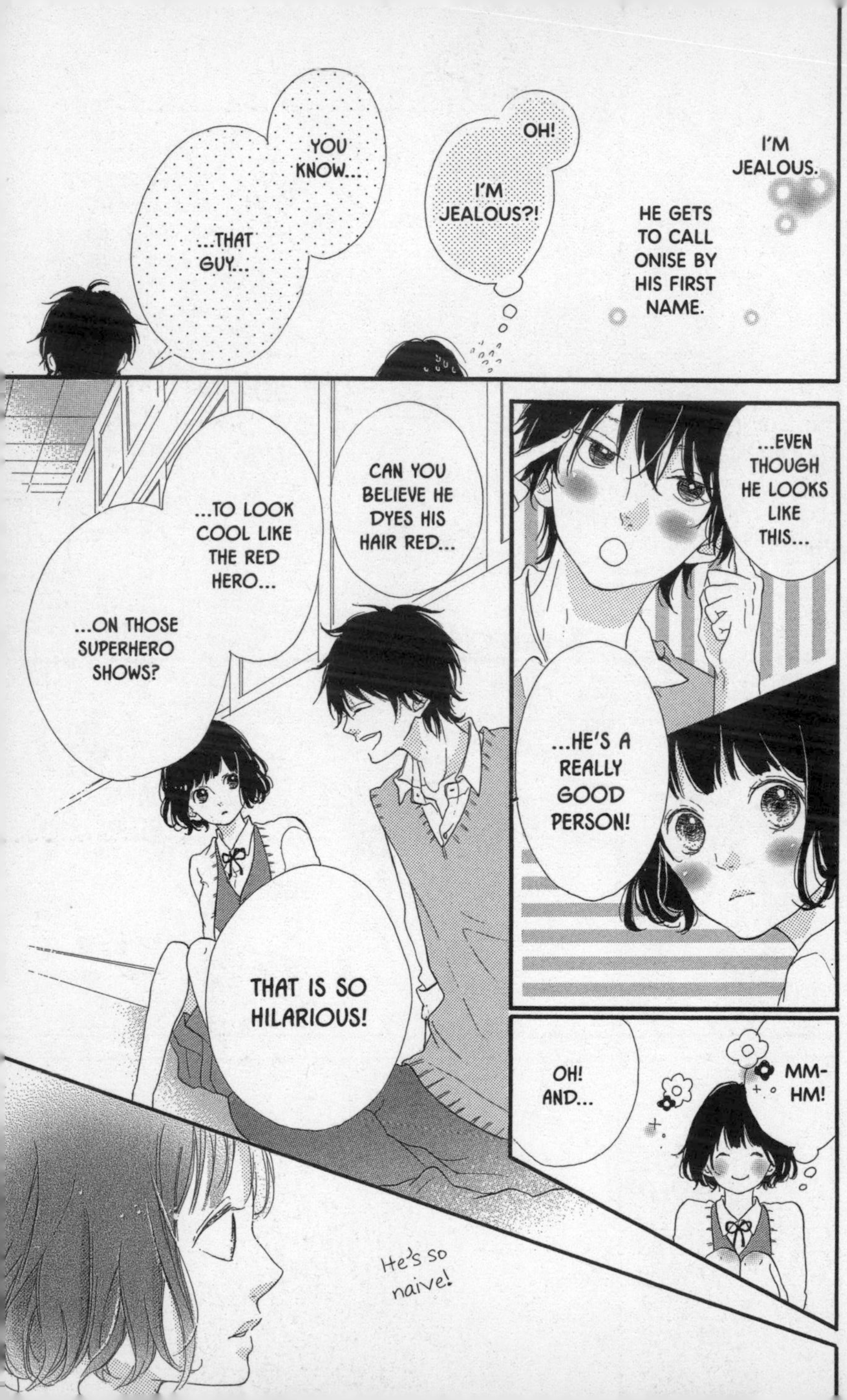
I'M JEALOUS.
HE GETS TO CALL ONISE BY HIS FIRST NAME.
OH!
I'M JEALOUS?!
YOU KNOW...
...THAT GUY...
...EVEN THOUGH HE LOOKS LIKE THIS...
...HE'S A REALLY GOOD PERSON!
MM-HM!
OH! AND...
CAN YOU BELIEVE HE DYES HIS HAIR RED...
...TO LOOK COOL LIKE THE RED HERO...
...ON THOSE SUPERHERO SHOWS?
THAT IS SO HILARIOUS!
He's so naive!

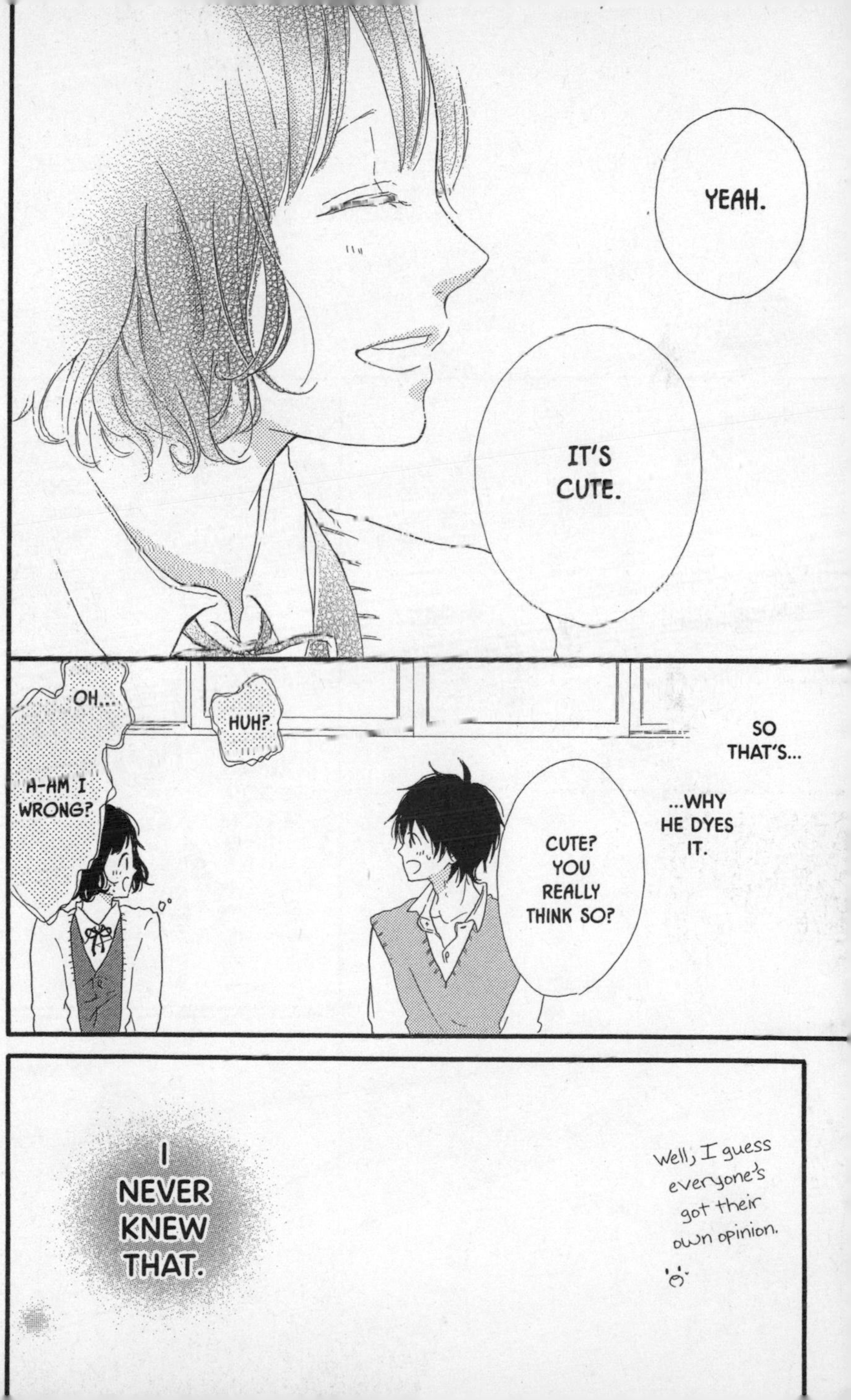
YEAH.
IT'S CUTE.
SO THAT'S...
...WHY HE DYES IT.
CUTE? YOU REALLY THINK SO?
HUH?
OH...
A-AM I WRONG?
Well, I guess everyone's got their own opinion.
I NEVER KNEW THAT.

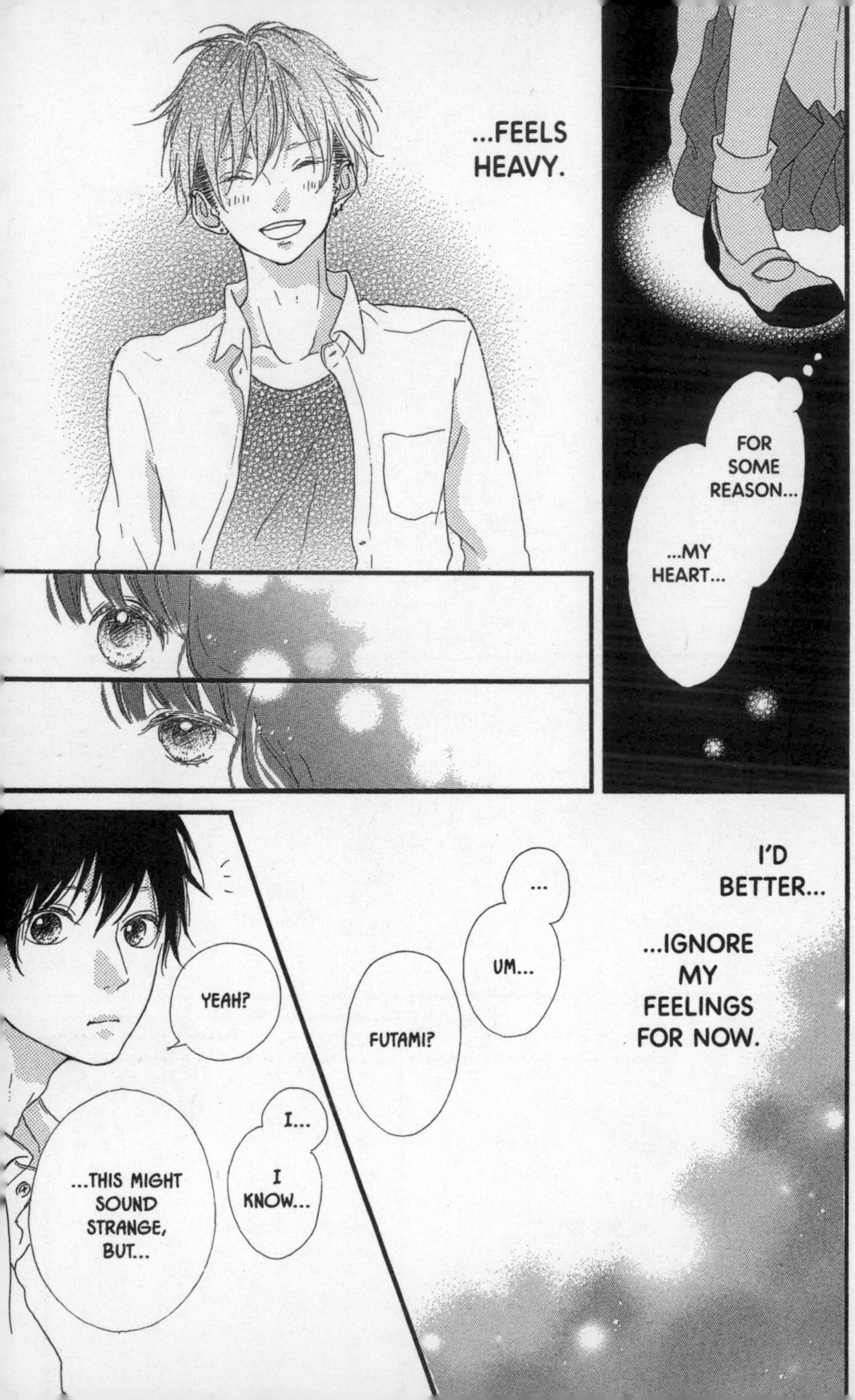
FOR SOME REASON...
...MY HEART...
...FEELS HEAVY.
I'D BETTER...
...IGNORE MY FEELINGS FOR NOW.
...
UM...
FUTAMI?
YEAH?
I...
I KNOW...
...THIS MIGHT SOUND STRANGE, BUT...

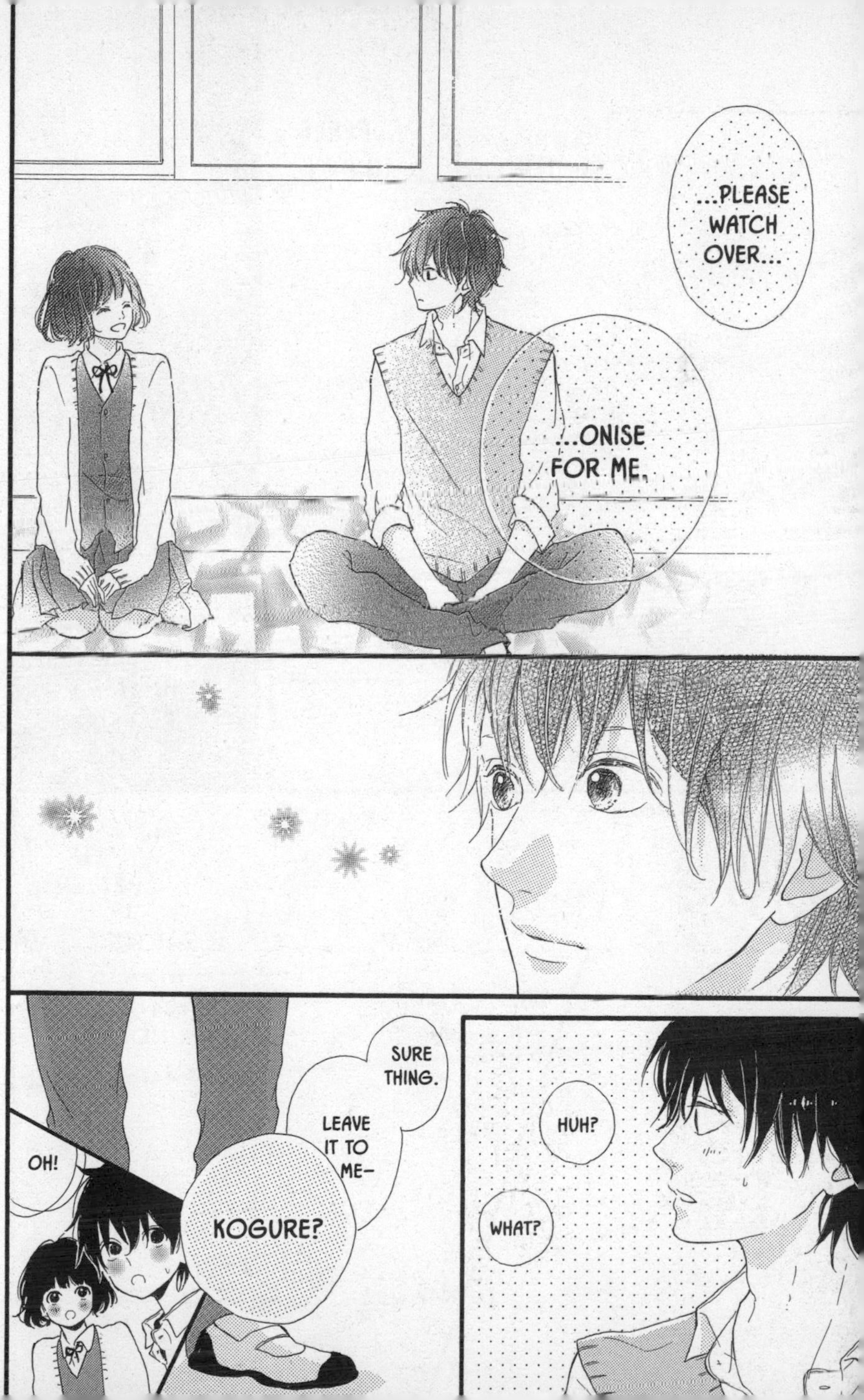
...PLEASE WATCH OVER...
...ONISE FOR ME.
HUH?
WHAT?
SURE THING.
LEAVE IT TO ME–
KOGURE?
OH!

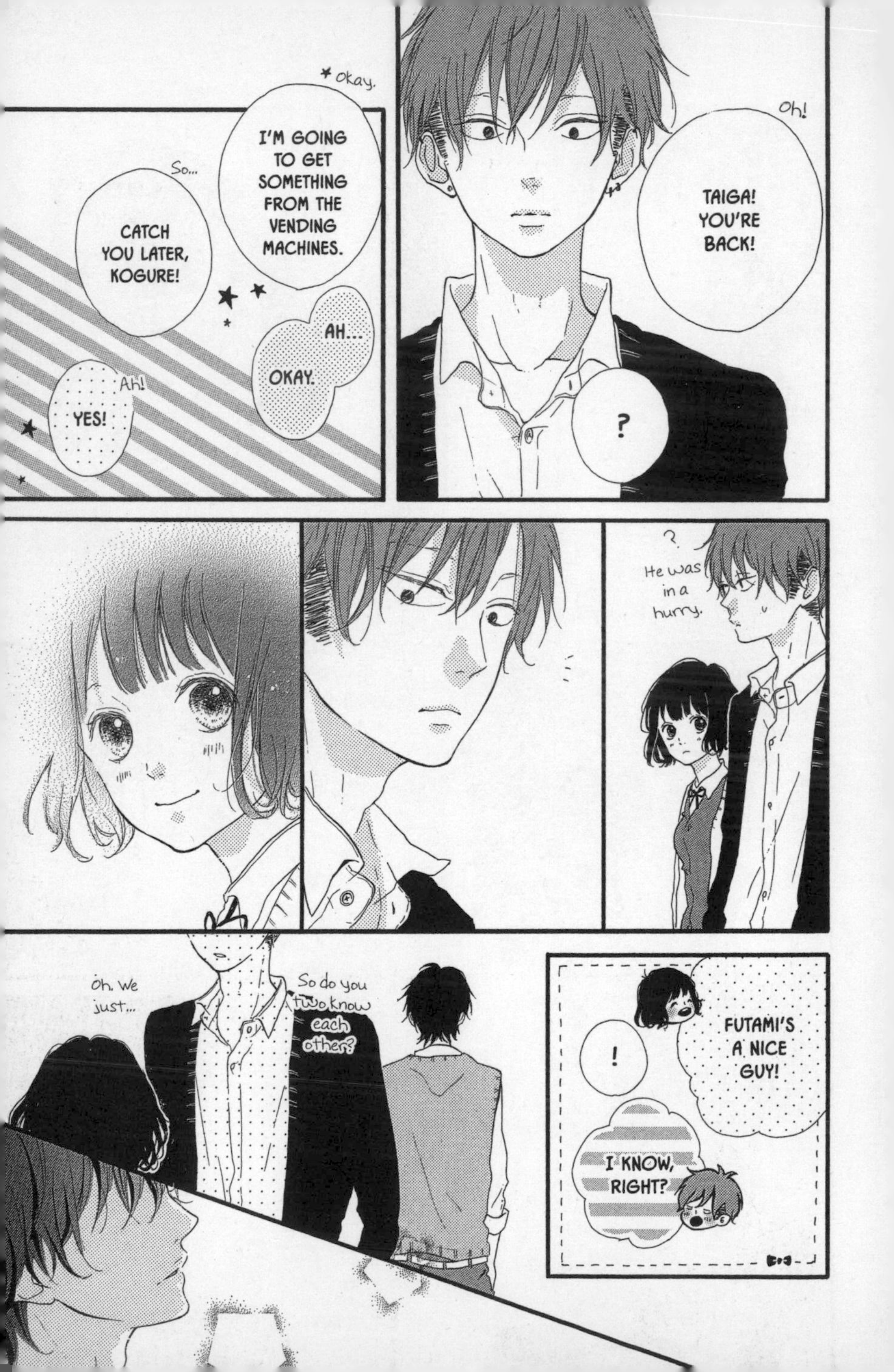
Oh!
TAIGA! YOU'RE BACK!
?
Okay.
I'M GOING TO GET SOMETHING FROM THE VENDING MACHINES.
So...
CATCH YOU LATER, KOGURE!
AH... OKAY.
Ah!
YES!
?
He was in a hurry.
FUTAMI'S A NICE GUY!
!
I KNOW, RIGHT?
So do you two know each other?
Oh. We just...

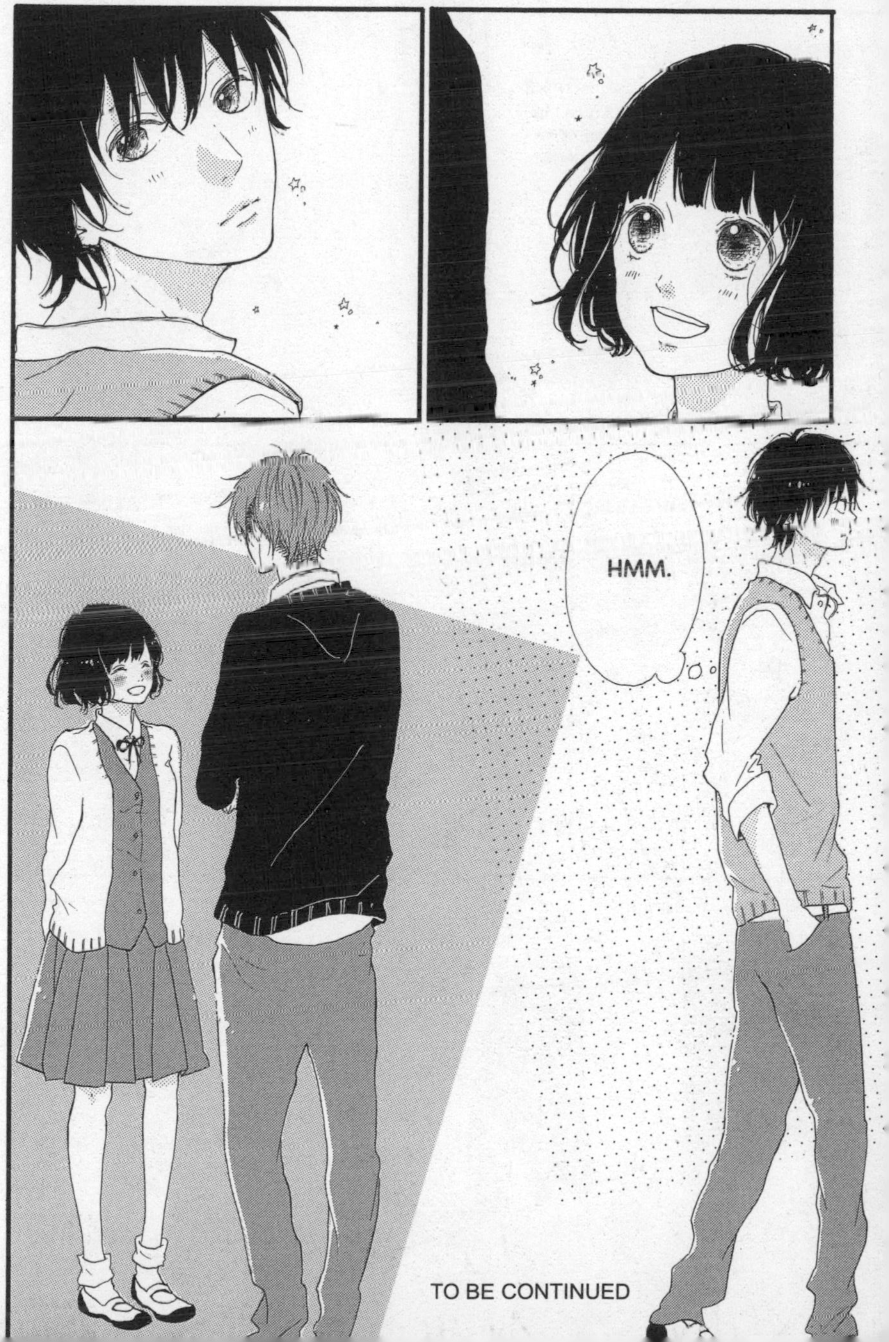
HMM.
TO BE CONTINUED

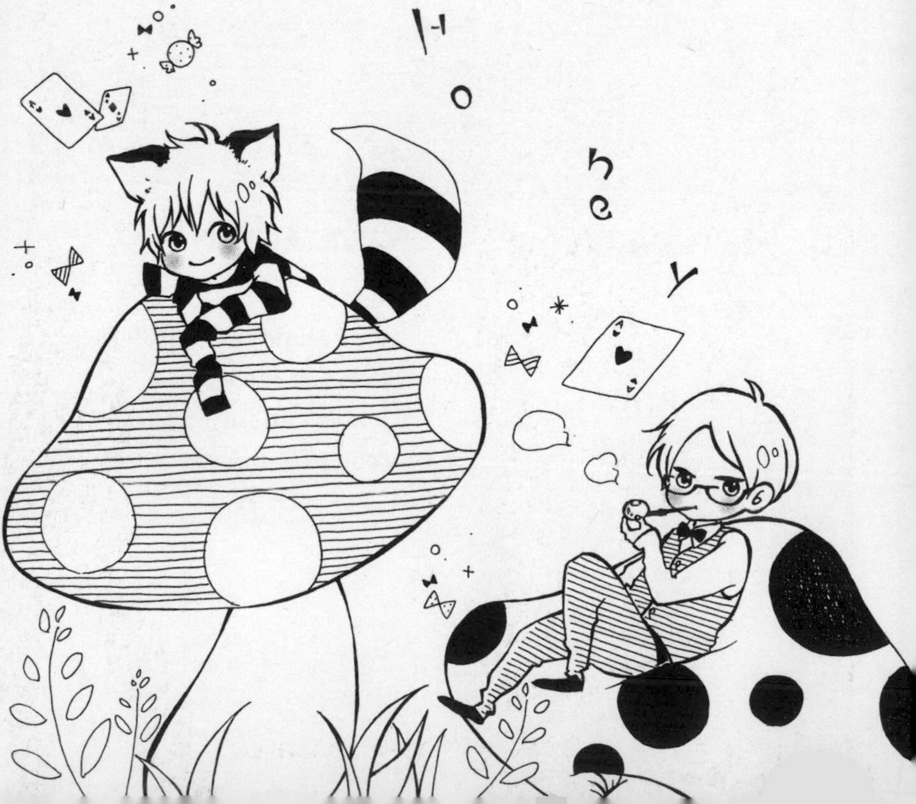
Honey

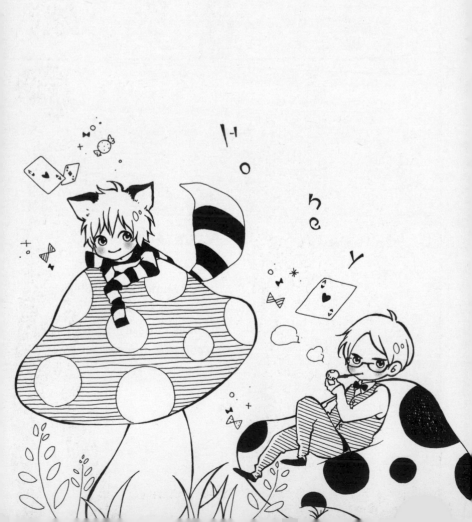

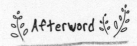 Afterword

Thank you for reading all the way to the end. I thought about

drawing not only illustrations but some behind-the-scenes

stuff from the story, but there wasn't anything important

enough, so I gave up on that idea. (laugh)

Oh! I also had some really goofy things in here because I really

enjoy that kind of stuff, but I apologize to anyone who

doesn't. That being said, if I have the time and space in

volume 3, I may do it again. (laugh)

Thank you for picking up

this volume!

I hope you enjoy volume 3!

♡ 2013.6 (E) GURO Ama

❀ Special thanks ❀

My editor and designer.

Everyone involved.

My mother, Nanae,

Ayu, Meikko, my dogs,

my readers who always

support me, and you for

choosing this book.

❀ SOCIAL MEDIA ❀

Find Shojo Beat here:

Twitter: @shojobeat

Tumblr: OfficialShojoBeat

Facebook: OfficialShojoBeat

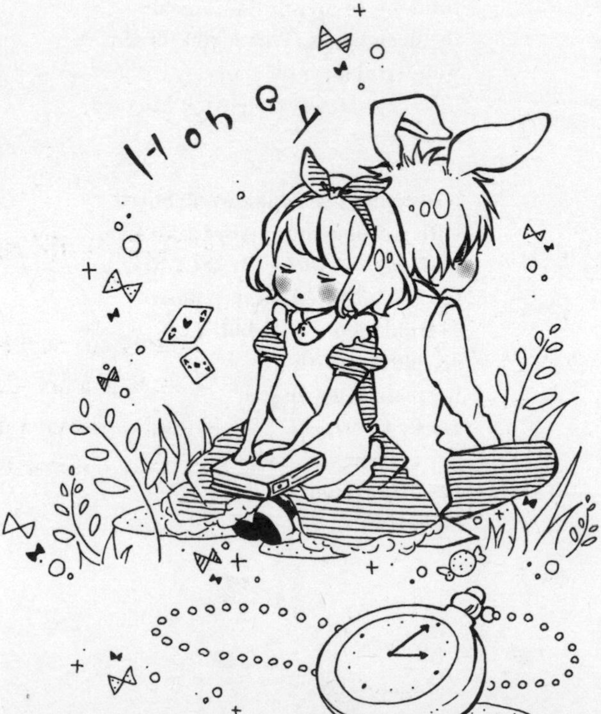
Honey

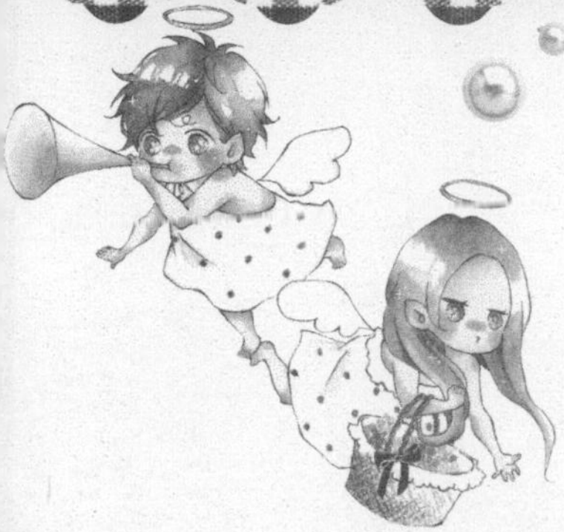

I loved how cute the cover design was for the first volume, so I changed the color for volume 2. It's so cute and purple. There were plenty of other choices, and they were all adorable. I kept thinking to myself how amazing the designer is. Thank you for the wonderful designs!

—Amu Meguro

Newcomer Amu Meguro debuted with the one-shot manga *Makka na Ringo ni Kuchizuke O* (A Kiss for a Bright Red Apple). Born in Hokkaido, her hobbies are playing with her niece and eating. *Honey So Sweet* is her current series in *Bessatsu Margaret* magazine.

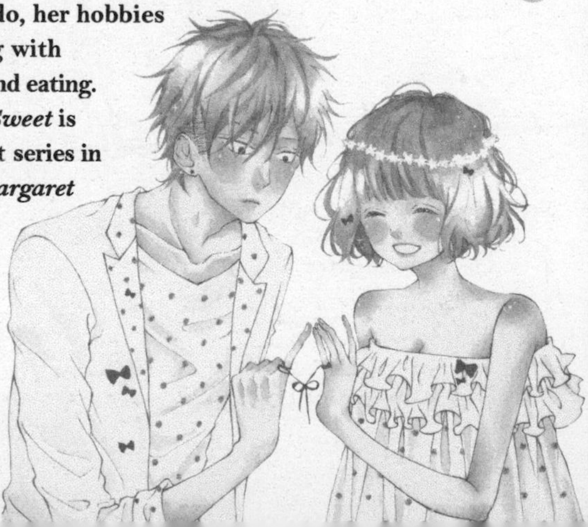

Honey So Sweet

Shojo Beat Edition
Volume 2

STORY AND ART BY
Amu Meguro

Translation/Katherine Schilling
Touch-Up Art & Lettering/Inori Fukuda Trant
Design/Izumi Evers
Editor/Nancy Thistlethwaite

First published in Japan in 2012 by SHUEISHA Inc., Tokyo.
English translation rights arranged by SHUEISHA Inc.

Printed in the U.S.A.

Published by VIZ Media, LLC
P.O. Box 77010
San Francisco, CA 94107

10 9 8 7 6 5 4 3 2
First printing, April 2016
Second printing, February 2018

Written by the creator of **High School Debut!**

KAZUNE KAWAHARA — Story
ARUKO — Art

Takeo Goda is a GIANT guy with a GIANT *heart*

Too bad the girls don't want him!
(They want his good-looking best friend, Sunakawa.)

Used to being on the sidelines, Takeo simply stands tall and accepts his fate. But one day when he saves a girl named Yamato from a harasser on the train, his (love!) life suddenly takes an incredible turn!